LIFE AND LETTERS OF JOHN WINTHROP

Volume I

LIFE AND LETTERS
OF
JOHN WINTHROP

By Robert C. Winthrop

Volume I

DA CAPO PRESS • NEW YORK • 1971

A Da Capo Press Reprint Edition

This Da Capo Press edition of the
Life and Letters of John Winthrop
is an unabridged republication of the
first edition published in Boston in 1864-1867.

Library of Congress Catalog Card Number 72-152833

SBN 306-70147-2

Published by Da Capo Press, Inc.
A Subsidiary of Plenum Publishing Corporation
227 West 17th Street, New York, N.Y. 10011
All Rights Reserved

Manufactured in the United States of America

LIFE AND LETTERS

OF

JOHN WINTHROP.

1588—1630.

Vandyke.   C.H. Sharpe.

SPES VINCIT THRONUM

From an original Portrait in the
Senate Chamber of Massachusetts.

Jo: winthop
Govr

GOVERNOR OF MASSACHUSETTS.

1630 _ 49.

LIFE AND LETTERS

OF

JOHN WINTHROP,

GOVERNOR OF THE MASSACHUSETTS-BAY COMPANY
AT THEIR EMIGRATION TO NEW ENGLAND,

1630.

BY

ROBERT C. WINTHROP.

BOSTON:
TICKNOR AND FIELDS.
1864.

BOSTON
STEREOTYPED BY JOHN WILSON AND SON,
No. 5, Water Street.

University Press, Cambridge:
Printed by Welch, Bigelow, and Company.

PREFATORY NOTE.

THERE is nothing in this volume which calls for any other preface than that which is supplied in the Introductory Chapter; but I am unwilling that it should go forth without a word of grateful acknowledgment to my valued friends, the Rev. CHANDLER ROBBINS, D. D., and CHARLES DEANE, Esq., A. M., for the aid they have given me in preparing it for the press.

I have also been indebted to CHARLES FRANCIS WINTHROP, Esq., of New York, to H. G. SOMERBY, Esq., and to W. H. WHITMORE, Esq., for papers and references; and to Dr. JOHN APPLETON, the Assistant Librarian of the Massachusetts Historical Society, for the preparation of the autographs and seals in the Appendix.

Nor could I pardon myself for omitting the name of the late FRANCIS B. WINTHROP, of New London, from whom many of the most interesting materials of the volume were procured; and who has since fallen a victim to disease contracted while he was serving as a volunteer in the army of the American Union.

ILLUSTRATIONS.

TO THE

MASSACHUSETTS HISTORICAL SOCIETY,

WHO HAVE HONORED ME WITH THEIR PRESIDENCY FOR EIGHT YEARS PAST,

𝔗𝔥𝔦𝔰 𝔙𝔬𝔩𝔲𝔪𝔢

IS RESPECTFULLY INSCRIBED.

CONTENTS.

CHAPTER V. ✓

CHAPTER XVIII.

CHAPTER XIX.

LIFE AND LETTERS

OF

JOHN WINTHROP.

CHAPTER I.

INTRODUCTORY.

DURING a brief visit to England in the summer of 1847,
I ran down to Groton, in the county of Suffolk, to see
the old home of my ancestors. · It is one of a cluster of
little rural villages, five in number, — Boxford, Groton,
Edwardston, Great Waldingfield, and Little Waldingfield,[1] — which lie midway between the larger towns of
Hadleigh and Sudbury, in the south-west corner of that
thriving agricultural county. The landscape around them
has no peculiar features either of beauty or of grandeur;
but clothed, as it was, in the matchless verdure of an
English summer, it presented a picture of quiet love-
liness which one would not willingly have lost. They
are all included in the old Hundred of Babergh; and
most of them have been associated in other ages with
some famous. person, or some celebrated family, or
some memorable event, which has saved them from

---

[1] Assington and Polstead might, perhaps, have been fairly included in the same
group.

being wholly unnoticed in the local histories of England. Thus we are told by Camden, in his "Britannia," that Edwardston was "formerly inhabited by the honorable lords Montchensy, of whom Warin married the daughter and heiress of that most potent William Marshall, Earl of Pembroke, who, by marrying William de Valence, of the family of Lusignan, in France, brought the title of Pembroke into the family. This Warin de Montchensy," continues Camden, "was a man of eminent rank and fortune, being accounted the Crassus of England at that time; leaving by will upwards of two hundred thousand marks."[1] Great Waldingfield, too, we learn, was once the lordship of James Butler, Earl of Wiltshire, and afterwards of the Earls of Essex; while, at Boxford, Queen Elizabeth secured a precious memorial of herself by founding a free grammar-school. Little Waldingfield and Groton appear to have been the least known, or certainly the least noted, of them all; and even the name of the latter would seem to have disappeared, of late years, from more than one of the Suffolk-County maps, as if the place had lost any importance which it ever possessed, and had become too inconsiderable to be the subject of particular designation. Meantime, it is pleasant to remember that at least two Grotons have grown up in New England, — deriving their name directly from the Groton of Old England, — which have already established no doubtful claim to an honorable mention by our American Camdens, and which

---

[1] Gough's Camden, vol. ii. p. 74. The British Crassus or *Crœsus*, — whichever Camden intended to call him, — who gave such celebrity to Edwardston, died in 1255.

will serve to keep the name fresh and fragrant on this side of the Atlantic for many generations to come.[1]

But the Groton of Suffolk County, in Old England, has by no means yet lost its local habitation or its ancient landmarks. I was there on a Sunday, and went to the parish church in which the Winthrops worshipped before they came to America. The grand old service of prayer and praise, in which they had united so long ago within the same sanctuary, had just commenced when I entered; and I could almost imagine, as I joined in the responses, that the venerable walls gave back an echo of welcome, as to a not unrecognized voice. Every thing concurred in awakening the memory of those who had gone before me, — the pulpit from which they had listened to preachers of their own presentation, the font at which so many of them had been baptized, the chancel around which they had knelt to receive the bread of life. There, on the crowning pane of the altar window, was the same *Sursum Corda*[2] which must have lifted their hearts in many an hour of trial and trouble. There, in the humble vestry, was the old parish register, the second entry on whose time-stained leaves gave the date of the death of the head of the family in 1562. There, too, was the tomb in which the father, the grandfather, and possibly the great-grandfather, of the first emigrant to New England had been successively buried. It still bore the family name and arms; and, by a strik-

---

1 Groton in Connecticut, the scene of the heroic Ledyard's death on the 6th of September, 1781; and Groton in Massachusetts, within whose original limits were the birthplaces of the Prescotts and Lawrences.

2 The "Lift up your Hearts" of the Liturgy. Taken from the old Communion Service, as described by St. Cyril, Archbishop of Jerusalem, A.D. 325.

ing coincidence, it had just been repaired, — almost as if in anticipation of the arrival of one who might be presumed to take a peculiar interest in its condition. It was outside the church, but close against the walls, just beneath the window which opened from the rector's pew, in which I sat during the service. The inscription was almost illegible; but enough could be deciphered to verify an ancient copy, which gives it as follows : —

"CŒLUM PATRIA : CHRISTUS VIA.

HIC . JACET . CORPUS . ADAMI . WINTHROP . AR . FILII
ADAMI . WINTHROP . ARMIGERI . QUI . HUJUS . ECCLESIÆ
PATRONI . FUERUNT . ET . DOMINI . MANERII . DE . GROTON
PRÆDICTUS . ADAMUS . FILIUS . UXOREM . DUXIT . ANNAM
FILIAM . HENRICI . BROWNE . DE . EDWARDUSTON . PER
QUAM . HABUIT . UNUM . FILIUM . ET . QUATUOR . FILIAS
HANC . VITAM . TRANSMIGRAVIT . ANNO . DOMINI . 1623
ÆTATIS . SUÆ . 75 . ANNA . VERO . UXOR . EJUS . OBIIT
1628 . HIC . QUOQUE . CONSEPULTA . EST.

BEATI . SUNT . PACIFICI . NAM . II . DEI . FILII
VOCABUNTUR."

The family records furnish the following translation : —

"HEAVEN THE COUNTRY : CHRIST THE WAY.
Here lies the body of Adam Winthrop, Esq.,
son of Adam Winthrop, Esq.,
who were Patrons of this Church,
and Lords of the Manor of Groton.

The above-named Adam, the son, married Anna, the daughter of Henry Browne of Edwardston, by whom he had one son and four daughters. He departed this life in the year of our Lord 1623, and of his own age 75. But Anna, his wife, died 1628.[1] She also is buried here with him.

Blessed are the peacemakers; for they shall be called the sons of God."

After the service was ended, I was directed to the site of the old family mansion. Not one stone was left upon

---

[1] It should have been 1629, as shown by the Parish Register of Groton.

GROTON CHURCH, *Suffolk Co., England;*

With the Tomb of ADAM WINTHROP, Esq., *ob.* 1562, and of his son ADAM WINTHROP, Esq., *ob.* 1623, Lords of the Manor and Patrons of the Living.

another, of the house in which John Winthrop, the Governor of Massachusetts, and his son John Winthrop, the
Governor of Connecticut, had both lived, and beneath
whose roof were prepared and pondered the memorable
"Conclusions" which determined them to quit their native
soil. The outlines of the cellar, however, were distinctly
traceable; and there was one old mulberry-tree still
standing, in what was probably the garden-plot, which
might have afforded fruit and shade long before those
Conclusions were acted upon.[1]

The spot was well known to the neighbors as the former property, and place of residence, of the family; but
one of the traditions associated with it was, that the
Winthrops were *regicides*, and that there was money
buried by them in some part of the premises before
their *flight* to America. Perhaps it was supposed that I
had come over to search for it! At any rate, I believe
it was the monstrousness of this tradition which prompted
the resolution, which I then formed, that I would employ
my earliest leisure from public occupations in rendering
an act of filial justice to my progenitors. I did not,
indeed, imagine that this absurd story had obtained cur-
rency or credit anywhere except where I heard it, or
that there were not those on the spot who understood
its utterly apocryphal character;[2] and certainly I did
not forget that here, in New England, there are memorials enough, both of the elder and of the younger Win-

---

[1] Prof. Masson, in his Life of Milton, says, humorously enough, that "no fact in
universal biography is better attested, than that great men, wherever they go, plant
mulberry-trees." — Vol. i. p. 147, note (Am. ed.).

[2] My valued friend, Richard Almack, Esq., F.S.A., of Long Melford, accompanied
me, and knew almost as much of my ancestors as I did myself.

throp, to leave no room for such a mistake as this, even in the mind of any well-educated schoolboy. But it is not the less true, that there has been no extended biography of either of them; nor any book containing such an account of their lives, services, and characters, as would be likely to render them familiar to the modern public mind.

There is a brief Life of each of them in Mather's " Magnalia," and another in Belknap's " American Biography; " but these works belong to other times, and are rarely read or referred to at the present day, except by the historian or the antiquary.[1] The elder Winthrop has left an imperishable monument of himself in his annals; and the laborious and learned annotations of Mr. Savage have rendered that work, as published in 1825–6,[2] and still more in the new edition of 1853, a complete storehouse of our early New-England history. It is a work, however, too full of various and curious matter about other men and other things, to allow the conduct and character of its author to impress themselves, as distinctly as they ought to be impressed, upon the minds of those who read it. It furnishes only the raw material of a biography, rather than a biography itself, even during the period over which it extends; while it leaves the earlier and larger part of its author's life and fortunes almost entirely unnoticed.

---

[1] A compendious memoir of the elder Winthrop has also been included in the "Lives of the Governors of New Plymouth and Massachusetts Bay." By Jacob B. Moore. Boston, 1851.

[2] The History of New England from 1630 to 1649, by John Winthrop, Esq., first Governor of the Colony of the Massachusetts Bay, from his original manuscripts; with notes, &c., by James Savage, President of the Massachusetts Historical Society. The first volume was published in 1825; the second, in 1826.

But I will make no apology for what I have undertaken; trusting that it will do its own proper work of self-justification with those into whose hands it shall fall. Let me only add, that the resolution which was inspired by my visit to Groton in 1847, and by the strange story which I heard there, was fulfilled in manuscript not long afterwards; and that several of the following chapters* are now printed just as they were written many years ago. Meantime, however, not only has another brief visit to England, in 1859–60, furnished me with the opportunity of refreshing my remembrance of the Groton associations and localities, but, since my return home, a very large collection of original family papers has come into my possession, supplying information and materials of the utmost importance to my work, and giving me abundant cause for satisfaction, that I had so long resisted the temptation to publish what had been originally prepared. Indeed, the abundance of these new materials has been not a little embarrassing. They have compelled me to abandon not a few of my own speculations and conjectures, and to cancel more than one chapter on which I had bestowed the most pains, and in which I had taken the most pride. But the truth of history will gain largely by such changes; while the character and career which I have attempted to portray will lose nothing.

Dr. Johnson has somewhere expressed the idea, that the best kind of biography is *autobiography;* and that every man's life may be written by himself better than anybody else could write it for him. Whether this be true or not to its full extent, there can be no question that the most trustworthy sort of autobiography is that which has been written, accidentally and unconsciously, as it were, in familiar letters or private journals, or upon the records of official service. Certainly, any one who has materials of this kind within his reach would be almost as inexcusable for overlaying them by too much authorship, as he would be for overlooking them altogether. The life of John Winthrop the elder, most happily, has been thus written by himself. It may be read in the language of contemporaneous records, or in the still more familiar and agreeable language of his own private correspondence and diary; and if I shall have succeeded in so arranging his letters and journals, his confessions and experiences, that this old father of Massachusetts shall be found telling the story of a considerable part of his career in his own words, and furnishing an ample clew to the course and current of the rest of it, I shall have accomplished every thing that I have aimed at. And I shall be greatly mistaken, I do confess, if in this way there be not presented to fresh contemplation a character inferior to few which can be found, either in the earlier or the later history of our land.

I do not forget the caution suggested in the old couplet of the author of the " Night Thoughts," —

> " They that on glorious ancestors enlarge
> Produce their debt, instead of their discharge."

I hardly know, however, of a deeper debt which any one can incur, or of a more binding obligation which any one can discharge, — whenever circumstances may afford the means and opportunity of doing so, — than to bring out from the treasures of the past, and to hold up to the view of the present and of coming generations, a great example of private virtue and public usefulness; of moderation in counsel, and energy in action; of stern self-denial, and unsparing self-devotion; of childlike trust in God, and implicit faith in the gospel of Christ, united with courage enough for conducting a Colony across the ocean, and wisdom enough for building up a State in the wilderness. Nor could any one easily subject himself to a juster reproach, than that of shrinking from the discharge of such a debt, for fear of being thought inclined to exaggerate the importance, or to magnify the merits, of a remote ancestry.

More than two centuries have now passed away since the elder Winthrop was laid in his narrow tomb. Six entire generations of descendants have intervened between him and myself. At such a distance of time, and in this republican atmosphere, by no means favorable to the growth of family pride, I trust my sincerity will not be questioned when I say, with another and older poet, —

"Et genus et proavos, et quæ non fecimus ipsi,
    Vix ea nostra voco."

CHAPTER II.

EARLY HISTORY OF THE WINTHROP FAMILY.

THE name of WINTHROP may be traced back, in various spellings, for at least six centuries and a half. On the Rolls of Court of the County of York, in England, for the year of our Lord 1200, there is a record which begins with the name of Robert de Winetorp. There is a similar record for the county of Lincoln, seven years later, in which the name I. Winethorp is found. *Thorpe* is the Saxon word for " village," corresponding to the Dutch word *Dorp*. *Win*, or *wine*, has more than one signification; sometimes meaning " pleasant," sometimes " the beloved," and sometimes standing for that juice of the grape to which both these epithets are not unfrequently applied.

Dr. Johnson, quoting from Gibson, says that " *Win*, whether initial or final, in the names of men, may either denote a masculine temper, from ƿin, which signifies, in Saxon, ' war,' ' strength,' &c. ; or else the general love and esteem he hath among the people, from the Saxon ƿine ; *i.e.*, ' dear,' ' beloved.' In the names of places, it implies a battle fought there."

A recent American writer on Surnames [1] says, " *Win-*

---

[1] B. Homer Dixon, Esq.

throp probably means a pleasant thorp, or village." A still more recent and most humorous American writer on Suffolk Surnames [1] suggests that *Winthrop* means " wine village." Dr. Johnson's citation would indicate that it might bear a more personal and enviable signification than either.

An old pedigree of the Winthrop Family, of uncertain date, and of still more uncertain detail, commences by stating that " they came anciently from Northumberland;" that " they afterwards settled in a village not far from Newark, which was called 'Winthrop;'" that " from thence they came up to London, and owned Marribone (Marylebone) Park;" that " from thence they went to Groton, in Suffolk, where they lived many years."

The village of Winthorpe, in Nottinghamshire, still exists near Newark; but which generation of the family lived there, if any, we have not found it easy to ascertain. Winthorpe Hall is a well-known seat in the same neighborhood. It is a comparatively modern structure, however; having been built in 1760 by Dr. Taylor, physician to George II. [2] There is another village of Winthorpe, on the coast of Lincolnshire, of which we know nothing but the name.

The early history of the Winthrops is thus succinctly stated by Cotton Mather, in the *Magnalia Christi Americana* : —

" Mr. Adam Winthrop, the son of a worthy gentleman of the same name, was himself a worthy, a discreet, and a learned

---

[1] The late lamented Nathaniel Ingersoll Bowditch, Esq.
[2] Burke's Visitation of Seats and Arms, vol. i. p. 196.

gentleman, particularly eminent for skill in the law, nor without remark for love to the gospel, under the reign of King Henry VIII. ; and brother to a memorable favorer of the reformed religion in the days of Queen Mary, into whose hands the famous martyr, Philpot, committed his papers, which afterwards made no inconsiderable part of our martyr-books. This Mr. Adam Winthrop had a son of the same name also, and of the same endowments and employments with his father; and this third Adam Winthrop was the father of that renowned John Winthrop, who was the father of New England, and the founder of a colony, which upon many accounts, like him that founded it, may challenge the first place among the English glories of America." [1]

Now, Cotton Mather was certainly in the way of knowing something about the facts which he states in regard to the Winthrop Family. His grandfather, Richard Mather, was a friend of John Winthrop, the Governor of Massachusetts; and his father, Increase Mather, was a very intimate friend of Fitz-John Winthrop, the second Governor Winthrop of Connecticut, upon whom he preached a funeral sermon; [2] while Cotton Mather himself was the friend of Wait Still Winthrop, Chief-Justice of the Superior Court of Massachusetts (1708–1717), on whom he also pronounced an elaborate funeral discourse, appending thereto a Latin epitaph almost as long as the discourse itself. The family traditions, at least, must thus have been abundantly familiar to him. Yet we may find good

---

[1] Mather's Magnalia, book ii. chap. iv. .

[2] This sermon was reprinted in London (1710), and dedicated to the Lady Rachel Russell — the widow of the ever-honored martyr, William, Lord Russell — by Sir Henry Ashurst, bart.

reason for doubting whether he was correct in all his information, and particularly as to the profession of one of the Adams, who would appear, as we shall see hereafter, to have been a merchant or manufacturer, instead of a lawyer. Nor have we been able to ascertain any thing in regard to the relation of any brother of his to the papers of Philpot, the martyr. The name of Winthrop is nowhere mentioned, so far as we have discovered, among the friends of Philpot,[1] in the " Acts and Monuments " of Fox ; although the papers of that martyr occupy so considerable a space in his voluminous work. Perhaps it was a brother by marriage who was thus distinguished.

The earliest residence of the family, of which there is any precise record, was at Lanham, or Lavenham,[2] in the county of Suffolk, where the second Adam Winthrop mentioned by Mather was born, on the ninth day of October, 1498, " one year after the battle of Blackheath-field," as an old Latin pedigree (the earlier and larger part of it evidently drawn up by his son Adam) is particular in stating. If it had said " six years after Columbus had discovered the New World," or " the very year in which Vespucius made the voyage which gave his name to the whole American hemisphere," it would have been equally true, and the period would have been fixed more significantly for those who are now interested in ascertaining it. But the American hemisphere was of

---

[1] John Philpot, Archdeacon of Winchester, burned at Smithfield, 18th December, 1555.

[2] The Parish Register of Lavenham does not commence till 1558, or we might learn more of the family of the first Adam Winthrop. The beautiful Lavenham Church was partly built by " Thomas Spring, the rich clothier," who resided there, and with whose descendants the Winthrops were connected by marriage before 1600.

small account when that record was made out, and the
writer of it did not imagine that a reference to the New
World would have any peculiar significance for his own
posterity.

This Adam was the eldest son of Adam Winthrop and
Joane (or Jane) Burton, who is sometimes styled " the
daughter of D. Burton," and sometimes " the widow of
D. Burton, and daughter and co-heir of Lord Burnel." [1]
He seems to have been a person of pretty decided character. He left his father's residence at seventeen years
of age, and went to London, where he bound himself to
Edward Altham, as an apprentice for ten years. Edward
Altham was of an ancient family, and afterwards reached
the dignity of Sheriff of London (1531). His grandson,
Sir James Altham, was one of the Barons of the Exchequer; and the son of Sir James was that Richard Altham, the friend of Howell, to whom so many of the
" Familiar Letters " are addressed. Edward's own business, at this time, was that of a clothier, or cloth-worker,
— a business partly mechanical and partly mercantile
in its nature, and which stood at the head of the indus-
trial pursuits of that period. " The clothiers " (says the
author of the recent " Popular History of England,"
speaking of the middle of the fifteenth century) " stood
apart, as pursuing the most important branch of England's industry." And, in relating the events of the beginning of the sixteenth century, the same author bears
special testimony to the influence of the clothiers of

---

[1] The Burnels and Burtons were both Salop (or Shropshire) families, — the former
of great distinction; but I find no trace of any connection with the Winthrops in the
pedigrees of either of them.

Suffolk in resisting oppressive and unwarrantable taxation. "But for the artisans of Suffolk," says he, "England, at this period, would probably have passed into the condition of France, where the abuse of the royal power had long before deprived the people of their rights."[1] In the year 1526, when his apprenticeship had been served out, Adam was admitted to the liberty of citizenship in London, and sworn in on the 9th of September, "under the mayoralty of John Allen."[2] The next year (16th November, 1527) he married Alice Henry, or Henny, who is duly recorded as having been born of honest or honorable parents. By her he had the following children : —

I. THOMAS, born 8th November, 1528. Died in April, 1529.

II. WILLIAM, born 12th November, 1529. Died 1st March, 1581, at London; and buried at St. Michael's Church, Cornhill. *Vir sine fraude bonus, et pietatis amans.* His wife, Elizabeth ———, died in Kent, 2d June, 1578; having had six children, Jonathan, Adam, William, Joshua, Elizabeth, and Sarah.

III. BRIDGET, born 1st January, 1530. Died January, 1536.

IV. CHRISTOPHER, born 4th January, 1531. Died in the parish of Stocke, Essex, aged nine months.

V. THOMAS (2d), born at London, June, 1533, "on the day on which Anne Boleyn was crowned Queen of England." Died 1537.

---

[1] Knight's Popular History of England, vol. ii. pp. 114, 303.

[2] The mayoralty of John Allen was a memorable one, as will be seen from the following account of him in Stowe's Survey : —

"This lord mayor (who, for his singular wisdom, was made a privy councillor to King Henry VIII.) built a beautiful chapel here, wherein he was first buried; but, since, his tomb is removed thence into the body of the hospital-church, and his chapel divided into shops. He gave to the city a rich collar of gold, to be worn by the mayor: he gave a stock of five hundred marks, to be employed for the use of the poor of London, besides the rents of certain lands by him purchased of the king. To prisons, hospitals, and lazar-houses, within, and two miles without, the city, he was abundantly charitable." He died in 1554; and Weever, in his "Antient Funeral Monuments," gives an elaborate Latin epitaph, which was inscribed on his tomb, in the "Hospital of St. Thomas of Acars, or Mercer's Chaple," in London.

Adam Winthrop was married for the second time, in 1534, to Agnes Sharpe, daughter of Robert Sharpe, of Islington; she being eighteen years of age," and he thirty-six. By her he had the following children : —

I. ALICE, born 15th November, 1539 ; married Sir Thomas Mildmay, and had William, Francis, George, John, Henry, and Thomas. She died 8th November, 1607 ; and the writer of the Latin pedigree inscribes against the date of her death, *Cujus erat vitæ vita medulla meæ.*

II. BRIDGET, born 3d May, 1543, "on the Festival of the Ascension." Married Roger Alabaster (of a distinguished Hadley family), and had William,[1] George, John, Thomas, Sarah. Died in Tharfield, Herefordshire, 4th November, 1614.

III. MARY, born 1st March, 1544. Married Abraham Veysie.

IV. V. JOHN and ADAM, twins, born 20th January, 1546. Adam died in six months. John married Elizabeth, daughter of Robert Risby, of Thorpe Morieux, Suffolk County; and died in Ireland, 26th July, 1613.[2]

VI. ADAM (2), born 10th August, 1548. Died 1623, at Groton Manor. He will form the subject of our next chapter.

---

[1] This was Dr. William Alabaster, who is thus described in Fuller's Worthies (vol. ii. p. 343): "A most rare poet as any our age or nation has produced: witnesse his Tragedy of 'Roxana,'" &c. "He was made Prebendary of St. Paul's, and Rector of ye rich parsonage of Tharfield, in Hartfordshire." He had turned Papist during a visit to Rome; and on that account, after coming back to England, had been imprisoned in the Tower. But, of course, he had renounced the Pope before obtaining "the rich parsonage." He died in 1640.

[2] He has been supposed to have left a son, from whom came Stephen Winthrop, of Bandon (1658): among whose numerous descendants may be named the late Benjamin Winthrop, Esq., of London, Governor of the Bank of England, 1804–5; his son, the late Benjamin Winthrop, Esq., of University College, Oxford, and of Lincoln's Inn, London; his nephew, the Rev. Benjamin Winthrop, M.A., of Wolverton, Warwick; and the late Winthrop Mackworth Praed, M.P., the lamented poet and statesman. The family records leave the first link of this connection in some doubt; but a letter in my possession, dated "Bandon Bridge in Ireland, the 5th day of March, 1637," addressed "To her lovinge & aproued good frend and Kinsman, Mr. John Winthrop in New England," and signed, "Your lovinge Cosen Joane Winthorp, daughter to Willyam Hilles," settles the question, that the Winthrops of Bandon were of the same family with those of Groton. Joane Hilles, daughter of William Hilles, of Holton Hall, Suffolk County, was married to Adam Winthrop, a cousin of our Massachusetts Governor Winthrop, early in 1600; and had a son, named Adam, in April, 1601. Joane writes that her husband had been dead three years in 1637. He was undoubtedly the son of William Winthrop, of St. Michael's, Cornhill, London; and thus the Bandon Family may have been descended from William, and not from John.

VII. CATHARINE, born 17th May, 1550. Married, and had children. Died[1] ——.

VIII. SUSANNA, born 10th December, 1552. Married D. Cottie, and had children. Died at Coventry, 9th August, 1604.

Adam Winthrop, whose children have thus been enumerated, seems to have become prominent in the ranks of the clothiers, and to have obtained a distinguished position in that famous Clothworkers' Company of London, into which royalty itself, half a century afterwards, thought it no scorn to seek an entrance. King James I. (we are told) incorporated himself into the clothworkers, as men dealing in the principal and noblest staple-ware of all these islands. " Being in the open hall, he asked who was master of the company: and the Lord Mayor answered, ' Sir William Stone;' unto whom the king said, ' Wilt thou make me free of the clothworkers?'—'Yea,' quoth the master, ' and think myself a happy man that I live to see this day.' Then the king said, ' Stone, give me thy hand; and now I am a clothworker.'"[2] It appears, from the court-books of this ancient company, that Adam Wyntrope was one of the stewards in 1537–8, quarter-warden in 1544, and upper-warden in 1545; and that he obtained the full dignity of master of the company in 1551.[3]

---

[1] Catharine is not named in her father's will, in 1562, when she could have been but twelve years of age. The old pedigree can hardly be correct in its indefinite statement, that she "married, and had children."

[2] 12th June, 1607. Howes' Continuation of Stow's Chronicle to 1631, p. 890.

[3] The company have recently erected a magnificent new hall, in which I saw (1860) a portrait of King James and one of Sir Samuel Pepys. The latter was master in 1677; and presented to them the rich "loving cup," which is still used on all festive occasions. George Peabody, Esq., the American banker, was admitted to the company, at a sumptuous banquet, after his recent munificent provision for the poor of London (1862), and one of the lineal descendants of Adam Winthrop, the Master of the Company in 1551, was present on the occasion.

In 1543, it is recorded in the old pedigree, that this Adam Winthrop was imprisoned in the Fleet for having had negotiations with foreigners, contrary to the edict of the king; and there detained until he had paid six hundred pounds into the royal treasury. These were the days when England was protecting her wool-trade by severe restrictions, and Adam may have incurred the penalty of some anti-free-trade enactment. These were the days, too, of violent and arbitrary religious persecutions; and it may be that he was found in correspondence or negotiation with reformers who had fled beyond the seas. This idea would accord with Cotton Mather's tradition about his brother and the martyr Philpot. At any rate, a fine of six hundred pounds would seem to indicate a considerable fortune, as well as a considerable fault, whatever it was. In 1548, he is stated to have been inscribed as an esquire (armiger) under the hand and seal of the young King, Edward VI.; and in the same year, "in the parish of St. Peter's, in the street called Gracious," his son Adam — the third Adam spoken of by Mather — was born.

Meantime, we learn from the history of Suffolk County, that "Groton, formerly the lordship of the Abbot of Bury, was granted at the dissolution to Adam Winthrop, Esq.; in whose family it continued till about the fourth year of Charles I."[1] The dissolution of the monasteries took place between the years 1536 and 1540; but the formal grant to Adam Winthrop, as recently found among the Patent Rolls in the Public Record Office in

---

[1] Excursions in Suffolk, vol. i. p. 78: London, 1818.

London, bears date 35 Henry VIII. (1544). The instrument, as translated by an expert from the original abbreviated Latin, began as follóws: —

" The King, to all those, &c., greeting. Know that we, in consideration of the sum of four hundred and eight pounds eighteen shillings and threepence, of lawful English money, paid into the hands of the Treasurer of our Court of Augmentation of the revenues of our crown by our beloved Adam Wynthropp (of which said sum we confess ourself fully satisfied and contented, and that the said Adam, his heirs and executors, are henceforth acquitted by these presents), of our special favor, certain knowledge, and mere intent, have given and conceded, and by these presents do give and concede, to the aforesaid Adam Wynthropp, all that our manor of Groton, in our county of Suffolk, with all its rights, members, and appurtenances, to the late monastery of Bury. St. Edmond's, in the same county, formerly belonging and appertaining," &c.

Adam seems to have established himself at Groton, for a part of the year, not long after this grant, and to have soon been called on to exercise the authority which it conferred. It appears, from the Registry of the Archdeaconry of Sudbury, that Roger Ponder was inducted Rector of Groton, Feb. 13, 1546; having been presented to the living by " Adam Wintrop, Lord of the Manor, and Patron of the Church." At Groton, too, this second Adam Winthrop died, in 1562; and an original bronze plate upon his tomb — now in my possession, and probably removed from the tomb when the longer inscription given in the introductory chapter was engraved upon the stone tablet — contained the following inscription: " Here lyeth Mr. Adam Wynthrop, Lorde and Patron of Groton, whiche departed owt of this Worlde the IXth day of November, in the yere of oure Lorde God MCCCCCLXII."[1]

In the old pedigree, from which all our scraps of Latin are taken, he is styled *vir pius, et veræ religionis amans.* There is a likeness of him still extant, having many of the characteristics of a Holbein; and which, if there be any "art to find the mind's construction in the face," portrays a man of an adventurous and fearless spirit. His last will and testament, as still extant in the Prerogative Court of Canterbury, England, was dated 20th September, 1562; and proved 15th January, 1563. It leaves to his wife, Agnes, the use of his house and furniture in St. Michael's, Cornhill, whenever she visits London. It names his sons, — William, John, and Adam; and his daughters, — Alice, Bridget, Mary, and Susan. These were, undoubtedly, all the children who survived him.[2]

The widow of Adam Winthrop was afterwards married to William Mildmay, of Springfield Barnes. She died 13th May, 1565, *femina præclaris condecorata donis;* and his daughter Alice married William Mildmay's son Thomas, who was afterwards knighted, and she became the Lady Mildmay. This was the Lady Mildmay from whom came "the stone pot with the silver lid," to which we shall find further reference hereafter, and which was preserved as an heir-loom in the family

---

[1] Edward Howes, writing to John Winthrop, jun., from London, 3d September, 1636, says, "Your Aunt Downing hath bespoken a black marble gravestone for your grandsire and grandmother." This was undoubtedly the period of the change.

[2] The will refers also to a sister Whiting; and to another sister, the wife of Richard Burd, of Ipswich, of whom I know nothing.

Holbein.   Jackman.

SPES VINCIT THRONUM

From the original in the possession of
Tho⁵. Cha⁵. Winthrop, Esq N.Y.

adam wyntkopp

OB. 1562.   ÆT. 64.

until a late day, when it was deposited among the treasures of the American Antiquarian Society, at Worcester, Massachusetts.

An ancient certificate from the Herald's Office, now in my possession, dated 1582, and in which, as in most other ancient instruments, there is a plentiful lack of punctuation, gives the arms of the family as follows: —

" To all and singular Nobles and Gentlemen of what estate dignity or degree (soever) bearing Armes to whom these presents shall come William Detheck also Garter principal King of Armes sendeth deu commendacions and greetings. Know ye that whereas by virtue of the ancient authority of my office from the Queenes most Excellent Majesty I am to take generall notice and to make publique declaration record and testimony for all matters and causes of Armes pedigrees and descents of all Noblemen and gentlemen through all her Majesty's Kingdoms Dominions principalities Isles and provinces To the end that like as some by their ancient names parentages kindreds and descent are generally known and anciently registered in the records of my office So others for theyre vertues va ntness dignities and deserts may be worthely approved and better discerned by these lawdable ensignes and tokens of honor and worshippe most necessary to be had and used in all the commendable acts of gentility. Wherefore having proof of this shield and cote of armes apperteyning to the name and ancestors of JOHN WYNETHROP Esquire, sonne of ADAM WYNETHROP of Groton in the County of Suffolk, Gentleman : I the said Garter principall King of Armes, according to the authority and custome of my office have thought good to declare blaze and exemplify the same shield or cote of Armes together with a creast or cognizaunce appropriate for achievement to the same viz, vizor *d'argent* three Chevrons *Gules Crénelé* over all a Lion rampant *Sables* armed and langued *azure*. And for his creast or cognizaunce a Hare proper running on a mount *vert* sett upon a helmet in a wreathe of his coullors with mantells and tassells as appeareth in this margent — To have and to hold use and enjoy the said shield and Cote of armes with the said three Chevrons and the Lion rampant together with the creast and cognizaunce of a Hare proper running upon a green hill and every part and parcell thereof unto the within named JOHN WYNETHROP, gent: and others the children issue and posterity of the said ADAM WYNETHROP of Groton of the sayd County of Suffolk Esquire lawfully begotten (observing their due differences) for ever. And that they may have use and beare the same Armes and Crests upon their Shields Targets Swords or Ensignes for Warre or in their rings signetts and seales for letters and evidences or in and upon their howses buildings edifices utensiles and liveries or otherwise eyther paynted carved or figured upon tymber marble glasse metall stones tombes or monuments : And finally for any other lawful warlike or vertuous and civile uses and exercises such as by the lawes of armes and customes for gent: apperteyneth : And this without any lawful impediment or contradiction of any person or persons. IN WITNESS and perpetual remembrance and testimony hereof I the said GARTER principall King of Armes have to these lettres patent subscribed my name and fastened the Seale of my office endorsed with the signet of my armes — YEOVEN at the office of Armes London the 24 day of June in the XXXIII year of the reigne of our Sovereigne Lady Elizabeth by the grace of GOD Queene of England France and Ireland defender of the faith.

1592
William Detheck Garter
principall Kinge off Armes."

The John Winthrop named in this certificate is unquestionably the same who has already been mentioned as born in 1546, and who removed to Ireland, and died there in 1613. It will be seen, however, that it was not an original grant of arms, but only an exemplification of " the shield and cote of armes apperteyning to his name and ancestors."

In addition to the children of Adam Winthrop heretofore given, the names of at least three more have found their way into a comparatively modern account of the family: viz., Robert, who is called of Scotland; Elizabeth, who is said to have married a Cottie; and Anne. No dates of their births or deaths, however, are anywhere given; and no mention whatever is made of them in the old Latin pedigree. The author of that pedigree could hardly fail to have known how many brothers and sisters he had; and he states expressly, that his father had four sons and one daughter by his first wife, and three sons and five daughters by the second wife. This would seem to settle the question, that Robert, Elizabeth, and Anne belonged to an earlier or a later generation.

In some accounts of the family, both manuscript and printed, it has been stated that Adam Winthrop, the father of these children, was once " Master of Trinity Hall, Cambridge, and Vice-Chancellor of the University."[1] This were, certainly, a feather in the family cap, not readily to be relinquished; but neither the Latin pedigree on which we have relied, nor the records of the university, which are still more conclusive, afford any authority for this statement. The career of Adam, as it may be gathered from the foregoing facts and dates, would seem quite inconsistent with his having

---

[1] Discourse on the death of Hon. John Winthrop, LL.D. and F.R.S., Hollis Professor of Mathematics and Natural Philosophy at Cambridge, New England; by Edward Wigglesworth, A.M., Hollis Professor of Divinity, 1779, p. 23.

held such an office; and we can only account for such an error having crept into print, by the conjecture, that the title, which really belonged to good Bishop Still, the reputed author of " Gammer Gurton's Needle,"[1]— whose sister, as we shall presently see, was married to Adam Winthrop's son, — was accidentally misplaced in transcribing the pedigree at some day long past, and became attached to a name to which it did not belong. John Still, afterwards Bishop of Bath and Wells, was Master of Trinity, and Vice-Chancellor of the University of Cambridge, between 1576 and 1592. It does not often happen, that, after the lapse of nearly three centuries, a borrowed plume can be so honestly accounted for, or so readily restored to its rightful owner. Meantime, however, we shall see, in our next chapter, that the son of this Adam Winthrop held an honorable and responsible relation to the University for many years.

---

[1] " The evidence that Bishop Still was the author of Gammer Gurton's Needle is exceedingly slight." — *Prof. Craik's Manual of English Literature.* London, 1862, p. 205.

CHAPTER III.

ADAM WINTHROP, THE THIRD OF THAT NAME. HIS FAMILY AND
PERSONAL CAREER. HIS POETRY, DIARY, AND ALMANACS.

ADAM WINTHROP (3d), the father of our Massachusetts
Governor, and the third son of Adam Winthrop and
Agnes Sharpe, was born in London, in the parish of
St. Peter's, and " in the street which is called Gracious "
(Gracechurch), on Friday, 10th August, 1548. Of his
early life and fortunes we have but few details. His
father died when he was but fourteen years of age ; and
his mother lived only three years afterwards, — having,
as we have seen, been married again in the mean time.
Of course, he had but a brief enjoyment of parental
care and culture. The family traditions, as perpetuated
by Cotton Mather, represent him to have been a lawyer ;
and he has sometimes been recorded as a serjeant-at-
law. A memorandum in one of his old account-books
proves that he was of the Temple in London in
1594 ; and that, on the 21st of February of that year,
he paid " to Mr. Marple, the chiefe buttler of the Temple," for all his pensions in advance, for " an Aide
Roule," and for the reparation of the church, the sum
of fifty shillings. A note of his " gaynes in lawe "
during the preceding year, amounting only to seven or
eight pounds, would not indicate, however, a very exten-

sive practice at that period of his life, whatever it may have been in his earlier years. After this date, he seems to have resided almost altogether at Groton, and to have occupied himself mainly with agricultural pursuits.

It is not easy to decide exactly at what period, or under what circumstances, he became lord of the manor. It would have been natural, that the Groton estate, at the father's death, should have gone first to the eldest son, William; but the London property to which he succeeded may have been considered sufficient for him. At any rate, we find a royal license of alienation among the Patent Rolls of 1557–8, under which the Groton estate was entailed upon the second son, John, who became lord of the manor on his father's death in 1562.[1] A similar license of alienation is found among the Patent Rolls of 1594, when John removed to Ireland; agreeably to which, the estate was sooner or later conveyed to Adam. But John appears to have made occasional visits to the manor for several years after his removal to Ireland; and as late as the 3d of October, 1601, we find him keeping a court at Groton Hall, when Adam says in his diary, "We had pike to dynn[r] that was iii qrt[rs] of a yarde longe, *ut puto*."

Cotton Mather would seem to imply that Adam was once the recipient of royal favor, in the following anecdote which he tells in connection with the younger John

---

[1] This second son John, as lord of the manor, presented Thomas Howlet to the living at Groton, 27th March, 1568, in place of Henry Browne, who had been inducted as rector 5th April, 1563, in place of Peter Forman, deceased, at the nomination of Agnes Wynthropp, widow of Adam (2d).

Winthrop's mission to England, in 1661–2, to obtain the charter of Connecticut: "I have been informed, that while he was engaged in this negotiation, being admitted unto a private conference with the king, he presented his majesty with a ring, which King Charles I. had, upon some occasion, given to *his grandfather;* and the king not only accepted his present, but also declared that he accounted it one of his richest jewels; which, indeed, was the opinion that New England had of the hand that carried it." This ring has become historical, and has been the subject both of story and of song. A lively version of the anecdote, and of the marvellous influence of "the bauble" in securing the charter for Connecticut, may be remembered in the third chapter of Cooper's charming tale of "The Wept of Wish-Ton-Wish;" and Trumbull and Pitkin have incorporated the tradition into the graver pages of history.[1] Doubtless it must have had some foundation in fact; and a miniature of Charles II. is still in possession of some of the descendants[2] of the Connecticut governor, which is said to have been given to him by Charles himself on the same occasion. But, if the ring were ever given to Adam Winthrop, it must have been while Charles I. was still only a prince, as he was not crowned until two years after Adam's death.

There are abundant proofs that this Adam Winthrop was a man of good education and of high social stand-

---

[1] Hollister's recent History of Connecticut repeats the story (vol. i. p. 208); and Miss Caulkins, the historian of New London, has written a pretty ode upon it: but Roger Wolcott, in his elaborate Poem on the Agency of Winthrop in procuring the Charter, published in 1724, does not allude to it.

[2] The family of the late brave and brilliant Major Theodore Winthrop, who fell at Big Bethel, June 10, 1861.

ing. The old pedigree, from which we have cited so
many scraps of Latin, would bespeak him to have been
not altogether wanting in scholarship,[1] mingled, perhaps,
with a sufficient share of pedantry. The late Rev.
Joseph Hunter, of London, in the following extract
from his valuable communication upon "Suffolk Emi-
grants," made to the Massachusetts Historical Society in
September, 1847, furnishes evidence that he was not
without some humble pretensions as a poet; his verses
having been thought worthy of preservation in a miscellany of the poetry of the time: —

"Adam Winthrop" (says Mr. Hunter) "received, as a
present from 'his sister, Lady Mildmay,' in 1607, 'a stone
pot, tipped and covered with a silver lid,' which is still preserved as a relic in the family. Mr. Savage, to whose edition
of Winthrop's History I owe this information, has not shown
us which of the Lady Mildmays of his time (for there were
several) stood in the relation of sister to Adam Winthrop:
but in his communication to the society, of information collected by him in England in the year 1842, he gives an extract
from the parish-register of Groton, which distinctly shows
that it was Thomas, son of William Mildmay, who married
Alice Winthrop, the sister of Adam; and he correctly states,
that this Thomas Mildmay was Mildmay of Springfield Barnes
in Essex, was knighted, and that thus the daughter of Winthrop became Lady Mildmay. This lady is, indeed, distinctly
described by Morant, in his 'History of the County of Essex'
(vol. ii. p. 24), as Alice, daughter of Adam Winthrop, of
Groton. Morant further informs us, that Sir Henry Mildmay,
of Graces, in the parish of Baddow, near Chelmsford, was
the issue of this marriage. This Sir Henry and his family
are the Mildmays who are named occasionally in the Winthrop

---

[1] The Latin is generally in hexameter or pentameter verse.

Letters. He lived till ʻ1639, when he died at the age of sixty-one. The wife of this Sir Henry was a near neighbor and friend of the Winthrops, a daughter of Gurdon of Assington,[1] the next parish to Groton, the family intended by the Governor, when, in his first letter to Groton from the new country, he desires to be remembered to all at Assington ; and this Lady Mildmay (not the Lady Mildmay originally a Winthrop, as might at first be supposed) is the lady to whom the lines which follow were addressed by Adam Winthrop. There is something pleasing in them ; and we may observe, that they exhibit something of the same feeling which we may collect from some passages of his son's writings belonged to him. The child who was thus welcomed to the world, became, in due time, member for his county, and was ' the implacable political enemy of Sir John Bramston' (Autobiography of Sir John, p. 122). The lines are preserved in a miscellany of poetry of the time, now No. 1,598 of the Harleian Manuscripts.

" *Verses made by Mr. Adam Winthropp to the Ladie Mildmay at y*ᵉ *Byrth of her Sonne Henery.*

MADAM,

I singe not like the swanne, that readye is to dye ;
But with the Phœnix I rejoyce, when she in fire doth frye.
My soule doth praise the Lord and magnifie his name,
For this sweete babe which in yoʳ wombe he did most finely frame.
And on a blessed day hath made him to be borne,
That with his giftes of heavenly grace his soule he might adorne.
God graunt him happie days in joye & peace to lyve,
And more of this most blessed fruite hereafter to you give.
                                                                Amen.

Ah me what doe I meane, to take my penne in hande,
More meete it were my aged Muse should reste and silent stande.
For pleasure take I none in music's sweetest laies,
Nor do delight, as I was wonte, in them to spend my daies.
Yet when the joyfull newes did come unto my eare,
That at this time a sonne was borne of you, my Ladie deare :
My hɑrte was filde with joye, my spirits revived all,
And from my olde & barren brayne these verses rude did fall :

---

1 Amy Gurdon was Sir Henry's second wife. His first marriage is thus given in Adam Winthrop's diary, 1 June, 1609 : " My nephiew Sʳ. Henry Mildmay was married to Sʳ. Willᵐ Harris his daughter of Cricksey."

Welcome sweete babe thou art unto thy parents deare,
Whose hartes thou filled hast with joy, as well yt doth appeare.
The day even of thy byrth, when light thou first didst see,
Foresheweth that a joyfull life shall happen unto thee.
For blessed is that daye and to be kept in mynde,
On which our Saviour Jesus Christ was borne to save mankinde.
Growe up therefore in grace, and feare his holie name,
Who in thy mothers secreat wombe thy members all did frame ;
And gave to thee a soule thy bodie to susteyne,
Which when this life shall ended be, in heaven with him shall reigne.
Love him with all thy harte, and make thy parents gladd,
As Samuell did, whom of the Lord his mother Anna had.
God graunt that they may live, to see from thee to springe,
Another like unto thyselfe who may more joy them bringe.
And from all wicked wayes, that godles men do trace,
Pray daylie that he will thee keepe by his most mightie grace.
That when thy dayes shall ende in his appoynted tyme,
Thou mayest yelde up a blessed soule defiled with noe cryme.
And to thy mother deere obedient be and kinde,
Give eare unto her godlie words and print them in thy mynde.
Thy father likewise love and willingly obey,
That thou may'st long possesse those lands which he must leave one daye.
                                        FINIS." [1]

Mr. Hunter did not venture to give the exact date for these verses; but we shall presently find conclusive authority for saying, that the child whose nativity they celebrated was born on Christmas Day, 1619. We could hardly commend them as a birthday ode or a Christmas carol for the present generation; though we doubt not that many "ruder verses" have fallen from "old and barren braynes," both in that day and in this. They are only valuable, however, as giving a glimpse of domestic life nearly two hundred and fifty years ago, and as furnishing an amusing illustration of the character

---

[1] Mass. Hist. Coll., 3d series, vol. x. pp. 152–4. An original draught has enabled us to make some corrections in these verses, which are written by their author in long lines, as here printed.

and qualities of their author. How little could he have dreamed of their being reproduced after so long an interval, and subjected to the criticism, perhaps to the ridicule, of remote generations in a widely distant hemi-sphere!

But still less could he have dreamed of the survival to this day of his private diary, and of the family alma-nacs in which he had recorded so many of his own experiences and of the daily occurrences in his little household. Of the old Winthrop Almanacs, there are no less than fifteen remaining.[1] Two of them, it is true, bear date after Adam's death. The almanac for the year 1631 belonged to Governor Winthrop of Massachusetts, and contains but few memoranda, and those of no parti-cular interest. That for the year 1662 belonged to Governor Winthrop of Connecticut, and contains at least one memorable entry in his own handwriting: —

" This day, May 10 in the afternoon, the Patent for Connec-ticut was sealed.

But all the almanacs for the previous years were the property of our third Adam, and several of them con-tain highly interesting and characteristic memoranda in his plain and well-preserved handwriting; while his little Diary, embracing a great part of the period from 1594 to 1610, abounds with the details of his own life, and of the lives and fortunes of his friends and neighbors.

It appears from this Diary, and from the accounts

---

1 Twelve of them are in the library of the Massachusetts Historical Society, and three of the most precious of them — those for the years 1603-4, 1614-15, and 1621-2 — in my own possession. For the recovery of two of them, I was indebted to the unfailing kindness of my friend, George Livermore, Esq.

which form a part of the same manuscript volume, that he held the office of Auditor at Trinity College, Cambridge, for not less than sixteen or seventeen years; and that he was accustomed to spend a week or more every winter at Cambridge in examining the college-accounts. He was the Auditor of St. John's College, also, during a part, if not the whole, of the same period. Thus, as early as 1593, and again in 1597, we find him entering among his annual receipts a fee of eight pounds six shillings and eightpence from Trinity College, and a fee of thirteen shillings and fourpence from St. John's; while in his Diary we find the following records: —

"1601. The ivth of Decemb. I ridde to Cambridge & beganne the Auditt the 7th beinge Monday.

The xiiijth of Decembre I returned from the Auditt & did see the Sonne in the Eclips about 12 of the Clock at noone.

1604. The last of Novemb. I rode to Cambridge to keepe the Audit at Trinitie Colledge & I ret. the xvth of December.

1605. The iij^{d} of Decembr. I did ryde to the Auditt at Trinity Coll. & retourned the xvijth.

1608. The Seconde day of December I did ryde to Cambridge.

The xiith of December I retorned home from the Auditt."

In January, 1609–10, we find him recording the circumstances under which he resigned his auditorship, as follows: —

"The 22 & 23 (January) Mr. Dr. Meriton[1] came to speake wth me about the resigninge of my office in Trinity College to Mr. Brookes.

---

[1] Rev. George Meriton, D.D., who died Dean of York, 23d December, 1624, and was buried in the south aisle of York Minster.

The 27 I surrendered my Auditorship in Trinitye College to the M.ʳ fellowes & schollers before a pub. notary.

The iiij.ᵗʰ of Marche I dyned at D.ʳ Meriton's in Hadley & received of him a xx.ˡᵇ for my Auditorshippe.

1610. On Munday the xvi.ᵗʰ of Aprill Mr. Rich. Brooke the nue Auditor of Trinity College was at my house in Groton, to whom I dd. divers paper books & Roles touchinge his office."

From the following entry in his Diary, it appears that he held other offices also during the same period, of more or less interest and importance to the community in which he lived: —

" 1602. The vij.ᵗʰ of Aprill I was appointed by S.ʳ W.ᵐ Waldegraue and iij other Justices to be one of the Overseers of the poore & one of the Serchers of Cloth w.ᵗʰin Groton. *Juratus et obligatus.*"

A still more extended view of his various employments and avocations may be gathered from such entries as these: —

" 1606. The xv.ᵗʰ day of Aprill I kept a Court for my brother Snelling at Shimplinge.[1]

The xxviij.ᵗʰ I kept a Court at Groton Hall.

The 29 (June) I kept a Court at Shimplinge.

The 2 day (October) I kept a Court for Mr. Manocke at Toppefields.

The xxi.ˢᵗ I kept a Courte & leete at Shimplinge.

The xv.ᵗʰ (January) I satt upon a Commission with Mr. Clopton at Lang.ᵐ

The xviij.ᵗʰ (Marche) I did keepe a Court at Toppesfields.

1607. The 22 of July I was sworne one of the Grande Jury at the Assises then holden at Bury before my L. Coke. Mr. Ryce was the foreman.

---

[1] A parish in Suffolk County, not far from Lavenham.

34   LIFE AND LETTERS

The vi[th] of October I kept a leete & Court baron for Mr. Edward Newport at Bromley Hall in Essex.

1608. The last of June I made Rob: Waspes Will.

Oct. 24th I kept a Court at Bromley Hall."

Adam, be it remembered, at this busy period, was already a grandfather, and had passed his sixtieth birthday. But his diary and almanacs deal with many other persons besides himself, and with many other occurrences besides those in which he was himself an actor. We find him sometimes setting down with particular precision the religious observances of the time; as, for instance, in the following entries: —

" 1596. The ix of August my brother Weston [1] preched at Boxford, *sup*. 13 Marcū versu ultimo, *pie et eloquenter*.

1603. The vth day [August] was celebrated for the King's deliverance in Scotland the same day of the moneth An° [1583] from being murdered by the Erle of Gowry. Mr. Birde preached at Boxforde uppon the 12 psalme, *pie et docte*.

1605. The xviii[th] day of July Mr. Welshe the preacher of Little W [aldingfield] died, & was buried in the said Churche the 20th of July, Mr. Knewstub preached the funerall Sermon, & he wth other preachers carried his coffin on ther shoulders.

The first of August my Cosyn Munnings preched at Boxford a very godly & learned Sermon uppon the 5th chap. of Gen: v. 1. 2. 3.

The xxix[th] [August] Mr. Rogers [2] preached at Boxford, Jam. 4. 1. 2. 3. 4.

1606. The xiiii[th] of Sept. Mr. Sands preched at Groton.

1607. The last of Decembr. Mr. Willm Amyes [3] preached at Boxford uppon the 80 psalme, & first verse, *pie et docte*.

---

[1] Roger Weston, Vicar of Wormingforde, Essex Co., who had married a sister of Adam Winthrop's wife. He died 2d December, 1608.

[2] Doubtless of Dedham, Co. Essex.

[3] William Ames, the learned Puritan preacher and writer, the author of "Medulla Theologica," and professor in the University of Franeker in Holland in 1629.

1616. March 9. Mr. Sands preched at ye Communion.

1619. March 1. Ash Wedensday, the first day of Lent, Mr. Layfield preached at Boxforde.

8, 9. The Assizes at Bury. Mr. Mūninge preached before the Judges. Mr. Vertue preached at Boxforde.

1620. April 17. Mr. Rogers of Dedham preached at curfey.

My Cosen Jeremy Raven[1] preached at Boxforde on Sonday in the afternoone, 18 Junii, 1620. Psal. 136. v. 15."

Sometimes we find him recording events of wider and more public interest; as, for example, in the years 1602–3–4:—

"1602. On Wedensdaye the xxiiii of Marche Queen Elizabeth died & James the vith Kinge of Scotland was proclaymed the next day at London, & on Saturday the xxviith at Colchester & Sudbury wth the great rejoicings of all men.

The iiii of Aprill Dr. Nevill M^{r}. of Trinitie College in Cambrige & Deane of Canterbury went towarde Scotlande in the name of the Clergie.

The xvith of Aprill being Saturday the Kinges ma^{ty} came to the Citty of York.

The xviii of Aprill Mr. Clopton toulde me that the Kinge had sworne the Erles of Northumberland & Cumberland of his privy counsell & also the L. Tho. Howard & the L. Mountague, & that the Lord Howarde should be L. Chamberlayne.

The 21 the Kinge did come to Shrewsbury, the 22 to Newarke, the 23 to Bever Castle.

The 23 of Aprill the Justices of the Peace were sworne to the Kinge & appointed Justices by force of a nue Commission.

---

1 Doubtless a cousin of Adam Winthrop's wife. In Adam's account-book, he mentions having paid (as executor of his father-in-law, Henry Browne) a legacy of xl^{s}. to his uncle Raven, and another of the same amount to John Raven. John was a native of Hadleigh, and *Rouge Dragon* in the Herald's Office in 1589.—*Proceedings of Suff. Inst. of Archæology*, vol. iii. pp. 136 and 175.

The 28th day was the funeralles kept at Westm̃ for õ late Queene Elizabeth.

The —— day the Kings ma^ty was at Cambridge.

The third of May the K. came to Teboldes[1] to Sr. Robert Cecilles house.

Mem. that the K. ma^tie sett forth a proclamation giuen at Theobaldes[1] the vii^th of May against licenses granted by the late Q. to private persons of all monopolies & against prophaninge of the Saboth by interludes Bulbaitinge & all other games.

1603. March 15. King James Q. Anne and Henry ye prince of ˌWales rode through ye Cytty of London from ye Tower to Whighthall.

19. The Parleament began at Westminster where the K. made an Eloquent Oration to ye Lordes and Cõmons.

1604. the xxix^th (Aprill) my Cosen Munninge was at Groton & showed me a booke in Latine, *De Unione Britanniæ.*

24 Oct. It was proclaymed that England & Scotland should be called Great Brittaine."

Such entries as these, in any almanac or diary of modern days, would by no means imply any peculiar information on the part of the person by whom they had been made. Any one might easily copy them from a Court Journal or a Royal Gazette. But it must not be forgotten, that newspapers were quite unknown at the time these entries were made. The old story of the " English Mercurie," published by authority " for the prevention of false reports," and commenced under the special patronage of Queen Elizabeth and Burleigh, at

---

[1] Theobald's was a famous place for the royal sports in those days. While Sir Robert Cecil, then Earl of Salisbury, was entertaining the kings of England and Denmark there, his Britannic majesty is said to have become so intoxicated as to be obliged to be put to bed. Salisbury afterwards sold it to James, and it became his favorite residence. — *Knight's Popular History of England,* vol. iii. pp. 339–40. An odd place, certainly, for so pious a proclamation to date from!

the period of the Spanish Armada, seems now to have been entirely exploded.[1] The first genuine English newspaper was the "Weekly News" of 1622. It is quite possible that special bulletins or "Currantoes" of a royal progress may have been printed and circulated at the time; and we know that King James's Progresses were afterwards served up in a considerable tract, which has been incorporated into Nichols's elaborate work[2] on the same subject. But, unless Adam obtained his facts from some such public sources, he must not only have had his eyes and ears wide open to the movements of royalty, in order to keep the record so exactly from day to day, but must have been in the way of meeting those who could tell him something about them.

Here are other entries of somewhat the same general interest: —

"1595. The 3. 4. & 5 daies of October Sir W.[m] Waldegraue mustred all his sould.[rs], viz. 400, uppon a hill nere Sudbury.

The —— of Marche S.[r] Robert Winckfilde the ancientest Knight in Suff. died, & S.[r] Francis Hynde of Cambridgeshire the 21 of the same moneth.

1596. The vi[th] day of July the Assizes were holden at Bury. The same day was the Commencement at Cambridge & Mr. Overall[3] was made D.[r] of Divinitie.

1603. The 23 daie of July my brother Mildmay was made a knight at Whighthall.[4]

The 25th daye the Kings ma[tie] was crowned at Westm.[r]

---

[1] Encyclopædia Britannica, 8th ed., "Newspapers."
[2] Progresses, &c., of King James I. London, 1828. 4 vols. 4to.
[3] A distinguished son of Hadleigh, who died, Bishop of Norwich, in 1619.
[4] Sir Thomas Mildmay of Springfield Barnes.

1607. The viiiᵗʰ of Feb. beinge Shrove tuesday the L. Cokes seconde soonne maryed the daughter & heire of Sʳ George Waldegraue at Hicham.

1608. The xxvᵗʰ of July my lorde Coke chiefe Justice of the Comon Plaies came to Hicham to Sʳ G. Waldegraues *cum magno comitatu amicorū et famulorū stipatus.*

1609. The xiiiiᵗʰ (March) the Assizes were holden at Chelmesforde by Baron Altham only, & Sʳ Tho : Mildmay of Barnes in Springfield was highe shreve.

1617. May 9. Sir Fra : Bacon L. Keeper came to Westminster Hall with a great company of noblemen and others, to take his place in the Chancery.

24. Serjent Hutton was sworn one of the justices of the Comon Plees."

Sometimes he jots down the social incidents of his household, as follows : —

" 1596. The xvᵗʰ daye of Aprill Mr. Gawen Harvey the youngest soonne of Mr. George Harvey [1] highe shreve of Essex came to my house, & the xixᵗʰ daye he & my nephewe Henry Mildmay departed towardes Springfield in Essex.

The xiᵗʰ (July) my cosen Alibaster came to my house.

The xiii day my cosen Alib. *fatebatur se esse papistam.*

1601. On Saturday the viiᵗʰ of August my sister Mildmay, my cosen Thomas her sonne, my cosen Browne & his wife, came to my house & departed the xiiiᵗʰ. The ixᵗʰ day my sister Alib. & my sister Veysye came to my house where fyve of us that are bretheren & systers mette & made mery wᶜʰ we had not doone in xvi yeres before. [2]

---

[1] Both father and son were afterwards knighted, and were known respectively as Sir George Hervey and Sir Gawin Hervey of Marks Hall, Essex. In one of the old almanacs, the death of the father is thus noted: " Aug. 8, 1605, Sir George Harvy Lieutent of yᵉ Tower died, æt. 72." They were of the same stock with that of the present Marquis of Bristol, as may be seen on the pedigree appended to the account of the Hervey Family by my valued friend, the Venerable Lord Arthur Hervey, Archdeacon of Sudbury. — *Proceedings of Suffolk Institute of Archæology,* vol. ii. No. 1.

[2] Of the five brethren and sisters present on this occasion, Adam and his wife were of course, two. The other three were his sisters Alice Mildmay, Bridget Alibaster, and Mary, the wife of Abraham Veysye, of Ipswich

1603. The xxith (Sep.^r) my cosen Alibaster came to my house & shewed me his pardon dated the xth of Septembre.

1604. The xiii day of August Sr Isaac Appulton came to speake wth me.[1]

1608. The iiiith (October) Sr Robert Crane sent his coche for me my wyfe & my daught^r Winthrop to dine with him at Chilton.

1617. September 11. Mr. Egerton and Mr. Knewstub *pernoctabant nobiscum.*[2]

1619. March 15. Sir Jo : Deane and my lady dined with us. Mr. Pilgrime preached at B.

1620. August 26. Sir Tho. Savage sent half a bucke.[3]

1621. March 4. Mrs. Clopton and Eliz. her daugh : dined with us.

May 24. Sir Hen : Mildemay and his lady dined here."

The entries are often still more purely domestic, and sometimes even ludicrously personal; as for example: —

" 1597. The 22 day of Aprill Grymble my great mastiffe was hanged, a gentle dog in the howse but eyes oft blind.

1601. The 2 of Jan. Mr Mannocke sent me iii yardes of Satten for a token of this nue yere.[4]

1603. The xith of Aprill I & my wyfe did ride to Bockinge to the christeninge of my Cosen Firmins childe, who was named Joseph.

1606. The viiith of Jan. father Smythe of Toppesfilde came to me & brought me a fatt capon, & James Betts a bottle of Secke. Also, M^{ris} Alston sent me a fatt goose & a bottle of muskadine on nue yeres daye.[4]

---

1 Four years later, the following entry is found : —
" 1608. The xiiijth of Sept. Sr Isaac Appulton, knight, died at Little Waldingfield."
2 The names of Knewstubs and Egerton are found among the signers of " The Millenary Petition " (subscribed by a thousand ministers), for a reformation of the church, in 1603–4; which led to what is known as King James's version of the Bible, 1611.
3 Sir Thomas was of Melford Hall, where the venison is still noted for its fatness. I was told, when I visited the Hall in July, 1859, that some of the deer had lately been purchased to stock one of the parks of the Emperor of the French.
4 New-Year's presents, it seems, did not wait until the 25th of March; which was the beginning of the year, according to Old Style.

1608. The 1 of November my daught.ʳ Fones' daught.ʳ was
christened. Sʳ Robᵗ Crane & his Lady were present & she
was witnesse wᵗʰ Mres. Sampson & Mres. Bronde & myselfe.
She named the childe Dorothey.

1610. The xiiiᵗʰ of June my Cosen Munninge & Mr. Marcellyne were at my house, at wᶜʰ tyme I did give my Cosen a
Scotch dagger & Mr. Marcellyne a nue knyfe.

1622. May 4. My son rode to London ; *barbam scidi.*
July 21. I brused my shin.
August 10. *Dies natalis mei* A. W. senʳ 1548, æt 73.
October 17. My wife had two of her great teeth pulled
out."

A fair sample of all the varieties of memoranda has
thus been furnished ; and more of them may perhaps be
given in our Appendix, as supplying names and dates
which may be of interest, and even of importance, on
the other side of the ocean, if not on this.

Nor is there wanting in these ancient diaries an occasional instance of the same fancy for rhyming, of which
we have already seen so considerable a specimen. Thus
the almanac for 1620, which seems to have been prepared as a keepsake for John Winthrop the younger,
when he was a boy, and in which many of the entries
are made as if in his person, contains the following
inscription on the fly-leaf : —

> " Nomine Johannes dictus, cognomine Winthrop,
>   Sum ; possessorem quem vocat iste liber.
>
> Though that yᵉ Sun doth shine most bright
> Yet dooth the Moone rule al the night.
> The Starres also their course doe keepe,
> When men are laide and faste doe sleepe.
> But God alone dooth rule them all,
> And by his woorde they rise and fall.
>   A. W. G."

It must be remembered, that Adam Winthrop, the
grandfather, was more than threescore and ten years old

when this was written; while the grandson, on whom he evidently doted, was a boy of hardly more than fourteen.

The first entry in this almanac, written in behalf of the grandson, is the following: —

"1619. Jan. 6. My cosin Henry Mildmay was baptized, being 12 daies olde. The same day, Mr. Chaplin preached at Boxforde."

This must have been the child to whom the birthday verses were addressed. No doubt there was a grand Twelfth-Night christening frolic at Graces,[1] at which the fond old grandfather figured largely as the poet-laureate.

There is another volume extant, besides the old almanacs, which also bears evidence to Adam Winthrop's poetical turn, both in English and Latin; and which contains abundant testimony, moreover, to his careful reading and precise information. This is the work entitled " A Perambulation of Kent, conteining the Description, Hystorie, and Customes of that Shyre: Written in the year 1570, by William Lambarde of Lincolnes Inne, Gent: first published in the yeere 1576, and now increased and altered after the Author's own last copie. Imprinted at London, by Edm. Bollifant, 1596."[2]

The book is in the library of the Massachusetts Historical Society, with an inscription on the reverse of the

---

[1] In the parish of Baddow, near Chelmsford, Essex County, the seat of Sir Henry Mildmay.

[2] In Adam's diary, at the end of the year 1597, he makes a special note, that he had lent his Perambulation of Kent to Mr. Nicholson, the minister of Groton.

fly-leaf, showing that it was given to Adam Winthrop by his friend Mr. John Grimwade. On the reverse of the titlepage, there is an elaborate Latin ode, in praise of the author, in Adam's handwriting, and plainly of his own composition. Having done his best to emulate the Horatian measures, he concludes by quoting Horace outright, as follows : —

"Dignum laude virum Musa vetat mori."

The book is dedicated to " the Right Worshipfull and vertuous Mr. Thomas Wotton Esquier ; " and Wotton himself appends to the dedication a most complimentary recommendation of it " To his Countriemen, the Gentlemen of the Countie of Kent." Whereupon our Adam is moved to take up his pen again, and indite two more Latin lines, which we spare our readers ; and then an English stanza in honor of Wotton, written in what seems to be a Saxon character, as follows : —

" Although this work great fame hath won
    By Lambarde's learned skill,
Yet greater praise to it doth come
    Through Wotton's friendly quill."

Autograph notes and references by Adam Winthrop are found in the margin of almost every page of this ancient volume, and show great familiarity with other books as well as with this. He seems particularly interested in schools ; and makes a special note, that "Mr. William Lambe erected a free schoole at Sutton Valence where he was borne, and appointed for yᵉ Mʳ 20 lb. and for the Usher 10 lb. yerelye." Again he says, " A free schoole in Tunnebridge, vide Stowe, in año 5 Ed. 6." On the blank leaves at the end of the volume is found,

in his largest and most careful hand, "A table of y^e
Martyrs wch suffered in Kent in the reigne of Queene
Mary," — fifty-seven in all. Sundry providential judgments upon the persecutors are carefully noted, and
everywhere the spirit of the Reformation is clearly
indicated.[1]

Many other interesting memorials of Adam Winthrop
are found among the family papers more recently discovered; and, among them, a manuscript commonplace
book, containing an account of "the manner and order
of ye execution of ye late Queene of Scottes, wth y^e
wordes wch she spake at hir deathe, truely sett downe
by Docto^r Fletcher, Deane of Peterborowe," with an
original Latin ode on her death; and also an account
of "The Confession & Execution of Sir Walter Raleighe,"
with the letter written to his wife the night before he
died. Both these accounts, as far as they go, seem to
be almost identical with those which have already found
their way into the authentic history of the sad events
which they describe; and they are only mentioned as
indicating the class of events to which Adam's commonplace book was devoted. Another little autograph book
contains a number of poetical versions into English of

---

[1] In the library of the Massachusetts Historical Society, there is also a little tract,
entitled "The Commendation of Cockes & Cockfighting: Wherein is shewed, that
Cockefighting was before the Coming of Christ," by George Wilson, 1607; which has
many notes by Adam Winthrop, both in Latin and in English, in prose and in poetry.
In the same volume with this tract is bound up "The Infallible True & Assured Witch:
or The Second Edition of the Tryall of Witchcraft, by John Cotta, Doctor in Physicke,
London, 1624." There is reason for thinking that this Dr. Cotta was the husband of
Adam's sister Susanna, who is named in the old pedigree as *D. Cottie.* An old family
memorandum refers to the Cottie, or Cotta, who married Adam's sister, as having
written a book on witchcraft.

Henry Peacham's "Emblemata Selecta." Our readers
will willingly excuse the omission of such compositions as
these; but they would not, perhaps, be as willing to spare
the following letters, which passed between the fond old
uncle and his loving niece, the Lady Mildmay, only a
year or two before his death, and which are found carefully copied into one of the same volumes. They belong
to the family history, and give a most agreeable impression of both parties to the correspondence.

The Lady Mildmay to Adam Winthrop.

"LOVINGE UNCLE, my longe silence in not testifienge my
thanckefulnes for yor kinde letters, and those good bookes, wch I
then received from you, may give you iust cause to thincke mee
unmyndfull of yor love : and so all yor kindnes bestowed on mee
buried in forgetfulness. I doe nowe with the acknowledginge
of my faulte herein crave pardon; assuringe you, good uncle,
that my illnesse, some good time before my deliverance, was
the greate cause of my silence. God hath bin wonderfull mercifull unto mee, not onlie in givinge mee safe deliverance, but
also in restoringe me to somme strengthe again : so as I have
good hope to see you·ere longe. Desiringe still the continu-
ance of yor good praiers for yor nephew, my selfe and all
ours; that God woulde more enlighten o.^r hartes with the
knowledge of his will, and give us more sinceritie in the performance of it. Thus good uncle wth myne & Mr Mildmaies
love remembred unto yor selfe & my Aunt, I committe you to
God, & to the worde of his grace, Desiringe him to multiplie
his favours uppon yor selfe & familie; to whose protection I
commende you, & will reste ever yours in all love,

"AMY MILDMAY.
"ffrom Graces
   the XXXth of August, 1621."

Adam Winthrop to the Lady Mildmay.

" Most lovinge neece most worthie to be loved and honored
alwaies by mee —
" I received pure honye, and not bare wordes in the letter
wch you sente unto mee. The sweetnes whereof dothe so delight mee, that I shall never forget the remembrance of yor love
therein expressed. I knowe not howe to value the price thereof
beinge so effectuallie & lovinglie shewed : but to recompence it
wth the like (thoughe I gladely woulde) I finde my selfe not able.
ffor you have ministered unto me a nue occasion to augment
my desire to love you, & to admire those excellent giftes &
graces of wisdome & learninge, wch I nowe plainelie see to bee
in you. Wherefore I thincke myselfe happie to inioye yor love,
and acknowledge it for a great blessinge that you vouchsafe to
thincke me worthie of it. The wch I doe faithfullie vowe by all
meanes to preserve and maintaine so long as we live together
in this transitory life."   (Adam Winthrop.)

The Lady Mildmay to Adam Winthrop.

"24 of November, 1621.

" Worthy uncle, If my meanes coulde in any measure
equall the height of my desire, I shoulde be studious to expresse
myselfe reallie thanckfull for the greate respecte wch I have
alwaies founde in yor selfe & familie : I praie God give mee
grace to walke woorthie of yor Love ; wch I have founde so constant, as I have greatlie marvailed why you shoulde bestowe
so great Love of one of so smale merite. It is God his mercie
unto me, to whom I doe desire to be thanckefull as the first, &
to yor selfe as the seconde. As for many, so this last token of
yor great love unto me, wch I cannot any waie requight, neither
are woordes of force to discharge so great a dett, as I doe, &
ever will acknowledge deservedly due unto you. And although,
good uncle, I do not saie, have patience & I will paie, yet I

doe desire that in yor Love you woulde be pleased to accepte of this verball acknowledgement, till a more actuall performance discharge somme parte of y.^t wch I owe. I have read wth great comforte a true description of the gratious life and blessed deathe of yor woorthie sister.[1] I doute not but her praires have, and will be effectuall to drawe goddes blessinges uppon her posteritie : I praie God perfitt his woorke of grace, where it is begunne in any of us : that wee maye walke as shee hathe given us an example. Thus, good uncle, fearinge my scribblinge lynes wilbe troublesome in the readinge, wth my best affection I commit you to God : Desiring him to continue his aboundant grace unto you; that you may bee as the light that shyneth more unto the perfitt daie : To whose protection I commit o.^r soules : & rest ever, yor lovinge thoughe unwoorthie neece,

" AMY MILDMAY."

Adam Winthrop to the Lady Mildmay.

"MOST KINDE LADIE, Yo.^r sweete lettres cominge from the aboundance of yor Love, were ioyefully received into the closet of my best affections, (though nowe furred wth age & no suitable harboure for suche a gueste.) The ioye thereof hath at length quickned me up to this slender testimony of my highe esteeme of yor love, &˙ my true desire to nourishe the same. Alas (good Ladie) can there any lovelye thinge appeare to you in so crazed a bodie & mynde, that beinge a burden to itselfe, accounts it great honor from the Lorde not to be offensive to my friends, nor despised of my betters : but to bee of such price (as you please to have mee) in a trulie noble & woorthie brest, would revive my conceite to some highe pitche of myne owne worthe, but that the continual sense of my infirmities holdes me still in my right temper. Beinge nowe warned by age to expecte my change daylie, I seeke the more to withdrawe my thoughts from other things, that I maie more seriouslie intende my preparations for it; as the most needeful

---

[1] I know not who this sister could have been, unless the Lady Tyndall, the mother of his son's third wife, were so called. But she had died July 20, 1620.

studie for all; especially for mee, whose time of dissolution is even at hande. Yet so longe as life and light upholde this hearte, I shall not cease to be myndefull of yo.ʳ Love; & (as my last & best meanes of requitall) laboure to laye up wᵗʰ the Lorde some pore blessinge of praier, wᶜʰ may be remembrᵉd upon you & yours, for yo.ʳ best wellfare, when I shall sleep with my fathers." (ADAM WINTHROP.)

On the 16th of December, 1574, this Adam Winthrop married Alice Still, daughter of William Still, of Grantham, Lincolnshire, and sister of Dr. John Still, then Master of Trinity College, Cambridge,[1] and afterwards Bishop of Bath and Wells. She and her first-born child died 24th December, 1577; and were buried together in Hadley Church. The old Latin pedigree adds, *Protinus æterno mittit utrumque Deo.* Adam's diary shows that his relations to the bishop continued to be intimate as long as they both lived, frequent letters passing between them, and frequent visits being interchanged by their children; and the name of Still has been preserved in the Winthrop Family, in memory of this connection, for many succeeding generations.

On the 20th February, 1579, Adam Winthrop married, for his second wife, Anne, the daughter of Henry Browne of Edwardston, clothier. We know little of this Henry Browne, except his occupation and the date of his death, which is thus noted in Adam's diary for the year 1596 : —

" The viiiᵗʰ day of January being Saterday my father Henry

---

[1] The first wife of Bishop Still was Anne, daughter of Thomas Alabaster of Hadleigh, in the county of Suffolk. She died 15th April, 1593. Roger Alabaster, who married Adam Winthrop's sister Bridget, was a nephew of Anne. The families were thus doubly connected. — *Hist. of Hadleigh; Proceedings of Suff. Inst. of Archæology* vol. iii., No. 1, p. 140.

Browne died at the age of 76 yeres & was buried in Prittlewell Church in Essex." [1]

A little note of his to Adam Winthrop is found
among the family papers, showing a good handwriting,
and concluding with the following postscript, which
proves that he was interested in other things besides
clothmaking: "I praye you send me my boke of
Marters." [2] Another little scrap of his writing is still
more significant: "Christ toke not o^r nature upon hym
to be a patrone to ye carver or paynter: he denied that
he came to breake the law & the prophets: & the law &
prophetes forbyd ymages."

Of his wife Agnes, not even the maiden name has
come down to us; but the old Latin pedigree says that
she died Dec. 17, 1590, and speaks of her as a woman
"whose heart acknowledged Christ as its master." [3]
A pleasant impression of their daughter Anne, who
had now become the wife of Adam Winthrop, will be
derived from the following letter to her husband, written
to him at London, doubtless soon after their marriage,
as it mentions no children. It exhibits her as an industrious and devoted wife, after the pattern which is furnished us in the Book of Proverbs: "She seeketh wool
and flax, and worketh willingly with her hands." Her
anxiety to have her Bible sent to her shows that she

---

[1] Adam Winthrop's account-book contains a note of all the legacies he paid as executor of Henry Browne, amounting to £297. Among them is one of £50 to John Speede,
who is called a grandson of the testator. This may possibly have been the historian.

[2] "The Book of Martyrs became, next to the Bible, the book most loved and treasured in the homes of Protestant England." — *Our English Home, Oxford*, 1860, p. 178.
Foxe's "Acts and Monuments of the Church, or Book of Martyrs," was first published
in England in 1563.

[3] Agnes ——, the wife of Henry Browne, died 17th December, 1590: *Fœmina quæ
Christum corde gerebat herum.*

knew how to value its examples and its precepts; and the little French postscript, in which she repeats her request that it may be returned to her as soon as possible by the wagoner, and speaks of it as a French Bible, indicates that she was familiar with at least one language besides her own.

Anne Winthrop to her Husband.

" I have reseyved, (Right deare and well-beloved) from you this week a letter, though short, yet very sweete, which gave me a lyvely tast of those sweete & comfortable wordes, whiche always when you be present with me, are wont to flowe most aboundantlye from your loving hart, — wherebye I perseyve that whether you be present with me, or absent from me, you are ever one towardes me, & your hart remayneth allwayes with me. Wherefore layinge up this perswasion of you in my brest, I will most assuredlye, the Lord assistynge me by his grace, beare alwayes the lyke loving hart unto you agayne, untyll suche tyme as I may more fully enioye your loving presence : but in the meane tyme I will remayne as one having a great inheritaunce, or riche treasure, and it beinge by force kept from him, or hee beinge in a strange Contrey, and cannot enioye it; longethe contynually after it, sighinge and sorrowinge that hee is so long berefte of it, yet reioyseth that hee hathe so greatt tresure pertayninge to him, and hopeth that one daye the tyme will come that hee shall inioye it, and have the wholle benyfytt of it. So I having a good hoope of the tyme to com, doe more paciently beare the time present, and I praye send me word if you be in helthe and what sucsese you have with your letters. I sent to Cokynes (?) for the capones and they are not yet fate, as soon as they be redye I will send them. I send you this weke by my fathers man a shyrte and fyve payer of hoses. I pray sell all thes, if ye wold any for your owne werying I haue mor a knyttynge. I pray send me a

pound of starche by my fathers man. You may very well
send my byble if it be redye — thus with my verye hartye comendacions I byd you farewell Comittinge you to almightye God
to whome I commend you in my daylye prayers as I am sure
you doe me, the Lord kep us now & ever Amen.

"Your loving wife   ANNE WINTHROPPE.

"Je vous rende grace de la bien souvenance que vous avez
de moy bible francois, Je vous prie de l'envoyer en bréf par
le Rouillièr.

"If my brother Wintropp be at Londone I pray forgett not
to saye my very hartye Comendacions unto him."

By this second wife, Adam had five children. Four
of them were daughters, as follows: —

ANNE, born Jan. 5, 1580-1; died Jan. 20, 1580-1.
ANNE, born Jan. 16, 1585-6; married Thomas Fones,[1] Feb. 25,
1604-5; died May 16, 1618.
JANE, baptized June 17, 1592; married Thomas Gostling,[2] Jan. 5,
1612.
LUCY, born Jan. 9, 1600-1; married Emanuel Downing,[3] April 10,
1622.

Two years after the birth of the second of these

---

[1] An ancient pedigree of the Fones Family goes back six generations behind Thomas
to "Wᵐ Fownes of Saxbie, Esq.," who married a daughter of "Sʳ Robᵗ Hyelton, kt:"
Thomas is styled "Citizen & Apothecary of London."

[2] Gostling, or Gostlyn, was a clothier of Suffolk County.

[3] Emanuel Downing was a lawyer of the Inner Temple, London; and afterwards,
for many years, a resident in New England. He had married for his first wife a daughter
of Sir James Ware, the father of that learned Sir James Ware who has been styled the
Camden of Ireland. By her he had several children. The first child of his second
marriage (with Lucy Winthrop) was the somewhat celebrated Sir George Downing,
who was of the first class of graduates at Harvard College (1642), and whose diplomatic
services under both Cromwell and Charles II. are too well known to history to require
further allusion. One of Sir George's sisters was the second wife of Governor Simon
Bradstreet. Another (Mary) married Thomas Barnardiston, of the old knightly family
of Barnardistons at Kedington, Suffolk County, England. The death of their son,
without issue, secured the endowment of Downing College.

daughters, and under the date of 1587, the following record is found in the very words of the happy father : —

" JOHN, the only sonne of Adam Winthrop and Anne his wife, was borne in Edwardston abovesaid on Thursday about 5 of the clocke in the morning the 12 daie of January anno 1587 in the 30 yere of the reigne of Qu : Eliza : "

Edwardston has already been mentioned as a little village in Suffolk County, immediately adjoining Groton. The mother had probably gone there to pay a visit to her parents. Or perhaps Adam Winthrop may have had a country residence there, before he came into possession of the Groton estate.

CHAPTER IV.

BIRTH AND EARLY YEARS OF JOHN WINTHROP. HIS EDUCATION
AND FIRST MARRIAGE.

JOHN WINTHROP, who came to America in 1630 as
Governor of Massachusetts, was born, as we have seen,
at Edwardston, near the family seat at Groton, in the
county of Suffolk, England, on the twelfth day of January, 1587, old style; or, as we now should register it, on
the twenty-second day of January, 1588. It may help
to fix the period more distinctly in our minds, if we
remember that less than a year had elapsed since the
tragical death of Mary, Queen of Scots; and that, before
another year should pass away, the grand Spanish Armada
would be hovering on the coast of England. He was the
only son of Adam Winthrop, the third of that name, and
Anne Browne, of Edwardston; and the particularity
with which his birth is recorded — the precise day of
the week, and even the precise hour of the day — might
almost seem like the prognostication of a more than
ordinary career. But the record ends here, and we
have no details of his childhood. His parents lived
until within a few years of his coming over to New
England, the mother dying only a twelvemonth before
his embarkation; and with the exception of a few
years of his married life, and of such absences from
home as his education or his professional pursuits may

have occasioned, he appears to have resided generally with them at Groton Manor.

The domestic incidents which have been gleaned from the old diary and almanacs of his father, in the previous chapter, will have given a sufficient idea of the influences and associations which attended his boyhood. His home was plainly the scene of a liberal hospitality, where he must not only have had the affectionate supervision of intelligent and well-informed parents, but where he must have enjoyed the advantage of the best social intercourse which the neighborhood afforded. The judges and lawyers on their circuits, and the ministers of the adjoining parishes in Suffolk and in Essex on their occasional exchanges, besides the numerous leading characters of the county with whom the family was connected or acquainted, were evidently the frequent and welcome visitors of Groton Manor. An. ancient plan of the manor-house has been preserved, — taken, perhaps, as a souvenir of scenes that were to be left for ever, — and its hall and great parlor, its pantry and buttery and bake-house and brewing-house, bespeak an ample provision and accommodation for many more than its regular inmates. The old Bible of Adam Winthrop, too, is still extant; from which, though of too late an imprint to have been the companion of his childhood, the son may have acquired something of that familiarity with the sacred text, which is so marked a feature at once of the private correspondence and of the public discourse of his mature manhood.[1]

1 This Bible is now in the valuable collection of George Livermore, Esq., of Cambridge; who procured it from the library of the late Rev. Dr. Homer, of Newton;

There is ample evidence, in his life and writings, that he must have enjoyed a good education; but we know not at what schools it was commenced, nor how far it was prosecuted beneath the paternal roof. As his name had never been discovered upon the records of either of the great universities of England, it has naturally been taken for granted that he was never a student at either of them. At least one of his descendants, however, had long ago been led to doubt the correctness of this conclusion. We remembered to have seen in Gifford's " Memoirs of Ben Jonson," that no note of that great poet's matriculation was to be found at Cambridge; and that, by some accident, there had been an omission of names in the University Register from June, 1589, to June, 1602.[1] Now, in June, 1602, Winthrop would have been far advanced in his fifteenth year; and, from the history of his subsequent career, we had considered it by no means impossible that he might have completed a longer or shorter collegiate course even at that early age. Lord Campbell, in his " Life of Sir Edward Coke," says that the sixteenth year was a late age for entering the university, according to the custom of that time; and Lord Macaulay has reminded us, in one of his masterly essays, that Bacon entered Trinity College, Cambridge,

---

to whom it was probably given by the late Hon. William Winthrop, of Cambridge. It is the quarto copy of King James's Bible. The Old Testament bears date 1614; and the New Testament, 1615. It is bound up with the Book of Common Prayer, printed in 1615; with the Genealogies recorded in Scripture, by John Speed, 1619; and with Sternhold and Hopkins's version of the Psalms, 1618. A careful list of the books of the Old and New Testament is found on the reverse of the titlepage, in the unmistakable hand of Adam Winthrop.

[1] The statement was confirmed by the Rev. Joseph Romilly, M.A., the Registrar of the University.

in his thirteenth year, and left it in his sixteenth. Winthrop's friend John Cotton, our Boston minister, was at Trinity College, Cambridge, at thirteen years of age; Shakspeare's friend, the Earl of Southampton, entered Cambridge University at twelve; and Isaac Walton's Dr. Donne entered Oxford in his eleventh year.

We had seen, moreover, an account of John Winthrop's "Christian Experience," drawn up by himself, and signed with his own hand, in New England, on the forty-ninth anniversary of his birthday (1636–7), in which he expressly alludes to his having been at Cambridge "about fourteen years of age." He does not say that he was at the university; but he speaks of having fallen into a lingering fever at Cambridge at that age: and it was not altogether easy to conjecture for what purpose his parents could have sent him there, at that early period of his life, except in order to pursue his studies. On the whole, we were not without some confidence in the opinion, that he had derived a part of his education, at least, from that venerable institution in Old England, whose name and image were destined, under his own auspices and by the bounty of another of her undoubted children, — the ever-memorable John Harvard, — to be so soon and so successfully reproduced in New England.[1] Our readers, we are sure, will share with us in the satisfaction we experienced, when, after this opinion and the grounds of it were already in type, the following entry revealed itself to us in the old diary of Adam Winthrop: —

---

[1] The foundation of our New-England Cambridge University dates back to 1636. Its endowment by John Harvard, whose name it bears, was only two years later.

"1602. The 2ᵈ of December I rode to Cambridge. The viiiᵗʰ day John my soonne was admitted into Trinitie College."[1]

We shall presently see how long he remained at the university, and under what circumstances he left it. Meantime, we must not omit the brief account of his earlier years, which he has furnished in the " Christian Experience," to which reference has just been made. It gives us the idea of a very precocious youth, with a strange mixture of wildness and sobriety in his composition; manifesting at one moment a strong tendency towards religion, and at the next an equally strong susceptibility to worldly temptations. His language must undoubtedly be taken with some grains of allowance for the peculiar phraseology and forms of expression which belonged to the times in which it was written, and also for that spirit of unsparing self-examination and self-accusation which was characteristic of all the Puritan leaders. But it shall speak for itself: —

" In my youth," says he, " I was very lewdly disposed; inclining unto and attempting (so far as my heart enabled me) all kinds of wickedness, except swearing and scorning religion, which I had no temptation unto in regard of my education. About ten years of age, I had some notions of God: for, in some frighting or danger, I have prayed unto God, and found manifest answer; the remembrance whereof, many years after, made me think that God did love me; but it made me no whit the better. After I was twelve years old, I began to have some more savor of religion: and I thought I had more understand-

---

[1] The date of this admission, it will be perceived, is six months later than the period covered by Gifford's statement; but I learn from Mr. Romilly that there is no admission-book earlier than 1625.

ing in divinity than many of my years; for, in reading of some good books, I conceived that I did know divers of those points before, though I knew not how I should come by such knowledge; (but, since, I perceived it was out of some logical principles, whereby out of some things I could conclude others.) Yet I was still very wild and dissolute; and, as years came on, my lusts grew stronger, but yet under some restraint of my natural reason, whereby I had that command of myself, that I could turn into any form. I would, as occasion required, write letters, &c., of mere vanity; and, if occasion was, I could write savoury and godly counsel.

"About fourteen years of age, being in Cambridge, I fell into a lingering fever, which took away the comforts of my life: for, being there neglected and despised, I went up and down mourning with myself; and, being deprived of my youthful joys, I betook myself to God, whom I did believe to be very good and merciful, and would welcome any that would come to him, especially such a young soul, and so well qualified as I took myself to be; so as I took pleasure in drawing near to him."

One would think that a child, who at ten years of age prayed unto God in moments of fright or danger, and "found manifest answer" to his prayer; and who at twelve years of age "began to have more savor of religion," and, in reading good books, discovered that he had "more understanding in divinity" than many of his years, — was in a pretty hopeful way. But as John Winthrop, in his mature manhood, in his wilderness retreat, and from that lofty eminence of personal purity and piety on which he had now planted himself, looked back over the course of his life, and found so little to reproach himself with except the follies and frailties of childhood, he seems to have been impelled to magnify every youthful peccadillo to the full measure of a deadly sin, in order that there might be something on which to exercise the cherished graces of confession, humiliation, and self-abasement. It may be, however, that he really was as wild a lad as his words would seem to imply, and that the corruptions of his youth weighed heavily on his conscience in later years.

Suffice it to say, that we hear of his juvenile delinquencies from nobody but himself. No trace of parental rebuke, or even anxiety, can be found in the diary or letters of his father. On the other hand, it is matter of tradition, that he was made a justice of the peace at the age of eighteen years, and that, very early in life, he was exemplary for his polite as well as grave and Christian deportment.[1] He certainly lost no time in giving what Lord Bacon calls " hostages to fortune ; " for, at the age of seventeen years and three months, we find him a husband, and, soon after he was eighteen, a father. The following entries in his father's diary seem to prove that he was in attendance on the college-terms for about eighteen months after his admission : —

" 1602.   The 2 of Marche my soonne went to Cambrige.
1603.   The 23th of July my soonne came from Cambrige.
The xth [February] my sonne went to Cambrige. .
1604.   The xxiiiith of Aprill my sonne retourned from Cambridge.
The xxviith (July) my sonne did ride to Cambridge."

These are the only references, in Adam's diary, to his son's connections with the University ; and they are soon succeeded by the following : —

---

1 Mather's Magnalia, b. ii. ch. iv. ; Hutchinson's History of Massachusetts, vol. i. p. 21, note.

"1604. The vth of Novembre my soonne did ryde into Essex wth Willm Forth to Great Stambridge.

1605. The xxvith of Marche I & my soonne did ride to Mr. John Foorthes of Great Stambrige in Essex.

The xxviiith day my soonne was sollemly contracted to Mary Foorth by Mr. Culverwell minister of Greate Stambridge in Essex *cum consensu parentum*.

The ixth (Aprill) my sonne did ryde into Essex.

The xvith of Aprill he was married at Great Stambridge by Mr. Culverwell, *Ætatis suæ* 17 [*annis*] 3 *mensibus et* 4 *diebus completis*.

The viiith of May my soonne & his wife came to Groton from London, and the ixth I made a marriage feaste when Sr Thomas Mildmay & his lady my sister were present. The same day my sister Veysye came to me, & departed on the 24th of Maye. My dawter Fones came the viiith of May & departed home the xxiiith of Maye."

And thus we have the whole story of the courtship, the wedding, and the honeymoon, — the journey to London, the family gathering at Groton, and the marriage-feast at the manor.

It was undoubtedly this early marriage which brought his college-life so prematurely to a close. The serious illness at Cambridge, to which he alludes in his " Christian Experience," may perhaps have broken up his studies, and discouraged him from pursuing them further; but, so far as the record runs, the charms of Mary Forth must be held responsible for his failure to obtain a degree. She was the daughter and sole heir of John Forth, Esq., of Great Stambridge,[1] in the county

---

1 Mr. Savage gives the authority of Sir Charles George Young, Garter King at Arms, for stating John Forth to have been of Stondon; but Adam's diary, and his old almanacs and the Latin pedigree, call it expressly *Great Stambridge*.

of Essex. John was the sixth son of William Forth, of Hadleigh and Butley Abbey or Priory, in Suffolk; and was connected with many ancient and distinguished families. William's wife, the grandmother of Mary, was a Powell of Wales; and a long Welsh pedigree is still extant, duly emblazoned with all the empalements and quarterings, tracing her back, through twelve generations of Ap Howells and Vaughans and Gwarinddys and Broadspeares, to Godwyn of Cornwall. The mother of Mary Forth .was Thomasine, the only child of —— Hilles, in the county of Essex. Her uncle, Robert Forth, was high-sheriff of Suffolk County in 1569; and his second son, William, was knighted at Greenwich, 3d July, 1604. Her own immediate family was a wealthy one; and she brought to her husband " a large portion of outward estate."

Besides other blessings resulting from this marriage, Winthrop, in his " Christian Experience" of 1636–7, attributes to the associations to which it introduced him a high degree of spiritual improvement, if rather it should not be called a complete and radical change of heart and life.

" About eighteen years of age," he says, " being a man in stature and understanding, as. my parents conceived me, I married into a family under Mr. Culverwell his ministry in Essex; and, living there sometimes, I first found the ministry of the word come home to my heart with power (for in all before I found only light) : and, after that, I found the like in the ministry of many others; so as there began to be some change; which I perceived in myself, and others took notice of. Now I began to come under strong exercises of conscience (yet by fits only) : I could no longer dally with religion. God put my soule to sad tasks sometimes, which yet the flesh would shake off and outwear still. I had, withal, many sweet invitations; which I would willingly have entertained, but the flesh would not give up her interest. The merciful Lord would not thus be answered; but notwithstanding all my stubbornnesse, and unkind rejections of mercy, hee left mee not till he had overcome my heart to give up itself unto him, and to bid farewell to all the world, and until my heart could answer, ' Lord! what wilt thou have me to do?'

" Now came I to some peace and comfort in God and in his wayes : my chief delight was therein. I loved a Christian, and the very ground hee went upon. I honoured a faithful minister in my heart, and could have kissed his feet. Now I grew full of zeal (which outranne my knowledge, and carried mee sometimes beyond my calling), and very liberall to any good work. I had an unsatiable thirst after the word of God; and could not misse a good sermon, though many miles off, especially of such as did search deep into the conscience."

We know nothing of Mr. Culverwell but his name, and that only from this ancient confession of Winthrop's; but the humble village-curate, to whose faithful ministry the father of the Massachusetts Colony has thus traced his earliest and strongest impressions of the power of the word, may well be considered to have earned a title to remembrance which many a lordly prelate of his day might have envied.[1]

Of the life and fortunes of Winthrop for the next ten or twelve years, but few details have survived, and those of

---

[1] His name, as we shall find by one or two of his letters given hereafter, was Ezekiel; and Allibone, in his invaluable Dictionary of Authors, makes him the author of several religious treatises. He may have been the father of Nathaniel Culverwell, "Master of Arts, and lately fellow of Emanuel Colledge in Cambridge," who wrote the "Elegant and Learned Discourse of the Light of Nature," &c. London, 1652. This volume is in the library of my friend Charles Deane, Esq., of our Cambridge.

a purely domestic character.   The only important entries relating to him in his father's diary are the following: —

" 1608.   The xth of October my soonne & his wyfe departed from Groton to dwell at Stambridge in Essex.

1609.   The xith of August my soonne was taken wth a fierce ague, and the xviijth I ridde to Stambridge to see him & returned the xxiith.

The xxvth (October) my soonne kept his first Court at Groton Hall, where a Recouery was sued against Ed. Robtson."

This holding of his "first Court at Groton Hall" in October, 1609, was doubtless in consequence of his having attained his majority in the early part of that year.   It might seem to indicate, also, that he had returned to reside at Groton, and perhaps that he had already become Lord of the Manor.   But his father's diary comes to an end soon after this date ; and we have no means of deciding these questions.   We incline, however, to the opinion, that he continued to make Stambridge his principal place of abode for several years longer, — perhaps until the death of his father-in-law Forth in 1613.

The wife of his youth bore him six children; the eldest of whom (born at Groton on the twelfth, or, as we should now style it, on the twenty-second day of February, 1606) is known to history as John Winthrop, the Governor of Connecticut, "the heir of all his father's talents, prudence, and virtues, with a superior share of human learning."[1]   We shall find frequent occasion to

---

[1] Savage ("History of New England," vol. i. p. 64, note), unconsciously, perhaps, translating Cicero, who says of a son of P. Africanus, *Ad paternam enim magnitudinem animi doctrina uberior accesserat.*

mention him in this volume, though he might fitly become the subject of a separate memoir. Of the other children, two were sons, — Henry [1] and Forth,[2] — of whom we shall· see something as we proceed. Of the three daughters, two were named Anne, and are shown, by the parish-register at Groton, to have died successively in their earliest infancy; while Mary, the eldest, lived to come to America, and was married (about the year 1632) to the Rev. Samuel Dudley, son of Governor Thomas Dudley.[3]

Within eleven years after her own marriage, Mary Forth, the mother of these children, died, and was buried in the family tomb at Groton, 26th June, 1615.[4] So soon and so sadly was the first chapter of John Winthrop's domestic history brought to a close. He was then not yet twenty-eight years of age, and the oldest of his children was little more than nine. We need but to turn the page to find that other and not less bitter bereavements awaited him at too early a day.

Before turning that page, however, we may here find an appropriate place for such passages from an old autograph manuscript of Winthrop's as relate to this first period of his life, and as may exhibit still more clearly the early development of his moral and religious character—

1 "1607. The xx[th] of Jan. my soonnes second sonne Henry was christened at Groton. Mr. Sands & my b. Snelling were his godfathers." — *Adam's Diary.*

2 "1609. The xxx[th] day of Decemb[r]. my sonne's third sonne was borne at Stambridge, in Essex." — *Ibid.*

3 She died 12th April, 1643; having had four children, at least two of whom survived her.

4 "Mary Forthe, the wife of John Winthrop, was borne on Wednesday, the first day January, Año 1583." She was thus four years older than her husband.

racter. He was a man who evidently, from his youth upwards, held much communion with his own conscience, and frequently employed his pen in making record of its rebukes and compunctions. We have already given extracts from his " Christian Experience," written in 1636–7; and we shall have further occasion to refer to it hereafter. But a much earlier " Experience " has recently come to light, dating from the first week in February, 1606, — soon after the commencement of his married life, and within a few days of the birth of his eldest son. It is an imperfect manuscript, stained and torn in many places, and quite illegible in others; many pages missing and many passages effaced, and plainly intended for no eye but his own. It may be doubted, indeed, whether any eye but his own has ever carefully perused it until now. But no one, we think, will regret that some parts of it have escaped the ravages of time. It begins as follows: —

" EXPERIENCIA a 2 Februarij : 1606.[1]

" Worldly cares thoughe not in any grosse manner outwardly, yet seacreatly, togither wth a seacret desire after plesures & itchinge after libertie & unlawfull delightes, had brought me to waxe wearie of good duties and so to forsake my first love, whence came muche troble & danger.

" Then in that time, having not perfect peace wth God, but throughe the perswasiō of the enimie, distrustfulness beganne to arise, whenas the Lorde sent but a smale triall, my wife but beinge taken wth a fitt of an ague, myselfe beinge not prepared wth a peaceable conscience, it did much harme me, whereuppon I promised to be prepared better.

---

[1] He was, at this date, but eighteen years of age.

" Beinge in this trobble I was wholy unable to raise up my selfe, neither could I pray a great while, yet at length I desired the Lorde & he herde me, so as uppon the cōfessiō of my sinnes, wᶜʰ I did wᵗʰ much cōforte, I found mercie & grace to amende.

" In that weeke that my wife was delivred, by reason of the present occasion & of an ague wᶜʰ I had taken, I gave myself to negligence and idlenesse wᶜʰ I could not shake off a good while after : it also brought wᵗʰ it māy other sinnes as caringe for this worlde etc., & one morninge a great fitt of impatience, for matter betwixt my wife & my mother, wᶜʰ I pray God for-give me.

" Where there is not a reverend trēbling at the comittinge of smale sīnes & those but in thoughte or worde, there is no feare of God, & where there is no feare there is no faithe : therefore marke this.

" It is wonderfull how the omissiō of the leaste dutie, or com-issiō of evill, will quench grace & estrange us from the love of God.

" Feb : 8. I founde that on Saterday in the affternoone deferringe readinge & prayer til 3 of the clocke, for the per-forminge of a needelesse worke, my herte was verie muche unsettled.

" On Sūday beinge the 9 of March : beinge at sermō at Groton, I let in but a thought of my iornie into Essex, but strait it delighted me, & beinge not verie carefull of my heart, I was suddainely, I knowe not how, so possessd wᵗʰ the worlde, as I was led into one sinne after an other, and could hardely recover my selfe, till taking myselfe to prayer before I was too farre gonne, I found mercie.

" The 20 of Aprill, 1606, I made a new Covenant wᵗʰ the Lorde wᶜʰ was this :

" Of my part, that I would reforme thesse sinnes by his grace, pride, covetousnesse, love of this worlde, vanitie of minde, unthankfulnesse, slouth, both in his service & in my callinge,

not preparinge myselfe wth reverence and uprightnesse to come
to his word : Of the Lords part that he would give me a new
heart, joy in his spirit, that he would dwell wth me, that he
would strengthen me against the world, the fleshe, & ye Divell,
that he would forgive my sinnes and increase my faith.

     " God give me grace to performe my promise & I doubt not
but he will performe his. God make it fruitfull. Amen."

     After this introduction, there follows a little catalogue
of " sinnes," running through many days of many months,
registered as in an account-current against himself, but
written partly in cipher, and with so many abbreviations
and secret signs as to be quite unintelligible to any eye
but his own. Turning in despair from this private confession, we find no difficulty in deciphering the following
pleasant testimony to the character of his wife : —

     " Decembre 12. It must be only God that must worke in
the hearte, as by this experience ; — when I used the best
meanes I was able to perswade my wife etc., & that when I had
the best spirit, yet I could not prevaile not so muche as to
make hir to answeare me or to talke wth me about any goodnesse ; but yet one time when I did but only aske a questiō,
by the way as it were, & that when there were many thinges
wch justly made me feare a repulse, yet it pleased God even
then to so open hir hearte as that she became very readie and
willinge to lay open hir hearte to me in a very comfortable
measure ; whereby I see that Praïer must do it, if ever any
good be done, for I had praied often to God in that matter :
and she proved after a right godly woman."

     The last line of this passage was evidently written
with different ink and at a different period from that
which precedes it. It may have been added after death

had sealed the account between him and his first wife, and as a final tribute to her virtues. It is the only testimony which remains to the character of Mary Forth. One little note of hers is left among the old family papers, addressed to her "sweet husband;" and ending, "your loving wife until death:" but it relates wholly to the procuring of a new serving-maid, and has nothing in it worthy of preservation. Its only interest is derived from its being indorsed by her son, Governor Winthrop of Connecticut, as having been "written by Mrs. Mary Winthrop, wife to John Winthrop, Esq., sometymes Governor of New England." The son seems to have saved it, as the only memorial of his mother. His own noble character and conduct, as we shall see them hereafter developed, are the best evidence of her having been a good and godly parent as long as she was spared to her children.

A little further along, we find a passage unquestionably written after much that follows it, and intended for his own warning as to some of the resolutions and experiences which he had previously recorded. It may be not less useful to those who would construe his confessions justly, and it is given here with that view: —

" In these following Experiences there be diverse vowes, promises to God, or Resolutions & purposes of my heart, occasioned throughe the ofte experience of my weaknesse in such things, & my great desire of keeping peace & holdinge communion wth God, many of w^h I have in tyme observed that I have great need to repent (in some of them) my unadvisednesse in making them, consideringe that they have proved snares to my Conscience, & (in others of them) my wretchednesse & sinne in not carefully observing them. Mr Cartwright in his Answ : to the Rem : Acts 5. 4.[1] givethe some directions on this pointe."

We may now proceed, without further interruption or explanation, with the remaining passages which relate to the period embraced in the present chapter.

" 1610 Jan. After I had muche displeased my God by followinge idle & vaine pastymes, as sittinge late up at ——,[2] wth my unkinde omittinge my family exercise, I was muche unsettled, as there was cause, yet God (when I thought his anger was even hote against me) drewe me to repentance & showed me· sweet mercye.

" 12. But a little after beinge out of order againe through the force of a newe temptatiō ; & mine owne rebellious wicked hearte yieldinge itselfe to the slaverye of sinne, had brought me into the Lords hands againe, yet my God, the true naturall father of the prodigall, seeinge me but have a minde to returne, mette me in his fatherly love & brought me into his favo.[r] notwithstandinge all my unkindnesse.

" 17. Then by little & little by want of diligent care & observation of my hearte & wayes I lost the former freshnes of my affections, & so beganne to fall to idleness, takinge pleasure in vanitie againe, but God crossed me in my delights, & when I perceived God was angry wth me I had no harte to any dutye, till readinge the 33 of Job : v. 29 : the Lorde moved me to come to him againe, so I returned & found favor, yet not suche affections as before.

" 1611. The 22 of August it plesed God to sende me a sore sicknes wherein besides the worke of Gods Spiritt upon my conscience, I did most evidently perceive his great mercie & care in supportinge me, easinge the paine, givinge me pacience, & muche cherefullnes, & willingnes to abide his good will, &

---

[1] The reference was probably to " The Answere to the Preface of the Rhemish Testament," by Thomas Cartwright, the great Puritan writer and preacher.

[2] The place is designated in the manuscript by an unintelligible sign.

before the sicknes was come to the hight, God in mercye cutt it off by sending me wthout any meanes a great relief.

" One thinge wch I observed in this sicknes was that God visited uppon me many of my bould runninges out against conscience, wch I then when I comitted them passed over wth slight repentance, & now had suerly smarted well for them if I had not now stopped them by searious & speedye turninge to God, whereuppon I resolved not to be so bould to sinne againste my conscience in tyme to come.

" Another thinge wch I resolved uppon good grounde was to leave all my working & inventions of all sorts, especially the doinge of such things as required any labour or tyme, & to content my selfe wth such things as were lefte by o^r forefathers, & that for divers reasons as

" First "

A missing page deprives us of the reasons of this most conservative resolution. We proceed with the pages which are left: —

" I had prayed ofte & earnestly for the mortifyinge of divers corruptions, & I have certainely founde that God hathe hearde me for some of them, weakeninge the force of them by meanes that I never thought of.

" Dec : 15. I acknowledge a speciall providence of God that my wife taking upp a measse of porridge, before the children or anybodye had eaten of it, she espied therein a greate spider.[1]

" Findinge by muche examination that ordinary shootinge in a gunne, etc : could not stande wth a good conscience in my selfe, as first, for that it is simply prohibited by the lawe of the land, uppon this grounde amonst others, that it spoiles more of the creatures then it getts :   2 it procures offence unto manye :   3 it wastes great store of tyme :   4 it toyles a mans bodye

---

[1] This may, perhaps, occasion a smile; yet it would not be easy to say why a special providence might not as well be recognized in the discovery of the spider which would have poisoned the porridge, as in " the sparrow which falleth to the ground."

overmuche :　5 it endangers a mans life, etc :　6 it brings no
profite all things considered :　7 it hazards more of a mans
estate by the penaltye of it, then a man would willingly parte
with :　8 it brings a man of worth & godlines into some contempt : — lastly for mine owne parte I haue ever binne crossed
in usinge it, for when I haue gone about it not wthout some
woūdes of conscience, & haue taken muche paynes & hazarded
my healthe, I haue gotten sometimes a verye little but most
comōnly nothinge at all towards my cost & laboure :[1]

"Therefore I haue resolved & covenanted wth the Lorde to
give over alltogither shootinge at the creeke ; — & for killinge
of birds, etc : either to leave that altogither or els to use it,
bothe verye seldome & verye secreatly.　God (if he please) can
giue me fowle by some other meanes, but if he will not, yet, in
that it is [his] will who loves me, it is sufficient to uphould my
resolution.

"That wch I promise for my selfe, I likewise promise for
my servants, as farre as the former reasons agree to them.

"Beinge further resolved that pœnall Statutes doe binde the
person to obedience in these indifferent thinges, I have proposed
not to breake the intention of this Lawe, etc : this further I
hould for this matter, that thoughe lawe cannot binde from the
use of the creatures, yet it may limitt the maner of taking
them.

"1611 Jan : 1.　Beinge admonished by a christian freinde
that some good men were ofended to heare of some gaminge
wch was used in my howse by my servants, etc : I resolved
that as for my selfe not to use any cardings etc, so for others
to represse it as much as I could, during the continuance of my
present state, & if God bringe me once to be whollye by my
selfe, then to banishe all togither.

---

[1] Bad luck with his gun, though the last reason assigned, may have given the
original impulse to much of this philosophy about shooting.　It certainly forms an
amusing climax to the argument.　The Governor was evidently not a good shot in his
youth.

" 28. In my sleepe I dreamed that I was wth Christ upon earthe, & that beinge very instant wth him in manye teares, for the assurance of the pardon of my sinnes etc : I was so ravished wth his love towards me, farre exceedinge the affection of the kindest husbande, that being awaked it had made so deep impression in my hearte, as I was forced to unmeasurable weepings for a great while, & had a more lively feelinge of the love of Christ then euer before. This followed the same night after I had bine visitinge Jesus Christ in his faithfull servant, old Hudson, to whom as by my presence & helpe I afforded muche comforte, so God recompensed me wth comfort againe. And heerein I see great cause to complaine of the weaknes of my faithe that cannot see Christs helpe as neere, now he is in heaven, as it appeared when he was on earthe.

" I see that I cannot ev^r feele the same measure of the love of Christ heere, but this is my comforte that I shall have the full fruition of it in heaven.

" Feb. Gettinge my selfe to take too muche delighte in a vaine thinge wch I went about wthout the warrant of faithe, I was by it by degrees drawne to make shipwracke of a good conscience & the love of my father, so as my heart beganne to growe hardened & inclininge to a reprobate minde ; prayer & other duties beganne to growe irksome, my confidence failed me, my Comfort left me, yet I longed after reconciliation, but could not obtaine it ; I earnestly sought to repente but could not gett an heart unto it, I grew wearye of myselfe, unprofitable to others, & God knowes whither ever I shall recover that estate wch I loste ; — O that this might be a warninge to me to take good heede how I greive the good spiritt of my God & wounde my conscience, & that as the penninge of this is in many teares, so the readinge of it when occasion shalbe may be a stronge motive unto sobrietye.

" I finde that often sinninge bringes difficulty in repentinge & especially the bould runninge out against knowledge & conscience.

" After the comittinge of such sinnes as have promised most contentment and comoditie, I would ever gladly have wanted the benefitte, that I might have bine ridde of the sinne. Whereuppon I conclude that the profitt of sinne can never countervaile the damage of it, for there is no sinne so sweet in the comittinge, but it proves more bitter in the repentinge for it.

" I do certainely finde that when I sett myselfe seariously to prayer etc : thoughe I be very unfitt when I beginne, yet God dothe assist me & bowes his eare to me, especially when I aske as one that would obtaine.

" I have trembled more at the comittinge of some newe sinne, althoughe but smale in comparison, then at the doing of some evill that I have been accustomed to, though muche greater ; therefore I see it is good to beware of Custome in sinne, for often sinninge will make sinne light.

" I sawe my greate follye in that I placed so muche felicitye in present outward thinges & in the hope of thinges to come, whenas I am suer that I shall have them but for a shorte tyme, if at all. The danger & hurte of these earthly ioyes I finde to be greater in that they deminishe the ioye of my salvation : wherefore I have resolved by the grace of God, to holde my affections in a narrower compasse, & not to suffer my hearte to delight more in any thing then in the comforte of my salvation.

" Sep : 8. 1612. ffinding that the variety of meates drawes me on to eate more than standeth wth my healthe, I have resolved not to eate of more then 2 dishes at any one meale, whither fish, flesh, fowle or fruite or whittmeats etc : whither at home or abroade ; the lorde give me care & abilitie to performe it. I founde that the pride of my hearte, viz : these great thoughts of mine owne gifts, creadite, greatnes, goodnes etc : were like a canker in my profession, eatinge out the comfort of all duties, deprivinge God of a principall parte of his right in my hearte, wch I daylye perceived, when it pleased God to lett me see my meanenes in his exceeding greatnes : whereuppon I resolved to make it one of my cheife petitions to have that grace to be poore in spirit : I will ever walke humblye before my God, & meekly, mildly, & gently towards all men, so shall I haue peace.

" May 23 1613. When my conditiō was much straightned, partly through my longe sicknes, partly through wante of freedome, partly through lacke of outward things, I prayed often to the Lorde for delivrance, referring the meanes to himselfe, & wᵗʰ all I often promised to putt forthe myselfe to muche fruitt when the Lorde should inlarge me. Nowe that he hathe set me at great libertye, givinge me a good ende to my teadious quartan, freedome from a superior will & liberall maintenance by the deathe of my wifes father (who finished his days in peace the 15 of May, 1613) I doe resolve first to give myselfe, my life, my witt, my healthe, my wealthe to the service of my God & Saviour, who by givinge himselfe for me, & to me, deserves what soever I am or can be, to be at his Cōmandement, & for his glorye :

" 2. I will live where he appoints me.

" 3. I will faithfully endeavour to discharge that callinge wᶜʰ he shall appoint me unto.

" 4. I will carefully avoide vaine & needles expences that I may be the more liberall to good uses.

" 5. My propertye, & bounty, must goe forthe abroade, yet I must ever be careful that it beginne at home.

" 6. I will so dispose of my family affaires as my morning prayers & evening exercises be not omitted.

" 7. I will have a speciall care of the good educatiō of my children.

" 8. I will banish profanes from my familye.

" 9. I will diligently observe the Lords Sabaoth bothe for the avoidinge & preventinge worldly busines, & also for the religious spendinge of suche tymes as are free from publique exercises, viz. the morninge, noone, & evening.

" 10. I will endeavour to have the morninge free for private prayer, meditatiō & reading.

"11. I will flee Idlenes, & much worldly busines.

"12. I will often praye & conferre privately wth my wife.

"I must remember to performe my fathers Will[1] faithfully for I promised him so to do; and particularly to paye Mr. Meḡes 40[2] a yeare till he should be otherwise provided for.

"September 17, 1613.   There mett at Mr Sands, Mr. Knewstubs, Mr. Birde & his wife, Mr. Chambers, John Garrold & his wife, John Warner & his wife, Mr. Stebbin, Barker of the pryorye, & I with my companye, where we appointed all to meete againe the next yeare on that frydaye wch should be neerest to the 17 of September, & in the meane tyme every of us eache fryday in the weeke to be mindefull one of another in desiring God to grante the petitions that were made to him that daye, etc.

"Securitie of heart ariseth of over much delighte in the things of the world.   Perk: fol: 609:   See there the excellent issue of this temptatiō in Gods children.   Item. 784. 799."

This last paragraph is separated from that which goes before it by a black line, and is written in a large round hand, as if to designate it as the sum and substance of the whole matter.   The reference is, undoubtedly, to one of the religious treatises of William Perkins, of Christ's College, Cambridge; who died in 1602, and whose works were published in several folio volumes.   Some of our readers may remember a pleasant story about "Master Perkins" and Arminius in Izaak Walton's charming biography of Sir Henry Wotton.

---

[1] He evidently refers to the will of his wife's father, John Forth, Esq., whose death (May 15, 1613) he had just mentioned.

[2] Neither the name nor the amount can be made out with confidence. It appears to be 40.^{lb} to Mr. Megges, or Meigs.

CHAPTER V.

SECOND MARRIAGE. CLOPTON FAMILY. DEATH OF SECOND WIFE.
CHRISTIAN EXPERIENCES.

JOHN WINTHROP appears to have been married again,
on the 6th of December, 1615. His second wife was
Thomasine Clopton, daughter of William Clopton, Esq.,
of Castleins, a seat near Groton. She was of that
famous family of Cloptons which Sir Simonds D'Ewes,
having married one of them himself, has thus celebrated
in his Autobiography : —

"There is scarce a second private family of nobility or gentry, either in England or in Christendom, that can show so
many goodly monuments of itself in any one church, cathedral
or parochial, as remain of the Cloptons in that of Melford, in
the county of Suffolk, this present year (1638) : where may
be seen and viewed about threescore portraitures, anciently set
up, of men and women, with their coat-armors on most of
them, in stone, brass, or glass ; besides some gravestones on
which are no statues, and divers portraitures of glass in the
great east window of the chancel, either wholly gone or much
defaced. All which figures and representations, as appears
by the epitaphs engraven on the tombs and flat marbles, and by
the inscriptions placed under the portraitures in glass, were
there fixed and set up in memory of the Cloptons themselves
(of which there are about twenty lineals and collaterals of the
male line) ; and the rest are to perpetuate the remembrance
of their wives and daughters and sons-in-law." [1]

---

[1] Sir Simonds D'Ewes, Autobiography, vol. i. p. 338.

Winthrop, alas! was destined but too soon to have an interest in these Clopton tombstones, and to realize but too sadly that —

> " The boast of heraldry, the pomp of power,
> And all that beauty, all that wealth, e'er gave,
> Await alike the inevitable hour."

A year and a day had scarce elapsed since her marriage, when Thomasine Clopton, with her infant child, was committed to the dust, and Winthrop's home was again left unto him desolate.

No wonder, that, under such successive and severe bereavements, his spirit should have been sorely tried and exercised. No wonder that he was oppressed with melancholy, and that he should have been led to conceive and entertain many misgivings as to his religious condition. He had previously made no small progress in overcoming whatever of worldliness there was in his nature. He had even contemplated an abandonment of his profession as a lawyer, with a view to take orders as a clergyman.

"I grew," says he, in reference to a period just previous to this affliction, "to be of some note for religion (which did not a little puff me up), and divers would come to me for advice in cases of conscience; and, if I heard of any that were in trouble of mind, I usually went to comfort them: so that upon the bent of my spirit this way, and the success of my endeavors, I gave myself to the study of divinity, and intended to enter into the ministry if my friends had not diverted me. But as I grew into employments and credit thereby, so I grew also in pride of my gifts and under temptations, which set me on work to look to my evidence more narrowly than I had done before."[1]

---

[1] Christian Experience, 1636–7.

It was, however, at the precise period of these sad domestic visitations, which occurred just as he was entering upon his thirtieth year, that he describes his condition as having been most critical and his soul most desponding.

"I was now," he proceeds, "about thirty years of age; and now was the time come that the Lord would reveale Christ unto mee, whom I had long desired, but not so earnestly as since I came to see more clearly into the covenant of free grace.   First, therefore, hee laid a sore affliction upon me, wherein he laid me lower in mine own eyes than at any time before, and showed mee the emptiness of all my gifts and parts; left mee neither power nor will, so as I became a weaned child.   I could now no more look at what I had been or what I had done, nor be discontented for want of strength or assurance.   Mine eyes were only upon his free mercy in Jesus Christ.   I knew I was worthy of nothing; for I knew I could do nothing for him or for myself.   I could only mourn and weep to think of free mercy to such a vile wretch as I was. Though I had no power to apply it, yet I felt comfort in it. I did not long continue in this estate; but the good Spirit of the Lord breathed upon my soule, and said I should live. Then every promise I thought upon held forth Christ unto mee; saying, 'I am thy salvation.'   Now could my soule close with Christ, and rest there with sweet content, so ravished with his love, as I desired nothing, nor feared any thing, but was filled with joy unspeakable and glorious, and with a spirit of adoption.   Not that I could pray with more fervency or more enlargement of heart than sometimes before; but I could now cry, 'My Father,' with more confidence."

This "Christian Experience" of John Winthrop, from which we have now quoted all that seems to throw light upon his earlier years, but of which the whole will be given hereafter in the order of its date, is in many respects a remarkable paper. It is written in a stern spirit of self-condemnation and self-abasement; and, as we have already suggested, might give room for the idea that its author had been a much less exemplary young man than he probably was, were not the peculiar elements of his character and the peculiar circumstances of his condition, both at the time of which he speaks, and still more at the time at which it was written,[1] taken into consideration in reading it. But viewed in this light, or, indeed, in any light, it presents a striking picture of a pious soul struggling under the doubts and despondencies which so often beset the religious temperament, and which the peculiar trials of his lot were so well calculated to aggravate. There is, too, a zeal and a fervor of expression in it, — in some passages rising almost to the height of poetry, — which, to a religious heart, give it a charm not unlike that which belongs to some of the devotional writings of Baxter or of Bunyan, or even to the Confessions of St. Augustine.

Nor can less, certainly, be said of the earlier " Experience," to which we turn again for additional illustrations of his character and circumstances at the precise period of his life which we have now reached, and for some account of the wife whose loss he had just been called to deplore. We proceed with the story just as it stands in the stained and moth-eaten manuscript,

---

[1] It was written during the height of the Antinomian controversy in New England, when the whole Colony was agitated, and almost rent asunder, by religious excitements.

omitting only such words or passages as have been obscured or obliterated by time. Few descriptions of a death-bed have survived the lapse of two centuries and a half in such minute detail as that of Thomasine Clopton: few, certainly, have afforded more incidents illustrative at once of the habits of the period and the character of the parties concerned. As a mere picture of the domestic history of so remote a day, it could not be read without a lively interest.[1] The hopes and fears, the prayers and watchings, the wandering thoughts and delirious fancies, "the temptations of the enemy," the parting words, the passing bell, the last sighs and tears, are all recounted with a pathos and a vividness which almost make us witnesses of the scene, and partakers of the sorrow. The diary begins two days before the death took place, and on the first anniversary of her wedding-day. The events which succeeded must have been noted down from hour to hour; though the narrative may, perhaps, have been drawn up more deliberately after all was over. The exquisite tribute to her character, with which it closes, was evidently added after the first pangs of the bereavement had somewhat subsided.

"Dec: 6 1616. God will have mercie on whom he will have mercie, & when & how seemes best to his wisdome & will. And his mercie is free, meere mercie, w^thout any helpe of o^r owne worthe or will; so as for all good actions, we adde nothinge either to the deed or the doer; but, as a man shootinge

---

1 It may help to fix in our mind the exact period at which it was written, if we remember that Shakspeare died during the same year at Stratford upon Avon, where he had lived in a house (New Place) which had been built by Sir Hugh Clopton, probably of the same stock with Winthrop's wife.

a birde through a hedge or a hole in a wall, the hedge dothe
no more but cover the author, though the birde may think
the blowe came from the hedge, so surely the Lord hathe
shewed me (in prayer & meditation whereunto he himselfe
onely drewe & inabled me, sending the affliction & sanctifieinge
it to that ende) that there was never any holye meditation,
prayer, or action that I had a hand in, that received any
worthe or furtherance from me or anythinge that was mine.
And untill I sawe this & acknowledged it, I could never have
true comfort in God or sound peace in mine owne conscience,
in any the best that I could performe. But when sometymes
I fell into a holye prayer, meditation etc : if I hapened but to
lett my affections to cast an eye towards myselfe, as thinking
myselfe somebodye in the performance of suche a duty in such
a manner, etc : suche a thought would presently be to my comfort & peace as colde water caste upon a flame; whereby I
might see that God by suche checkes would teache me to goe
wholly out of myselfe, & learne to depende upon him alone ;
wch he himselfe of his meere favour give me grace to doe constantly. For it is not possible that any good thinge should
come from me as of myselfe, since the verye least conceit that
ascribes any thinge to myne owne worthe or abilitie in the best
dutye, not only takes awaye all meritt from it, but makes it
lothesome & sinfulle in Gods sight.

"In this tyme of my sorrowe for my wifes weaknesse, I
founde it a speciall meanes for the humblinge & cleeringe of
my hearte & conscience, even to meditate upon the Comandments & to examine my life past by them, & then concludinge
wth prayer, I founde my hearte more humbled & Gods free
mercie in Christ more open to me then at any tyme before to
my remembrance.

"On Saturdaye beinge the last of November 1616, Thomasine, my deare & lovinge wife, was delivered of a daughter,
wch died the mundaye followinge in the morninge. She tooke
the deathe of it wth that patience, that made us all to merveile,
especially those that sawe howe carefull she was for the life of

it in hir travaile.   That daye soone after the deathe of the
childe, she was taken wth a fever wch shaked hir very muche,
& sett hir into a great fitt of coughinge, wch by teusday morninge was well alayed, yet she continued aguish & sweatinge,
wth muche hoarsenes, & hir mouthe grewe verye soare, & muche
troubled wth blood falling from hir head into hir mouthe &
throate.

"On Wensdaye morninge those wch were about hir, & hirselfe also beganne to feare that wch followed, whereupon we
sent for my Cosin Duke ;[1] wch when she understood she tould
me that she hoped when he came he would deale plainly wth
me, & not feed me wth vaine hopes ; whereupon I breakinge
forthe into teares, she was moved at it, & desired me to be
contented, for you breake mine heart (said she) wth your griev-
ings.   I answered that I could do no lesse when I feared to be
stripped of suche a blessinge :   She replied, God never bestowes
any blessinge so great on his children but still he hathe a greater
in store, & that I should not be troubled at it, for I might see
how God had dealt wth Mr. Rogers before me in the like case.
And allwayes when she perceived me to mourne for hir, she
would intreat & persuade me to be contented, tellinge me that
she did love me well, & if God would lett hir live wth me, she
would endeavour to shewe it more, etc ;   She also desired me
oft that so longe as she lived I would not cease prayinge for her,
neither would be absent from hir, but when I had necessary
occasions.

"On thursdaye at noone my Cosin Duke came to hir, &
tooke notice of hir dangerous estate, yet expectinge a farther
issue that night he departed, sayeing that before Saterdaye we
should see a great change.   After his departure she asked me
what he said of hir, wch when I tould hir, she was no whitt
moved at it, but was as comfortably resolved whither to live or
die.

---

1 " On Thursday the xi of November (1596) Anna Snellinge was married to John
Duke."   She was the daughter of John Snellinge of Shimpling, who is constantly
called by Adam Winthrop " my brother Snellinge."

"On thursdaye in the night she was taken wth deathe, & about midnight or somewhat after called for me, & for the rest of hir friends. When I came to hir she seemed to be fully assured that hir tyme was come, & to be gladde of it, & desired me to praye wch I did, & she tooke comforte therein, & desired that we would sende for Mr. Sands, wch we did. In the meane tyme, she desired that the bell might ringe for hir, & diverse of the neighbours came into hir, wch when she perceived she desired me that they might come to hir one by one, & so she would speake to them all, wch she did, as they came, quietly & comfortably. When the bell beganne to ringe, some said it was the 4 aclock bell, but she conceivinge that they sought to conceale it from hir, that it did ringe for hir, she said it needed not, for it did not troble hir. Then came in Mr. Nicolson whom she desired tó praye, wch he did.

"When Mr. Sands was come she reached him hir hande, beinge gladd of, his cominge (for she had asked often for him). He spake to her of diverse comfortable points, whereunto she answered so wisely & comfortably, as he & Mr. Nicolson did bothe mervaile to heare hir, Mr. Sands sayinge to me that he did not looke for so sounde iudgem^t in hir: He said he had taken hir allwayes for a harmelesse younge woman, & well affected, but did not thinke she had been so well grounded. Mr. Nicolson seeing hir humblenesse of minde & great comfort in God, said that her life had been so innocent & harmlesse as the Devill could finde nothing to laye to her charge. Then she desired Mr. Sands to praye but not praye for life for hir; he answered then he would praye for grace. After prayer she desired me that I would not lett Mr. Sands goe awaye, but when he shewed hir the occasion he had, she was content upon promise that he would come againè. This was about 5 of the clocke on fridaye morninge.

"Friday morninge about 6 of the clocke my Cosen Duke came to us againe, & when he had seene how things fell out that night, he tould us that that was the dismall night, wherein she had received hir deathes wounde, yet she might languish a daye or 2, yet after he had felt hir pulse, he said that if the next night were a good night wth hir, there was some hope lefte.

" Fridaye morninge she beganne somewhat to cheere, & so continued all that daye, & had a very good night that night followinge, & beganne hirselfe to entertaine some thought of life, & so did most of us that were about hir. But on Saterday morninge she beganne to complaine of could, & a little after awakinge out of a slumber, she prayed me to sett my heart at rest, for now (said she) I am but a dead woman, for this hand (meaninge hir left hande) is dead allreadye, & when we would have persuaded hir that it was but numme wth beinge under hir, she still constantly affirmed that it was dead, & that she had no feelinge in it, & desired me to pull off hir gloves that she might see it, wch I did ; then when they would have wrapped some clothes about it, she disliked it, tellinge them that it was in vaine, & why should they cover a dead hande : when I prayed hir to suffer it, she answered that if I would have it so she would, & so I pulled on hir gloves, & they pinned clothes about hir hands, when they had doone she said O what a wretche was I for layinge my legge out of the bedd this night, for when I should pull it in againe it was as if it had come throughe ye coverlaye, (yet it seemed to be but hir imaginatiō or dreame for the women could not perceive it).

" The feaver grewe very stronge upon hir, so as when all the tyme of hir sicknesse before she was wont to saye she thanked God she felt no paine, now she beganne to complaine of hir breste, & troubles in hir head, & after she had slumbered a while & was awaked, she beganne to be tempted, & when I came to hir she seemed to be affrighted, used some speeches of Satans assaultinge hir, & complained of the losse of hir first love, etc : then we prayed wth hir, as she desired, after prayer she disliked that we prayed for life for hir, since we might see it was not Gods will that she should live.

" Her feaver increased very violently upon hir, wch the Devill made advantage of to moleste hir comforte, but she declaringe unto us wth what temptations the devill did assault hir, bent hirselfe against them, prayinge wth great vehemence for Gods helpe, & that he would not take away his lovinge kindnesse from hir, defyinge Satan, & spitting at him, so as we might see by hir setting of hir teethe, & fixinge her eyes, shakinge hir head & whole bodye, that she had a very greatt conflicte wth the adversarye.

"After she a little paused, & that they went about to cover hir hands wch laye open wth her former strivinge, she beganne to lifte up hir selfe, desiringe that she might have hir hands & all at lib^{tle} to glorifie God, & prayed earnestly that she might glorifie God, althoughe it were in hell. Then she beganne very earnestly to call upon all that were about hir, exhortinge them to serve God, etc: (And whereas all the tyme of hir sicknesse before she would not endure the light but would be carefull to have the curtaines kept close, nowe she desired light, & would have the curtaine towards the windowe sett open, & so to hir ende was much grieved when she had not either the daye light or candlelight, but the fire light she could not endure to looke upon, saying that it was of too many colours like the raynebowe.)

"Then she called for hir sisters, & first for hir sister Mary,[1] & when she came she said, sister Mary, thou hast many good things in thee, so as I have cause to hope well of thee, & that we shall meet in heaven, etc.

"Then she called for hir sister Margerye,[2] whom she exhorted to serve God, & take heede of pride, & to have care in hir matchinge that she looked not at riches & worldly respects, but at the feare of God, for that would bringe hir comfort at hir deathe although she should meet with many afflictions.

"To her Eliz:[3] she said, serve God, take heed of lyeinge. I doe not knowe that you doe use it, but I wish you to bewarre.

---

[1] Mary married George Jenny, of London.
[2] Margery married Thomas Dogget, of Boxford
[3] Elizabeth married George Cook, of Ipswich.

"Hir sister Sampson[1] she exhorted to serve God, & to bringe up hir children well, not in pride & vanitye, but in the feare of God.

"To hir mother she said that she was the first childe that she should burye, but prayed hir that she would not be discomforted at it; when hir mother answered that she had no cause to be discomforted for hir, for she should goe to a better place, & she should go to hir father, she replied that she should goe to a better father than hir earthly father.

"Then came my father & mother, whom she thanked for all their kindnesse & love towards hir.

"Then she called for my children & blessed them severally, & would needs have Mary brought that she might kisse hir, wch she did.

"Then she called for my sister Luce, & exhorted hir to take heed of pride & to serve God.

"Then she called for hir servants: to Robt she said, you have many good thinges in you, I have nothinge to accuse you of, be faithfull & diligent in yor service.

"To Anne Pold she said that she was a stubborne wenche, etc: & exhorted hir to be obedient to my mother.

"To Eliz: Crouff she said, take heed of pride & I shall nowe release you, but take heed what service you goe into.

"To Anne Addams she said, thou hast been in badd servinge longe in an Alehouse etc: thou makest no conscience of the Sabaothe; when I would have had thee gone to ·Church thou wouldst not, etc:

"Then came Mercye Smith to hir, to whom she said thou art a good woman, bringe up thy children well, you poore folks comonly spoyle yor children, in sufferinge (them) to breake Gods Sabaothes, etc:

"To an other she said you have many children, bring them up well, not in lyeing, etc:

"To an other she said God forgive yor sinnes whatsoever they be.

---

[1] Bridget Clopton married John Sampson, of Sampson's Hall in Kersey.

"To goodwife Cole she said, you are a good woman, I thanke you for all yo.ʳ paines towards me, God reward you.

"To Hen: Pease she said, be diligent & faithfull in yo.ʳ worke, or els when death come, it wilbe layd before you; I pray God send yo.ʳ wife good deliverance, she may doe well, though I die, bringe up my god-daughter well, lett hir not want correctiō.

"To hir keep.ʳ she said, be not discouraged, although I die, thou hast kept many that have doone well, thou hast but one child, bringe it up well.

"Hir payne increased verye muche in her brest, wᶜʰ swelled so as they were forced to cutt the tyeings of hir waystcote to give hir ease: whilst she laye in this estate she ceased not (albeit she was verye hoarse, & spake wᵗʰ great paine) one while to exhorte, another while to praye. Hir usual prayer was Come Lord Jesus; When Lord Jesus, etc: hir exhortation was to stirre up all that sawe hir, to prepare for death, tellinge them that they did not knowe how sharpe & bitter the pangs of deathe were, wᵗʰ many like speeches.

"In this tyme she prayed for the Churche, etc: & for the ministerye, that God would blesse good ministers, & convert such ill ones as did belonge to him, & weed out the rest. After this we might perceive that God had given her victorye, by the comfort wᶜʰ she had in the meditatiō of hir happinesse, in the favour of God in Chᵗ Jesus. Towards afternoone hir great paynes remitted, & she laye very still, & said she sawe hir tyme was not yet come, she should live 24 howres longer; then when any asked hir how she did, she would answer pretily well, but in hir former fitt, to that question she would answeare that she was goeinge the way of all flesh. Then she prayed me to reade by hir, when I asked hir where, she answeared, In some of the holye gospells, so I beganne in John the 14, & read on to the ende of the 17ᵗʰ Chapter. And when I pawsed, at the ende of any sweet sentence, she would saye this is comfortable: If I stayed at the ende of any Chapter for hir to take rest, she would call earnestly to read on, — then she desired to take a little rest.

"She often prayed God to forgive the sinnes of hir youth, etc : & desired me ofte to praye for hir, that God would strengthen hir with his holye spirit. After, she desired me againe to reade to hir the 8ᵗʰ to the Romˢ, & the 11ᵗʰ to the Hebˢ, whereby she received great comfort, still callinge to reade on, then I read the 116 ps. this is a sweet psalm (said she) then I read the 84 psal : the 32, 36, 37, & other places.

"In the eveninge Mr. Sands came againe, & prayed, & soon after she tooke him by the hand & tould him she would bidd him farewell, for she knew it was a busie night wᵗʰ him. After, we went to prayer, & when we had doone, ' O what a wretche am I (said she) to lose the ende of this prayer, for I was asleepe.'

"After we had continued in readinge etc, untill late in the night, she asked who should watche wᵗʰ hir, & when we tould hir, she was satisfied, & disposed hirselfe to rest.

"In the night she prayed one of the women that watched wᵗʰ her to read unto hir : whilst I was gone to bedde, she asked often for me, & about 2 of the clocke in the morninge I came to hir. Now it was the Sabaothe day, & she had now & then a brunt of temptation, bewaylinge that she could not then be assured of hir salvation, as she had been. She said that the devill went about to persuade hir to cast of hir subiec- tion to hir husbande, etc :

"That Sabaothe noone, when most of the companie were gone downe to dinner, when I discoursed unto hir of the sweet love of Christ unto hir, & of the glorye that she was goeinge unto, & what an holye everlastinge Sabaothe she should keepe, & how she should suppe wᵗʰ Christ in Paradise that night, etc : she shewed by hir speeches & gestures the great ioye & stead- fast assurance that she had of those things. When I tould hir that hir Redeemer lived, & that she should see him wᵗʰ those poore dimme eyes, wᶜʰ should be bright & glorified, she an- swered cheerfully, she should. When I tould her that she should leave the societie of freinds wᶜʰ were full of infirmities, & should have communiō wᵗʰ Abram, Isaacke, & Jacob, all

the prophets & apostles & saints of God, & those holye mar-
tirs (whose stories when I asked hir if she remembred she
answered yea) she would lifte up her hands & eyes, & say, yea
she should.   Suche comforte had she ag^t deathe that'she stedfastly professed that if life were sett before hir she would not
take it.

"When I tould hir that the daye before was 12 monthes she
was maried to me, & now this day she should be maried to
Ch^t Jesus, who would embrace her wth another manner of love
than I could, 'O husband (said she, & spake as if she were
offended, for I perceived she did mistake me) I must not love
thee as I love Christ.'

"Hir hearing still continued, & hir understandinge very perfecte, hir sight was dimmed, yet she knewe every bodye to the
laste.   If I went from hir she would call for me againe, &
once asked me if I were angry wth hir that I would not staye
wth her.

"While I spake to hir of any thinge that was comfortable,
as the promises of the Gospell, & the happie estate she was
entringe into, she would lye still & fixe her eyes stedfastly
upon me, & if I ceased awhile (when hir speeche was gone)
she would turn her head towards me, & stirre hir hands as
well as she could, till I spake, & then would be still againe.

"About 5 of the clocke, Mr Nicolson came to hir & prayed
with hir, & about the ende of his prayer, she fetched 2 or 3
sighes, & fell asleepe in the Lorde.[1]

"The Wensdaye followinge beinge the 11 of Dec. she was
buried in Groton chancell by my other wife, & hir childe was
taken up, & laid wth hir.

"She was a woman wise, modest, lovinge, & patient of
iniuries; but hir innocent & harmeles life was of most observation.   She was truly religious, & industrious therein; plaine
hearted, & free from guile, & very humble minded; never so

---

[1] The following memorandum is inscribed in the margin: "Decemb: 8th 1616. An:
ætat: 34 come 12 of Feb. foll: et ætat. meæ 29."

adicted to any outward thinges (to my iudgm.ᵗ) but that she could bringe hir affections to stoope to Gods will in them. She was sparinge in outward shewe of zeale, etc. but hir constant love to good christians, & the best things, wᵗʰ hir reverent & carefull attendance of Gods ordinances, bothe publiqe & private, wᵗʰ hir care for avoydinge of evill hirselfe, & reprovinge it in others, did plainly shewe that truthe, & the love of God, did lye at the heart. Hir lovinge & tender regard of my children was suche as might well become a naturall mother : ffor hir cariage towards myselfe, it was so amiable & observant as I am not able to expresse ; it had this onely inconvenience, that it made me delight too muche in hir to enjoye hir longe."

CHAPTER VI.

EARLY RELIGIOUS EXPERIENCE (CONTINUED), 1616–17.

AFTER the tribute to the memory of his wife which has been given at the close of our last chapter, there is a blank space in Winthrop's little autograph volume; and then it proceeds with the religious emotions and expe-riences of the succeeding year. Now and then a date will be found, marking the precise period at which different passages were written. There is no date, how-ever, to the first passage. It was probably written not many weeks, perhaps not many days, after the sad scenes which had been so minutely and touchingly recorded. We give it all just as we find it. We should hardly be pardoned for interrupting the progress of such a confession by any comments of our own; much less for mingling any other matter in the same chapter with a self-communion so free from all mere worldly considerations.

"I finde by often experience that the most usuall thinge that breakes off my comfort in God, & delight in heavenly things, is the entertaininge the love of earthly things; — for having so often given myselfe unto the Lord, by particular solemne

Covenants, as upon my recoverye out of my quartan, the
deathe of my former wife, deliverance from speciall sicknesses,
etc, & now againe upon the renuinge of my repentance in this
last affliction by the deathe of my other wife, the Lord will not
endure it that I should steale my affectiō from him, to sett
it againe upon the world; so as I perceive. that lett me doe
what duties I will, yet if my heart be roaminge after pleasure,
glorie, profitt, etc : he abhorres bothe me & my service ; so as I
see that if he may not have my heart, he will have nothinge : —
Heerupon it hathe fallen out often that I have bestowed a great
deale of tyme in prayer, & other duties, & have founde no
other answeare but a wounded & discontented minde, & all
because I have brought an heart haltinge betweene God & the
worlde, desirous of his favour, & yet not resolved upon the
deniall of this worlde & myselfe ; not weighinge that sentence
of Christ ' He that wilbe my disciple, must denie himself,' &c :
Againe on the other side sometymes upon a short meditation,
or prayer, a secreat grone, or desire sent up into heav̇en, etc.,
I have founde unspeakable peace & comforte, for then my
heart would repose itselfe in God, & yield to him sayinge w^{th}
Paul, Lord, what wilt thou have me to doe? Whereupon I
conclude that I cannot serve 2 masters ; if I love the world,
the love of the father can have no abidinge in me. This be-
numbs the hand of faith, casts a mist before the eyes of it,
cooles the zeale of prayer, quenchethe the spirit, & all spirituall
affections, & layes the heart open to the force of all temptal-
tions.

"Now to repell all suche lusts, pleasures, profitts or whatsoever, that would steale awaye my heart from my God, I will
meditate upon these & such other scriptures :

"If then ye be risen wth Christ, seek those things wch are
above &c :

"Love not the world, neither the things of the world &c :

"My sonne give me thy heart :

"They are not of the world, as I am not of the world :

"Demas hath forsaken me & imbraced this present world :

" — The world is crucified to me & I to the world :

" 2 Pe. 1. 4.   Flee the corruptions wch are in the world through lust :

" 1 Pe. 2. 11.   As strangers & Pilgrimes abstaine from fleshly lusts that fight against the soule.

" Althoughe the losse of my wife were to me a grievous thinge, yet God, in his more than fatherly mercie, drewe my minde from beinge too intentive upon it, by givinge me cause to looke into myselfe, & when he had shewed me mine owne nakednesse & unworthinesse, & thereby sett me on woork to follow him unweariably in prayer, (not onely in sett & solemne manner upon my knees, but by ofte & earnest liftings up of my heart, as I was walkinge, & sittinge, havinge good incouragement, by his presence & assistance, to provoke me thereunto,) wherein I could not tell whither were greater my sorrowe, ioye, desire or feare, often tymes ; & giving me to finde muche sweetnesse & more than ordinary rellishe in the readinge of his holye worde, & in meditation, etc : I founde in one fortnight, suche an abundant recompence of my losse, as I might saye wth the prophet, O Lord thou hast caused my ioye to surmount my griefe an 100 foulde.   O my soule, prayse the Lord, & all that is w^{th}in me prayse his holye name ; wch forgiveth thee all thy sinnes, & healeth all thy Infirmities :   My soule, what wilt thou returne unto the Lord for all his benefitts ? take the cuppe of salvation (wch he houldeth forthe unto thee) & thanke him wth all thy might ; Love him wth all thy soule, & wth all thy strengthe ; & for his loves sake lett all thy delight be in the saints that are on the earth.   Wronge not his trueth so muche, as to distrust him either for thy resurrectiō to glorye, or thy perseverance in grace.   He hathe given thee his Soñe, who is as able to sanctifie thee as he is to save thee ; thou art nowe no more thine owne ; he hathe sealed thee for him selfe,· by that spirit of adoption, that spirit of trueth & Comfort, wch the world nor all the devills in hell cannot take from thee.   O Heavenly father strengthen the weake faith of thy most unwor-

thie servant; & stablish the worke thou hast wrought in me
unto the ende. Amen, Amen.

" It is a very hard thinge to love Christ as well in contempt
as in glorye, & to acknowledge & confesse him in his base
estate, as being exalted. It was an easye thinge to think
gloriously of the martirdome of such as were glorious in worldly respects, as learninge, honor, eminency of place, or great
birth, etc : & on the other side no easye thinge to reade the histories of suche as were vile, & base, & had no other ornament
but naked truethe, wthout some contemptible thoughts abatinge
the worthe & estimation of their cause & sufferings. These
things did somewhat trouble me, untill I considered that Christ's
Kingdome was not of this worlde, & that a Christian as he
must beare the Crosse, so he must denye himselfe, wch is the
harde thinge. O Lord, for J : C : sake strengthen me hereunto.

"Rom : 7 : 18 : — In me (that is in my fleshe) dwelleth no
good thinge. I am carnall, sould under sinne ; Dead in sinnes
&c.

" Before I beleeved these things, as cominge from the mouthe
of God who sees what is in mans heart, & therefore sees that
all the imaginations of the thoughts of his heart are onely evill
continually, my heart would ever be readye to attribute somewhat to its owne worthe & power, in the well doeing of any
dutye, notwthstandinge that I have founde the contrarye by
muche experience ; for sometymes when my heart hathe been
but weakly prepared to prayer so as I have expected little comfort, etc : yet God hath filled me wth suche power of faith,
sense of his love, etc : as hath made my heart mealt wth ioye,
etc : Againe at another tyme, when I have settled my heart
unto prayer, of purpose to quicken up my drowsie affections,
& to strengthen my faith, etc : yet I could not, wth all my
labour, althoughe continuinge longer, & in greater fervency
then ordinary, gett my faith strengthened, or my heart humbled & broke, or the feelinge of the love of God shedd abroad

in my heart, but the rather more doubtings & discouragements, etc : yet when I have been forced wth wearinesse to give over, even in the very partinge Christ hathe shewed himself unto me, & answered all my desires. And hereby he hath taught me to trust to his free love, & not to the power or selfeworthe of my best prayers, & yet to lett mee see that true prayer, humble prayer, shall never be unregarded.

" When I was a boye I was at a house, where I spied 2 small bookes lye cast aside, so I stole them, & brought them awaye wth me ; & since when they have come to my minde I have grieved at it, & would gladly have made restitution, but that shame still letted me ; & when I had thought I had stilled my conscience, by consideringe the smallnesse of the value, my willingnesse to restore, etc : yet would not my conscience be quiet, but in everye affliction, especially in this last, in the deathe of my wife, it mett wth me at every turne, neither could I be ridde of the checkes of it untill I did (through Gods direction) finde a meanes to make satisfaction ; wch doone, I had peace, & was in muche better lib^tye of heart than before, Gods holy name be praysed.

" It is a better and more safe estate to be prepared to die then to desire deathe, for this comonly hath more selfe love wth it then pure love of God :   And it is a signe of more strength of faithe, & Christian courage, to resolve to fight it out, then to wish for the victorye.

   " The fleshe is eagerly inclined to pride, & wantonnesse, by wch it playes the tirant over the poore soule, makinge it a verye slave ; the workes of o^f callings beinge diligently followed, are a speciall meanes to tame it, & so is temperance in diet, for idlenesse (under wch are all suche workes as are doone to fullfill the will of the fleshe rather then of the spirit,) & gluttonie are the 2 maine pillars of the fleshe hir kingdome.   See Eccl : 1 : 13.

" After I had somewhat shaked off my afliction, & had held in to a temperate course, & had been pretily wayned from the worlde, & had brought under my rebellious fleshe, & pretylye tamed it by moderate & spare diet, & houldinge it somewhat close to its taske, by prayer, readinge, meditation & the workes of my callinge, not suffering it to be idle nor yet to be busied in suche things as it did desire, etc : after a monthe or 5 weeks continuance thus, this wilye fleshe beganne to fainte, & seemed as thoughe it could not longe hould out, it grewe aguishe & lumpishe, etc : so as if Christ had not heere holpen me, I had through too light beleefe, & foolish pittie, lightened it of the burthen & letten it have more lib^{tie} to mine owne overthrowe ; but God being mercifull to me, forced me (even against my will) to lay more loade upon it, & to sett it a greater taske, for he lett in suche discomforts, of anguish, feare, unquietnesse, etc, upon my soule, as made me forgett the grones of the fleshe & take care to helpe my pore soule, & so was the fleshe forced to be more stronge & lively, when it was putt to greater labour ; yet as soone as the soule was at quiet againe, the fleshe fell to his former course, & grewe exceedinge discontented, when it remembered the fleshe potts of Egypt, the former pleasure, ease, recreations, mirthe, etc : wch it had wont to enioye. And even like a horse in his travaile wilbe eager to runne into suche an Inne, as he hathe been used to baite at, so this wanton bruitishe fleshe at suche tymes of the daye, as it was wonte to have most libertie to those former lusts & follies, at such tymes would it be most discontent wth its imprisonment, & most madde after his wonted baits of pleasure, etc : And in these temptations I was sometymes very hard putt to, yet hathe Christ (whose I am whollye) hitherto so strengthened me, that the fleshe hathe loste grounde in all these assaults. And these things doe turne to my great benefitt, throughe the free & neverfailinge mercie of my heavenly father, so as I am resolved, by his grace (O Lord lett not thy grace faile me, I feare indeed greatly mine owne frailetye, but I neither hope nor desire, O Lord thou knowest, to stand by mine owne

strengthe, wisdome, etc : but onely by faithe in Christ Jesus,)
I am resolved, I saye, to stand to the Covenant of my bap-
tisme, renued so often since ; & forsomuche as Christ hathe
freed me from the fearfull & woefull slavery of the world &
the flesh, I will not backe to prison againe, though I die for
it. (Yet O my poore soule, thou knowest, that if thou wert
even now left to thy selfe, thou shouldst even in this instant be
made a slave againe, but O my heavenly father, for Jes : Christ
his sake keepe me ; If thou wilte, correct, humble, or trye me ;
let me fall into thy hands, for thou art mercifull, but give me
not up into the impure hands of these barbarous enemies the
world & the fleshe ; lett not the habitation of thy holy spirit be
poluted by them, nor lett thy temple become a denne for
theeves). Throughe Christ Jesus the world is crucified unto
me, & I to the world ; I owe nothing to it, nor to the fleshe,
but have bidden defiance to them wth my whole heart, & I am
resolved (Lord strengthen mee, O strengthen me my God &
father) that come life, come deathe ; come healthe, come sicknesse ; come good reporte or evill reporte ; come ioye, come
sorrowe ; come wealthe, come povertie ; come what may, I
will never yield me a prisoner to these enemies, I will never be
reconciled unto them, I will never seeke their wealthe nor pros-
peritie all the dayes of my life ; for I knowe that if I enter
friendship wth them, they will cause me to eate of their sacri-
fices, & so wthdrawe my hearte from my God to runne roaminge after them & to committ Idolatrye wth them.

"Jany 20.   Our Sess^{ns} [1] were, against w^{ch} (fearinge greatly
mine owne frailtie) I did prepare myself by earnest prayer etc :
& my tyme, as I rode, I spent as well as I could in good meditations, & kept my course of prayer etc : as well as conveniently I could while I was there, refraininge my mouthe, eyes,

---

[1] It will be observed, that Winthrop makes frequent reference, during the whole
period covered by these self-communings, to his engagements in attending the sessions
of the courts, and to his discharge of his duties as a magistrate.

& cares from vanitie, as well as I could, & so it pleased God that I brought home my peace & good conscience wth me, yet my love of goodness some what abated, wch I perceived not till a daye or 2 after, when I began to be somewhat loathe to prayer & good communicatiō; the fleshe beginninge to favoure itselfe, but it pleased God by prayer to quicken me againe. When I was at Sess^{ns} I kept a continuall watche (as neere as I could), but yet when I sawe & heard the great accompt & estimation that the wisdome, glorye, wealthe, pleasure & such like worldly felicitie was in wth all, methought I hearde all men tellinge me I was a foole, to sett so light by honour, credite, welthe, iollitie etc : wch I sawe so many wise men so much affecte & ioye in, & to tye my comforte to a conversation in heaven, wch was no where to be scene, no way regarded, wch would bring my selfe & all my gifts into contempt, etc : These & the like baites did Sathan laye for me, & wth these enymies he did ofte tymes sore shake my faithe ; but Christ was in me, & uphelde my resolution, & he will uphould it (I truste & praye) that my faithe shall never faile. O Lord keepe me that I be not discouraged, neither thinke the more meanly of the portion wch I have chosen, even to walke wth thee, & to keepe thy Comandments, because the wise ones of this world doe not regarde but contemne these things. Thou assurest my heart that I'am in a right course, even the narrowe waye that leads to heaven : Thou tellest me, & all experience tells me, that in this way there is least companie, & that those wch doe walke openly in this way shalbe despised, pointed at, hated of the world, made a byworde, reviled, slandered, rebuked, made a gazinge stocke, called puritans, nice fooles, hipocrites, hair-brainde fellowes, rashe, indiscreet, vain-glorious, & all that naught is ; yet all this is nothinge to that wch many of thine excellent servants have been tried wth, neither shall they lessen the glorie thou hast prepared for us. Teache me, O Lord to putt my trust in thee, then shall I be like mount Sion that cannot be removed. Amen.

"Feb: 3. I went towards London, & returned soone, the 11. I went forthe sickly, but returned (I prayse God) safe, & healthie. Whereas I was wont to lose all my tyme in my iournies, my eyes runninge upon everye obiect, & my thoughts varieing wth everye occasion, it pleased God that I nowe made great use of my tyme, bothe in prayeing, singing, & meditatinge wth good intentiō & muche comforte. Amongst other things, I had a very sweet meditation of the presence & power of the Holy Ghost in the hearts of the faithfull, howe he reveales the love of God in o^r hearts, & causeth us to love God againe ; howe he unites all the faithfull in deed & in affection : howe he opens o^r understandings in the misteries of the gospell, &, makes us to beleeve & obeye : & of the sweet consent betweene the worde & the spirit, the spirit leadinge & directinge us in all things according to the worde : I am not able to expresse the understandinge wch God gave me in this heavenly matter, neither the ioye that I had in the apprehension thereof. Other meditations I had of my sinnes & unworthinesse, of the exceedinge mercies of God towards me, etc : & nowe & then to refreshe me when I grewe wearye I had a prayer in my heart, & sometymes I sunge a psalm. I founde it verye hard to bringe my heart heerunto, my eyes were so eager of wanderinge, & my minde so lothe to be heald wthin compasse ; but after I gatt into it, I founde great sweetnesse therein, it shortned my waye & lightned all suche troubles & difficulties as I was wont to meet wth.

"After my returne I founde wthin a 4 or 5 dayes when I should beginne to settle to my ordinary taskes, etc : that the fleshe had gotten head & heart againe, & beganne to linger after the world ; the society of the saints seemed a contemptible thinge, meditations were few, prayer was teadious, & fain would the fleshe have been at an ende before I beganne : I grewe drowsie & dull in every good dutie ; it made me marvaile at my selfe when I remembred my former alacritie ; I prayed & I wept, yet still I grewe more discouraged : — God beinge mercifull unto me, heerby to revive me, at length I fell to prayer & fastinge, whereto the fleshe was as unwillinge as the bear to the stake, yet it pleased God that hereby I recovered life & comforte, & then I founde plainely that not keepinge a strict watche over my appetite, but feedinge more liberally than was meet, or then before, of late, I was wont, the fleshe waxed wanton, & would no longer weare the yoake, but beganne to growe iollye & slouthfull, as it had wont to doe, & to minde earthly things. O the deepe deceitfullnesse of my heart; if God had lefte me, I had even nowe forsaken him, & embraced my former follye & worldly delights. But blessed be the Lord that remembred me in the day of perill, & saved me; O my God doe not forsake me in the tyme of need.

"I finde by ofte & evident experience, that when I hould under the fleshe by temperate diet, & not sufferinge the minde or outward senses to have everye thinge that they desire, & weane it from the love of the worlde, I ever then praye wthout wearinesse, or ordinary wanderinge of heart, & am farre more fitt & cheerefull to the duties of my callinge & other duties, performinge them wth more alacritie & comfort then at other tymes.

"Not longe after fallinge into a light ague, I tooke occasion thereby to favour myselfe more then I needed, & Sathan made use of this oportunitie by reason of the weaknesse of my head to fill my heart, first wth wandering thoughts, so drawinge me from good meditations, & then enticinge me to delight in worldly thoughts, wch at last my heart did embrace so eagerly, as I could not for my life gett my minde from them, but they interrupted my prayers, brake my sleepe, abated the wonted relishe of heavenly thinges, tooke awaye my appetite from the worde, made the duties of my callinge teadious, & filled me wth muche discomforte, so as I thought upon that sayeinge, All is vanitie, & vexatiō of spirit.

"I see therefore I must keepe a better watche over my heart, & keepe my thoughts close to good things, & not suffer a vaine or worldly thought to enter, etc: least it drawe the heart to delight in it. And therefore I propose (so farre as God shall give me grace) to stint myselfe to my tymes in this sort, except necessarie occasiō makes me to alter :

"ffirst, for the forenoone to spende it whollye in the service of God & duties of my callinge. After dinner [1] I will allow an howre to my worldly affaires, & if need shall so require somewhat more, otherwise (when it will stand wth my health & other conveniences) in visitinge some neighbour or etc :, & then to my studye againe. And when my Callinge will give me libertie, to some other profitable studye as occasiō shall serve. (As soone as I had written this, Sathan beganne to tempt me, wth his wonted baites of worldly pleasure, in a thinge wherein I have muche busied my thoughts to finde out the lawfullnesse, & conveniencie, etc : & when I would have putt it out of my minde, Sathan suggests to me, that I should sinne except I did presently determine in my heart whither I would doe it or not, (& by this sleight he had ofte circumvented me) but it pleased God to putt into my mouthe to answeare him thus, Avoyd Sathan, this is not the tyme for to think or resolve upon these thinges, they have their tyme sett out for them, & when that tyme comes I will resolve & doe as God shall guide me : thus by this meditation it pleased the Lord to strengthen me at that tyme, blessed be his holy name, Amen.)

"Mr. Sands : In indifferent thinges my perswasion must be my guide.

"It was delivered me by Mr. Sands as upon his best Judgm^{t} & experience, that a Christian is bounde to make use of his Sabaothe businesse all the weeke after, & that so to doe would keepe away muche uncomfortable discontent from a Christian minde, as thus : A man should sett apart some tyme of the daye throughe the weeke, to goe over the things wch he hathe learned in the Sabaothe, either in his prayer or meditatiō ; & a

---

[1] The hour for dinner was probably not later than eleven or twelve. "In the time of Elizabeth, the gentry dined at eleven, and the merchants at twelve." — *Our English Home*, p. 34.

man doeing this of conscience, as Gods ordinance, God would blesse it. And as of o: hearinge so of o: prayers, readinge, meditatinge etc, looke what speciall affections are stirred up in us by any of these on the Sabaothes, we should worke upon them in the weeke dayes; for certainly the Sabaothe is the markett of o: soules.

"When a man leads a life secluded from the comon delights of the worlde, & gives himselfe to walke whollye wth God, he shall heare many sayinge, He will shorten his dayes, he will pine himselfe, he will be overrunne wth melancolie &c : But suerly a man so livinge, shall doe more honor to God, & service to his Churche in a very shorte life, then another (although a true Christian, also) livinge at more lib^tie shall doe in a muche longer tyme : for the more differinge that a mans conversation is from the comon course of the worlde, the more occasiō & matter there is of the observation of Gods work in him : And since there are so many that in an overmuche respecte to their owne outward felicitie take more lib^tie in these outward things then standeth wth Gods will, who shall forbidd others (there beinge so fewe suche) to tender God more fruits of their love & thankfullnesse, by abridging themselves in the number & measure of suche outward comforts as they might lawfuly inioye. But yet I see no grounde for suche opinions, for besides that God hathe numbered o: dayes etc, there are many places in scripture wch may make us looke that holynesse should lengthen o: life, & sweeten it, but none to make us feare that it should discomfort or shorten it. O Lord, enhable me to live righteously & holyly, & I shall not be muche carefull of livinge longe or hapylye.

"I had been overtaken, & turned out of my course by entertaininge the love of pleasures, & worldly cares into my heart, wch brought me out of peace wth my God, & tooke aweaye my delight in prayer & other duties, & made me utterly unfitt for studye in my Callinge. In this estate my heart could not be

at rest, I could not live so ; I humbled myselfe & sought pardon & peace againe, & I oftentymes was well comforted &
persuaded of it, but it was soone gone againe, & I returned
backe to my former unsettled & voluptuous course, yet rest-
lesse therein.   The Sabaothe came, I arose betymes, & read
over the covenant of certaine Christians sett downe in Mr.
Rogers booke, & therew^th my heart beganne to breake, & my
worldly delights wch had heald my heart in suche slaverye before, beganne to be distastefull & of meane account wth me, I
concluded wth prayer in teares ; & so to my family exercise, &
then to Churche, my heart beinge still somewhat humbled
under Gods hande, yet could not gett at lib^tie from my vaine
pleasures : After dinner & o^r famyly exercise, I read Mr.
Perkins treatise of the estate of a Christian, &c, thereby as
my heart grewe more humbled, so my affections were more
reclaimed.   I went to Boxsted[1] Churche in the afternoone
where I heard wth some affection & found sometymes a comfortable consent in prayer ; being returned I went into my chamber
to prayer, but beinge hot & weary wth goeinge I was forced to
leave.   I layde me downe upon the bed allmost overcome w^th
discontent arisinge partly of my wearinesse etc.   I could not
bringe my minde to think seariously of any good thinge, but it
beganne to wander & be idle, so I arose, & knelt downe to
praye againe, but could not ; then I endeavored to praye
standinge, & so strivinge wth the Lord for helpe ag^nst my weaknesse.   At last he enabled me to my full content, & then my
heart gave in, & I renounced my beloved pleasures, & was
willinge to denye my selfe ; then was my minde & conscience at
sweet rest, & I desired nothinge so much as Christ Jesus & the
fellowship of his holy Spirit ; then my soule despised &
abhorred my former beloved vanityes ; then was I content to
be at Gods allowance, that I might enioye his love & the light
of his countenance, althoughe it were wth bread & water.   Then

---

[1] This seems to be Boxsted, a parish in Suffolk County, not far from Lavenham. It
may have been intended for Boxford, which was nearer to Groton.

I sawe playnely that the usuall cause of the heavinesse &
uncomfortable life of many Christians is not their religion, or
the want of outward comforts (for Gods presence in favour
brings all sufficiency wth it, as Psal : — In thy presence there
is fullnesse of Ioye &c.) but because their consciences enforce
them to leave some beloved unlawfull lib^tie before their hearts
are resolved willingly to forsake it : whereas if we could denye
o^r owne desires & be content to live by faithe in our God, the
Christian life would be the only merrye & sweet life of all.   O'
Heavenly Father I beseeche thee give me grace to watche &
be sober, & lett thy favour & my peace in it be ever of more
account wth me then all the world besides it.   Amen.

" After this, settlinge myselfe to walke uprightly wth my God,
& diligently in my callinge, & havinge an heart willinge to
denye myselfe, I found the Godly life to be the only sweet life,
& my peace wth my God to be a true heaven upon earthe.   I
founde God ever p^rsent wth me, in prayer and meditation, in
the duties of my callinge, etc : I could truely loath my former
folly in preferringe the love of earthly pleasures before the love
of my heavenly father.   I did wonder what madnesse was in
me, that I should leave the fellowshippe of my Saviour, to keepe
fellowshippe wth unfruitfull works of darknesse ; I was not then
troubled wth the common cares & desires that I was wont to be
taken up w^th, as of food, apparell, credit, pleasure, etc : but
was well contented wth what God sent : what can I say ? I finde
a change in my heart & whole man, as apparent as from darknesse to light.   God of his mercie continue & increase it.   I
finde w^thall that I was readye upon every obiect or occasion, to
embrace the delight in earthly things againe, wch I see plainly
will soone gett w^thin me againe, if I slacke my watchfullnesse
never so little, so as I resolve by Gods grace to keepe my heart
wth all diligence, & to sett a watche over my mouthe, eyes,
ears, etc, when I am alone, in companye, at home, abroad, in
every business, service of God, etc.   O Lord my God, for
Jesus Christ his sake inable me heerunto, and strengthen the
poore weake faithe of thy unworthy servant.

"Before the week was gone about I beganne to lose my former affections, I uphelde the outward dutyes, but the power & life of them was in a manner gone; I prayed as I was wont, but I could not finde that comfort & feelinge w^h I had; I did the duties of my Callinge, but not so cheerfully & fruitfully : & still the more I prayed & meditated, etc : the worse I grewe, the more dull, unbelievinge, vaine in heart, etc : so as I waxt exceeding discontent & impatient, beinge sometymes ready to frett & storme ag^t God because I founde not that blessinge upon my prayers & other meanes that I did expecte; but O Lord forgive me : Searchinge my heart at last, I founde the world had stollen away my love from my God, & that I was growne from depending upon him to trust to my prayers & outward dutyes, & so not diligently observing my heart, as I should have done, the devill had gotten wthin me, & had deceived me. Then I acknowledged my unfaithfullnesse & pride of heart, & turned againe to my God, & humbled my soule before him, & he returned, & accepted me, & so I renewed my Covenant of walking wth my God, & watchinge my heart & wayes.   O my God, forsake me not.

"When I had some tyme abstained from suche worldly delights as my heart most desired, I grewe very melancholick & uncomfortable, for I had been more careful to refraine from an outward conversation in the world, then to keepe the love of the world out of my heart, or to uphold my conversation in heaven; wch caused that my comfort in God failinge, & I not daringe to meddle wth any earthly delights, I grewe into a great dullnesse & discontent : wch beinge at last perceived, I examined my heart, & findinge it needfull to recreate my minde wth some outward recreation, I yielded unto it, & by a moderate exercise herein was muche refreshed; but heere grewe the mischiefe : I perceivinge that God & mine owne conscienee did alowe me so to doe in my need, I afterwards tooke occasion, from the benefite of Christian lib^{tie}, to pretend need of recreation when there was none, & so by degrees I ensnared my heart so farre in worldly delights, as I cooled the graces of the spirit by them : Whereby I perceive that in all outward comforts, althoughe God allowe us the use of the things themselves, yet it must be in sobriety, & o.^r hearts must be kept free, for he is jealous of o.^r love, & will not endure any pretences in it.

" Havinge occasiō of conference wth a Christian friend or 2, God so blessed it unto us, as we were all much quickened & refreshed by it; the matter of o.^r conference was not doubtfull questions to exercise o.^r witts, etc : but a familiar examination of o^r owne experiences. Growinge dull in prayer, & unwillinge thereunto, I founde one great cause to be, that I was discouraged, because I could not find that my prayers were heard; thereupon examininge farther I founde the cause of that to be, that I had not prayed in faith, as well as in affection of desire, for I remembred that where I was wont to come to God in assurance to be heard because of his promise, I knewe then that my prayers were answered, & I came many tymes wth as good a will to prayer, as I was wonte, when being hungry, to come to my meals. Wherefore O Lord I beseeche thee strengthen & increase my faithe.

" Lookinge over some lettres of kindnesse that had passed between my first wife & me, & beinge thereby affected wth the remembrance of that entire & sweet love that had been sometymes between us, God brought me by that occasion in to suche a heavenly meditation of the love betweene Christ & me, as ravished my heart wth. unspeakable ioye ; methought my soule had as familiar & sensible society wth him, as my wife could have wth the kindest husbande; I desired no other happinesse but to be embraced of him ; I held nothinge so deere that I was not willinge to parte wth for him ; I forgatt to looke after my supper, & some vaine things that my heart lingered after before ; then came such a calme of comforte over my heart, as revived my spirits, sett my minde & conscience at sweet liberty & peace : I thought upon that speeche of the Churche, Cant. 5. 2. — It

is the voice of my welbeloved that knockethe, &c :   O, there's
my husband (saies the lovinge wife) &c : then she runnes, then
she ioyes, out of the armes goes the childe, awaye goes every
impedim^t, she hathe enough that she heares his voice, whom
hir soule loves : O my Lord howe did my soule mealt wth ioye
when thou spakest to the heart of thy poore unworthy handmayd ! — ffurther when I considered of suche lettres as my wife
had written to me, & observed the scriblinge hande, the meane
congruitye, the false orthog ; & broken sentences, etc : & yet
founde my heart not onely acceptinge of them but delighting in
them, & esteeminge them above farre more curious woorkman-
ship in an other, & all from hence, that I loved hir; It made
me thinke thus wth myselfe :   Can I doè thus through that
droppe of affection that is in me, &c : & will not my Lord &
husband Ch : Jesus (whose love surpassethe knowledge, & is
larger than the ocean) accept in good parte the poorest testi-
monies of my love & dutye towards him ?   O if I had faithe
to believe this, how abundant comfort would it afford me in my
weakest services, since they are sent up to him that lookes not
at the forme or phrase, etc : but findinge them to come from one
in whom he delights, he accepts wth all favour the sincere sim-
plicity of the heart, & covers all imperfections wth the skirt of
his love.   O my God increase my weake faithe I humbly pray
thee.

"This affection continued still wth me, & the love of Christ
was ever in my heart, & drewe me to be more enamoured of
him.   Then I ofte remembred that in Jer : 2. 2.   I remembred
thee wth the kindnesse of thy youth, & the love of thy mariage,
&c : wch made me to recall to my view the love of my earthly
mariages, wch the more I thought upon, the more sensible I
grewe of the most sweet love of my heavenly husband, Christ
Jesus ; his spirit persuaded my heart, that if I could so entirely
affecte & delight in suche as I had not laboured for &c : onely
for this consideration that they were to become a parte of my
selfe ; needs must his love towards me be exceedinge measure,

that had made me, died for me, sweatt water & bloud for me,
etc, & maried me to himselfe, so as I am become truely one w^{th}
him : then I was persuaded that neither my sinnes nor infirmities could putt me out of his favour, he havinge washed awaye
the one wth his owne bloud, & coveringe the other wth his un-
changeable love : This comfort that I had in his sweet love
drewe me to deale wth him as I was wont to doe wth my earthly
welbeloved, who beinge ever in the eye of my affection, I
greedily imployed everye opportunitye to be a messinger of the
manifestation of my love, by lettres, &c : so did I now wth my
deare lord Christ ; I delighted to meditate of him, to praye
to him, & to the Father in him (for all was one wth me), to
remember his sweet promises, etc : for I was well assured that
he tooke all that I did in good parte. I considered that he was
suche an one as should ever be livinge, so as I might ever love
him, & allwayes present, so as there should be no griefe at
partinges : O my Lord, my love, how wholly delectable art
thou ! lett him kisse me wth the kisses of his mouthe, for his
love is sweeter than wine : how lovely is thy countenance ! how
pleasant are thy embracings ! my heart leapes w^{th}in me for ioye
when I heare the voice of thee my Lord, my love, when thou
sayest to my soule, thou art hir salvation. O my God, my
kinge, what am I but dust ! a worme, a rebell, & thine enemie
was 'I, wallowinge in the bloude & filthe of my sinnes, when
thou didest cast the light of thy Countenance upon me, when
thou spreadest over me the lappe of thy love, & sayedst that I
should live. Then didest thou washe me in the everflowinge
fountaine of thy bloud, thou didest trime me as a bride prepared
for hir husbande, my clothinge was thy pure righteousnesse,
thou spakest kindlye to the heart of thy most unworthy servant, & my fleshe grewe like the fleshe of a young childe, etc :
And now lett me ever be wth thee, O my Redeemer, for in thy
presence is ioye, & at thy right hande are pleasures forevermore. Shadowe me, & guide me wth thy love, as in the days
of my mariage, that I may never swerve from thee to runne
after earthly vanityes that are lyeinge & will not profitt.

Wholye thine I am (my sweet Lo : Jesus) unworthy (I acknowledge) so much honor as to wipe the dust off the feet of my Lord & his welbeloved spouse, in the day of the gladnesse of their heart, yet wilt thou honor me wth the societye of thy mariage chamber.   Behould, all yee beloved of the Lord, knowe & embrace wth ioye this unspeakable love of his towards you.   God is love, assuredly.

["I doe finde by experience of some good tyme, that a spare diett, & abstinence from worldly delights, is a great meanes of keepinge bothe bodye & minde fitt & lively to holye duties; I was wont, when I supped liberally, that I was sleepye & unweeldye in my familye exercises, & nowe, when I eate but little (& that ordinarily but bread & beere), I am cheerful & unweariable in them.] [1]

"The unspeakable comfort that I had in the former sweet comunion wth my Lord Jesus Christ filled me with such ioye, peace, assurance, boldnesse, etc, as I was many tymes readye to incline into the other extreme of lightnesse & securitye, but God gave me grace, when I beganne to wax wanton, to looke into my sinnes & corruptions, & by the consideration of them I was after kept under, &c.

"July 13.   Beinge the Sabaothe daye, findinge some tyme before that all was not well betweene my God & me, wch I perceived by the couldnesse of my prayers, & the unquietnesse & tremblinge of my conscience, & the lightnesse & continuall wanderings of my heart, I sighed & groned often, prayinge earnestly that God would open my heart, & lett me see what it was that did so disturbe my peace, &c.   I often set to

---

[1] These brackets are in the original. Bread and beer might seem to us nowadays rather a coarse supper; but coffee and tea were unknown in England at that day. "The first cup of coffee ever drank in England" is said to have been drunk at Oxford in the year 1637; and the introduction of tea was some years later. — *Our English Home:* Oxford, 1860, pp. 189, 190.

examine my heart but could not, I was still caried awaye wth wanderinge thoughts, etc, but at last it pleased God by little & little to affecte my. heart, & to bringe me to the sight of my selfe ; & then did I see as evidently as the sunne when it shines, that my heart was withdrawne from my God, the fleshe had prevailed ag^{nst} the spirit, & had drawne me into a lukewarme religiō, servinge God & yet seekinge greedily the ease & plea- sure of my wanton & idle fleshe, wch had made me cast off the life of every dutye, & had turned all zeale into a counter- fait discreation. And my conscience did especially accuse me for my remissnesse in my callinge of magistracie, in that I had not been painfull in the findinge out & zealous in the punish- inge of sinne ; & for that I spent my dayes so idlely & unpro- fitablye, givinge too muche tyme to sleepe, recreations, &c. Thereupon I prayed earnestly unto the Lord for pardon, & for grace to hate these my sinnes, & to amende them, & I promised & covenanted wth the Lord to be more zealous & diligent, & to walke more constantly wth him, and I desired the Lord that when so ever I should decline from this Covenant, that I might not have any peace, but feele his anger untill I were returned againe.

" After this I was as one weaned from his mothers breasts, my comfort & peace wth my God returned, I had bouldnesse & confidence in prayer, then againe did I finde that the only sweet estate was to walke wth God & be upright : & the only safe estate to denye my selfe, the worlde, &c, & to holde this idle wanton fleshe unto its taske, & to keepe watche unto sobrietye. O Lord I beseech thee, continue this in the purpose & heart of thy servant forever : cause me to looke ever to thy service & glorye. Thou (I am assured) wilt looke to my com- forte : whatsoever thou doest wth me, give me not up to the vilde slaverye of the world & the fleshe : O Lord I am thy servant.

" Remittinge my care & watche, & givinge lib^{tie} to the fleshe,

I was againe unsettled, & then my conscience could swallowe
foule faults w^{th}out any great remorse, when as sometymes it
would have stucke at the least evill.   I returned to my selfe
againe & renewed my repentance.   I resolved to keepe a better
watche, & to holde under the fleshe by temperate diet, & diligence in my callinge, for I founde that there was no peace in
any other course.   All pleasures are vanytye in the use & vexatiō in the ende, & the fruit of idlenesse is shame & guiltinesse.
It wounded my heart in the eveninge when I looked backe &
sawe the daye misspent in the service of the worlde, & in fullfill-
inge the will of my fleshe.   Disuse in any good thinge causethe
the greatest unwillingnesse & unfitnesse ; I sawe it was saufeste
for me ever to be well doinge, & to be fully resolved of Gods
good allowance of all that passeth either mouthe, heart or
hande ; faith would teache me to looke to approve my selfe to
God in every thinge, & so to goe on, according to the occasion
of every dutye, & leave the successe to ˙God.   But O my
unbeliefe & my fearfullnesse !   Lord strengthen my faith, &
incourage thou me.

    "Upon this last resolution I setled my selfe to my study, &
to suche duties as I was necessarily occasioned unto, & so by
Gods assistance I kept my peace, &c., meetly well for all that
weeke followinge ; for I was ready upon every occasion to starte
aside, yet keepinge a carefull watche over my hearte, I quickly
perceived when it was straglinge, & so the sooner brought it in
againe.
    "I plainly perceive that when I am not helde under by some
affliction, either outward or inwarde, then I must make my
fleshe doe its full taske in the duties of my callinge, or suche
other service wherein it takes no pleasure.   Otherwise it will
waxe wanton & idle, & then findinge sweetnesse in earthly
thinges it will growe so weary of Gods yoake, as it will not be
borne any longer, except the fleshe by stronge hande be brought
under againe.
    "Sometymes my faithe hathe been so deadhearted in the

promises as no meanes could quicken me up to apprehende the mercies of God, although but in the ordinarye sence of my sines. At an other tyme againe, God hathe lett in upon my heart suche a floud of mercie as in the quickest sight of sinne that ever I had I could not have been brought to make question of pardon. And upon such an offer I have first layde holde of mercye & forgivenesse, & after turned to the acknowledginge & bewaylinge of my sinnes : for there is no confession so franke as that wch comes from the sence of free pardon.

" Order & observatiō makes many duties easye wch otherwise wilbe very tedious & difficult.

" A wilde colte must be well tamed in the ploughe, & then a childe may backe him; so this wanton heart of o^{rs} till it be well tamed wth afflictions, or suche duties in o^r callings as are not pleasinge nor easy to the fleshe, there is no rulinge it ; it will neither be kept to prayer, nor hearinge, nor meditation, etc ; but it will flinge out 20 wayes, & be runninge ag^t every wall, &c : but beinge thoroughly tempered & tamed, &c, it will goe on quietly & soberly in any dutye. It is great wisdome for a Christian to keepe the fleshe ever under by service that it may be sober, for if it gett lib^{tie} there is no rulinge of it : An unruly horse will more weary himselfe in one miles travaile then a sober horse in 10 : so it is when we goe about any dutye where o^r hearts looke for their lib^{tie}.

" My disposition is ever fittest upon the first apprehension of any thinge ; if it once hange of hande, & that I begiñe once to beat my head about it, & meet wth any rubbe or discouragement, I cannot for my life proceed to make any dispatche, &c ; as in writinge of lettres, &c, whilest I have some tymes been over carefull & studious for the forme, I have cleane lost bothe my matter & invention, & on the other side when I have gone on wth more readinesse & lesse curiositie, I have doone farre better in conclusion bothe for matter & forme.

"I have observed that in all my exercises of conscience, when I have been most frighted with guiltinesse of sinne, my carelessenesse in hearinge Gods worde hathe muche more troubled me then my carelesse & could prayer; & my omissions more then my commissions; & the omittinge mercie & the dutyes of my callinge of magistracie more then all thinges besides.

"I finde often tymes that cominge out of good companie, I am sometymes more disquieted, other tymes more unsetled then before: what the reason should be I knowe not, except that beinge taken up wth too muche regard of their persons, I neglect to watche well over my heart; or that God sends it as a punishm^t upon me, for not makinge that good use of such companye as I ought; or whither their godlinesse dothe stirre up & checke some secret evill w^thin me that disquiets my minde.

"I have observed that after a gleame of any speciall ioye, whither in heavenly things or in earthly, there hathe followed a storme of dumpishnesse & discomfort, that hathe abolished the memorye of the former ioye; but especially when I have suffered my heart to take too much ioye in any earthly thinge, I have been sure (for the most parte) in the turninge, to meet wth a fitt of melancollike discontent, that hathe beene farre more burdensome then the other was pleasinge; so as I thinke it good wisdome for me to keepe to a meane in my ioyes, especially in worldly things; moderate comforts being constant & sweeter, or saufer, then suche as beinge exceedinge in measure faile as much in their continuance; for they beinge waysted by passion, are resolved into payne, even as the bodye is most sensible of could, when it hathe beene thoroughlyest warmed by the heat of the fire.

"My heart getting loose one Sab: daye throughe want of due watchfullnesse & firme resolutiō, it gate so deepe into the world as I could not get it free, but it followed me to Churche

& home againe ; but heer was not all the hurt of it, for I founde evidently, that this sufferinge my heart to take lib^{tle} to the profaning of the Sabaothe, made it utterly unfitt for dutye all the week followinge, so as it cost me muche strife & heartsmart before I could bringe it into order againe ; therefore I purpose, by Gods grace, to keepe a better watche over my heart upon the Sabaothe.

" The onely meanes to keepe o^r hearts from beinge taken up & cumbered wth the thoughts & cares of worldly things is, to gett o^r treasure in heaven, for where o^r treasure is, there will our hearts be. Luke : 12.

" Novemb : 1617. I went to London, not so well prepared for suche a iournie as had been meet, & it was a monthe before I returned, wherein God had muche mercie upon me, preservinge me & bringinge me home in safety ; yet my soule was waxed leaner, & my love & faithe muche decayed, as I did suspecte while I was gone, yet could not so evydently perceive as when I came to settle to mine ordinary course at home. But above all I founde my faithe to be very muche shaken, wch was throughe want of carefull nourishinge of it in the meditation of the worde of God. Oh I see, if we leave, or slightly exercise o^rselves in the worde, Faithe will starve & die, & o^r hearts imbrace any dotages of mans braine sooner then Gods eternall truethe, as I founde by dangerous experience : O Lord forgive my great infidelytie & forgettfullnesse of thy goodnesse, & stablishe me wth thy truethe. Oh that I might ever have a care to looke to my Faithe as I would doe to my life ; & thanks be to the Lord that dothe not forsake me.

" I founde this experience while I was at London, that havinge there no matters to distract my minde, but beinge free from my ordinary cares & temptations wch I was wont to meet wth at home ; as I had ease & leisure, & little or no occasion of sorrowe through my faintings, &c, under temptation, wch I was wont to meet wth at home ; so on the other side I founde as slender comforte, & fewe or noe quicknings or stirrings of the

Spirit in me, but was still & quiet, wthout any great sence either of guilt or peace ; whence I gather that he wch would have suer peace & ioye in Christianitye, must not ayme at a condition retyred from the world & free from temptations, but to knowe that the life wch is most exercised wth tryalls & temptations is the sweetest, & will prove the safeste. For such tryalls as fall wthin compasse of o^r callinges, it is better *to arme & wthstande them* then to avoide & shunne them. I founde as readye & familiar accesse to God in prayer, singinge, &c, in my travaile, as if I had been in my chamber, & it is an excellent meanes to season the heart, & to shorten the tediousnesse of the iournie.

" Still I finde by continuall experience that the usuallest thinge that turnes me out of my course & breakes off my peace wth my God is the imbracinge the love of earthly thinges, & seekinge a kind of secure & commodious settlinge in these thinges ; wch as it greatly delights the wanton fleshe, so it as fast quenchethe all delight & appetite to heavenly thinges ; it blinds the iudgement, takes awaye all affection, & dulles all gifts bothe of bodye & minde, makinge all unservisable, &c : I still pray, O Lord, crucifie this world unto me, for suerly the love of thee & the love of the world cañot stand togither.

" I have founde this infallibly true by ofte experience since, & I am fully resolved, that if I will keepe the love of God, I must cast quite off the love of the world.

" I finde it a most difficult thinge to use constantly the practice of meditatiō, the want whereof is an occasion that I am ofte unsettled, for suche thoughts & considerations as doe keepe the heart well ordered will passe & vanishe awaye if they be not revived & uphelde by meditatiō. O my God helpe & inable me.

" I was wonte to be muche disquieted wth feare of reproache & of an ill name wth the moste where I lived, so as I have been drawne by suche foolish respects to doe or leave undone many things to the woundinge of my conscience ; especially to avoide a suspition of ingratitude, basenesse, unfriendlynesse, &c. But the Lord openinge my heart to consider of the vanytie of all suche things, as that they are trifles of no continuance, & of leaste benefite (as if we thinke of suche as we knewe that are nowe dead & gone, who whilst they lived were also either taken up wth suche vaineglorious conceipts, whereof they neither had any true comforte whilest they lived, nor being dead have retained any fruit, or left any memorye of them,) I see it is the best wisdome for a Christian to labour to approve himselfe to God in keeping faithe & a good conscience, wch wilbe a readye comfort to a man in his life, & will bide wth him after deathe, & to sett light by the unprofitable & suer-fadinge favour of the world, wch a Christian man may as well be wthout, as a gent. may spare a kennell of hounds, & wth w^{ch}, he that will have it, shall never want a disquiett minde. I will saye wth Paul, I passe not for mans iudgment.

" Ob : A good name is to be sought after &c : Ans : Walke wth God, & never feare but thou shalt be honored of the Godlye.

" I have observed, that after some true woorke of mercie, I have founde speciall operation of Gods spiritt.

" O what a difference there is betweene the reigne of the fleshe & of the spirit; that like the reigne of Ahaz full of troubles, full of shiffts, & helplesse ; but this like Solomons, plentifull, peaceable, &c,. When the fleshe hathe prevailed in me, all hathe been out of order, full of blindnesse, slouthe, vanytye of minde, captivitye to sinne, strangeness towards my God, a guiltie heart inclininge to rebellion, no comfort in prayer, no delight nor savour in the worde, no ioye in Christ, etc ; sometymes secure in carnall ioyes, & on the suddaine as uncomfortably deiected ; discontented wth everythinge ; still taken up wth earthly cares, feares, desires, &c, all for the bellye, the glorye, &c, (in a worde) all unhappie. But the spirit renewinge his strengthe, brought a newe face of all things wth it, & was to the whole man & conversation, as the

authoritye of Mordecay to the afflicted Jewes, ioye & gladnesse, peace wth God, peace wth heart, peace wth all : my soule
yieldinge itselfe to God in the acknowledgmen^t of its owne
unworthynesse, could yet comfortably repose it selfe in the
merits of Christ ; nowe could it abhorre & tremble at the
memorye of its former vanityes & ungodlinesse : nowe could
it mealt into teares & sighes to remember its unkindnesse &
ingratitude ; now could praye wth confidence, & yet in feare
& reverence ; nowe Christ onely was desired, as my onely portion, my conversation was in heaven, & God was my refuge,
whatsoever occasiō was offered to affright me. O that I could
ever walk in the spirit.

"Ever ag^t a Communion, the neerer it grewe, the more
would Sathan labour to unfitt me for it, seekinge to diminishe
the reverende account & singular benefite of it, & so to steale
from me all appetite unto it ; & w^thall persuadinge me that I
was sufficiently prepared unto it, when (upon better consideration wch God in mercie hathe brought me unto, in my order of
p^rparing my familye) I have founde myselfe muche wantinge,
& especially in desire & appetite unto it, for wch particular I
meane to examine my heart better heerafter (by Gods grace),
Amen.

"My heart beinge againe overtaken, & forward in the thinges
of the world, as pleasures, ease, eatinge & drinkinge &c, I lost
my sweet peace wth my God ; the more my heart delighted in
& lingered after the former things, the more unquietnesse &
anguishe of minde grewe upon me : faine I would haue had my
peace againe, but could not gett my heart to seeke it earnestly ;
amonge other things I looked over some things wch I had written
heere before, concerninge the manifestatiō of Christs love unto
me, my unspeakable ioye therein, & the advised & cheerful
Covenants that thereupon I had made, for walking wth my God
in faithe & holynesse, deniall of the world & myselfe &c :
when I considered w^th.all how I had broken those Covenants,

how unkindly I had requited my good God, &c, it brake my heart, & forced me to an humble & searious submission, in abundance of teares; I truely & cleerly sawe my follye, in settinge so muche by this vaine world, & esteeminge to satisfie the intemperate desires of this wanton fleshe; I renewed my former Covenants wth my God, whom I beseech (for Ch: sake) to incourage & inhable me to performance.

" Jan: 10, 1617. Afterwards findinge myselfe snared by the worlde, I could not be at rest untill by readinge Mr. Boultons discourse of true happinesse, I was brought to a more thorough discoverye of my sinfull heart & wayes, & thereupon to more sounde repentance & resolution of reformation; when againe upon sounde. deliberation beinge free from all passion, or oppression of melancholie, I did quietly, cheerfully & absolutely resigne up myselfe againe unto my God, covenantinge to walke faithfully wth him, & prayeing fervently yet wthout any distemper of affection, &c, that he would rather take me out of the worlde or cast me into any affliction, sicknesse, povertye, disgrace, or whatsoever, so himselfe would not faile me in them, then to give me up to the slaverye of the worlde, to mine ould profane, idle, voluptuous, & foolishe heart; & so I begge still of him for the Lo: Jes: sake.

" ffeb. I kept on my course but yet up & downe, for the fleshe still gathered to itselfe, & sought its owne ease, pleasure, glorye, &c, & my heart grewe towards the worlde againe, so as the sweet relishe & estimation of Christ & salvation was even gone, untill God againe opened mine eyes to see my carnal affections, my slouthfulnesse, vanitye of minde, pride, falseheartednesse, infidelitye; no love to him in Christ, nor love to his saintes; my too muche account & estimation of the worlde, too busylye imployinge my thoughts in caringe for & delightinge in earthly things: so as I am thoroughly persuaded that the love of the worlde even in a smale measure, will coole, if not kill, the life of sinceritye in Religion, & will abolishe the verye

memorye of heavenly affections :   O Lord, crucifie the world
unto me, that though I cannot avoyd to live amonge the baites &
snares of it, yet it may be so truely dead unto me & I unto it,
as I may no otherwise love, use, or delight in any the most
pleasant, profitable, &c, earthly comforts of this life, then I doe
the ayre wch I continually drawe in, or the earthe wch I ever tread
upon, or the skye wch I ever behould.   O why should I doate
wth greater affection on other thinges wch are of lesse use?

"I purpose by Gods grace to meditate more often upon the
certainty & excellencye of my everlastinge happinesse through
Christ, & of the vanitye & perill of all worldlye felicitye.   This
one thinge I observe wthall, that whilest we seeke to make o^r
earthly habitations comodious for the ease, quiet, & outward
comfort of o^r lives, we doe but provide for the encrease of o^r
sorrowe, for by suche meanes we doe the more animate & arme
the fleshe ag^t the spirit, so as it will cost us the more strife to
mortifie it & holde it under.   Lord teach me wisdome from
hence.

"Upon searche of my heart, & the sight of my secret sinnes
& corruptions wch still prevayled against me, I grewe into much
feare, discomfort, & heavynesse.   I was wthout ioye ; in God I
could finde none, (I seemed so unworthye) ; In worldly things
I durst take none (althoughe the devill did make me continuall
& large offers,) but resolved wth myselfe rather to continue in
my perplexed estate then to have helpe by any other meanes
then from the Lorde ; so I prayed earnestly & gave my selfe to
waite wth patience, & in due tyme I found, accordinge to that
of the Prophet Esaye 30. 15., in quietnesse & confidence was my
strength.

"When I have enioyed sweet peace wth my God then I have
been shye of the smalest occasions of offending him, & have
readylie & cheerfully denyed myne owne will, delight, content,
& credite, &c ; but afterwardes when my peace was gone, & I

had lost my lib^tie of heart & comunion wth Christ, then I fell to
them againe, & althoughe I could remember that I had formerly
shunned them, &c, yet I could not then finde what it should be
that should make me part wth things of so great necessitye &
use as then I esteemed them : but againe so soone as my peace
returned upon any renewinge of my repentance, & that the love
of God was shedd abroad in my heart, &c, then I could see
cause enoughe to make me willingly to contemne greater matters : For suerly there is no treasure like a good conscience, no
pleasure like the fellowshippe wth Christ Jesus, no ioye on earthe
like the Comunion of Saints : methought it was a happinesse
unmatchable, that I could quietly repose my heart in the bedd
of Gods promises ; — wch I never could doe but when I had
fully denyed & given over myselfe unto him, & still as I sought
myselfe God lefte me.

"Havinge been longe wearied wth discontent for want of suche
imployment as I could find comfort & peace in, I founde at last
that the conscionable & constant teachinge of my familye was a
speciall businesse, wherein I might please God, & greatly further their & mine own salvation, wch might be as sufficient
incouragement to my studye & labour therein as if I were to
teache a publick Congregation ; for as to the pleasing of God
it was all one, & I perceived that my exercise therein did stirre
up in me many considerations & muche life of affection, w^ch
otherwise I should not so often meet w^th ; so as I purpose by
Gods assistance, to take it as a chiefe parte of my callinge, &
to intende it accordingly.

"God by his great mercie brought me to a sight of my sinnes,
& so to repentance, never (I hope) to be repented of, true Repentance, sweet thoughe sharpe repentance ; O most happie, &
wholesome Repentance, more welcome to me then all earthly
pleasures, — for want of it (it havinge been longe absent) my
poore soule was allmost famished ; when by it God opened
before mine eyes the state of my soule, O what a poluted con-

science found I; what impure affections, what unruly desires, what blindnesse of minde, what fearfull hardnesse of heart, wch althoughe it were shaken & stirred to consideration & slight relentings, sometymes ofte in a day by occasion of readinge, or prayer, &c, yėt it soone shooke off all suche motions, & grewe more stiff necked ag^t God, untill it was allmost at that passe that it could not repente : But when it pleased God to have mercye upon me, & to sett my wickednesse upon me, I thought then suerly he would be doone wth me, for my former boldnesse in sinninge & daliance wth the breache of his Comandements : but I founde him more gracious then I durst conceive, or make use of for the present ; my former rebellion, ingratitude, self love, slouthe, carnallitie, tyme servinge, &c, came so freshe before me, & shewed so foul & odious unto me : Oh that not onely my eyes, but that my very heart could melt in teares, that I might mourne night & daye for my sinnes ag^t my good Father. O when shall I be ridde of the burthen of this sinful fleshe ! Would any that had knowne the sweet mercies that I had received from him, ever have beleeved that I should have turned from him, to goe roaminge after worldly pleasures ? Could I so soone forgett the pleasures, etc, wch his presence was wont to afforde me, as I had learned out of Psal : 16. & 36. & prov : 3.

" Amongst other sinnes wch I founde in my selfe, I sawe my great unbeleefe was one of the cheifest, for I had not nourished my faithe in Christ & in his worde, but had given waye to doubtinge & distrust so farre, as I had neere lost the use of Gods worde, wch althoughe I continued to read dailye, yet my faithe was so weakned through difficulties & delayes, as I had lefte off to live by faithe in the worde : & so for want of faithe my prayers failed, my meditations, readinge, & all grewe teadious & unprofitable, I had no heart to any Christian dutye, I thoughte all was in vaine. Heerupon I prayed earnestly & mourningly to have my faithe strengthened, & God soone heard me & by occasion in my familye exercises, I fealt my

faithe beginne to revive as a man out of a dreame. I acknowledged the infallible truthe & certainty of Gods most pure &
perfecte worde ; my heart leaped wthin 'me when I considered it,
I embraced it, I cast my selfe in to it : as fast as temptations
came either to feare, doubt, of difficultie or danger, &c, the
very first thought of Gods worde, Gods trueth, did easyly dis-
pell them ; & whereas before all my care was to gather peace
to my heart from the smalnesse of my infirmities &c, nowe my
comforte was in bringinge them (smale or great) unto the bloud
of Christ, & by applyinge the promise I founde howe the crim-
son sinnes might be made white as well as the palest-coloured.
Gods trueth caried all before it : I founde my heart, upon this
meditation, willinge to sett upon any dutye, whilest I behelde
my warrant in Gods book : & whereas sometymes many things
did discourage me from dutye, as the iudgm^t of the greatest
parte, the unlikelynesse of successe, the evill acceptation of
others, the feare of losse, disgrace, health, &c, now I remembred what Christ sayed, ' Woe to the world because of offences,
& blessed are they that shall not be offended in me : ' I perceived that these & suche like rubbes to o^r faithe were the
offences that Christ dothe partlye meane there, & I see that
they that will take offence from the opinion of others, their
owne corrupt reason, comon experience, &c, shall never enioye
the comforte of livinge by faithe, for the Childe of God must
breake throughe all these & saye wth Paul, Rom :   Let
God be true & every man a liar. O Lord I have sinned in
that I have not beleeved thy worde that I might sanctifie thy
name before thy people, but by thy grace I shall not dare heerafter once to doubt of thy holy & eternall truethe : Let it be
sufficient encouragem^t & warrant to me in any thinge, that it is
thy Comandm^t, thy promise &c.

"Resist the Devill & he will flee from you : this have I found
true by ofte experience, for whereas upon the Sabbaothe & in
hearinge of the worde &c, my heart would be most pestered
wth worldly thoughts, &c, so as I should have stronge desires

to be thinkinge of some suche things at those tymes, wch at other tymes I should not regarde; & from these snares I could not free myselfe, until it pleased the Lord, in prayer, to discover unto me that it was Satan that did thus followe me wth his assaults; whereupon I sett myselfe ag^t him by applyinge such places of scripture, as did best oppose his temptations: & thus doeinge, I have ofte tymes had my heart set at lib^{tye} from suche worldly thoughts & other his snares: The Lorde be praysed forever."

CHAPTER VII.

THIRD MARRIAGE. THE TYNDAL FAMILY. LETTERS OF WINTHROP
AND OTHERS.

In the year 1618, John Winthrop was once more established in domestic life. His third wife was Margaret Tyndal, daughter of Sir John Tyndal, knight, of Great Maplested, in the county of Essex. This has been correctly supposed to be the same Sir John Tyndal who had been assassinated two years before by a man named Bertram, on account of a decision, involving only the trifling sum of two hundred pounds, in a case which had been referred to Sir John as a Master in Chancery. Bertram, it seems, shot him in the back just as he was entering his chamber in Lincoln's Inn, and then hung himself in prison before he could be brought to trial. Lord Bacon, then Sir Francis Bacon, and Attorney-General of the Crown, examined the case soon afterwards; and wrote as follows to the favorite, Villiers, afterwards Duke of Buckingham: —

"I send, therefore, the case of Bertram, truly stated and collected, and the examination taken before myself and Mr. Solicitor: whereby it will appear to his majesty, that Sir John Tyndal, as to his cause, is a kind of martyr; for, if ever he made a just report in his life, this was it." [1]

---

[1] Bacon's Works, London, 1824, vol. v. p. 452.

A few days afterwards, Bacon wrote to the king him-self, as follows: —

"For this wretched murderer, Bertram, now gone to his place, I have, perceiving your majesty's good liking of what I propounded, taken order that there shall be a declaration con-cerning the cause in the King's Bench, by occasion of punish-ment of his keeper; and another in Chancery, upon the occa-sion of moving for an order, according to his just and righteous report.   And yet, withal, I have set on work a good pen, and myself will overlook it, for making some little pamphlet fit to fly abroad in the country." [1]

We know not whether this "little pamphlet" is still in existence; but here is an original letter, which is quite too interesting to be omitted in this connection, and which, being found among the family papers, removes all doubt that the murdered Master in Chan-cery, in regard to whose fate Bacon and his royal master took so lively an interest, was the father of Winthrop's wife.   It is a letter from her own brother, Arthur Tyndal, then a lawyer of Lincoln's Inn, to their widowed mother, immediately after the occurrence.

Arthur Tyndal to his Mother.

"To the right wor[ll] the Lady Tyndale at her house in Much Maplested in Essex.

"MY DEARE & LOVEINGE MOTHER, — It much refresheth my sorrowfull heart to understand & see the true effects of chris-tianity and of Gods holy Spirit in you, which are with patience and with a most humble humiliaĉon to the Almighty to beare these more then ordinarie afflictions and to waite and expect his mighty delivrances.   He is all sufficient and wise, and as he hath humbled us to the dust so he can and will exalt us againe,

---

[1] Bacon's Works, London, 1824, vol. vi. p. 134.

if we give glory unto his name in these bitter tymes of tryall.
He hath wrought wounderously alreadie in stoppeing the
mouthes of malicious & naughtie people. For the vilde wretch
that had pretended a wronge donne to him by my father &
laboring to maintaine it, God not sufferinge the blood of his
saints to lye too longe unrevenged delivered this caitiffe over to
Sathan, who on the last Sabboth in the forenoone hanged himselfe in prison, in a most marveilous sort dispairinge of Gods
mercie. All the grave examiners of that busines proclame
my fathers integritie, and say if it had been theire case they
must have been subject to the pistol too, for they would have
donne as he did. Thus it hath pleased God to justifie my
father, & every day more & more his upprightnes will appeare.
Good mother, comfort your selfe in the Lord ; he will againe if
we make right use of this, restore us againe to comfort, so that
we repine not, but with [y]earninge affections of soule & body
love him & magnifye him in all these his woundrous workes.
I have acquainte my uncle ffrancis with your letter [who]
offerethe still mercie unto us, & we are concluded of a course
for th'administracōn with which my brother Deane will thorowlie
acquainte you. The taylor cannot this weeke dispatch your
blacks, but the ribbyns and those trifells I send downe, & the
gownes shall come the next weeke or at such tyme as Betts
shall retorne with his coache. I pray remember my duty to
my good uncle your comforter & to all with you & at Dynes, &
to motion the buyinge of the reversion of the lease land to Sir
John Deane. I pray the Lord to be all our comforters.
Amen.   " Your most dutifull Sonne
                                    " ARTH : TYNDALE.
" LYNCOLNES INN 22ᵗʰ of No: 1616."

Morant's " History of Essex County " contains an
elaborate pedigree of the Tyndal Family, running it
back to the time of Edward I., and connecting it with
more than one of the crowned heads of Europe ; and
Nichols, in his " Historical Anecdotes of the Eighteenth

Century," states that Sir John Tyndal, the great-grandfather of Margaret Winthrop, and afterwards his son
Humphrey Tyndal, D.D., were actually waited upon to
assume the crown of Bohemia, as among its rightful
heirs.[1]

It would have been more in keeping with the character of Margaret, as we shall see it developed hereafter,
if her lineage could have been traced distinctly back to
the famous reformer, and translator of the Bible, William Tyndal, of ever-honored memory ; and an old
family pedigree does actually so trace it. In the more
authentic pedigrees of the Tyndals, however, the name
of the translator of the Bible is placed in the margin,
as one who would gladly have been included, and who
was probably a collateral relation, but as not being in
the same line of descent with Margaret's father, Sir
John. It is, however, more relevant to the family
history to notice, that the wife of Sir John was Anne
Egerton, widow of William Deane, Esq. ; from whom
the name of Deane soon afterwards found its way into
the Winthrop Family.

And here we are able to furnish a curious specimen
of the courtship of the old Puritan time, in the shape of
three original letters to Margaret Tyndal on her engagement and approaching marriage. One of them is from
Winthrop's father, welcoming her as his future daughter.

---

[1] Nichols's Hist. Anec., vol. ix. p. 304. Morant says, " Dr. T. Fuller (Hist. of Camb.,
p. 81) relates an improbable tradition concerning Humphrey Tyndal: viz., that, in the
reign of Q. Elizabeth, he was proffered by a Protestant party in Bohemia to be made
King thereof; which he refused, alledging, That he had rather be Queen Elizabeth's
subject than a Foreign Prince." — *Hist. of Essex*, vol. ii. p. 280.

It is written in his largest and most careful hand, and evidently with a pen made or mended for the purpose. It is as follows: —

Adam Winthrop to Margaret Tyndal.

"I am, I assure you, (Gentle Mistress Margaret) alredy inflamed wth a fatherly Love and affection towardes you : the wch at the first, the only report of your modest behaviour, and mielde nature, did breede in my heart; but nowe throughe the manifest tokens of your true love, & constant minde, wch I perceyve to be setteled in you towardes my soonne, the same is exceedingly increased in mee. So that I cannot abstaine from expressinge it unto you by my pen in absence, wch my tounge and mouthe I hope shal shortely declare unto you in presence. And then I doute not, but I shal have just cause to prayse God for you, and to thincke my selfe happy, that in my olde age I shal injoye the familiar company of so virtuous and loving a daughter; and passe the residue of my daies in peace and quietnes. For I have hetherto had greate cause to magnifie his holy name for his loving kindenes & mercy shewed unto mee in my children, and in those to whom they have been maried; that bothe I have alwaies deerly loved and affected them, and they also most lovinglye and dutifully have used mee. And therefore I assure you (good Mistress Margaret) that whatsoever love and kindenes you shal vouchsafe to shewe heereafter unto mee, I wil not only requite it wth the like, but also to the utter most of my power redouble the same. And for that I woulde fayne make it a little parte of your fayth to beleeve, that you shal be happye in matchinge wth my soonne, I doe heere faithfully promise for him (in the presence of almighty God,) that he will alwaies be a most kinde and lovinge husbande unto you, and a provident stuarde for you and yours during his lyfe, and also after his deathe. Thus wth my harty comendacions to your selfe, and to the good Lady your deere mother, confirminge my true Love and promise unto you, by a token of a smale value, but of a pure substance, wch I sende you by this trusty bearer, I doe leave you to ye protection of the most mighty Trinitye.   this last of Marche 1618.   Your assured frende   "ADAM WINTHROP."

The two other letters are from Winthrop himself, written in his most characteristic vein, and full of those earnest expressions of affection and of piety in which he ever delighted to indulge.   The first of them, it will be observed, has relation to some objections which Margaret's family and friends had made to the match, and which she herself seems to have resolutely resisted.   The precise nature of " the unequall conflicte " is not stated. It would not be surprising, however, that Margaret's brothers and sisters should have raised some question in regard to her becoming the third wife of a man who was as yet without any considerable fortune or fame, and who had four young children to be taken care of.   Winthrop, it seems, was able to assure her that she could rely on a maintenance of eighty pounds a year; which would be equivalent to at least four hundred pounds in these days. But religious considerations evidently turned the scale. Margaret and her mother clearly sympathized with Winthrop's earnest religious convictions, and would not listen to the more worldly, or certainly more prudent, views of others of the family.   But the letter will explain itself : —

John Winthrop to Margaret Tyndal.

" To my dearest freind & most heartyly beloved Mrs Marg^t Tyndall.

" Havinge seariously considered of that unequall conflicte wch for my sake thou didst lately sustaine, & wherein yet, (although the odds were great), God beinge on thy side, thou gatest the victorye, I have had from hence a large provocatiō to acknowledge Gods providence & speciall favour towards me, & to give him thankes for so great experience as hathe been offred me heerby of thy godlinesse, love, wisdome, & inviolable constancie; — wch as in itselfe it deserves all approbatiō, so in me it is of suche vertue as the more I thinke of it, the more it drawes & knitts my heart unto thee, and hathe setled that estimatiō of thy love therein, as (I am truely persuaded) nothinge but deathe shall abolishe or diminishe it.   Such an invincible resolutiō could not have been founde in a poore fraile woman, had not thine armes been strengthned by the mightie God of Jacob.   He it was wch gave an other spirit to thyselfe & that good Lady thy mother, wth Caleb & Josuah, constantly to followe the Lord against all the discouragements of the greater parte, — yea when my selfe, too cowardly & unkindly ioyned armes wth thine opposers against thee : But nowe doe I knowe that thou lovest me, & heerby we may bothe be fully assured that this thinge comethe of the Lorde : Therefore it is my desire to confirme thy heart in this resolutiō; not that I feare any change (farre be suche a thought from me) but for that I wishe thee a large additiō of comfort to thy constancie, wch may molifie & heale up the scarres of such wounds as may yet remaine of thy late conflicte.   And now I will take lib^{tie} to deale freely wth thee since there is no need of persuasiō, nor any feare of suspitiō of flaterye; & let me tell thee that as thou hast doone worthyly & Christianly, so thou hast doone no otherwise than became thee being one professinge to feare God & beleeve in him : for (what so ever I am or may be, yet) beinge, in thy accompt, a servant of God & one that thou mightest well hope to be furthered to heaven by (Amen I say), & beinge offred unto thee by God, & thy selfe beinge as warrantably called to embrace the opportunitye as a woman might be, I see not how thou couldst have had peace to thine owne heart if thou hadst refused it; but thou mightest iustly have feared least, for wthdrawinge thy heart from God & leaninge to thine owne reason, he should have given thee over to some suche matche as should have proved a plauge to thy soule all thy dayes : Let worldly minds that savour not the things of

God, & that indeed have no parte or portion in the least of Gods promises, bende all their care & studye to secure themselves of an earthly happinesse ; let them make sure of great portions wth their wives & large Ioyntures from their husbands ; they doe but their kinde, & I confesse it concernes them very muche to looke especially to suche things, for there is nothing else wch they can have comfort or happinesse in, havinge no parte in Christ & beinge strangers from the covenant of grace ; & therefore if they should be barred of their great hopes in these outward things, their God, their heaven, their ioye & all, were gone, their heart would dye w^{th}in them like Naball : Therefore God letts suche many tymes catche what they can scramble for, he fills their bellies wth his hidd treasure, they live in ease & pleasure, they nourishe their hearts as in a daye of slaughter, but he sends leannesse into their soules, & in the ende when they are called to a reconinge, what fruit can they shewe forthe of all their labour, care, etc., but vanitye & vexatiō of spirit? And so they dye under a secure, or tormented conscience, wch followes them to their owne place. But you, whom God hathe ordayned to a better ende, he lookes you should be guided by an other rule ; he telles you that you are a pilgrime & stranger in this life, that you have no abidinge cytye heere but must looke for one to come : He wch is your Kinge telles you that his kingdome is not of this world, if you desire to reigne wth him in his kingdome you must be content to be an underlinge wth him in the world's kingdome, & must looke for afflictiō heere, for the servant must not looke to be above the master : He telles you that the first worke in his service is to denye y^{or} selfe ; he bidds you never to cheapen about the pearle except you be resolved to sell all for it, & never to thinke to gett him & his love except you can be content for his sake to leave, yea to hate father, mother, friends, goods, & y^{or} owne life : for he telles you plainly that you can not serve 2 masters ; so as if you love the world, the love of the Father cañot be in you : If you would knowe of him, who are the blessed, looke at that 5 of Math : & amongst all those 8 beatitudes you shall finde never a worde of riches, or honor, or ease, etc., but when the scripture speakes of suche things it setts a *caveat* upon them, as temptations, snares, riches of iniquitye, the choakes of the hopes of salvatiō, branded wth these 2 speciall observations by Christ & his Apostles — ' But the cares of the world & the deceitfulnesse of Riches & the Lusts of other thinges enter in & choake the worde, &c : ' And ' w[ch] while some have lusted after, they have erred from the faithe & have pierced themselves through wth many sorrowes.' — And tell me then what it will profite a man to winne the worlde & to loose his soule ? It is the dearest purchase that must cost a man the losse of his soule. Who would take Demas his bargaine ? And yet (no doubt) he was of the opiniō that our comōon protestants are of in these dayes (who in the depthe of their devise wilbe wiser than Christ & his Apostles,) he thought he had founde an easyer waye to heaven then other men, he thought to save his soule & yet keepe & love the world too : But he was deceived, & so shall they also, for the mouthe of the Lord hathe spoken it ; let them please themselves never so muche wth their owne conceits in the meane tyme. Nowe for thee, I dare bouldly saye to thee that thou hast doone wisely in seekinge first the kingdome of heaven, & making sure for the better parte w[ch] shall not be taken from thee : for if it be a Rule of policie amongst the men of this world, to adventure upon the least hope of vertue in suche matches where there is assurance of a great portion, so as dayly examples of the contrarye ill event cannot drive such par- tyes from that grounde : how muche more commendable is it in thee (& woorthy of thy profession, w[ch] esteemes Godlinesse as the greatest gaine) when havinge mett w[th] (at least in thy per- suasion) sufficient assurance of holynesse, thou canst be content to conceive hope of outward happinesse even from doubtfull conditions : And heerin thou canst want no incouragement for hope of good successe, amongst so many promises & examples as make for thy cause : Looke upon the blessinge of Salomons choyse ; he sought onely wisdome, & God added all outward prosperitye : Consider Ruthes choyse, who for the love of the God of Israell forsooke hir owne countrye & friends to partake wth the povertye of a desolate widowe : but how did God recompense her in the ende ? You may see the like in Moses, who if he had had the counsell of the wisdome of our tymes might have looked to have kept his greatnesse in the Court, & yet not have hindred his salvatiō, ɲor wanted Gods favour. I need instance no more, for the Scriptures & our owne tymes afforde many examples, wch all consent in this, to persuade suche as beleeve God & have their treasure in heaven, to make sure for salvatiō, & to cast the care of their present, incertaine, transitorye conditiō upon the love & wisdome of him that is their father & God all-sufficient, who hathe undertaken to care for them. And heerin I am persuaded (notwithstandinge callinge for a diligent & faithfull use of all good meanes) that a Christian cannot too boldly relye upon God whilst he yields himselfe in obedience to his will : for it dothe so fittly agree to the nature of a young childe, whereunto we must be like if ever we shall come in heaven : it is so called for, in all places of Scripture, as Psal : 37. 5. Rolle thy way upon the Lord, trust in him & he shall bringe it to passe : the whole Psalme is excellent to this purpose : So Phil : 4 : 6. 7 : Be carefull for nothinge, but in every thinge by prayer & supplicatiō, etc. But especially that in Luke, 12 : 22, &c : Take no thought what you shall eate, &c : And observe how Christ urgeth that exhortatiō by the examples of the Lillies & Ravens, whence he gathers an unanswerable argument, verse 28 : If God so clothe the grasse, &c : will he not clothe you? &c : The too frequent & cumbersome cares, feares, doubtings, etc, that the minds & mouthes of most Christians are taken up wth in these dayes, doe plainly discover that men live not by faithe ; & that heaven is not their home, when they sett so muche store by the things of this worlde. Men are not satisfied wth such competencie as God allowes them, but hunt as eagerly after risings & increasings, as if it were the onely ende of their life : when yet we are exhorted to have our conversatiō wthout covetousnesse, & to be content wth what we have, for he hath promised that he will not faile us nor forsake us, &c : And Salomon in all his wisdome & experience tells us

that it is the blessinge of God that makes riche wthout addinge
sorrowe : But the tymes seem nowe to be changed, & the prises
of Salomons merchandice to be muche abated, as if you reade
the 3 of the Proverbes from the 13 verse to the ende of the 18th
you will thinke as I saye. But I forgett myselfe in runninge so
farre in this argument : but I take the more lib^{tie} (as I sayd at
first) because I would confirme that in thy heart whereunto God
hathe allreadye persuaded thee ; & God of his mercye persuade
us bothe to a constant followinge of the hope of salvatiō wch is
layd up for us in Christ, & so shedd abroad his love in our
hearts by that spirit of Adoption, as beinge assured that our
names are written in the booke of life, we may reioyce wth
ioye unspeakable & glorious. Amen.

" By this wch I have allreadye written I may seeme to confirme
those obiections wch thy freinds have moved, & to grant that
there should be great causes of discouragement offered thee in
outward respects : But I trust I shall make it appeare that thou
shalt have no wronge or disparagement by matchinge wth me,
all things beinge indifferently considered : I confesse it is possible
that I may die verye soone, & then thy maintenance for a while
may be some what lesse then convenient ; but it is more likely
that I may live a fewe yeares wth thee, wch will certainly better
thy conditiō. But whether I live longer or lesse while, I can
lett thee see how, wth a little patience, thy meanes may be better than 80^{lb} a yeare ; yet can I promise no more for present
certaintye then I have formerly acquainted thy freinds wth ;
neither would I that thou shouldest make this knowne to them.
I had rather that they should finde it then expecte it. What-
sover shall be wantinge of that wch thy love deserves, my kindest affection shall endeavour to supplie, whilst I live, & what I
leave unsatisfied (as I never hope to be out of thy debt) I will
sett over to Him who is able, & will recompence thee to the
full : & for the present, I wish thee to followe the prophets exhortatiō Psal : 27. 14. Waite on the Lord, be of good courage,
& he shall strengthen thyne heart ; Waite I say on the Lorde."[1]

---

[1] The paper is torn at this point, and the signature and date are thus wanting.

The second of these letters bears date after all the
family differences were at an end, and only a week or
two before the marriage. The grave suggestions which
it contains, in regard to the bridal apparel which Margaret was engaged in preparing, will occasion a smile.
They would hardly be relished, we imagine, by any young
lady to whom they might be addressed under the same
circumstances at the present day. But the scriptural
allusions and applications which are introduced so
abundantly into this letter are still more remarkable.
Winthrop had evidently studied the Song of Solomon
most diligently. It seems to have been one of his favorite books. We have already observed him more than
once, in his religious experiences and confessions, borrow-
ing the ideas and images of that " mystical allegory of
the union of Christ with his Church." We shall find
him again, hereafter, in several of his letters, adopting
the same analogies and comparisons between earthly
marriages and the marriage of the Church to Christ.
But this particular letter is replete with them; and the
language of it might seem not a little extraordinary to
those who are not sufficiently familiar with " the Canticle
of Canticles " (as it was formerly styled in the sacred
calendar) to recognize the source from which so much of
his phraseology and so many of his figures are derived.
The other scriptural references will readily explain themselves; but that to " Cant: 2." might hardly be so obvious to a common reader. It must not be forgotten, too,
that the rites of matrimony, in those days, were always
concluded by the administration of the holy Communion
to the bride and bridegroom; and the early part of the

letter has evident allusion to that solemn sacrament. This letter, however, like the others, shall speak for itself.

John Winthrop to Margaret Tyndal.

"To my best beloved Mrs Margaret Tyndall at Great Maplested, Essex.

" Grace mercie & peace, &c:

"My onely beloved Spouse, my most sweet freind, & faithfull companion of my pilgrimage, the happye & hopefull supplie (next Christ Jesus) of my greatest losses, I wishe thee a most plentifull increase of all true comfort in the love of Christ, wth a large & prosperous addition of whatsoever happynesse the sweet estate of holy wedlocke, in the kindest societye of a lovinge husbande, may afford thee. Beinge filled wth the ioye of thy love, & wantinge opportunitye of more familiar comunion wth thee, wch my heart fervently desires, I am constrained to ease the burthen of my minde by this poore helpe of my scriblinge penne, beinge sufficiently assured that, although my presence is that wch thou desirest, yet in the want thereof, these lines shall not be unfruitfull of comfort unto thee. And now, my sweet Love, lett me a whyle solace my selfe in the remembrance of our love, of wch this springe tyme of o^r acquaintance can putt forthe as yet no more but the leaves & blossomes, whilest the fruit lyes wrapped up in the tender budde of hope ; a little more patience will disclose this good fruit, & bringe it to some maturitye : let it be o^r care & labour to preserve these hopefull budds from the beasts of the fielde, & from frosts & other iniuryes of the ayre, least o^r fruit fall off ere it be ripe, or lose ought in the beautye & pleasantnesse of it : Lett us pluck up suche nettles & thornes as would defraud o^r plants of their due nourishment ; let us pruine off superfluous branches ; let us not sticke at some labour in wateringe & manuringe them : — the plentye & goodnesse of o^r fruit shall recompense us abundantly : O^r trees are planted in a fruitfull soyle ; the grounde, & patterne of o.^{r} love, is no other but that betweene Christe & his deare spouse, of whom she speakes as she finds him, My welbeloved is mine & I am his : Love was their banquetting house, love was their wine, love was their ensigne ; [1] love was his invitinges, love was hir fayntinges ; love was his apples, love was hir comforts ; love was his embracinges, love was hir refreshinge : love made him see hir, love made hir seeke him : [2] love made him wedde hir, love made hir followe him : love made him hir saviour, love makes hir his servant.[3] Love bredd o.^{r} fellowshippe, let love continue it, & love shall increase it, untill deathe dissolve it. The prime fruit of the Spirit is love ; [4] truethe of Spirit & true love : abounde wth the spirit, & abounde wth love : continue in the spirit & continue in love : Christ in his love so fill o.^{r} hearts wth holy hunger & true appetite, to eate & drinke wth him & of him in this his sweet Love feast, wch we are now preparinge unto, that when o.^{r} love feast shall come, Christ Jesus himselfe may come in unto us, & suppe wth us, & we wth him : so shall we be merrye indeed. (O my sweet Spouse) can we esteeme eache others love, as worthy the recompence of o.^{r} best mutuall affections, & can we not discerne so muche of Christs exceedinge & undeserved love, as may cheerfully allure us to love him above all ? He loved us & gave himselfe for us ; & to helpe the weaknesse of the eyes & hande & mouthe of o.^{r} faithe, wch must seeke him in heaven where he is, he offers himselfe to the eyes, hands & mouthe of o.^{r} bodye, heere on earthe where he once was. The Lord increace o.^{r} faithe.

" Nowe my deare heart let me parlye a little wth thee about trifles, for when I am present wth thee my speeche is preiudiced by thy presence, wch drawes my minde from it selfe : I suppose nowe, upon thy unkle's cominge, there wilbe advisinge & counsellinge of all hands ; & amongst many I knowe there wilbe

---

[1] Cant: 2.   [3] Jo: 3. 16. Deut: 10. 12.
[2] Jer: 2. 2. Ezek: 16. [4] Gal: 5. 22.

(We have transferred to the foot of the page the above references, which are found in the margin of the original letter, at the points designated.)

some, that wilbe provokinge thee, in these indifferent things, as matter of apparell, fashions & other circumstances, rather to give contente to their vaine minds savouringe too muche of the fleshe &c, then to be guided by the rule of Gods worde, wch must be the light & the Rule; for allthoughe I doe easyly grant that the Kingdome of heaven is not meat & drinke, apparell &c, but Righteousnesse, peace &c: yet beinge forbidden to fashion o^{r}selves like unto this world, & to avoyde not onely evill but* all appearance of it must be avoyded, & allso what soever may breed offence to the weake (for wch I praye thee reade for thy direction the xiiijth to the Rom :) & for that Christians are rather to seeke to edifie then to please, I hould it a rule of Christian wisdome in all these things to followe the soberest examples: I confesse that there be some ornaments wch for Virgins & Knights daughters, &c, may be comly & tollerable, wch yet in so great a change as thine is, may well admitt a change also: I will medle wth no particulars, neither doe I thinke it shalbe needfull; thine owne wisdome & godlinesse shall teache thee sufficiently what to doe in suche things: & the good assurance wch I have of thy unfained love towards me, makes me perswaded that thou wilt have care of my contentment, seeing it must be a cheife staye to thy comfort: & wthall the great & sincere desire wch I have that there might be no discouragement to daunt the edge of my affections, whyle they are truly labouring to settle & repose themselves in thee, makes me thus watchfull & iealous of the least occasion that Sathan might stirre up to o^r discomfort. He that is faithfull in the least wilbe faithfull in the greatest, but I am too fearfull I doe thee wronge, I knowe thou wilt not grieve me for trifles. Let me intreat thee (my sweet Love) to take all in good parte, for it is all of my love to thee, & in my love I shall requite thee: I acknowledge, indeed, thou maist iustly say to me as Christ to the Pharisies, Hypocrite, first cast out the beame that is in thine owne eye &c, for whatsoever I may be in thy opinion, yet mine owne guiltie heart tells me of farre greater things to be reformed in my selfe, & yet I feare there is muche more

than in mine owne partiall iudgment I can discerne; iust cause
I have to complaine of my pride, unbeleefe, hardnesse of heart
& impenitencie, vanitye of minde, unrulinesse of my affections,
stubbornesse of my will, ingratitude, & unfaithfullnesse in the
Covenant of my God, &c. therefore (by Gods assistance) I
will endeavour that in myselfe, wch. I will allso desire in thee.
Let us search & trye o.^r hearts & turne to the Lord : for this is
o.^r safetye, not o.^r owne innocencye, but his mercie : If when we
were enemies he loved us to reconciliatiō; much morè, beinge
reconciled will he save us from destructiō.

"Lastly for my farewell (for thou seest my lothenesse to parte
wth thee makes me to be teadious) take courage unto thee, &
cheare up thy heart in the Lorde, for thou knowest that Christ
thy best husbande can never faile thee : he never dies, so as
there can be no greife at partinge; he never changes, so
as once beloved & ever the same : his abilitye is ever infinite,
so as the dowrye & inheritance of his sonnes & daughters can
never be diminished.   As for me a poore worme, dust & ashes,
a man full of infirmityes, subiect to all sinnes, changes &
chances, wch befall the sonnes of men, how should I promise
thee any thinge of my selfe, or if I should, what credence
couldst thou give thereto, seeinge God only is true & every man
a lyar.   Yet so farre as a man may presume upon some experience, I may tell thee, that my hope is, that suche comfort as
thou hast allreadye conceived of my love towards thee, shall
(throughe Gods blessinge) be happily continued; his grace
shalbe sufficient for me, & his power shalbe made perfect in my
greatest weaknesse :. onely let thy godly, kinde, & sweet carriage towards me, be as fuell to the fire, to minister a constant
supplie of meet matter to the confirminge & quickninge of
my dull affections : This is one ende why I write so muche unto
thee, that if there should be any decaye in kindnesse &c.
throughe my default & slacknesse heerafter, thou mightest have
some patternes of o.^r first love by thee, to helpe the recoverye
of suche diseases : yet let o.^r trust be wholly in God, & let us
constantlye followe him by o.^r prayers, complaininge & moan-

inge unto him of owne povertye, imperfections & unworthynesse, untill his fatherly affectiō breake forthe upon us, & he speake kindly to the hearts of his poore servant & handmayd, for the full assurance of Grace & peace through Christ Jesus, to whom I nowe leave thee (my sweet Spouse & onely beloved). God send us a safe & comfortable meetinge on Mondaye morninge. Farewell. Remember my love & dutye to my Ladye thy good mother, wᵗʰ all kinde & due salutations to thy unkle E : & all thy brothers & sisters.

    " Thy husband by promise
           " JOHN WINTHROP.
" GROTON where I wish thee. Aprill 4. 1618.

" My father & mother salute thee heartyly wᵗʰ my Lady & the rest.

" If I had thought my lettre would have runne to halfe this lengthe I would have mayde choyce of a larger paper."

We should hardly know where to look for love-letters of the olden time more quaint and curious than those which have just been given. Sir Simonds D'Ewes, in his Autobiography (1626), gives a letter of his own " to Mistress Clopton," whom he was about to marry; saying, that, it " being the only line I sent her during my wooing-time, and but short, I have thought good to insert it in this place."[1] We cannot plead their brevity as an apology for inserting Winthrop's letters; and we have no belief that the two which have so strangely survived the lapse of years were all that he wrote between his engagement and his marriage. But they are too characteristic, both of the man himself and of the times in which he lived, to be suppressed or abbreviated. Were

---

[1] Autobiography of Sir S. D'Ewes, vol. i. p. 316.

they less than two centuries and a half old, we might, perhaps, have some compunction about betraying the confidences of private and domestic correspondence; but re-appearing, as they have done, from the old original files in which they have so long slumbered, at the very moment when this volume was taken seriously in hand, they may be almost said to have asserted their own claim to be included among the illustrations of the character of their author. And most striking evidence, certainly, do they bring to that deep-seated and prevailing love of God in his heart, which strengthened and purified all his other affections, and which seemed itself to be purified and strengthened in turn, even by those very earthly ties and domestic attachments which have so often estranged other hearts from the highest objects of their love.

The wedding took place at Great Maplested, not many days after the date of the last of these two letters. Adam Winthrop had recorded the precise day on which it occurred, on the fly-leaf of one of his old almanacs; but the paper has so crumbled with age, that the date cannot now be deciphered with confidence. We have before us, however, Adam's distinct record, that Margaret Tyndal, his son's wife, came first to Groton on Friday, the 24th of April, 1618. That was a memorable advent in the family history. It was the commencement of a new era in Winthrop's personal fortunes. The clouds and darkness which had overshadowed so many of his earlier years were now about to disappear, and nearly thirty years of undisturbed domestic enjoy-

ment were in store for him. Yet little could Margaret
have dreamed of the precise career which awaited her.
Had she foreseen that only eleven or twelve years would
have passed away before she should be called on to
resign all the luxuries and comforts of civilized life, to
traverse a stormy ocean, and to take up her abode in a
distant and dreary wilderness, —there to live, and there
to die, — she might well have faltered as she crossed the
threshold of Groton Manor. Haply she might even
have regretted that she had not listened to the remonstrances of sisters and brothers, before linking her
fortunes with one whose religious faith and fervor
might induce him to engage in so formidable and appall-
ing an enterprise.

But we must not anticipate the course of her destiny;
and still less must we distrust that constancy and
courage of which we shall find her giving such abundant evidence hereafter. Resuming, rather, the direct
thread of our narrative, we may find here an appropriate
place for two brief letters from that same Mr. Culverwell (Ezekiel by name) by whom Winthrop had been
married to the wife of his youth, and to whom, in his
" Christian Experience," he attributed his earliest religious impressions. One of them was written on occasion
of his marriage to Margaret Tyndal, and the other on
the approaching birth of their first child. They certainly
give a pleasant impression of the venerable pastor, by
whose " weary, shaking hand" they were penned; while
they bear most agreeable testimony to the " true Christian love" of him to whom they were addressed.

Rev. Ezekiel Culverwell to John Winthrop.

"To the Worp[ll] his especiall friend Mr. Winthrop at Groton.

"WORSHIPFULL & BELOVED MR. WINTHROP, — I have receaved your letters which well resemble their parent in constansy of true christian love, which yf I should not accordingly intertaine it should be my great fault. The occasions of my love being increased, no reason my love should be abated. I am now bowned with a dubble bond, one to you, another to your wife; to you both I say, yea for you both I pray, God make your comforts like to ours which you [know] were not common. I know no better means thereof than the constant strife between us who should get the better hand in kindnes & duties of our place. I ever complaned I was behind & she the like. Let it be so with you & you shalbe both great gayners. But this will not be obtained yf God be any looser by your bargane. Let him therefore have your hearts & he will give them back ech to other. For myselfe I have had this spring much peine & never look to recover my weaknes in my feet & peines of the stone which both have some mitigation that I may endure them. I have indeed as you well deem oft remembered you & joyed in the accomplishment of your mariage, & wilbe ready to further your comforts wherein me lyeth, & thus my weary shaking hand makes me to end — The Lord every way prosper your mariage.

"Yours ever in Christ   "EZ. CULVERWELL."

Rev. Ezekiel Culverwell to John Winthrop.

"To the Wop[ll] his very kinde friend Mr. John Winthrop at Groton.

"RIGHT WORTHILYE BELOVED, — I take very thankfully your loving respect of me, & God forbid I should so sinne as to cease to pray for you & yours, of whom I conceave good hope that they be that blessed seed, of whom it shalbe veryfyed which Esa 61, 9. did foretell. And to this end make it (as you

doe) your chiefe studye to trayne them up in the nurture &
admonition of the Lord, which I understand from their infansy
to nurse them up in knowledge & practise of christianity as
their capacity will bear.   I hear your wife is neer her tyme, I
pray God give like successe to my poor prayers for you which
of late I have found with others, who have craved my help in
like case.   Thus much certify your sweet natured & modest
wyfe (as I conceave) for her comfort, that (as neer as I can
gesse) I wilbe with her at her need.   I would be glad to hear
how she fits her self to your course.   I doubt not but my
much respected Lady Tindal wilbe with you, whom I pray
salute in my name, & merily require her to pay her debts, I
meane of prayers for me, which I must looke to in myselfe
both for her & you both.   Concerning my helth its oft crasy,
but noe regement fitts.   I am growing into an astma, that is a
shortnes of breath with wheesing & a dry cough.   I desire &
labour to be ready for my change, & so I comit us all to the
providence of our heavenly father.

"Yours while his owne   "Ez. Culverwell.
"Mar. 12. 1618.

"I hope you haue heard of my daughter's fruitfulnes, two at
a byrth : 4 which could not make 2 yeers.   7 living.   the poor
man hath his hands full, yet I thank God he thrives both
wayes which is rare & good."

Here, too, we may find a place for a letter from Margaret's brother, Deane Tyndal, Esq., written a year or
two after her marriage, which furnishes ample evidence,
that whatever family misgivings . there may originally
have been as to the wisdom of the match, the most cor-
dial and affectionate relations had now been established
between Winthrop and at least one of her brothers:
another of whom, we shall find hereafter, actually
accompanied him to New England.

Deane Tyndal to John Winthrop.

"To my verie loveing brother Mr. John Winthrop att his house in
Groton give these.

"KINDE BROTHER, — I acknowledg your great love in
sending to see us, and condemne myselfe of neglect in that
kinde; wch I protest (and that trulye) hath not proceeded
from anie forgetfullnesse of my sister, or you, but the snow,
& cold weather, hath kept me and mine from sturing farr from
home. Now I understand by your messenger that the wayes
be pasable, it shall not be longe (if it please God) before I will
visit you, for I much desier to see my sister and you, whose
good I daylie wish and praye for. Sr John Deane and his Ladie
after a troublesom and dangerous iournie are safe come home.
They report that it is of credit that the Kinge of Bohemia and
his whole armie are overthrone, the Citie of Prage taken by
Burquoy, the Kinge and Queen fled, and som afferme he is not.
This sadd newes we heare here. I have sent you Camden.
My wife, I thanke the Almightie, was never better soe neere
hir time. And thus wth thankes for all your kindnesses, my
wives and my owne love and unfayned affections being remembred to our best beloved sister and yourselfe I rest

      "Your assured loving brother   "DEANE TYNDALE.
"The second of Decr 1620."

Here, again, may be given another of the Lady Mildmay's pleasant letters, addressed about this period, though
unhappily without any exact date, to her cousin, John
Winthrop : —

The Lady Mildmay to John Winthrop.

"GOOD COSEN, — I hartelie thancke you for this good messenger, & also for yor lovinge & proper lettre. I acknowledge
myselfe so unworthie of so greate respecte as every waie unable

to make the least requital unto you for it.   I assure myselfe it is a special blessinge of God uppon me & my posteritie, that he hathe moved the heartes of yor selfe, wife & lovinge parents, to be so myndfull of me.   Howe available God hath iudged the praiers of his servants, one for another, his holy worde besides o.^r owne experience hath made knowne unto us.   The Lorde knowes howe barren this place (wherein he hathe set me) is of grace, as also myne owne weakenes in it : and therefore he movethe his servants to upholde me by their praiers, as Aaron & Hur staied up the hand of Moses : least he should saie unto me, as he saide to the Churche of Sardis, Thou hast a name that thou lyvest, but thou art deade.   The Lorde I trust will keepe me from that deadnes.   And seinge he hathe given me an other sonne, as a pledge of his mercy, I have cause to reioice as by yor letter it appereth you doe.   I beseeche the Almightie that his blessinge may be uppon him, that his frends may have more cause to reioice in his second birthe then in his first, when they shall see that the Lorde hathe fitted him for his owne service.   Thus good Cosen wth the remembrance of my love to yor selfe & yor good wife, I committe you to God & reste ever yours to the uttermost of my power.

"AMY MILDMAY."

And here, also, we may give the few passages of Winthrop's little autograph volume of religious experiences which relate to this period, — the first of them bearing date, according to the old style, on the 24th of March, 1618; or, as we now should write it, the 3d of April, 1619.

"On Wensdaye the 24th of Marche 1618, Marg^t my wife was delivered of a sonne,[1] whereof I desire to leave this testimonye of my thankfullnese unto God, that she being above 40

---

[1] This was Stephen Winthrop, who was colonel of a regiment in the civil wars of England, and a member of one of Cromwell's parliaments.

houres in sore travayle, so as it beganne to be doubted of hir life, yet the Lord sent hir a safe deliverance. Heerby I had occasion to finde the great power & benefite of prayer: for Mr Sands first prayeing wth hir in hir trouble, & after myselfe, it pleased God (althoughe she was not delivered many houres after) yet to increase hir strengthe, & afterwards, I perceiving hir danger, I humbled myselfe in fastinge & mourninge, I searched my heart for some sinnes, & made up my peace wth my God, & so getting a more large & melting heart to goe unto the Lord, I sett myselfe to prayer, & gave not over untill God had sent hir deliverance.

"The daye after hir deliverance she was taken wth a burning feaver, wch heald hir so, as after the viiith daye was passed my Cosin Duke made little reconinge of hir life, but wthin one daye after, beinge the 10th daye of hir sicknesse, diverse godly min^{rs} meetinge togither did in their prayer remember hir case in partic^{r}, & that very daye & houre (as neere as might be guessed) she founde a sensible release of hir disease. The Lord be blessed forevermore.

"Aug. 22, 1619. I had been drawne from my stedfastnesse, & walked in an unsettled course, for the space of a yeare & more, before this tyme: I had made diverse attempts to returne againe, but they still vanished, my zeale was cooled, my comfort in heavenly things was gone, I had no ioye in prayer, nor in the Sabaothe, nor in Gods word, nor in the Comunion of Saints, or if I had any, it was so soone gone, as it was not to be regarded; & now it pleased God to open mine eyes againe upon a Sabaothe daye, & I founde the cause of all to be, that I had againe embraced this p^{r}sent worlde, eagerly pursuinge the delights & pleasures of it, & I might easyly observe that as the love of the world p^{r}vayled, so the love of God & all goodnesse decayed. Heerupon (by Gods grace) I have ag^{ne} resolved to renounce this worlde, & to holde in my affections to the love & estimation of heavenly things; the Lord in mercye inable me hereunto.

"It is a policie of Sathan to discourage us from duty by settinge before us g.ᵗ appearances of danger, difficulty, impossibilitie, &c, wᶜʰ when we come to examine or make triall of, are found indeed to be nothinge so ; but even as a foole being tyed by a thredd or a strawe, thinkes himselfe unpossible to stirre, & therefore stands still, so dothe Sathan make advantage of oᵘ foolishe & *fearfull* dispositiō. In these discouragements &c, it is sufficient oft tymes to sett us at libᵗˡᵉ, if we doe but consider that it is the tempter, &c.

" When I thinke it were good (in some partic.ʳ pleasures, &c) for the peace of my Conscience, to leave suche or suche a thinge undone, &c, it is a usuall obiectiō of my heart — But I shall gaine nothinge by leavinge it &c : so as I see it is good for a man to applie to himselfe that promise of God to Ab : I am thy exceedinge g.ᵗ reward : & wᵗʰ Moses to have respect to the recompence of the Reward : Heb : 11. & therefor to have the eye of ffaithe allwayes fixed upon life ev.ʳ lastinge, for by nature we are all disposed to saye as the wicked in Job : What profite shall we have, &c :

" It appeares by divers pʳcepts of God to Israell, Deut   , of talkinge wᵗʰ their children &c, about God, & by the practice of the faithfull in the tymes of persecution, that we should have religion in as familiar practice as oᵘ eatinge & drinkinge, dealings about earthly affaires &c, & not to tye it onely to the exercises of Divine worship, wᶜʰ makes that there is so little free speeche of heavenly matters, & that men are readye to blushe at the speakinge or hearinge thereof, as if it were some streininge of modestye.

" 1620 : Aprill 7 : beinge frydaye. About one of the clocke in the morninge Adam my sonne was borne.
" I have cause for ever to remember the goodnesse of the Lo : & the power of prayer, for my wife beinge in longe & very difficult travaile I humbled my selfe in earnest prayer to God

for hir, & beinge in the next chamber, as I arose from prayer
I heard the child crye. I desire of God, I may make more
accompt of prayer, havinge so ofte founde the sweet successe
of it. I perceive the Lo : will keepe faithfully his promises w^th
his Children.

"I haue founde that a man may master & keepe under many
corrupt lusts by the meere force of reason & morall considerations (as the heathen did) but they will returne ag^n to their
former strength : there is no way to mortifie them but by
faithe in Christ, & his deathe : that as he, when sinne &c, had
him at the greatest advantage in the grave, yet then gate the
full victorie of sinne &c, by arisinge from under it ; so a Ch^n.
beinge in him by faithe, is made really partaker of his Conquest.

"1620. Januarye 12. Ridinge throughe Boxford wth Mr.
Gurdon in his coache, my sonne Henrye beinge wth me & one
of Mr. Gurdons men, enteringe into the towne the coachmen
was throwne off & the horses ranne throughe the towne over
logges & highe stumpes untill they came upon the causye right
ag^t the Churche, & there were snarled in the logges, &c ; & the
coache beinge broken in peeces, toppe, botom & sides, yet by
Gods most mercifull providence we were all safe : blessed be his
holy name.

"The water of Bethlem that David offered unto God was not
an offeringe that had any promise of acceptance, neither for the
worth of it could challenge any : yet (no doubt) it was well
pleasinge unto God, because it was a deniall of himselfe for
Gods sake in that particular lust of his ; we many tymes have
the lesse heart to beat downe o^r particular lusts in thinges that
are indifferent, or of so smale consequence as we think that God
will have no respecte to us for it. But afterwards even in suche
thinges God is well pleased that we doe denye o^r selves, & the
sacrificinge of any longinge affection to the Love of o^r God
(though it be but either a little water, an apple, a triflinge plea-

sure, &c,) is of greater account wth him then some workes of a farre more glorious appearance.

" Many thinges w[ch] fall out by the ordinarye course of nature &c, are not easylye discerned to be guided by any speciall providence of God, as the Eclipses of the Sunne &c, thunders, tempests, &c, the effects whereof are ofte very strange ; but God who had from the beginninge determined of suche effects, did w[th]all appointe that the course of naturall causes should concurre at the same tyme : so that heerby his glory is the greater, in effectinge thinges extraordinary, & yet not changing the order of causes. Thus when God in iustice hathe appointed that a wicked man shalbe cut off, he hath w[th]all appointed that suche a disease, suche a battail &c, or age it selfe shall concurre at the same instant for effecting of it, so that thoughe he dye of meer age, yet he dies by the force of Gods judgm[t]. So when God sayes that the righteous men are taken awaye from the evill to come, & we see good men ag[t] such ill tymes die of pure age, yet it is truely fullfilled that they are taken away from the evill to come ; for he who had determined of the occasion of their takinge awaye, had determined allso, that they should be borne wth age fitt for that occasion."

In connection with the foregoing account of the birth of two of Winthrop's children, we may appropriately give the following statement in relation to them, as found in the clear and careful chirography of Adam Winthrop, their grandfather. He was doubtless particularly gratified, in his old age, to have one of them called by his own name; and we can imagine the satisfaction with which he took up his best pen to record the details of their birth and baptism. It is the last writing of the fond old grandfather which remains to this day. Of course, he puts his little namesake down first.

"Adam Winthrop, the second soone of John Winthrop Esquire & Margaret his third wife, was borne in Groton, on frydaie ye seventh day of ye moneth of April, in the yere of our Lorde, one thousand sixe hundred and twentie ; and in ye beginninge of ye eightene yere of the reigne of our Sovereigne Lorde James Kinge of Great Britanne.

"He was baptised by Mr. Nicholson, the parson of Groton, and named Adam by Adam Winthrop his grandfather, Philip Goslin the elder, Jane Goslin his fathers sister, & Mary Cole the wife of Joseph Cole, who were his godfathers and godmothers.

"Steven his elder brother by father & mother, was borne on [Wednesday] the 24 day of Marche, in the yere of our Lord, 1618. Margaret their mother nursed the younger, and not the elder.

"Sir John Tindal, knight, was their grandfather by their mother : And the Ladye Anne Tindal was their grandmother, who lyved after they were borne ; & died the 20th day of July 1620. She was godmother unto Steven, & Mr. Steven Egerton her brother, and Mr. Deane Tindal her sonne were his godfathers.

"Sir John Deane, knight, is their unckle by their grandmother, ye lady Tindal : & Mr. Deane Tindal & Mr. Arthure Tindal are their unckles, by their grandfather Sir John Tindal."

Before concluding this chapter, we may find room for a Will which was made and executed by Winthrop soon after the birth of the second of these children. Though superseded by one afterwards made in New England, it furnishes the best and most authentic evidence of his condition and circumstances at the exact period of his life which we have now reached. Nor is it without many characteristic features both of style and of substance. It is as follows :—

"JOHN WINTHROP.

[SEAL.]

" In the name of God, amen. This tenth day of May, in
the year of our Lord God 1620, and in the eighteenth year of
the reign of our sovereign Lord, King James of England,
etc., and of Scotland the fifty-third, I, John Winthrop, of
Groton, in the county of Suffolk, Esquire, being (I praise
God) of sound mind and memory, and in good health of body
(upon serious consideration of the frailty and uncertainty of
this momentary life, occasioned by the Lord's watchword, and
frequent examples of such as I have observed to have been
snatched away suddenly and in their best health and strength),
do make and declare by these presents my last will and testament in manner following : —

" First, I commend my soul into the hands of God, who
made me and redeemed me, and hath renewed me into the
image of Christ Jesus ; by whom only I am washed from my
sins, and adopted to be the child of God, and an heir of ever-
lasting life, and that of the mere and free favor of God, who
hath elected me to be a vessel of glory for the only manifestation of his infinite mercy, and accordingly hath called me outwardly by his word, and inwardly and effectually by his holy
spirit, into this grace wherein now I stand and rejoice under
the hope of the glory to come. My body I yield to the earth,[1]
there to be decently bestowed, as waiting for the hope of the
resurrection of the just. Now, for such temporal goods as I
shall leave behind me, I do commit them to the care and disposition of Margaret my wife, [Mr. Adam Winthrop my father,
Anne Winthrop my mother,[2]] and John Winthrop my son,
whom I do make and ordain executors of this my last will and
testament, to this end, and upon this confident persuasion, that
they will have a mutual love and due regard each to other and
to all the rest of our family, and that they will faithful perform

---

1 At this point of the original instrument, the following words are inscribed in the
margin: "I desire to be laid near my godly and loving wives, — if conveniently it may
be."

2 The words in brackets are partially erased in the original.

this my last will and testament. Item, I give unto my said wife all those my lands and tenements which I lately purchased of William Forthe of Neyland, gentleman; viz., the two tenements, and six acres of land, lying by Leven Heath, in the occupation of [blank] Coker, and ten acres of woodland lying near the same tenements : which land and woods are called by the several names of Masterman's Cross, Masterman's Grove, Stubbins Cross, Stubbins Grove, and Homylie's Grove, or by what other names soever ; and also one close of pasture-ground, called Little-pond Field, containing about eight acres, lying at the end of Neyland Town, towards Buers ; and also three acres of meadow lying in Lowe's Meadow, in the parish of Assington, just by the said end of Neyland Town : all which said parcels of land, meadow, and wood, are more particularly expressed in a certain deed of feoffment from the said William Forthe to me made, bearing date the twenty-seventh day of July, 1617. To have and to hold the said tenements, land, meadows, pastures, and woods unto my said wife for term of her life ; and, after her decease, to remain to Adam, my son, and to his heirs. I give unto my said son John all that messuage wherein I now dwell, together with all the appurtenances, and all that indenture of lease, or term of years, which I have in the same, and in certain acres of land therewith let, being now in my occupation, situate in Groton aforesaid, and being parcel of the rectory of the same parish. Item, whereas I have one parcel of land called Upper Crabtreewent, containing about twelve acres, lying in Groton aforesaid, and now in the occupation of Philip Gostlin the elder, which I have left out of former conveyances, to this end, that I might lay it unto the parsonage of Groton, in satisfaction of the like quantity of land which I have of the same, I do hereby admonish my said son, and streightly charge him before the Lord, that he so dispose hereof as may be best to God's glory, the peace of his own conscience, and the due recompense of the faithful incumbent ; as myself purpose to do, if God spare me life to a fit opportunity.

"Item, for Mary, my daughter, I will that my executors

shall pay her grandfather Forthe his legacy of £240, to be paid her at her age of eighteen years ; and, withal, I do commit her to the care of my executors, to be well and Christianly educated with such goods as I shall leave unto them. [¹ Item, I will that my said executors shall pay unto Luce Winthrop, my sister, one hundred and twenty pounds ; one hundred whereof is due to her upon an agreement between my father and me upon the setting-over his whole estate unto me. Item, I will that they shall pay unto Ezekiel Bonde threescore pounds and [blank] that which is behind and due to him of· such legacies as my said father was to pay unto him.] Item, I will that my son[s, Henry and] Forthe, shall be brought up and disposed of by my executors in learning, [or else in some honest calling such as they shall prove most fit for,] out of the rents and profits as they are to have by the will and testament of their said grandfather, Mr. Forthe, when they shall attain to certain ages, as in the said will is expressed. My other two sons, Stephen and Adam, I commend to the care of their mother, to be brought up in the fear of God by the help of such lands and goods as I shall leave unto her. Item, I will that my executors shall pay my son Henry £13. 6s. 8d. yearly out of those lands which should fall to him by his grandfather Forthe's will, at his age of twenty-four years. Item, I make my loving wife and John my son² executors of this my last will and testament ; entreating and charging them that they will provide that all my debts may be truly paid and satisfied out [of] such lands and goods as I shall leave unto them ; for performance whereof I do give unto my son John the lease of the house I dwell in, with the lands thereunto belonging and therewith occupied.

"Published in the presence of

" HENRY WINTHROP,

SAMUEL GOSTLIN."

---

1 The erasure in the original of the words enclosed in brackets indicates the changes which had occurred in his family and affairs during the six or seven years next after the will was made, and of which we shall see the details as we proceed with his life.

2 John was at this time only in his sixteenth year.

It would appear from this instrument, that, in 1620, Winthrop's father and mother, and sister Lucy, were living; and that he had five sons and one daughter, — John, Henry, Forth, Mary, Stephen, and Adam. He seems also to have possessed an ample landed estate, and to have provided for its equitable distribution at his death. But the striking feature of the will is the testimony which it supplies, not only to his own religious faith, but to his anxious care that his children should be " well and Christianly educated," and " brought up in the fear of God."

It would seem, too, from this instrument, that the lordship of the Manor of Groton had already been assigned to John Winthrop by Adam, his father; and an original record, of which the following is a copy, confirms this idea, and may not be entirely without interest, as an illustration of the legal forms and customs of the place and the period: —

" Groton.

" MEMORANDUM that the 14th daie of November Anno Domini millessimo sexcentessimo decimo octavo (1618) et domini Jacobi regis Angliæ &c decimo sexto, Johannes Nutton, senr., came before John Winthrop Esq., lorde of the manor of Groton and out of the Court of the said manor in the presence of Adam Winthrop, gent, John Doget and Steven Gostlin two customary tenantes of the said manor, did surrender into the hands of the said John Winthrop all that his moitie and portion of the customary lands which he holdeth of the said John Winthrop as of the manor aforesaid to the use of the said John Winthrop and his heirs, and the said John Winthrop being so seized of the moitie aforesaid did presently in the presence of the said Adam Winthrop, John Doget and Steven Gostlin, deliver out of his hands all that moitie and portion of the said customary lands unto the said John Nutton for the use of the said John Nutton and his heirs and assigns forever under these conditions here expressed, that is to say, that if the said John Nutton his heirs or assigns doe not yearly pay or cause to be paid unto Anne Gale the daughter of William Gale or her assigns during her life, three pounds four shillings of lawful money of England by sixteen shillings every quarter of the year, the first payment thereof to be at the feast of the nativity of our Lord God next coming after the date hereof and so forth every quarter, previous or within fourteen days next after every of the said days of payment at or within the church porch of the parish church of Groton aforesaid, that then this estate shall be void and that the said John Winthrop or his heirs shall be seized of and in the said moitie and portion of land to the only use and behalfe of the above named Anne Gale her heirs and assigns to be holden of the said John Winthrop his heirs or assigns of the manor aforesaid, by the rent customs and services before due and accustomed.

                  " By me   " JOHN NUTTON.[1]
" ADAM WINTHROP
    JOHN DOGET
        STEVEN GOSTLINGE."

This, we presume, is what would technically be called a surrender of a copyhold estate into the hands of the lord, for the uses therein designated, in the presence of two customary tenants. A year or two after this date, Adam Winthrop, the father, is found exercising the powers of a Coroner at Groton, under a commission from his son, as lord of the manor. And thus we have brought down the story of Winthrop's life to the memo-

---

[1] A family of *Newtons* were neighbors of the Winthrops at Groton.

rable year in which the Pilgrim Fathers of New England abandoned their temporary abode in Holland, and embarked in the " Mayflower " on the voyage which terminated at Plymouth Rock. We have found no evidence that he was in any degree interested in their movements, or even aware of them; much less that he had ever contemplated the idea that they were but the pioneers in a path in which he was so soon to follow.

CHAPTER VIII.

WINTHROP'S LETTERS TO HIS WIFE, 1620–1622.

THE materials for our Biography of John Winthrop begin now to grow somewhat less sombre in their character, and to present features of interest less purely domestic or religious. He could never have imagined that his private correspondence would be preserved for more than two centuries after his own death, to be published and read in a land of which, at the time when so much of it was written, he knew little more than the existence. But so it has happened. From the memorable year 1620, we have an almost unbroken series of his letters, with rarely an interval of more than two or three months between them, — furnishing the most satisfactory and authentic index to his occupations, condition, and character. Some of these letters have already been deciphered and printed by Mr. Savage, as an Appendix to his first and second editions of Winthrop's "History of New England." But even those have hardly had a fair chance, in such a connection, to attract the attention to which they are entitled. Few readers look for any thing interesting in an appendix, even if they take the trouble to examine what it contains. Meantime, many other letters have come to light, since this Biography was taken in hand, of by no means inferior value.[1] The whole of them will be given, in our successive chapters, in the order of their dates or of their subjects, and in the full confidence that they will be thought worthy of preservation and of perusal, not merely as containing frequent allusions to the private life and circumstances of their author and his family, but as charming specimens of the epistolary style of " auld lang syne." The simple beauty of their language, and the spirit of personal tenderness and pious trust in which they were composed, cannot fail of being appreciated by all who read them. Nor have his own letters alone survived the lapse of centuries. Letters of his wife, and of more than one of his children, are also left; and some of them, certainly, will be found worthy of a place on the same page with his own. It would not be easy, we think, to find private domestic correspondence of the same period, or indeed .of any period, which would better bear exposure, or which would reflect more credit on the character of the writers.

We begin with a letter to his wife, of Jan. 23, 1620, written evidently from London, though there is no place set down in the date. It will be remarked, that his stay in London on this occasion had some reference to the session of Parliament, of which we may find an explanation hereafter.

---

[1] Of the ten letters from Winthrop to his wife, given in this chapter, all but the last one are new. The letters published for the first time in this work may be distinguished from those taken from the Appendix to the History of New England by the fact that the spelling of the latter was modernized by the copyist. It has not been thought important to restore the old spelling; but a few corrections have been made in them, after a careful comparison with the originals.

John Winthrop to his Wife.

" To my verye lovinge wife Mrs. Winthrop at Groton in Suffolk.

" MY TRUELY BELOVED & DEARE WIFE, — I salute thee
heartylye, giving thankes to God who bestowed thee upon me,
& hath continued thee unto me, the chiefest of all comforts
under the hope of Salvation, which hope cannot be valued : I
pray God that these earthly blessings of mariage, healthe,
friendship, etc, may increase our estimation of our better &
onely ever duringe happinesse in heaven, & may quicken up
our appetite thereunto accordinge to the worth thereof : O my
sweet wife, let us rather hearken to the advise of our lovinge
Lord who calles upon us first to seeke the kingdom of God, &
tells us that one thinge is needfull, & so as without it the gaine
of the whole world is nothinge : rather then to looke at the
frothye wisdome of this worlde & the foolishnesse of such
examples as propounde outwarde prosperitye for true felicitye.
— God keepe us that we never swallowe this baite of Sathan :
but let us looke unto the worde of God & cleave fast unto it,
& so shall we be safe.

" I know you have heard before this of my coming to London : I thank God we had a prosperous journye & found all
well where we came : I doubt not but thy desire wilbe now to
heare of my returne, which (to deale truely with thee) I fear
will not be untill the middest of next weeke : for the Parl: is
putt off for a week ; & I have many friends to visit in a short
tyme : but my heart is allready with thee & thy little lambes,
so as I will hasten home with what convenient speed I may :
In the meane tyme, I will not be unmindfull of you all : but
commend you dayly to the blessinge & protection of our heavenly Father.

" The newes from Bohemia is very badd, as that there is a
generall defection from the Kinge of Bohemia &c : Secretary
Nanton is commanded to keepe his howse : the King is gone
to Theobalds & many wilbe idle untill he returne.

"Remember my dutye to my father & mother, my love to Mr. Sands & all the rest of my true freinds that shall ask of me, & my blessing to our Children; & so giving thee commission to conceive more of my Love then I can write, I rest

           "Thy faythfull husbande   "JOHN WINTHROP.

"My brother salutes you all.

"JAN. 23 1620.

"My brother Tindall & my sister wilbe at Groton before Lente (if God will), there would be some fowles provided & some Ale etc."

Five or six months after the date of the letter just given, Winthrop having, in the mean time, returned to Groton, his wife was called away to her old home, in Essex County, by the illness of her mother (Lady Tyndal), whither she is soon followed by the second letter of our series.

John Winthrop to his Wife.

"To my lovinge friende Mʳˢ Winthrop at Chelmsey House[1] in Great Maplested, Essex.

"MY DEARE WIFE, — I beseeche the Lorde oᶠ good God to blesse thee & thy little babe wᵗʰ all spirituall blessings in heavenly things, & wᵗʰ a comfortable supplye of all things needfull for this present life, wᵗʰ such a portion of the true wisdome as may cause us allwayes to discerne of the worthe & excellencie of Chᵗ Jesus, to take him as oᶠ onely portion, & to love him wᵗʰ all oᶠ heart, as oᶠ best thanke offeringe for his unspeakeable love & mercie in redeeminge us from oᶠ sinnes by his owne death, & adoptinge us into the right of the inheritance of his fathers Kingdome. To him be glory & prayse for ever, Amen.

"Albeit I cañot conveniently come to thee yet, I could not

---

[1] Morant, in his History of Essex, calls it Chelmshoo House.

but sende to knowe how thou doest, & in what state thy good mother continueth, wth the rest of o.^r freinds : That wch we nowe foresee & feare in hir,[1] we must looke to come to o.^r selves, & then neither freinds nor goods, pleasure nor honor, will stande us in any stead, onely a good conscience sprinkled wth the blood of Ch.^t shall give us peace wth God & o.^r owne sowles.

"We are all heer in good health (I prayse God) yet not well contented untill thou returnest to Groton, but I will not hasten to abridge thy deare mother of that comfort wch she may receive in thy companie. My sweet spouse, let us delight in the love of eache other as the chiefe of all earthly comforts : & labour to increase therein by the constant experience of eache others faithfulnesse & sinceritye of affection, formed into the similitude of the Love of Ch.^t & his Churche. Looke for me on thursday or friday (if God will) & remember me to thy good mother & all ye rest as thou knowest my dutye & desires, etc. My parents salute thee ; many kisses of Love I sende thee : farewell. [JOHN WINTHROP.]

" JULY 12. 1620."

And here is another letter, addressed to his wife while she was paying the same or another visit at " Muche Maplested." It has no date of time or place ; but was evidently written from Groton, and probably in the course of this same year 1620.

John Winthrop to his Wife.

" To my verye lovinge Wife Mrs. Winthrop at Muche Maplested in Essex."

" MY SWEET WIFE, — I beseeche o.^r good God to blesse thee ever. I am gladd to heare of thy welfare, & doe think very

---

1 The Lady Tyndal died eight days after this letter was written, 20th July, 1620.

longe to see thee, but I must now staye untill a convenient tyme. Tomorrow M.ʳ Sands preachethe wth us, & if I should be from home I knowe not howe some would take it, but my purpose was to have come to thee in the afternoone, till I considered that you would not be conveniently lodged by reason of thy brother Arth: sicknesse (although for my parte any would content me), so as I thinke fitter to come on Wensdaye morninge, & so to goe dine at Dines hall ¹ & home in the afternoone, for I must of necessitye be at home on thursdaye, because I must meet M.ʳ Gurdon at Boxford in the morninge, & after dinner my sister Luce must ride to M.ʳˢ Bacons. I praye God send us a comfortable meetinge, & a prosperous iornye, wch he will surely doe, if we depende on him, wth resolution to be stirred up by his benefits to love & serve him better. O what great cause have we to love him above thousands whose portion in all good things is farre inferio.ʳ to o.ʳˢ ! althoughe this alone were sufficient to enforce us to love him wth all our hearts, that he hath redeemed us from hell, & appointed us to eternall happinesse, when we were as deeply under the curse as the most reprobate. Let o.ʳ prayer be (my good wife) that he would quicken up the faithe & feelinge of these things in us, that at lengthe we might come to take as muche delight in the meditation & exercise of heavenly things, as the most covetous earthlinge dothe in his lands & goods.

"Thy lovinge husband   "Jo : Winthrop.

"Till we meet, farewell my sweet wife. If I should not fetche thee untill thou didst write me for that ende, I mervaile how longe thou wouldst stay there.

"ffather, mother, etc, comend their love to thee & all the rest. remember my dutye & love as thou knowest, etc. My mother hathe been ill at ease ever since thou wentest, but is now better, I prayse God."

---

¹ Dynes Hall, the principal manor of Little Maplestead, then the seat of Sir John Deane, a son of Lady Tyndal by her first husband.

The two next letters were written from London during the following year, with only a day's interval between them ; and then we have a third, written after his return to Groton, and when his wife had again gone to visit her relatives in Essex.

John Winthrop to his Wife.

" To my most lovinge & deare wife Mrs Marg^t Winthrop at Groton in Suffolk.

" MY DEARLY BELOVED WIFE, — the blessinge of o.^{r} heavenly father be upon thee & all o^{rs} : & he who hath preserved & prospered us hitherto, wthout o.^{r} meritts of his free goodnesse, continue us in his favour, & the comfort of each others Love, unto o.^{r} last & most happie change. I trust by the blessinge of God to be restored safe to thee on Saturdaye next : for my heart is at home, & specially wth thee my best beloved, yet the businesse I came for is come to no passe, & there is cause to feare lest it will not be effected this week : therefore be not over confident of my returne untill tuesdaye next weeke : but I hope I shall write to thee againe if I be likely to staye. O.^{r} freinds heere are all in healthe : I am much streightened in tyme, & therefore cañot satisfye my selfe in writinge as I desire, gather the rest out of thyne owne faithfull assurance of my Love : so wth the sweetest kisses, & pure imbracinges of my kindest affection I rest

" Thine   " JOHN WINTHROP.

" Remember my dutye to parents & loveinge salutations to suche good freinds as thou knowest I desire, etc.

" LONDON. May 9 : 1621.

John Winthrop to his Wife.

" MOST DEARE & LOVINGE WIFE, — I wrote unto thee by o.^{r} neighbo^r Cole, beinge then uncertaine of my returne, yet I hoped to have been wth thee on Saterday but it so fallethe out, that I am inforced to staye except I should leave my sister

Goldinge [1] destitute, & the businesse I came for w^{th}out effecte, wch I cannot now faile wth comforte & good reporte. Therefore I must intreat thy gentle patience untill this businesse be dispatched, wch I hope wilbe betymes the next weeke. In the meane tyme thou art well persuaded that my heart is wth thee, as (I know) thine is wth him to whom thou hast given thyselfe, a faithfull & lovinge yokefellowe : who truely prising this gifte as the greatest earthly blessing, provokes thy Love to abounde in those fruits of mutuall kindnesse, etc, that may adde a daylye increase of comfort & sweet content in this happinesse. I would willingly offer a request unto thee, wch yet I will not urge (not knowing what inconveniences may lye in the waye) but it would be very gratefull to me to meet thee at Maplested on Wensday next, but be it as God shall guide thy heart & the opportunitye. It is now neere XI of the clocke & tyme to sleepe, therefore I must ende. The Lord o^r heavenly father bless & keepe thee & all o^{rs}, & let this salutation serve for all, for I know not how safe a messinger I shall have for these. Remember my dutye & Love as thou knowest how to bestowe them.   farewell,

"Thine   "JOHN WINTHROP.

"I send thee divers things by Wells in a trusse.
"MAI 10: 1621."

John Winthrop to his Wife.

"To my very lovinge wife Mrs Winthrop at Muche Maplested, Essex.

"MY DEARE & LOVINGE WIFE, — I am exceedingly streightened in tyme, throughe the suddaine opportunitye of sendinge this messinger, yet I could not but write unto thee as I maye. God be blessed, I came home in peace & found all very well, & so we continue, & I hope we shall all meet in peace & comfort on friday. I have sent a horse for my uncle.

---

[1] This is plainly *Goldinge* in the original; though I know of no such sister.

Thus with most hearty remembrance of my fond & faithfull love to thee, I comende thee (to the Lord) who blesse & directe us allwayes & all o.^r children.

"Thine as his owne   "JOHN WINTHROP.

"Remember me very kindlye to all as thou knowest my desire; my parents salute thee & thine.

"JUNE 27: 1621."

The next letter, in the order of date, was addressed, during the same year, to his brother-in-law, Thomas Fones. The first wife of Fones, Anna Winthrop, had died two years and a half before this time (May 16, 1619); and he had been married again, Aug. 28, 1621, to Priscilla, daughter of Rev. John Burgis, D.D.[1] Fones seems now' to have been suffering from a long illness, and Winthrop writes him a letter of congratulation on his incipient recovery.

John Winthrop to Thomas Fones.

"To my very lovinge Brother Mr. ffones at the three fawnes in the old Bayly, London.

"MY GOOD BROTHER, — I received your lovinge lettre, & doe prayse God for that beginninge of yor recoverye, & the good health of the rest of yor familye. I hope the Lord will now visite you in his riche mercie, & doe you good & comforte you accordinge to all the evill wch you have endured: He hath shewed you great trobles & adversities, but he will returne & receive you, &c, to the ioye & strengthening of yor Faith, & the raysinge up the heart of my good sister, w^{ch}, I knowe, hath suffered much discomfort in yor longe troubles. ffor o^r selves, the Lo: continues very gratious towards us, blessed be his holy name: my wife is sitting up againe, & I

---

[1] Old MS. pedigree of the Fones Family, lately found among the Winthrop papers.

trust shalbe restored to hir former health in due tyme. We might rejoyce greatly in o.ʳ owne private good, if the sence of the present evill tymes, & the feare of worse did not give occasion of sorrowe. The Lo: look mercifully upon this sinfull lande, & turne us to him by some repentance, otherwise we may feare it hath seene the best dayes. I will write no more at this tyme, being (as yet) to seeke of a messinger for these. Let us still continue mindfull of each other in o.ʳ prayers, & the confirminge of o.ʳ mutuall Love, for it may meet w.ᵗʰ tryalls. Thus w.ᵗʰ all our lovinge salutations to yo.ʳselfe, my good sister & little cosins, I commende you to the grace & peace of the Lo: Jesus, & will rest alwayes

           "Yo.ʳ lovinge brother   "JOHN WINTHROP.
"JAN.ʸ 29, 1621.

"My receipt of Hand is due this terme, I pray let one of yo.ʳ folkes pay it for me.

"I pray send us a little of yo.ʳ Juice of Liquorice."

We proceed to give three more letters to his wife, two of them written in April, and the third in October, of the succeeding year; or rather of the same year, allowing for the change of style. The two first of them were undoubtedly written while Winthrop had gone to attend the wedding of. his sister Lucy, whose marriage to Emanuel Downing is recorded as having taken place on the 10th of April, 1622.

John Winthrop to his Wife.

"MY DEARE WIFE, — I prayse God, we are come safe to Londō, where we finde all well. We are now at Redrife at a kinsmans of my brother Downings, where we are most kindly entertained: we have ofte wished thee with us, but wishes are vaine: I trust, God will give us to meet againe shortlye in peace & sweet comfort, in the fruition of o.ʳ mutuall Love;

in the meane tyme let this staye o.^r hearts, that no distance of
place or space of tyme can sever us, in respect of o.^r true &
fervent affections to each other; whereof every occasiõ shall
give us more assurance. I am too much streightened in
tyme to write to hir whom I love so dearly (it beinge now XI
of the clock this tuesday night); thy kind heart must gather
a great deale of matter from a fewe scribled lines. I will adde
no more, but beseech the Lo : to blesse thee & all o.^r younge
ones, & send us a ioyfull meetinge. Remember my dutye to
parents & Love to all whom thou shalt think fitt : my brother
Downing & sister salute thee most kindly etc. farewell my
sweet wife, farewell.

    " Thy faithfull lovinge husband   " JOHN WINTHROP.

" REDERIFE, April 9. 1622."

John Winthrop to his Wife.

" MY DEARE WIFE, — albeit I am now cõminge towards
thee, yet that thou mayest knowe that I am allwayes mindfull
of thee, I would take every opportunitye of confirminge thy
good assurance of it, desiringe to offer some such refreshinge
to thy minde, as may prepare a cheerefull countenance for my
welcome to thee. I prayse God, we are all in health, and
prosper well in o.^r affaires hetherto : & doe hope in the Lo : for
a safe returne. Let us labour to gett a thankfull heart to him
for his free love & constant bounty towards us & o.^{rs}. I heare
by this bearer J : Go : that thy selfe & all o.^{rs} are in health &
I prayse o.^r good Lo : for it, but thy lettre miscaried by the
waye. Thy Love in my kinde welcome shall supplye all : The
Lo : blesse thee & thy little lāmes & send us a comfortable
meetinge at Groton & at last to meet in o.^r Fathers house in
heaven : farewell my sweet wife

    " Thy faithfull lovinge husband   " JOHN WINTHROP.

" Take & imparte salutations & dutyfull remembrances from
all of us to whom thou knowest.

" LONDON. Aprill 18 1622."

John Winthrop to his Wife.

"MY SWEET WIFE, — Blessed be God, by whose providence and protection I am come safe to London. Here I find them all in health, and a great deal of kind welcome. Only thy company is wanting, which they much desire.

"I doubt my brother's coming to Ipswich will be deferred till the spring; for Mr. Hore (who should hire his house) and he are broken off. Thus man purposeth, but God disposeth. Oh that we could learn at length to trust his wisdom, love, power, etc., and cast our care upon him, and leave our own carnal wisdom, fear, confidence, etc! Then should it go well with us assuredly. Then should we have our rest in that true peace which passeth understanding. But it is our wretched infidelity that keeps good things from us. Let us, therefore, pray earnestly, and labor for this precious faith: it will recompense all our cost.

"For such news as is here, this bearer can sufficiently inform you, and so may spare my labor; and, besides, I am hasted into the city about my business. When I shall return, I cannot yet tell; but thy love will make me lose no time. Therefore, for the present, with my brother's and sister's kind salutations to thee and to my parents, to whom I commend my love and duty, I heartily commend thee and our little ones and all our family to the gracious protection and blessing of the Lord. So I rest

        "Thy faithful, loving husband,   "JOHN WINTHROP.
"LONDON, Oct. 19, 1622."

We may conclude this chapter with a letter from the Rev. Henry Sands, the venerable pastor whose name so often occurs in Winthrop's early Experiences, and whose death will be found particularly noticed at a later date. It gives a pleasant impression of the writer, and proves how much Winthrop was relied upon in the church-affairs of his neighborhood.

Henry Sands to John Winthrop.

"To my Worship[u] well-aproved good friend Mr. John Wintrop at Honton Hall (?) these.

" SIR, — I do understand that Stoke Vicarage is not yet given. It is a great parish. I do frō my hart persuade my selfe that at Naylond would be a good Church of God if they had a good minister. Theare is one or two. There is one M[r] Watson felow of Trinitie Colledge. I take the next yere to be his yere of Bachelo[r] of Divinitie. A Gentleman borne, hath of his owne some xx or xxx[l] a yere. A mā of gret lerning for his tyme & verie quiet. Theare is another, one Mr. Gilgate, sonne unto M[r] Gilgate that dwelt at Langham, one whome I thinke M[r] Manocke knew & a verie quiet honest mā. A sufficient scholer. A bachelo[r] & so I thinke it may be he will contynue, for he is of some good resonable yeres. Let me intreat yo[u] end[r] in the affection that I know yo[u] beare to the Churche of God to look into it & help. If extremitie of buisnes had not hinderd I would haue bene w[th] yo[u] afore this tyme & I purpose afore weekes be ended to come to yo[u]. In the meane tyme the thing is p[r]sently to be done. Let me intreat importunitie to the uttermost you can. I pitie the Church. The Lord stirre up all o[r] harts to love it & labo[r] for the good of it. I take my leave thus hastely this hande being wearie. Comending my selfe to yo[r] owne selfe & M[ris] Wintrop, Not forgetting M[ris] Hanna,

" Yo[r] Worships exceedingly behoulding to you

" HEN. SANDS."

CHAPTER IX.

LETTERS TO HIS SON AT TRINITY COLLEGE, DUBLIN; DEATH OF
HIS FATHER; AND LETTERS OF FORTH WINTHROP.

WE turn now to another correspondent of Winthrop's,
— his eldest son, John Winthrop, jun., afterwards the
Governor of Connecticut. He had been prepared for
college at the somewhat celebrated Free Grammar
School, at Bury St. Edmund's, founded by Edward VI.
in 1550, and which has maintained a high reputation
to the present day. Among its distinguished pupils
within the last half-century, it boasts of Lord Cranworth,
the late Lord Chancellor of England, and of Dr. Blomfield, the late Bishop of London, — whose armorial
shields have recently been suspended on the walls of its
principal hall.[1] The younger Winthrop was now (1622)
in the seventeenth year of his age; and was a student
at Trinity College, Dublin,[2] where he remained for several years, and is believed to have been graduated in due
course. The letters addressed to him by his father at
this period are models of old-fashioned paternal advice
and affectionate counsel. It would be difficult, indeed,

---

[1] I saw them when I visited the school in July, 1859, in company with the Rt. Hon.
and Rev. Lord Arthur Hervey, now the Archdeacon of Sudbury.

[2] This institution, founded in 1591, had received a charter in 1613 from James I.,
with all the privileges of a University, and with an endowment which secured its prosperity and permanence.

to find a nobler illustration of the apostolic injunction to
parents, that they should "bring up their children in
the nurture and admonition of the Lord," than in these
letters of John Winthrop to his son.

They deal mainly with domestic events, and require
little explanation or comment. One of them furnishes
an idea of Winthrop's pecuniary circumstances, by his
proposal to allow thirty pounds per annum, or more "if
occasion be," for his son's expenses at college, — no
inconsiderable sum, we imagine, for those days.[1] Another suggests that he was not altogether contented with
his condition in England in 1623, by the expression in
a postscript, " I wish oft God would open a way to settle
us in Ireland, if it might be for his glory there." His
thoughts had evidently not yet been turned towards
America; and perhaps the expression only meant, that
he was disposed to settle where some of his family were
already living, and where his son was at college. Another of these letters contains the account of the death
of Winthrop's father at the age of seventy-five, with this
beautiful tribute to his memory: " He hath finished his
course ; and is gathered to his people in peace, as the ripe
corn into the barn. He thought long for the day of his
dissolution, and welcomed it most gladly. Thus is he gone
before ; and we must go after, in our time. This advantage he hath of us, — he shall not see the evil which we
may meet with ere we go hence. Happy those who

---

1 Prof. Masson says, Milton's father must have made up his mind, in sending his
son to Cambridge, to pay fifty pounds a year, in the money of that day, for the expenses
of his maintenance there. There was some difference, probably, between Cambridge
and Dublin. — *Life of Milton*, vol. i. p. 77, Am. ed.

stand in good terms with God and their own conscience: they shall not fear evil tidings; and in all changes they shall be the same."

All the letters alike bear testimony to the satisfaction which Winthrop enjoyed in the character and conduct of his son at college, and how glad he was to hear that this "dutiful and well-deserving child" "declined the evil company and manners of the place he lived in, and followed his study with good fruit." The younger John Winthrop gave early indication of that purity of life, and devotedness of purpose, which made him so distinguished in after-years; and it is to be regretted that none of his answers to his father's letters during his college-life have been preserved. If, however, they were all written in Latin,—as we find, from his father's replies, that some of them were,—they will be the less missed by the general reader.

We proceed with the father's letters in their order:[1]—

John Winthrop to his Son.

"To my beloved son, John Winthrop, at the College in Dublin.

"DEAR SON,—Though I have received no letters yet from you, I cannot pass by any opportunity, without some testimony of my fatherly affection, and care of your welfare; for which respect I am content to have you absent from me in so far a distance: for I know, that, in respect of yourself, *patria ubicunque bene;* and, in respect of the Almighty, his power and providence is alike in all places; and, for mine own comfort, it shall be in your prosperity and well-doing wheresoever.

---

[1] All the letters in this chapter, except the five last, are in the Appendix to the History of New England.

"Because I cannot so oft put you in mind of those things which concern your good as if you were nearer to me, it must be your care the better to observe and ruminate those instructions which I give you, and the better to apply the other good means which you have. Especially labor, by all means, to imprint in your heart the fear of God ; and let not the fearful profaneness and contempt of ungodly men diminish the reverent and awful regard of his Great Majesty in your heart. But remember still, that the time is at hand when they shall call the [mountains to] hide them from the face of Him whom now they slight and neglect, &c.

" I have written to you more largely by one Mr. Southwell, and now am at little leisure. When you write back, let me know the state of your college, &c., and how you like, &c. ; and remember my love to your reverend tutor. Your grandfather, grandmother, and mother salute and bless you. Your brothers and sister are in health (I praise God). The Lord, in mercy, season your heart with his grace, and keep you from the lusts of youth and the evil of the times. So I rest

"Your loving father,

"JOHN WINTHROP.

"GROTON, Aug. 6, 1622."

John Winthrop to his Son.

" To my beloved son, John Winthrop, at the College near Dublin.

" MY BELOVED SON, — I beseech the Lord to bless thee with grace and peace. I give him thanks for thy welfare ; and hope, through his mercy, that this infirmity which is now upon thee shall turn to thy health. I received two letters from thee, written (I perceive) in haste ; but they were welcome to me and the rest, to your grandmother, mother, &c., who all rejoice in your good liking. I sent you two letters a good while since ; which I hope will not miscarry, though they be long in going. The further you are from me, the more careful I am of your welfare, both in body and soul ; the chief means whereof lyeth in your own endeavor. Your friends may pray for you and counsel you ; but your own diligence and watchfulness must be added to make you blessed. God hath provided you a liberal portion of outward good things. You must labor to use them soberly ; and to consider that your happiness lieth not in meat, drink, and bodily refreshings, but in the favor of God for your part in a better life. I purpose to send you, by this bearer, such books as you writ for : only Aristotle I cannot, because your uncle Fones is not at London to buy it, and I know not whether you would have Latin or Greek. I purpose also to send you some cloth for a gown and suit ; but, for a study-gown, you were best buy some coarse Irish cloth. I shall (if God will) write to you again by Mr. Olmsted. For the carriage of such things as I send you by John Nutton, you must remember to pay him, because I cannot tell here what they will come to. I have written to your uncle to send over my gelding. If you see that he forget it, you may put him in mind. Your grandfather and grandmother will write to you. Your mother salutes you with her blessings. We are all in health (I praise God). Remember my love to your good tutor. The Lord in mercy bless and keep you, and direct and prosper your study. Amen. So I rest

"Your loving father,   "JOHN WINTHROP.

"GROTON, Aug. 31, 1622."

John Winthrop to his Son.

"To my beloved son, John Winthrop, at Trinity College, in Dublin, Ireland.

"MY DEARLY BELOVED SON, — I do usually begin and end my letters with that which I would have the A and Ω of all thy thoughts and endeavors : viz., the blessing of the Almighty to be upon thee, not after the common valuation of God's blessings, like the warming of the sun to a hale, stirring body ; but that blessing which Faith finds in the sweet promises of God and his free favor, whereby the soul hath a place of joy and refuge in all storms of adversity. I beseech the Lord to open thine eyes, that thou mayest see the riches of this grace, which will abate the account of all earthly vanities ; and, if it please him to give thee once a taste of the sweetness of the true wisdom which is from above, it will season thy studies, and give a new temper to thy soul. Remember, therefore, what the wisest saith : 'The fear of the Lord is the beginning of wisdom.' Lay this foundation, and thou shalt be wise indeed.

"I am very glad to hear that you like so well in Ireland. If your profiting in learning may be answerable, it will much increase my comfort. I was not greatly troubled to hear that your body did break out; but rather occasioned to bless God, that sent you so good a means of future health. I must needs acknowledge the great care and kindness of your uncle and aunt towards you. It may be much to your good, if you be careful to make right use of it, as I hope you do ; for I hear you love your study well. You must have special care that you be not insnared with the lusts of youth, which are commonly covered under the name of recreations, &c. I remember the counsel of a wise man : *Quidquid ad voluptatis seminarium pullulat, venenum puta.* Think of it (dear son), and especially that of Paul to Timothy : ' Exhort young men that they be sober-minded.'

"I sent you some books by J. Nutton. I could not then buy the rest, nor such cloth, &c., which I would have sent you, because your uncle Fones was not then in London ; and I have no friend else that I can make bold with. I have now a piece of cloth to make your doublet and hose, if I can send it by Mr. Olmested : if not, then desire your uncle to fit you there. It is only some little more in the price ; and I have found, that, except one send by some friend, the carriage and custom (besides the hazard) costs so much, as there will be little saved. You may line your gown with some warm baize, and wear it out, for else you will soon outgrow it ; and, if you be not already in a frieze jerkin, I wish you to get one speedily : and howsoever you clothe yourself when you stir, yet be sure to keep warm when you study or sleep. I send you no money, because you may have of your uncle what you need. I hope you will be honestly frugal, and have respect to my great charge and small means, which I shall willingly extend to the utmost to do you good.

" Your grandfather, grandmother, and mother salute and bless you. We all, with your brothers and sister, are in health (I praise God). Forth is at Bury; but he fell so between two forms, as he had like, between both, to have fallen back to Boxford.

" Your uncle Gostlin and aunt are in health, and he means to write to you. Your good host and hostess at Bury inquire much of you, and desire always to be remembered to you : so did your master there, when I last saw him. I purpose to write two or three lines to your good tutor, in token of my thankful acceptance of his loving pains with you.

" We are daily in expectation of Mr. Olmested's coming by us, who appointed to have set forth on his journey above a fortnight since : otherwise I had adventured some letters by London before this, though we received none from you since John Nutton came to us. I hear not yet of my gelding. It will be fit, that, at the quarter's end (if your uncle forget it), you ask him money for your tutor. The Lord bless you ever. So I rest

"Your loving father,   " JOHN WINTHROP.
"OCT. 16, 1622.

" Commend me to Mr. Downes the stationer."

John Winthrop to his Son.

"To my beloved son, John Winthrop, at Trinity College, in Dublin, Ireland.

" MY DEAR SON, — I received your letters, with the bill of charges enclosed, &c. I bless God for the continuance of your health, but especially for the good seed of his true fear, which I trust is planted, and grows daily in you. I perceive you lose

not your time, nor neglect your study; which as it will be
abundantly fruitful to my comfort, so much more to your own
future and eternal happiness, and especially to the glory of
Him who hath created you to this purpose. I pray, continually, that God will please to establish your heart, and bless
these good beginnings. For the money which you have spent,
I will pay it, and what else your uncle shall appoint me, so
soon as I receive my rents. And for your expenses, seeing I
perceive you are considerate of my estate, I will have as great
regard of yours; and, so long as your mind is limited to a
sober course, I will not limit your allowance less than to the
uttermost of mine own estate. So as, if £20 be too little (as
I always accounted it), you shall have £30; and, when that
shall not suffice, you shall have more. Only hold a sober and
frugal course (yet without baseness), and I will shorten myself
to enlarge you. For your apparel, desire your uncle to furnish you for this present; and, if I can find out a means to
send you things against winter at a more easy rate, I will provide for you, as I would have done before this, but that I
thought (the charges of sending and hazard considered) you
were as good provide them there. Your mother is lately delivered of another son (his name is Deane),[1] and is reasonable
well (I praise God), with your grandmother, brothers, sister,
uncle and aunt Gostlin, &c.; but your grandfather is very
weak, and (we fear) in his last sickness. They all salute you,
and rejoice in your welfare. Goodman Hawes was here, and
salutes you also. Remember my love to your tutor, &c. The
Lord bless you always. Amen.

       " Your loving father,   " J. WINTHROP.

" I wrote to you lately, and to your uncle and aunt; and,
since, I wrote another letter to your aunt.

" MARCH 25, 1623."

---

[1] Baptized at Groton, March 23, 1622.

John Winthrop to his Son.

" To my loving son, John Winthrop, at the College in Dublin, Ireland.

" Son John, — The blessing of the Lord be upon thee, and upon thy studies unto a most happy success. I received divers letters from thee since Christide, and I have written three. I hope thou hast received them before this. I bless God, and am heartily refreshed to hear of thy health and good liking, — especially to see those seeds of the fear of God, which (I hope and daily pray) will arise to timely fruit. He who hath begun that good in you will perfect it unto the day of the Lord Jesus : only you must be constant and fervent in the use of the means, and yet trust only to God's blessing.

" I was purposed to defer writing to you till your uncle Gostlin should have come; but, his journey being put off on the sudden, I am enforced to borrow of the night to write these few lines unto thee. Concerning thy charges, I have written my mind in a former letter; but, lest that hath miscarried, know that my good persuasion of thy tender regard of my estate, and confidence of a sober course, shall make me to extend myself to the farthest of my ability for thy good, be it £30 per annum, or more, if occasion be. And, though I have sent over no money all this time, it was not through any neglect of thee, but upon that assurance which I had of thy uncle and aunt their care of thee, he himself willing me to send no money till he sent for it; and now, since Mr. Goad is dead, I know not to whom to pay it. But make you no question; for (God willing) I will discharge every groat. And for your apparel and books, I find it so difficult and troublesome, &c., to send things over, as I would wish you to provide there for the present.

" I have written to your uncle of the change that it hath pleased the Lord to make in our family.[1] The Lord give us and you to make a right use of it. Time will not permit me

---

[1] The death of his father, Adam Winthrop, to which he alludes more particularly in the next letter.

to write more. Your grandmother and mother salute and bless you. Remember me very kindly to your good tutor and Mr. Downes, &c.

"Your loving father, "J. WINTHROP.
" APRIL 20, 1623.

" Send me word in your next how Mr. Olmsted and that plantation prospers. I wish oft God would open a way to settle me in Ireland, if it might be for his glory. Amen.

" Commend me to my little cousins, and to my god-daughter Susannah Nutton, to Richard, and the rest of the family."

John Winthrop to his son.

" To my [son] John Winthrop, at Trinity College, in Dublin, Ireland.

" MY WELL-BELOVED SON, — I received thy letters of the 26th of May this 26th of June ; and, the messenger being presently to return, I cannot satisfy myself in writing to thee as I desire. Let it suffice for the present, that I humbly praise our heavenly Father for his great mercy towards thee in all respects ; especially for the hope, which I conceive, that he hath pleased to make thee a vessel of glory for thy salvation in Christ Jesus. And I heartily rejoice that he hath withdrawn thy mind from the love of those worldly vanities, wherewith the most part of youth are poisoned, and hath given thee to discern of, and exercise thyself in, things that are of true worth. I see, by your epistle, that you have not spent this year past in idleness, but have profited even beyond my expectations. The Lord grant that thy soul may still prosper in the knowledge of Jesus Christ, and in the strength of the Spirit, as thy mind is strengthened in wisdom and learning ; for this gives the true lustre and beauty to all gifts both of nature and industry, and is as wisdom with an inheritance. I am sure, before this, you have knowledge of that which, at the time when you wrote, you were ignorant of ; viz., the departure of your grandfather (for I wrote over twice since). He hath finished his course ; and is gathered to his people in peace, as the ripe corn into the barn. He thought long for the day of his dissolution, and welcomed it most gladly. Thus is he gone before; and we must go after, in our time. This advantage he hath of us, — he shall not see the evil which we may meet with ere we go hence. Happy those who stand in good terms with God and their own conscience : they shall not fear evil tidings; and in all changes they shall be the same.

"The rest of us (I praise God) are in health. Your grandmother and mother salute and bless you in the Lord. We all think long to see you; and, it is like, myself shall (if it please God) go over to you, before I shall be willing you should take so great a journey, and be so long withdrawn from your happy studies, to come to us. It satisfieth me that I know you are well and can want nothing, and that (I believe) God blesses you. I shall continue to pray for you, and will not be wanting, to my power, to further your good in every thing; and know this, that no distance of place, or length of absence, can abate the affection of a loving father towards a dutiful, well-deserving child. And, in that I have not sent you money all this time, it is upon that assurance which I have of your uncle's and aunt's care of you, and his free offer to forbear me till he should send. But I have written to him to receive £30 or £40 of some of Dublin, who have occasion to use money in London; and they shall not fail to receive it again at my brother Fones his [house] upon the first demand. For Cooper's Dictionary, I will send it you as soon as I can; but it is so difficult and hazardable [1] (especially now, since Mr. Goad died), as I cannot tell how to convey that or any thing else to thee. Remember my kind love to your good tutor. And so, in haste, I end; and, beseeching daily the Lord Jesus Christ to be with thee and bless thee, I rest

"Your loving father,   "Jo. WINTHROP.
"GROTON, June 26, 1623."

---

[1] This volume, which it was "so difficult and hazardable" to send over to Dublin in 1623, is now safely in the library of the Massachusetts Historical Society in Boston.

John Winthrop to his Son.

" My dear Son, — The Lord bless thee, and multiply his graces in thee, to the building up of that good work which (I well hope) is truly begun in thee, and wherein I rejoice daily, and bless God, who hath pleased to call thee and keep thee in that good course which yields hope to all the friends of thy future happiness. Be watchful, (good son,) and remember, that though it be true, in some cases, that *principium est dimidium totius*, yet, in divinity, he who hath attained beyond the middest must still think himself to have but new begun : for, through the continual instigation of Satan and our own proneness to evil, we are always in danger of being turned out of our course ; but God will preserve us to the end, if we trust in him and be guided by his will.

" I received no letters from you since that in Latin, wherein you wrote for Cooper's Dictionary, which I sent you since by London ; and I have wrote twice since. I purpose to send by this bearer, Samuel Gostlin, a piece of Turkey grogram, about ten yards, to make you a suit ; and I shall have a piece of good cloth against winter, to make you a gown. All my care is how to get it well conveyed. I would have sent you some other things, with some remembrancers to your aunt and cousins, but that the occasion of sending this messenger was so sudden, as I could not provide them. If your uncle come over to Chester, you may come with him ; and there I hope to see you. Be directed by him and your tutor ; for though I much desire to see you, yet I had rather hear of your welfare than hazard it. And, if your uncle mean to come further than Chester, I would wish you not to come over now ; for I am not willing you should come to Groton this year, except your uncle shall much desire your company. Remember my kind love to your good tutor and to Mr. Downes : and excuse me to your aunt that I write not to her, for I have not leisure ; and, if occasion be, impart my joy in her safe deliverance, which we long much to hear of. What remains, this bearer can inform you of all our affairs. Put him in mind (as from me) to be sober, and beware of company. Your grandmother and mother salute and bless you ; your uncle Gostlin and aunt salute you ; your master at Bury (to whom I wish you to write at leisure),your good host and hostess, salute you also. *Vale.*   " JOHN WINTHROP.

" GROTON, Aug. 12, 1623.

" You shall receive by Samuel a twenty-two-shilling piece, if he have not occasion to spend it by the way."

John Winthrop to his Son.

" To my beloved son, John Winthrop, at Trinity College, in Dublin, Ireland.

"MY WELL-BELOVED SON, — I beseech our God and heavenly Father, through Christ, to bless thee ; and I humbly praise his holy name for his great mercy towards thee hitherto, which is a great occasion of my rejoicing. For there is nothing in this world that can be like cause of private comfort to me as to see the welfare of my children ; especially when I may have hope that they belong to Christ, and increase his kingdom, and that I shall meet them in glory, to enjoy them in life eternal, when this shade of life shall be vanished. Labor, my dear son, to have in highest esteem the favor of this God, whose blessing is better than life, and reacheth to eternity. Make him thy joy, by trusting in him with all thy heart ; and nourish the peace of a pure conscience in an undefiled body. I am glad also to hear that thou declinest the evil company and manners of the place thou livest in, and followest thy study with good fruit. Go on, and God will still prosper thee. To fall back will be far worse than never to have begun ; but I hope better of thee. Your grandmother, mother, brothers, and sister are in health (I praise God). How we do all here at London, this bearer can tell·you. Your uncle (Fones) wishes well to you. I would have you write him a Latin epistle at your leisure. You must be careful to visit your aunt, and help her to be cheerful in this time of your uncle's absence. Commend

me heartily to your reverend tutor; and think not of seeing
England till you may bring a hood¹ at your back.
"It shall satisfy me, in the mean time, to hear of your wel-
fare, which I daily pray for; and so I commend thee to the
Lord, and rest   "Thy loving father,
                                             "JOHN WINTHROP.
"LONDON, Oct. 3, 1623.

"I send two books by Richard. One of them is for your
aunt, the other for yourself. Read it over and again; and
God give a blessing with it."

John Winthrop to his Son.

" To my loving son, John Winthrop, at Trinity College, in Dublin,
                              Ireland.

"I sent you, in January last, the books which you wrote for.
'Imagines Deorum' is very dear, and hard to get.² I could
not find a second in London. It is a book that may be of some
use for the praise and antiquity of the monuments, abused by
the superstition of succeeding times; but you must read it with
a sober mind and sanctified heart. Your grandmother and
mother are in health (I bless God), and do salute and bless
you. Your brothers and sister, and the rest of your friends,
are likewise in health; only Adam hath a sore ague. Let me
hear, by your next, how your aunt bears this long absence of
your uncle, and how things goe in Ireland, at Mont Wealy,
and elsewhere, and what success hath been of the proclamation. Our Parliament here is begun with exceeding much
comfort and hope. The treaty about the Spanish match is
now concluded, by king, prince, and Parliament, to be at an
end; and, it is very like, we shall not hold long with Spain.
The Duke of Richmond and Lenox died suddenly that morn-

---

1 " An ornamental fold that hangs down the back of a graduate." — *Johnson.*
2 The volume here referred to is perhaps the same which is now in my possession,
entitled " The Image of God, or laie mãs booke, in which the right knowledge of God
is disclosed, and divers doutes besydes the principall matters — Newly made out of holi
writ bi Roger Hutchynson of Cambrydge." 1550.

ing the Parliament should have begun.   The Duke of Buckingham hath quit himself worthily, and given great satisfaction
to the Parliament.   God send a good end to these happy beginnings.   This bearer comes suddenly upon me, and is but a
stranger.   Therefore here I end; and with my loving salutations to your reverend tutor, and your kind friend his substi-
tute, with Mr. Downes, your little cousins, Richard, &c., I
est   " Your loving father,
                                        " JOHN WINTHROP.
" GROTON, March 7, 1623."

John Winthrop to his Son.

" To my beloved sonne John Winthrop at the Colledge in Dublin.

" MY DEARLY BELOVED SONNE, — I beseeche the Lord God
Allmighty to blesse thee & prosper the course wch thou art, by
his providence, entered into ; & to returne thee home in safetye
in his good tyme, wch though I thinke longe for, (& shalbe
still more greved at thy absence, if thy uncle & aunt should
returne into England before winter,) yet when I weighe all
considerations rather by judgment then affection, I had rather
thou should continue still till the springe, or till thou maiest
obtaine a degree, wthout w^{ch} (for ought I can learne) this tyme
wilbe loste : neverthelesse if yor uncle shall thinke fitt, &
yor selfe shall desire it, I shall give waye, & be gladd to have
you heere.   I receeved no letter from you since the 18 of
Maye : I must needs blame yor want this waye.   I expected
to have had many Latin Epistles ; but *vix unam et alteram
accepi, easq : vulgari penitus sermone exaratas ; — si quid aliud
in coniecturā inciderat præter communem causam ignaviam, paternus
Amor facile excusationē suppleret : sed si alio perfugio uti non
possis, quid restat quin culpam agnoscas et redimere studeas.*   My
true desire is that you may be a good proficient in y^{or} studyes,
but my most earnest prayers & wishes are, that you & y^{or}
studyes may be consecrated to Christ Jesus & the service of his
church ; for wch ende, I beseeche the Lorde to furnish you with
all meet gifts, & to sanctifye you throughout ; for I doubt not

but, if it please the Lorde to reveale himselfe once in you, & to lett you taste & see howe good he is, & what the worthe of Christ is to those who finde him, what riches, what pleasures, what wisdome, what peace & contentatiō is to be founde in Christ alone, you will willingly forsake all to follow him, & with Paul, those things wch sometymes seemed great advantage to you, to account them lost for Christ's sake.   I can give you but a taste of these thinges; be constant in hearinge, prayer, readinge & meditation, & the good spirit of God shall reveale unto you this great misterye of godlinesse, & shall shewe you more then any tongue or penne can expresse.   Amen.   Y^{or} grand mother & mother salute and bless you, y^{or} brothers & sister are all in health (I prayse God).   Y^{or} master at Burye salutes you, I merveile you never write to him; y^{or} good host & hostesse are well & salute you.   So wth itteratiō of my blessinge upon you, & my kinde salutations to y^{or} Revd Tutor, Mr. Downes, & all o^r frends, I rest

" Y^{or} lovinge father,   " JOHN WINTHROP.

"GROTON. June 20, 1624."

In more than one of the letters which have just been given, the elder Winthrop alludes to his son Forth, who was a schoolboy at Bury St. Edmund's, as his brother John had been before him.   We cannot conclude this chapter more appropriately than by giving two or three of Forth's own letters to his brother at this period. They furnish a good idea of the juvenile correspondence of the olden time, and contain many pleasant allusions to the scholars with whom he was associated, and to the masters by whom he was instructed.   They also settle a question of fact, which has frequently been raised, in regard to the uncle and aunt of the younger Winthrop, with whom he resided in Dublin, and to whom his father sent so many messages of remembrance. Forth speaks of them distinctly as his uncle and aunt *Downing;* thereby proving that Emanuel Downing, who had married Lucy Winthrop in 1622, resided at this time in Ireland, where probably their eldest son (Sir George Downing) was born in August, 1623.

Forth Winthrop was born Dec. 30, 1609; and was but about thirteen years old when these letters were written.

> "So young, so wise, they say, do ne'er live long."

But we will not anticipate his early fate.

Forth Winthrop to his brother John.

"To his very loving brother Mr. John Winthropp at Dublin in Ireland.

"'God　　be　　Imanuell　　with　　us　　&　　Jesus.'[1]

"LOVING BROTHER, — I received youer letters the 19 daie of Agust, by which I doe understand youer singular love to me-warde, & that althou the distans of place hath severed us one from another, yet I trust that neither sea nor land can braek of na diminish ou^r tru love and affectiō one towardes each other wch hath ever bene; & I trust that the sune shall cease his corse before ou^r love shall be abolished : and as we doe thus love one an other, how unfainiedly shold we love God for his sonne Jesus Christe; he loved us when we weare enimies not breathren. How, how I saie shold we love him : let us take heede that we lose not ou^r first love as Laodicea did, or begin well wth the Galatians but shold not goe on well, but shold have cause for to feare wth the Apostell least we are turned from

---

[1] It was a common practice, in the olden time, to write these sacred words as a caption to a letter, running them along the top of the successive pages.

God : and I hope mountaines or hills shold soner be cast into the sea, than that we shold lose ou^r first love : Let us follo the thing wch Solomon sayth in his Booke, Remember thy Creater in the daies of thy youth before the evil daies come : let us do as Esaie the proffit sayth, Wash you, mak you cleane, Turne you from you^r evill waies, & thow your Sines weare as crimsin yet will I mak them as snow : If we belong to God, God sayth to us, the keeper of Israel nether slumbereth or sleepeth, yet God will have his to suffer afflictions even as the church is alowed, for to mak us fitt : but I shall forget to wright to you of the things wch I have to wright : for as concerning you^r wrighting to me about my going to Bury : I am not yet gone thither but I purpose by God's grace for to goe about next Ester, it may be sōner or later : Abraham Caly is not as yet gone to Cambridg but he was admitted at ester, he is of S^t. Johns colledge & he purpos to goe the next Spring. all ou^r friends here about are in good helth. Thus desiring you for to writ to me of your welfare & of your frends I rest

" Your brother in all love to command

" FORTHE WINTHROP.

" GROTON this 2 of Sept. 1622.

" Charles Neuton is not yet gone to Cambridg, nether is admitted, but he hopes of great matters ; but I think they will prove but vaine : next Ester he hopes to get a place which I hope may prove good for him, in the end he shall be a good scholar."

Forth Winthrop to his brother John.

" To his verry lovinge Brother Mr John Winthropp at Dublin in Ireland at the College.

" LOVING BROTHER, — You wroght to me for to send you word of my going to Bury, & I sent you word as far as I knew about Ester time : but having knowledge of my father I now wright to you about that matter, ffor he tould mee about Michaelmas or soone after : the ræson I know not, but as you

know — *nunquam sera est ad bonos mores via*, so althou it weare
long before I goe, yet at leanth seein I goe it is sum comfort
unto mee : and as you wroght to mee ons, which I thank you
for, for to comfort mee & incorage mee to goe on in the corse
of learning : & shewed me the reason of it, *nam sine doctrina
vita est quasi mortis imago :* wch is a most true sainge, for many
men which in their youth have neclected learning & goodnes,
in ther age, when as it should doe them any, na most good &
steed, then they crie out of all, ther parents, themselves & all,
& wish that they had never seene the sunne ; is not this a woo-
full cause & worthy to be taken heed of : I pray you to send
me word so soone as you have a good occasion of the welfare
of your & our friends, thus having at this time no more to writ,
remembring our love to you I rest

" Your loving Brother   " FORTHE WINTHROP.

" My uncle ffones is about removing but he is not as yet settled there. he hath gotten him a place at Ipswich, a house
wher Mr Ward dwelt in. I pray you remember me to my
Uncle & Ante Downing — also to Richard his man. ffinis."

Forth Winthrop to his brother John.

" To his most lovinge Brother Mr John Winthroppe at Trinitie Coll:
neere Dublin, give thes. Ireland.

" MOST LOVINGE BROTHER, — I received youer letters the 16
of Aprill whereby I perceived your great love & respect towards
me which alwaise hath binne : I thank you for your good admo-
nitions which you in your letters sent me for to alwaise goe on
as I haue begunne ; knowinge that althow the waye to lerninge
seeme verry hard & difficult, yet the frute & end is sweet &
pleasant. I hope althow the distans of place hath set us one
from another yet nether sea nor land nor anythinge else can
part our affections one from the other : I had an intention to
have written to you by one of Bury that went over, but he went
over so speedilie as I cold nott have time to wright : but having

so fitt an opportunitie I will wright. I wold I cold find matter wherin I might expresse my mind to you: for sich are our sinnes to God as they dailie cry for vengans uppon us, & so littell love or charitie one to another in these daies as it is Gods mercy that we are nott consumed: But to retturne to the purpose: you wrote to me to send you word of what forme I am of, & how I like: I am of Tho: Chalmans: for when as I came first Mr Ward did putt mee to my choise whether I would be of Germin Wrights or the other, now Germins classe was so forward in Greke gram̄er as I cold verry hardly have over-taken them — so I wold be of the lower forme: we came up into the hie ende last Christide: As for my likinge of it, who cold mislike of sich a place havinge sich kind usage att schole: & I giue most hartie thanks to Almightie God for that he hath disposed it so for my good & benefight. As for our Borders, Tho: Wright & his Brother are gone to Cambridge: they went a fortnight before Ester: none else but Abraham Caly of whom before I wrote to you: All our frends are in good health, onely our grandmother is nott very well: Our grandfather is departed out of this miserable life to a perpetual rest: When as I came last from my master Mr Dickerson he was in good health & sent commendations to you. So did Mr Ward: Mr Dickerson is married last Ester: his wife is bigge wth child reddy to be delivered if nott she bee already: William Harbone is gone to Cambridge: he went that daie that Tho: Wright went: William Hall went to Cam: 2 monthes before; & Edmund Maier went to bee admitted then too, but he cold not. William Smith went to Cambridge this Easter: the 2 Classe as I sup-pose shall be turned to the hye one: Charles Neuton is gone to Cambridge very latly but of what Col: he is I cannott learne: Henery Bridon sendeth salutations to you: I am in good health I praise God for it: So are all our frends so far as I can learne; our new Brother Deane is well, praised be God for itt: Thus havinge nott more time I committ you to the almightie Jesus:

"Your loving brother   "FORTH WINTHROPPE.

"GROTON, April 17, 1623.

" As for the printed booke of quarters which you wroght word of I cannott reddilie find it nor how surely send it. But my father will find it & send it to you by my uncle Gostling who will come shortly.

" Remember me to my uncle & Ante Downinge & to Richard : "

Forth Winthrop to his brother John.

" To my verie lovinge Brother Mr John Winthroppe at Trinitie College neere Dublin give thes — Ireland.

" MOST LOVINGE BROTHER, — The longe absens of my wrighting to you may make you ether thinke the bond of brotherlie love is broken in me, or else that ungratefulnes, which to God is most detestable, hath possessed my mind, or rather that sum impediment of sicknesse or any other diseases by Gods just judgment for my sines & offences hath befalen upon me. But thankes be to the Almightie that thow my sines hath caled for great punishment yet through his great goodnes he hath removed them from me : I could not therfore at this time, havinge so fitt an opportunitie & so honest a messenger, but take the occasion, not knowinge when I shal have sich a fitt opportunitie, for as the poet saith

Fronte capillata, post est occasio calva:

so if I should neclect this occasion perhaps I might seldome or never enioy the like. I tharfore in hast wright to you desiringe you that you will not be greved because I have omitted & lett passe the time so longe, because I have nott had a fitt & good one to send bye : I wright now tharfore desiringe that you would send me word of the wellfare of your selfe & of my ante wth you, for wth us there is a verye great desease & at Cambridge many of the scholers are sicke of another sicknes : therefore I the rather wright unto you to know whether it be so wth you also. Thus I remembring my love hartilie to my ant & also to your selfe in hast I rest. — My host & my hostesse remember their love to you & also Abraham Calie for he

came from Cambridge a little while before.   Mr Gurdon the
elder is departed verie latlie out of this life.

    "Youer loving Brother   "FORTHE WINTHROPPE.

"I praie brother send me word whether you received the
letters which I sent you sins Whitsuntide or noe: lastlie I
praie wright to me as speedilie as you can:

"BURIE S^{rr} EDMONDS August 26. 1623."

CHAPTER X.

CORRESPONDENCE WITH HIS WIFE, &c. — 1623-5.

WE turn again to the letters from Winthrop to his wife, giving, in their order, a series of eight, which require but little explanation or preamble. All of them seem to imply that he was busily engaged in the practice of his profession; and one of them proves that he was taking an active interest also in the political affairs of his County. With them we are glad to be able, at last, to give one of his wife's replies, — the earliest which has survived the lapse of time. Her husband, in the first of this series, after welcoming her "sweet letters," reminds her that they were "without date." But the hint seems not to have been regarded; and, like too many of her sex in that day and in this, she habitually omitted to give the year of our Lord in which she was writing. Generally, however, she tells her simple story of affection or of household affairs in a way which leaves little danger of mistake as to the period of which she is speaking; or certainly so as to render it of little consequence, at this late day, whether we succeed or fail in conjecturing the precise year to which it may have belonged. Such letters never could have come amiss to her loving husband; nor will the satisfaction of those who read them now be materially impaired, we imagine, by the want of an exact date.[1]

John Winthrop to his Wife.

"MY DEARE WIFE, — Thy sweet Lettres (w^{th}out date) how welcome they were to me I cañot expresse : both in regard of the continuance of thy health & thy little ones, my mother & o^r whole familye, for wch I humbly blesse & prayse o^r good God & Heavenly father, & doe heartyly begge of him & trust in him for the continuance of the same mercie to thyselfe & all the rest : as also in respect of the manifestation of the constancie & increase of thy true love wherein (I seariously professe) I doe more reioyce then in any earthly blessinge : O how I prize the sweet societye of so modest & faithfull a spouse ! O that I could be wise to be thankfull & improve it, accordinge to that esteeme wch I have of it when I want it ! I am heere where I have all outward content, most kinde entertainment, good companye & good fare, &c : onely the want of thy presence & amiable society makes me weary of all other accomplem^{ts}, so deare is thy love to me, & so confident am I of the like entertainem^t my true affection findes wth thee : O that the consideration of these things could make us raise up o^r spirits to a like conformitye of sinceritye & fervencie in the Love of Christ o^r Lord & heavenly husband ; that we could delight in him as we doe in each other, & that his absence were like greivous to us : But the Love of this present world, how it bewitcheth us & steales away our hearts from him who is o^r onely life & felicitye ; but I must break off this discourse. The blessed protection & favour of the Lord be still wth thee & all o^r familye, & bring us togither againe in peace : thou & the rest are kindly remembred of all heere ; remember my duty to my mother & my love to all thou knowest I wish it. My brother ffones is gotten abroad againe, my sister is as she useth

---

[1] All the letters in this chapter are printed now for the first time.

to be, the rest of us are all in health (I prayse God). Our businesse goeth on, tho' slowlye as matters use, to do at Court. My brother sends Richard home this daye & meanes to stay awhile himselfe, to see further successe. Let Sam : come up on monday & bring my horse, for I will leave my brother heare awhile ; let him be heere on teusdaye betymes, for I would goe out of London the same daye. Heere is no newes but of the Princes beinge at sea, where he hath bin wind bound a great while : Thus embracinge thee in the true affection of a faithfull husband, I will so remaine

"Thine   "JOHN WINTHROP.

"I have nothinge to send thee but my love, neither shall I bringe thee anythinge but my selfe, wᶜʰ I knowe wilbe best welcome.

"LONDON, Octob 3. 1623."

John Winthrop to his Wife.

"MY MOST LOVINGE & DEARE WIFE, — I received thy kinde & welcome Lettres, & doe heartyly blesse oʳ mercifull God for his gratious providence over thee & all oʳ familye. Oh that we had hearts to love him & trust in him as his kindnesse is towards us : I am sory that I cannot returne to thee so soone as I made account, for cominge to Childerditch upon Saterday last, I found my Cosin Barfut [1] very ill, & decayinge so fast as on mundaye morninge I could not leave him, so staying wᵗʰ him about noone he comfortably & quietly gave up the Ghost :, I sawe Gods providence had brought me thither to be a stay & comfort to hir in that suddaine tryall, when none of hir freinds were wᵗʰ hir ; by this occasiō it was Wensdaye night before I

---

[1] I know nothing of this cousin Barfut. The name, spelt Barfoote, was not undistinguished at that time in England. Dr. John Barfoote is mentioned by Walton, in his Life of Hooker, as Vice-President of Corpus Christi College, Oxford, and Chaplain to Ambrose, Earl of Warwick, 1579. Walter Barefoote was Deputy-Governor of New Hampshire in 1685.

could gett to London : where (I prayse God) I found all well
except my brother ffones, who is aguish &c, as he useth to be.
The dayes are heere so shorte, & the weather so could, as I
can dispatch no businesse, so that it wilbe the ende of the next
weeke before I can gett home. Heer is no certain newes, but
much expected w^{th}in fewe dayes. Till I come, have care of
thyselfe & little ones (as I knowe thou doest) ; remember my
duty to mother & my love to Mr Sands & all the rest. So
wth my kindest Love to my sweet wife, & my blessinge to o^r
children, I comende thee & all the rest to the blessinge & protectiō of the Lord & rest, Thy faithful lovinge husband

"JOHN WINTHROP.

" My brother ffones & my sister & my brother Downinge
salute thee & my mother.
"DECEMB: 11. 1623."

John Winthrop to his Wife.

" To my very lovinge Wife Mrs. Winthrop at Groton in Suff^k,

" MY SWEET SPOUSE, — I prayse o^r good God, and doe
heartylye reioyce in thy welfare & of the rest of o^r familye,
longinge greatly to be with thee, whom my soule delights in
above all earthly things : these tymes of separation are harsh
& greivous while they last, but they shall make o^r meetinge
more. comfortable. It wilbe mundaye at night before I can
come home. In the meane tyme my heart shalbe with thee, as
it is allwayes, & as thy Love deserves : I am now at Childer-
ditche[1] from whence I cannot goe till Saterdaye, & it wilbe too
farre to come home, so as I intend to keepe the Lords daye at
Sr Henry Mildmaies.
" The newes heer is of a Parliament to beginne the XIIth of
ffebruary next. The Earle of Oxford came out of the Tower
upon Tuesdaye last. Other thinges I shall relate to thee when
we meet : onely I thought good to write least thou shouldst be

---

1 A parish in Essex County, about twenty miles from London.

troubled at my not cominge on Saterdaye night : Thus comending thee & all o^{rs} to the gratious blessinge & holye providence of o^r heavenly father, I heartylye embrace my sweet wife
in the armes of my best affections, ever resting

"Thy faithfull husband "J WINTHROP.

"CHILDERDITCH Jan: 1. 1623.

"Let this letter to Mr. Gurdon be sent so soone as you
receive it."

John Winthrop to his Wife.

"MY DEARE WIFE, — I am so streightened in tyme as I can
not write to thee as I desire, yet I would not let a weeke passe
wthout lettinge thee heare from me : I prayse God, I came well
to London, & found all well there, except my brother ffones
who is troubled wth his gout, & my Aunt Egerton who hath
kept hir bedd these six weekes. Heere is no parliam^t newes,
but this day is expected to bringe forth somewhat. I hold my
purpose of being at home on Wensday at the furthest (if God
will). Thus in much hast wth remembrance of my true love to
thy sweet selfe, my duty to mother & blessinges to o^r little
ones, wth lovinge Salutations from my brothers & sister heere,
I comende you all to the protection & blessinge of the Lord,
ever restinge

"thy faithfull husband "JOHN WINTHROP.

"LONDON, March 19. 1623."

John Winthrop to his Wife.

"MY MOST SWEET HEART, — I received thy kinde Lettre,
wch was truely wellcome to me, as a fruit of that Love wch I
have (& shall ever) esteemed above silver & golde, & cannot
but reioyce more in so kind a testimonie of it, then in the richest present thou couldst have sent me. Now blessed be the Lo :
our good God, who giveth us still matter of comfort in each
other & in those wch belonge to us : onely I am greived for our
2 little Lambes, the Lord keepe them & deliver them in his
good tyme. If heer be any thinge wch may be good for them I

will not forgett them. I prayse God we are all heer in health, & salute thee heartyly, wishinge thee heer ofte if it could be. Newes heer is none certaine. I purpose (if God will) to be at Graces on Saterday at night, & so to be at home on mundaye. In the meane tyme I cease not to cõmende thee & all o͏ʳ familye to the gratious blessinge & protection of o͏ʳ heavenly father, & so w͏ᵗʰ my dutye to my mother, blessinge to o͏ʳ children, & salutations to all etc, I kisse my sweet wife & remaine allwayes

"thy faithfull husband   "JOHN WINTHROP.

" Wells bringes downe a trusse.

"LONDON Octob: 30 1624."

John Winthrop to his Wife.

" MY SWEET WIFE, — I blesse the Lorde for his continued blessings upon thee and o͏ʳ familye : & I thanke thee for thy kinde lettres : But I knowe not what to saye for myselfe : I should mende & growe a better husband, havinge the helpe & example of so good a wife, but I growe still worse : I was wonte heertofore, when I was longe absent, to make some supplye w͏ᵗʰ volumes of Lettres ; but I can scarce afforde thee a few lines : Well, there is no helpe but by enlarginge thy patience, & strengtheninge thy good opinion of him, who loves thee as his owne soule, & should count it his greatest Afflictiõ to live without thee : but because thou art so deare to him, he must choose rather to leave thee for a tyme, than to enioye thee : I am sorye I must still prolonge thy expectatiõ, for I cañot come forth of London till Tuesdaye at soonest ; the Lorde blesse & keepe thee & all o͏ʳˢ & sende us a ioyfull meetinge. So I kisse my sweet wife & rest

"Thy faithfull husband   "JO : WINTHROP.

" My brother & sister salute thee. my sonne & daughter remember their dutye ; the match goeth on fast enough, I am like to bring them downe w͏ᵗʰ me.

" Thy Syder was so well liked that we must needs have more as soone as thou canst.

"Nov: 26. 1624."

Margaret Winthrop to her Husband.

"To hir very Lovinge husband John Winthrope, Esq. theese.

"MY DEARE HUSBAND, — I am sory it faleth out so that I coulde not send for thee at the time appoynted, by reson of my mans beinge from home, & the unfitnesse of your horsses for travill, that I must be constrained to forbeare sending for thee till I can get meanes, though it be with a great deale of greefe to me : I hope you will not impute or take it ill at my hands, for theare wants no will in me, but that I wanted abilyty to performe it. My sonne came safe home on fryday, and brought me thy kinde letter, with the nuse of all your welfayres wch I desyre the lord longe to continue to his glory & for the good of many others. I shall thinke the tyme very longe before I see thee ; I pray make hast for thou shalt be very welcome : I am much irdetted to my sister D for hir kindenesse to my daughter M. I pray tel hir I give hir many thankes for that, & al other fruits of hir love, and thus with my best respect rememberd to thy selfe & all the rest of our friends, I desyre the lord to send us a comfortable meetinge and commit thee to the lord.

"Your loving and obedient wife,

"MARGARET WINTHROPE.

"I have now received thy lovinge letter by goodman N. and rejoyce that the time is so near whearein I shall see thee. I am wel perswaded of thy love and can see it in a fewe lines as in a whole volem — my daughter M & hir welwiler shalbe very welcom to me if you pleas to bring them — My sonne F. and John[1] came home on Saterday late from theare roveinge, haveinge bin from home two dayes & I have well chid them for theare paynes ; I hope John wil make the more hast. Your good servant remembers hir service and thankes you for hir letter, she desyreth to be excused from rightinge, haveinge many other letters to right :

---

[1] The John here meritioned was evidently a servant, not her son ; as also was "Robt," who is named in one or two of the following letters.

my sister F wil tel John whare to have a pillyon for M.   I thinke she ware best ryde dubble." [1]

John Winthrop to his Wife.

" To my verye lovinge wife Mrs. Winthrop at Groton in Suff^k.

" MY SWEET WIFE, — I prayse God, we came safe to London, where we found all reasonably well : we came by Graces, my Lady is some what amended; I purpose (God willinge) to returne thither againe either to morrowe or on mundaye. Heer is little newes : the Coronation is put off till Maye & then to be performed privately : there is order given to the Bishops to proceed ag^t the papists by ecc^{tiall} [2] censures : & muche speeche of the Kinges purpose to bringe the Queene to our Church : there be divers Lords come out of Scotlande, their busines is supposed but not certainly knowne. As we came by Assington Mr Gurdon made a motion of choosing the master of the Wards [3] for one of the Knights of our shire, wch my brother Downinge & myself consideringe off, have written to Sr Robt Crane, Mrs Bacon, & some others about it : he is knowne to be sounde for Religion, firme to the Com : W : (for wch he suffered muche) & the meetest man to further the affaires of our Countrye, for our Clothiers businesses &c : I would have written to Mr Sands about it, but I have not tyme : remember us kindly to him & shewe him this. Thus wth all o^r hearty salutations (& my humble duty remembred to my mother) to my sister Downing, thy selfe, &c : beseechinge the good Lord so to continue his good providence over you all & ourselves, as through his mercie we may meet in peace, I rest thy faithful husbande

" JOHN WINTHROP.

" JANY, 14. 1625.

---

[1] I have had some misgivings about inserting Margaret's first letter here; yet several passages of it seem to be in direct answer to the letter of her husband which immediately precedes it. Her daughter Mary, however, must have been rather young at that time to be the subject of a match, or even of a "well-willer." She married Rev. Samuel Dudley, seven or eight years afterwards. No record is found of the precise date of her birth; but it could hardly have been before 1610.

[2] Clearly an abbreviation for *ecclesiastical.*

[3] Probably Sir Robert Naunton, who, as we shall see hereafter, was Master of the Wards about this time.

" Mr. Downinge is in London & we should meet with him anone. My brother Dow: would have written to my sister now, but having many lettres to write he must deferre till I come."

John Winthrop to his Wife.

" To his best beloved Mrs. Winthrope the younger, at Groton.

" MY SWEET WIFE, — I prayse God I came safe to London on fridaye, & have continued in health hitherto. Our friends heare are all in reasonable health. My brother Dow: is so full of businesse as I can scarce speake wth him. I went this morninge to knowe if he would any thinge downe, but he was gone to Westm^r: he tould me yesternight, he would deferre to write or send till I went. I thinke longe to heare how thy selfe & the rest doe, & till God give me opportunitye to re-turne, wch I hope wilbe the next weeke : If I wright not to the contrarye, let Robt come up on mundaye : but I shall write againe (God willinge) on frydaye next. I send thee stockens, starch, silke, & other thinges : If thou wantest ought els, write up this weeke. Heere is little newes stirringe, this bearer can tell thee all.

" God allmighty blesse & keepe thee & all ours, & our whole company, & grant us to meet with ioye & peace in his good tyme : be cheerfull my deare wife, & waite upon o^r good God, who hath allwayes taken care of us & ours, & will not faile o^r trust in him ; continue to praye for me, as I doe for thee. Thus wth all lovinge Salutations from all o^r good friends heere to my sister Downinge, thy selfe, wth all love & dutye to my good mother, hearty blessings to o^r children, & lovinge remem-brance to all the rest, I embrace thee in the best Affection of a lovinge husband & rest

"Thine ever   " J. W.
" FEB. 13. 1625.

" I have sent downe some oranges for my sister Downinge & thee. Comende me to my brother Gostlin & sister : good Mr Ley his wife & all o^r good neighbours."

We may conclude this chapter with a letter which has no address,[1] but which was undoubtedly written to one of his brothers-in-law, Fones or Gostlin, in London, about the same time with the two first letters in this chapter.

John Winthrop to —— ——.

"My good Brother, — I percieve my last weekes Lettre was not come to your hands when yours was written, though I doubt not but since it is, & therefore I will spare to write of any thinge in that : my mother (I prayse God) is well recovered & remembers hir love to you & to my good sister, & so dothe my wife, & we all are gladd of the continuance of your health & of all yours. If my Brother Downinge goe for Irelande soe suddainly, I thinke I shall not see you this winter. I have, assigned Haxall 2 trees which stande in the ditche waye between Mr. Brande & you ; we estimated them (being stubbed) at 2 lodes & $\frac{1}{2}$, so that what he hath more than his allowance now, must be abated at the next assignment (which he is well content with), if upon sisinge by workmen there fall out to be more. In that fence there be divers places where it cannot be discerned that there hath been any ditch or bancke, so as I have a purpose to meet Mr. Brande there one day & have it viewed & agreed upon. I wrote you in my last that Peyton Hall wilbe sould ; it is now offered to any that will buye it ; the rent is 300ᣔᵇ per an. & his price is 6000ᣔᵇ: but he must come downe a gret deall if he will sell togither, which (I thinke) will make him in the ende to parcell it out, which yet he is not willing to doe : I heare that it is all soccage tenure (except 40 acres) ; it is good land but very bare of wood & no royalty or other ad vantage belonging to it, nor any building, & farre from churchᣔ which defects, I suppose, will discourage any great purchaser, & Sir David must needs sell, and that speeᣔilve. Thus wᣔᣔ

---

[1] The address of this letter, and those of many others which precede and follow it seem to have been torn off for the sake of the paper; probably on this side of the ocean, owing to the scarcity of the commodity in New England in the early days of the Colony.

my heartyest salutations to your selfe, my sister & all yours, I commend you to grace & blessing of our heavenly father, who keepe & guide us in all our wayes, to feare & trust in him, so I rest

"Your lovinge brother   "JOHN WINTHROP.

"NOVEMBER 11. 1623.

"I praye when you goe by Paul's buye me the book of the relation of the Blackfryars accident,[1] & remember my Respects &c.

"You shall receive by Welles a Rundlett of our cider, it wilbe fitt to drink by Christyde, & if you like it, you shall have more in Lent, when I broache my hoggeshead.

"Broache it not too lowe at first because the grounds are in jt; you shal not need open it for there is mustardseed in it all-readye."

---

[1] The book here referred to was undoubtedly that of which Lowndes's Manual gives the following title: "The doleful Even Song, or a true Narration of that Calamity which befel Mr. Drurye, a Jesuite, and the greater Part of his Auditory, by the Downfall of the Floore of an Assembly in the Black-friers on Sunday, the 26 of Octob. last" [1623].

CHAPTER XI.

LETTERS TO HIS SON ABOUT HIS STUDY OF THE LAW, AND PLANS
OF LIFE, 1624–26; WITH SOME ACCOUNT OF HIS OWN PRO-
FESSIONAL CAREER IN ENGLAND.

JOHN WINTHROP, the younger, having completed his
course at Trinity College, Dublin, was in London in the
year 1624–5, staying with his uncle Fones, and engaged
in the study of the law. The five letters from his
father, which are here given in succession, were written
to him during the two or three years of his legal preparations.[1] The first of them (dated Feb. 22) refers to his
not having been yet " admitted," without saying exactly
to what: but the letter could have hardly more than
reached its destination before the admission had taken
place ; and the record is still extant, as follows : —

" John Winthrop, son & heir of John Winthrop of Groton, in the
County of Suffolk, admitted to the Inner Temple 28 Feb^y, 1624." [2]

These letters contain some interesting items of domestic and local life ; among which will be observed the
birth of another son, and the death and burial of the

---

1 These five letters, and all the other letters in this chapter except two, are here
printed for the first time.
2 I was indebted to my friend Judge Warren for this excerpt from the Temple Records, which he kindly searched at my request, while we were in London together, in
1860.　There was a subsequent record, as follows : " John Winthrop, gentleman, specially
admitted 29 June, 1628." This may have referred to the elder Winthrop.

worthy and venerable pastor of Groton, Henry Sands, between whom and the Winthrop Family there seems to have been so strong an attachment.

John Winthrop to his Son.

"To my beloved Sonne John Winthrop.

"MY BELOVED SONNE, — I beseech o^r heavenly father to blesse thee. I received yor lettre, & am gladd of yor healthe, but should yet be more gladd, if I could heare that you were resolved upon any good course for the employment of yor life & talents. I desire but that yor iudgm^t may be once rightly informed, & then lett God dispose of you as he please. I perceive you are not yet admitted, & I am now offered a place in the Temple wth Mr. Gurdons sonne, where you may have a Chamber freely for the most parte of the yeare; but I referre this & the rest to suche good advise as yor freinds there shall give you. God give you an heart to be guided aright in all yor wayes. I shall thinke longe to heare somewhat of yor settlednesse. Yo^r grandmother & mother salute & blesse you; they wth the rest of o^r family & yor new brother Nath,[1] are in reasonable healthe (I prayse God). So having many lettres to write, I will ende for this tyme, & comendinge you againe & againe to o^r heavenly father, I rest

"Yo^r lovinge father, most studious of yor welfare,

"J : W :
"FEB. 22. 1624.

"Remember me most kindly to yor good Aunt ffones."

John Winthrop to his Son.

"To my beloved Sonne John Winthrop.

"MY BELOVED SONNE, — I blesse o^r good God for the continuance of yor healthe & his blessinge upon you, & I daylye beseeche him of his great mercie to guide & prosper you in all

---

[1] He was baptized Feb. 20, 1624; and died young.

yor wayes, & to make you a true servant to his name & glorye heere, & in the ende give you a place in the kingdome of his glorye, Amen. I doe muche desire that you should familiar yor selfe wth Mr. Gurdon (to whom I desire to be kindly remembered), & for this ende & the better opportunyty of followinge yor studyes I shall wish you in Comons as soone as shall be fitt, but I would not hasten to preiudice yor healthe, & so I leave it. You write for sheetes, w^{ch} (if I had knowne yor want) should not have been now to provide : we have none at this tyme fitt for you, therefore desire yor Aunt ffones to helpe you buye some clothe & gett them made ; the lesse will serve because you lye alone. I have searched in the studye for the Grogeram but can finde none. If I meet wth it I will sende it you. Yo^r grandmother & mother are in healthe, they salute & blesse you ; Yo^r brother Deane is verye ill of an ague &c. The blessing of the Lord Jesus be ever upon you. So I rest yor lovinge father " JOHN WINTHROP.

" MARCH 15. 1624.

" I meane to speake wth olde Mr. Gurdon about the sale of Nusted as soone as I can."

John Winthrop to his Son.

" To my lovinge Sonne John Winthrop.

" MY BELOVED SONNE, — I beseeche the Lorde to continue & encrease his blessing uppon thee : I am glad to heare of thy wellfare : ffor y^{or} returne there is now a fitt opportunitye offered, for M^r. Gurdon comes upp uppon wensdaye or thursdaye, & you may come downe upon his horse, & sende downe suche thinges as you shall need heere by the Carrier or some of o^r honest neighbors, if you meet wth them. Sir Hen : Mildmaye & his lady are very desirous you should come by them, & were allmost displeased wth me that you came not by them as you went up. If you like not to come that waye (wch yet I had rather, but will not urge you) it may be my neighbo^r Cole wilbe ready to come wth you on friday. We are all heere in health, I prayse God. Y^or grandmother & mother salute and blesse you, but you comitt an error in not remembring your dutye to them, & y^or grandmother is not pleased that you never write to hir. So soone as Mr. Gurdons horse comes to towne, take charge of him & paye for his meale, allowing a peck of Oates a daye besides haye, & have care that he be well shodd & take no harme. farewell.

     " Yo^r lovinge father   " JOHN WINTHROP.

" APRILL 4. 1625."

John Winthrop to his Son.

" To his lovinge sonne John Winthrop at the three fawnes in the old Bayly, London.

" MY GOOD SONNE, — I received yor Lettre & the things wch you sent, & doe prayse God for his gratious protectiō over you in yor io^rnye, beseechinge his heavenly majestie daylye to take care of that soule & life &c, wch he hathe pleased to lende you, that himselfe may have glorye & you peace & safetye in the imployment of them. The suddaine newes of this messinger, & my other occasions hinders me from writinge to y^r 2 unckles this weeke; you must supplye that defecte by remembringe us all kindly to them & yor Aunts & cosins : We are in healthe as you lefte us (I prayse God), Luce & the rest, onely Robt hathe an ague. Mr. Sands is now hastinge to his last period, & not like (in mans Judgment) to live another week : The good Lo : in mercye carrye him on wth peace into the haven of rest, & teache us all how to make right use of suche a losse. Yo^r grandmother & mother salute & blesse you & yor sister ; I comende you bothe to his mercifull protectiō & holy government, & rest

     " Yo^r lovinge father   " JOHN WINTHROP.

" Nov. 6, 1626."

John Winthrop to his Son.

" To my lovinge sonne John Winthrop.

" MY GOOD SONNE, — I received yor lettre : & doe blesse
God for the continuance of yor healthe & of all o^r good friends
where you are. The. Lord longe continue peace and blessinge
to you all. We all likewise (through his mercye) continue in
healthe, onely Robt hathe been sick this señight, & Luce hath
had some gruchings of hir Ague againe, & this daye yor grandmother hathe not been well, but she hathe made shifte to goe
see Luce. I wrote the last weeke of the great declininge of o^r
Rev^d & worthye freinde Mr. Sands, whose ende was then at
hande, for he finished his course in happie peace on teusdaye
last about one of the clock in the afternoone, & was buried on
thursdaye afternoon, Mr. Stansby preaching upon 1 Sam :
25. 1. So as we are now very much destitute, Mr. Nicolson
beinge allmost blinde &c : So as we must looke out some
assistant for him, some single man, that may make shifte wth
smale meanes, while Mr. Nicholson lives. — Diverse of o^r neighbor ministers have comended to me Mr S.[1] of S^t Jo : & o^r parish
doe muche affecte & desire him : I praye God guide us all to a
good choyse, for he knowes I looke not at mine owne advantage, but the Churches wellfare. Yo^r grandmother & mother
salute and blesse you & yor sister. Remember us all to yor
good Aunts & 'Cosins. God Allmighty blesse you ever
" Yo^r lovinge father " JOHN WINTHROP.
[Nov. 1626.]

" Yo^r mother desires yor A : ffones to buye hir 4 : oz : more
of the blacke worsted she sent hir before. We want white
starche. I knowe not where you keepe. I praye goe see M^r.
Culverwell & carrye him my lettre ; & goe see my Cosin
Kayne wch was my Cosin Peitall, yor owne mothers deare

---

[1] Subsequent letters will show that this was Mr. Simonds.

freinde, & comende me & my mother to hir. She dwells in
Gratious Street, a little beneathe the Conduitt. Comende me
very kindly to Mr. Warre the elder if you see him.
"I heard not this weeke of Mr. Gurdon; if you see him,
remember me to him &c."

During the autumn of 1626, John Winthrop, the
younger, was evidently contemplating a matrimonial
arrangement. He seems to have asked his father's
advice on the subject; and one or two of the following
letters will be found to contain some very plain and prudent counsel in reply, not unworthy, perhaps, of a wider
application. As nothing came of the consultation, it
may be inferred that John did not fancy his " somewhat
crooked" cousin Waldegrave;[1] and perhaps that Miss
Pettual, or Peitall (whichever be the name),[2] did not
fancy John. Meantime, the father's concern for his son's
spiritual welfare was evidently not diminished by the
interest which he was taking in his temporal advancement. Nothing could be terser or more emphatic than
this: "Mr. Rogers hath set forth a little book of faith;
buy it."[3] But several of these letters deal also with public

---

[1] The father of Thomasine Clopton, the second wife of Gov. Winthrop, married a
daughter of Edward Waldegrave, Esq., of Essex County.

[2] I find on a copy of the Forth Pedigree, for which I am indebted to my friend
Richard Almack, Esq., of Long Melford, Suffolk County, Eng., that Elizabeth Forth, a
cousin of Winthrop's first wife, married a merchant of London, named Poyntell; and
this may, perhaps, be the true name.

[3] This was "The Doctrine of Faith, Wherein are practically handled twelve princi-
pall points, which explain the Nature and Use of it. By Jo. Rogers, Preacher of God's
Word at Dedham in Essex." It was dedicated to three ladies, one of whom was Win-
throp's cousin, the Lady Mildmay, as follows: "To the Right Worshipful, the Lady
Mildmay, wife of Sir Henry Mildmay of Graces, and to Mistris Helen Bacon of Shrib-
land Hall, and to Mistris Gurdon, wife to Master Branton Gurdon of Assington; the
Author prayeth all increase of Faith, many good dayes here, and eternall life in the
Kingdome of Heaven " It had reached the eighth edition in 1640.

men and public affairs, and show that their writer was taking an active interest in all that was occurring at the time. The letter of Dec. 18, in particular, would imply that he had been concerned in some exciting controversy at Bury. It undoubtedly related to the tyrannical measures of the Crown for extorting a forced Loan.

John Winthrop to his Son.

"To my loving Son, John Winthrop.

"MY GOOD SON, — I received your letter, and do bless God for the continuance of your health, and of all our good friends at London; but I had no letters from any of them. For the matter which you write of, I can give you no advice; for I must deal plainly and faithfully with all men, and especially with my inward friends. So it is, that I have had lately some speech with my cousin Waldegrave, about matching you with his younger daughter, which I have referred to your own liking; but yet I cannot in honesty enter treaty for another, till he hath some determinate answer. It is a religious and a worshipful family; but how the woman will like you, I know not, for she is somewhat crooked. I will neither persuade you to that, nor dissuade you from this or any other, which you shall desire, that may be fitting for my estate, and hopeful of comfort to you, which is not to be judged of only by wealth and person, but by meet parts and godly education. I trust you will mind well that saying, *Deliberandum est diu, quod statuendum est semel.*

"I praise God, we continue all in health, as you left us, and, when you are weary of London, will be glad to see you and your sister at home; but take your own time before the holidays. Your grandmother and mother salute and bless you and your sister. Your mother thanks you for the things which you sent her. Remember us very kindly to your uncles and aunts, and to all our cousins and good friends. The good Lord guide, protect, and bless you in all your ways.

"Your loving father,　　"JOHN WINTHROP.

"NOVEMBER 21, 1626.

"I pray buy me a pair of stirrup stockens, the warmest you can get; and when you go near the bridge, on Fish Street Hill dwells one that sells lines and packthread,—buy some lines to raise up the long net, and some packthread to do it. A hair line were best for the leads."

John Winthrop to his Son.

"To my lovinge Sonne John Winthrop at the house of Mr. Downinge in ffleet St over ag^{to} the Conduit, London.

"MY GOOD SONNE,—I received y^r Lettre & doe blesse the Lorde for the continuinge of yor healthe, w^{ch} (through his mercye) we all likewise enioye. ffor yor returninge home sooner or later, I leave you to yor selfe & yor good freinds wth whom you are : all the inconvenience of yor tarrienge is that I shalbe too burdensome to them, except I may paye for yor diet : but we shall agree for these thinges. ffor yor Clothes, I thinke fitt you should have a newe suite, & for that I will sende you up moneye so soone as it comes to hande. I spake last weeke wth my cosin Waldegrave &, in a lovinge respecte to each others good, we are both at lib^{tye}. Therefore if a good occasiō be offered you may certifie me of it. Mr. Simonds is now wth us, but yet not certaine of his acceptinge the place, for the meanes wch we can promise, whilest Mr. Nicholson lives, are so smale, as he is very doubtfull whither he maye leave so good & certaine a Conditiō for one y^t is smale & incertaine. If he refuse it, I knowe not where we can be so well in all respects. I praye God of his mercye dispose all for the best. All things continue heere as you lefte them : the Lorde blesse, directe, & prosper you allwayes. This is the prayer & salut^n wch yor grandmother, yor mother & myselfe sende to you & yor sister.

Comende us to yo͞r good Aunts & Cosins. S͞r Nath : Barnardiston lodged wth us one night last weeke & yo͞r brother is heer
still; but Mr. Smith came not. If there be any Curant^os or
other likely newes sende it downe, So I rest
" Yo͞r loving father   " JOHN WINTHROP.
"DEC: 4. 1626."

John Winthrop to his Son.

" To my lovinge Sonne John Winthrop at the three ffawnes in the olde
Baylye, London.

" MY GOOD SONNE, — I wrote not the last weeke, trustinge
to Lewes Kelby his coming to London, who failed, & went
not; & besides it was a tyme of muche businesse & distraction,
which tooke up my minde more than ordinarylye. What the
carriage & issue of these late affaires hath been in our Countrye, you shall knowe by my lettres to your unckle : I made
no other accompt but to have been at London before this letter,
but it hath seemed good to the Lords most wise providence to
dispose otherwise of it, as you may know by that my letter.
Sir Nath : Barnardiston came not to Burye till Saturday neare
noone, when all was doone, & when I was come out of towne
the Lords sent for him, but what conclusion he made with
them I doe not heare. When you have read your unckles letter,
I wish you would goe into Southwark to the Marshallsea, &
remember my Love and service to Sir Francis Barrington,[1] &
acquaint him how thinges have gone in our Countrye, but you
must doe it in private. I prayse God we are all here in health.
Your grandmother & mother salute & bless you. The good
Lord blesse you & sanctifie you throughout, & prepare & fitt
you a vessell for his kingdom, & guide us all wisely & faithfully in the middest of the dangers & discouragements of these
declining tymes : farewell.
" Your loving father   " J. WINTHROP.
" DEC^a 18 1626."

---

[1] Sir Francis was doubtless in prison for resisting the forced loan; as Sir Nath.
Barnardiston certainly was, not far from the same time.

John Winthrop to his Son.

" To my loving Son, John Winthrop, at the House of Mr. Downing, at the Sign of the Bishop, over against the Conduit, in Fleet street, London.

" MY GOOD SON, — I wrote the last week so far as my paper would reach. I hope you received my letters, which I desire to understand from you, for Jarvice his man had them. I bless God for your health and welfare; but we now think long to have you at home, for your brother[1] is to return to Cambridge, and then we shall be alone; but if there be any good occasion to stay you still, I will not urge your hasty return. Touching the matter of Mr. Pettuall, (though I can give no direct answer where nothing is propounded, yet) thus much in general, where I may have more money, I can depart with the more land. I pray God give you wisdom and grace to discern of meet gifts, and a disposition that may promise hope of a comfortable life in the fear of God; otherwise (if you can so content your own mind) you were better live as you are. But I commit this, and all our other affairs, to the only wise providence of our heavenly Father.

" We have had much ado for a minister, since Mr. Simonds refused it. Groton Church did not afford such variety of gifts in divers years before. We have many suitors, that would take it at a mean rate; but for such as are worthy, all the difficulty is to get maintenance enough. We are now (by God's providence) like to fasten upon a godly man, one Mr. Lea,[2] a curate at Denston in Suffolk, a man of very good parts, but of a melancholic constitution, yet as sociable and full of good discourse as I have known. All the parish are

---

[1] Forth, who had, in April before, been admitted of Emanuel, and matriculated 4th July, in the rank of pensioner.

[2] He was afterwards settled at Groton. The name was William Leigh. He was son of Ralph Leigh, a Cheshire man, who had been a soldier under the Earl of Essex at Cadiz; and married Eliz. Newton, a daughter of a fellow of St. John's, Cambridge, and a preacher at Bury St. Edmund's. — *Rev. Jos. Hunter, Mass. Hist. Coll.,* vol. x. 3d ser. p. 156.

very earnest with me to take him; but I have taken a little respite, because he is but a stranger to me, but well known to divers in the town. He was Mr. Simond's pupil. I purpose to send up £10 for my A. B.[1] if I can hear of any fit party; if not, you should receive some money of your uncle Downing for Mr. John Brande. Lay out £10 of that, and I will restore it, for I have the money by me. Be not known to any body of any money you receive for Mr. Brande; but fail not to write me word this week of the receipt of it. You may speak to your uncle about it, lest he should forget it. Mr. Rogers hath set forth a little book of faith. Buy it. I want a pair of plain, ordinary knives, and some leaf tobacco and pipes. You may buy these things at your leisure; as likewise some packthread and lines, hemp ones, if you will. Your grandmother and mother salute and bless you. The good Lord bless you ever. Farewell.

"Your loving father,   "JOHN WINTHROP.
"JANUARY 9, 1626.

"I, should have sent up some fowls this week if they had been fat."

We come now to a letter from John Winthrop, the younger, to his father, sent by an express messenger from London, which helps us to unravel a family mystery. The father, in a letter to his wife, of uncertain date, which has already been printed in the Appendix to the History of New England, and which will be found

---

1 An "A.B.," on our side of the ocean, would stand for a degree of Bachelor of Arts. Ten pounds would have been a large price to pay for one, however; and Winthrop would have been a little old at this period to purchase one. In England, too, the letters indicating such a degree are always reversed. But after having repeatedly puzzled my brain over this paragraph, in the notion that it might be a confirmation of the idea, that Winthrop had, in some way or other, entitled himself to a place on the University roll, it was an amusing relief to find, among the old family papers recently discovered, several little quarterly receipts, indorsed "Aunt Branch, £10"! The receipts are all signed "Reynold Branch;" and are given in behalf of his wife Elizabeth, for whom Winthrop held an annuity of forty pounds.

hereafter in this volume, tells her, " My office is gone ; " and it has never been exactly ascertained to what office he referred. Here is the clew ; and, in connection with it, we may find fit occasion for adding some brief account of Winthrop's professional career in England.

John Winthrop Jr. to his Father.

" To the Wor.ll his very loving father Mr. Winthrop at his house in Groton these deliver swift:

" MOST LOVING FATHER, — My duty remembred to your selfe, my mother & grandmother, w.th my love to my brothers & the rest of o.r freinds. The occasion of my sending thus hastily is this : that whereas M.r Lattimer one of the Atturnies of the Court of Wards is yesterday dead, so as now that place is void, my uncle Downing willed me to give you speedy notice of it & desire you to come up w.th all speed you can to London ; for the M.r is now out of towne & doth not returne till Saterday nexte, & he would have you be here before his comming home that you might ride some way out of towne to meete him, because he feareth that if it be not granted presently at his comming home, or before, the Kings or Dukes letter may be a meanes to make it be disposed of some other way ; therefore if you have a mind to it, my uncle thinkes it will be your best course to be heare upon friday at furthest, & he will use all the meanes he can to obteyne it for you, & in the meane tyme, if he can by any meanes, he will write into the country to the M.r about it. Thus hoping to see you soone at London I desire your prayers & blessing & so rest

     " Your Obedient Sonne   " JOHN WINTHROP.
" LONDON. Jan: 14, 1626.

" The bearer hath promised to be w.th you by tomorrow at night. I agreed w.th him for 5.s for the whole iournie, whereof I have given him 2 already, but if he performeth his promise I pray give him 5 or 6 more, for it wilbe cheaper then I could have had any other.

" Since the writing of my letter my uncle Downing himselfe hath written. We are all well save little George[1] who· hath hadd one sore fitt of an ague.

" I think there is no great hast of sending up my Cozen Jeames[2] so he be from Ipswich, therefore I thinke it would be good to keepe him at Groton still this cold wether."

We know not how far the father conformed to these urgent suggestions of his son. We doubt a little whether he hurried down to London, and rode " some way out of town" to meet the Master of the Wards, and waylay him with an application for a place just vacated by death. It does not look altogether in keeping with his dignity of character. Yet such things were doubtless done in those days, as they are in these, by worthy men. At all events, the appointment was obtained; and many papers are left, which prove that the elder Winthrop held this position for several years. Among them is the following letter, addressed distinctly " To my worthie lovinge ffryende Mr. Wynthrope, one of the Atturnies in his Highness Courte of Wards & Lyvereyes, at his chamber neere the inner, temple in Fleete Streete, London : " —

John Bowen to John Winthrop.

" MR. WINTHROPE, — I comend me unto you with thankes for your love & care in my buysines the last tearme &c. I have sent you the Comission & our answers hereinclosed accordinge to the effect of the sayd Commission, the which you shall

---

1 Afterwards Sir George Downing.
2 James Downing, the son of Emanuel by his first wife, and named after his grandfather Sir James Ware.

receave by my loveing ffrynd & kinsman Mr. Roger Mortymer
— prayinge you to deliver it into the office that there be noe
advantage had against us; & although it is returnable *mense*
michael: yet I doubt not but you will se that there be noe
advantage, beinge returned within the tearme, for verilye I
could not returne it rather, by any trustie messenger. I praye
you that you will motion the Court for dismission for us, that
we may may be at libertie to proceed in chauncerie where my
suyte dependeth, & that Lewis John Ap howell and Ann his
wiefe may be lycensed to proceede in the Comon lawe for the
lands in Merthrie & Llandeloy, as well by reason that they
are poore, as allsoe that the sayd ward is of full age & noe
longer in reason to be protected, therebie to keepe poore men
from theyre right, with delayes & deversitie of suites : if theyre
neede counsell to motion, uppon notice from you by this bearer,
I will send you fees for the same if I come not my self. Soe
not doubting of your care, I end with my best wishes & rest
           " Your assured Lovinge ffrynd :   " JOHN BOWEN.
"HAVERFORD WEST the 24 of October 1627.

    " You shall receave by this bearer the some of seaven shil-
lings to be disposed as you see cause, & whatsoever more you
shall disburs in the effectinge of the busynes, I will not miss
by Gods help to bringe it or send unto you. I have sent the
coppie of our answeres wherebie you may the better motion."

The Court of Wards and Liveries was first established
by Henry VIII. to remedy some of the abuses and ex-
tortions which had been practised by the notorious
Empson and Dudley, in the reign and under the authority of Henry VII. It had a large jurisdiction over
wards and their estates, over widows, and over lunatics.
Lord Coke gives a full account of it in his 4th Institute.
" The judges of this court," he says, " are the master,

the surveyor, the attorney, receiver-general, and the auditors."[1] Winthrop was evidently not " the attorney" thus included by Coke among the judges, but one of the practising attorneys of the court, whose number seems to have been limited, and who appear to have been the subject of special appointment by the Master, — sometimes, as it would seem, upon the suggestion of the king or his favorite minister.

Winthrop had long before been engaged in the practice of the law, in London and on the circuit, as his letters sufficiently show. As early as 1622, we find him telling his wife that he had " hasted into the city about his business;" and, from that time forward, there are but few of his letters, whether to his wife or to his son, which do not allude, more or less distinctly, to his professional avocations. A few fragmentary legal memoranda and fee-bills are found among his papers, bearing date 1622; several papers connected with his practice in the Court of Wards and Liveries, dated 1624; and a long docket of cases, running through 1626, '7, and '8. Some of the papers bear the original attest of Sir Robert Naunton, Master of the Wards, and one of his majesty's Secretaries of State and Privy Councillors;[2] and others that of Sir Walter Pye, one of his majesty's attorneys for the same court. The following letter from Sir Robert Naunton (the original of which is found among Winthrop's papers) would seem to show that the

---

1 4th Inst. 202.
2 Sir Robert Naunton was a native of Suffolk County. He was made Secretary of State 8th January, 1617–18; King James (it is said) having been previously so well pleased with his eloquence and learning as to appoint him Master of the Court of Wards.

Countess of Nottingham was among his clients. She may have sent the letter to him as an authority for his appearance as her counsel in the suit.

Sir Robert Naunton to the Countess of Nottingham.

" To the right ho^ble Margarett Countesse of Nottingham.

" After my very harty comendacons to yor good La^ipp, whereas there is a Bill of Complaint exhibited before mee into his Ma^ts Courte of Wards and Liveries, against yor La^ipp on the behalfe of the right ho^ble Charles Earle of Nott^s, unto which Bill by course of his Ma^ts Lawes awnsweere is to be made, to the intent the matter may receyve noe prejudice by anie delay, I have therefore thought good to desire yor La^ipp to send yor Sollicitor or Servant or some of yor La^ipps Councell unto the said Court the Seaven and Twentith of this instant November to peruse or take a copie of the said Bill, and that yor La^ipp would thereupon make some awnsweare thereunto, To the end the Cause may receive Tryall as to Justice apperteineth, And soe I doe bidd yor La^ipp most hartily farewell. From my howse nere Charing Crosse this ffoure and Twentith day of November 1627.   " Yo^r La^ips very loving freind

" ROB^T NAUNTON."

He would seem to have had the Lady Sackville also among his titled clients ; while his friend Brampton Gurdon employed him in a case in which appears the name of " John Brent," recently rendered so familiar by the brilliant story of one of Winthrop's descendants.[1]

The petition in this case may serve to illustrate still further the character of the Court, and the mode in which its proceedings were initiated.

---

[1] " John Brent," by the late Major Theodore Winthrop.

"To the right ho^{ble} Sr Robert Naunton k^t, M^r of his ma^{ts} Court of Wards and Liveries.

"The humble petition of Brampton Gourdon; Humblie sheweth unto yor honor That whereas one John Brent of Cossington in the Countie of Som^rset Esq. did about fourteene yeares since die seised of diverse lands wthin the said Countie & elsewhere leaving his sonne & heire wthin the age of twentie one yeares, and whereas after the death of the said John Brent an Inquisition was taken wthin the said Countie whereby it was found that some of the said lands weare holden of the Kings Matie in cheife by knights service & his Matie thereupon intituled to the custodie and wardship of the body & lands of the said heire, and for that Elizāb Brent mother of the said ward then was & yet is a popish recusant convict : and therefore disabled to have the custodie & education of her said sonne whereupon the custodie and tuition of the said Ward & his estate was comitted to one Richard Worth gent. brother of the said Elizabeth for his better education, but soe it is may it please yor honor that the said Richard Worth hath ever since the custodie soe to him comitted suffered the said Elizabeth to have the sole educacon of the said Ward, and thereby the said Ward through the continuall practise & industrie of his said mother wholie inclined unto the popish religion & hath for all the said tyme refused to repaire to his or anie other parish church and to conforme himselfe to the religion of the church of England to the eivell example of others & manifest hurt of the said Ward :

"May it therefore please yor hono^r to grant unto yor supliant the custodie & Wardship of the said Sonne & heire of John Brent, and he shall see that the said ward be brought up according to the religion of the Church of England, and yor petitioner shall praye."

Here is a letter, also, from Brampton Gurdon himself, at that time High Sheriff of Suffolk County, dated on the

20th of October, — unfortunately, without any designation of the year, but evidently belonging to this period, — the address of which shows that Winthrop then occupied a chamber in the Temple, and was engaged in similar practice.

Brampton Gurdon to John Winthrop.

" To my worthy good friend Mr. Winthrop at his Chamber in the Temple lane near the Cloyster, give these —

" GOOD SIR, — Let me entreat your favor to this bearer, Mr. Warford, who is a Master of Arts of six years standing. He hath spent three years here in my brother Sedlyes house as a schoolmaster wherein he hath approved himself. I have some few times heard him preach in publick, and often I have heard him pray in the family for which he deserveth well to be approved. My request is that you will help him in his suit to the Master of the Wards. He hath a presentation from Mrs. Gurny who is guardian to her son who wanteth a few months of being of full age. I know the Masters have right to present. Young Mr. Gurney cometh with him to manifest his good will for the furthering of him to this living. I am loth to make this my suit to the Master because I purpose, if God will, to wait upon his honor before such time as the King prick shrieves,[1] and to renew my suit again to him. I pray be helpful to Mr. Warford that he may be kindly delt with by the officers under whom he must pass, and so in haste with my commendations to you and to Mr. Downing I pray God to keep us.

"Your very loving friend   " BRAMPTON GURDON.

" MORLY this 20 of 8ber."

Winthrop's professional services appear also to have brought him more or less into connection with the Par-

---

[1] The custom of the sovereign pricking the names of sheriffs is well known to this day.

liamentary proceedings of the time. We find among
his papers no less than three original draughts of bills,
which either were, or were intended to be, introduced
into Parliament. They are wholly in his own handwriting, on large paper, with ample margins, and prepared as if for the consideration of a Legislative Committee. One of them is entitled "An Act to settle a
course in the assessing and levying of common charges
in towns and parishes;" another is "An Act for the
preventing of the multitude of causeless suits, and of
the great vexation of the inferior sort of people thereby;"
and the third is "An Act for the preventing of drunkenness and of the great waste of corn."

This last bill may be worth inserting here, as an illustration of the views entertained in those days on a subject
so much vexed and agitated in our own. It will hardly
add much to our means of solving that most difficult of
all social problems, — the preventing of intemperance;
but it may suggest that the difficulty was as great two
centuries and a half ago as it is now, and that, too, when
there was nothing stronger in common use than beer and
ale. The bill reads as follows: —

"*An Act for the preventing of Drunkenness and of the great waste
of Corn.*

"Forasmuch as it is evident that the excessive strength of
Beer and Ale in Inns and Alehouses is a principal occasion
of the waste of the grain of this Kingdom, and the only fuel of
drunkenness and disorder which by no laws could hitherto be
repressed, because they were not limited to a reasonable and
wholesome proportion in the strength of Beer and Ale:
"Be it therefore enacted by the King's most excellent majes-

ty, the Lords Spiritual and temporal, and the commons in this present Parliament assembled and by the authority of the same, that no Innkeeper, Taverner, Alehousekeeper, or keeper of other Victualling or Tipling house, after forty days next ensuing the end of this present session of Parliament, shall have in his, her, or their houses any more than one sort of Beer or Ale only, and the same to be of no higher or greater strength than after the rate of two bushells of malt to one hogshead ; and if any Innkeeper, Taverner, Ale-housekeeper, or keeper of any victualling or tiplinghouse shall brew other, or have in his or her house any more than one sort of beer or ale, or shall brew, utter, or have in his or her house any Beer or Ale whereunto shall be put more than two bushells of malt to one hogshead, then every such party so offending against the true intent and meaning of this Statute shall forfeit for every offence ten pounds, the one half to the Informer, and the other to the Benefit of the house of Correction of the same limits, to be levied by distress by warrant from the Court or justices before whom the same shall be tried. And if any such offender shall not have whereby he or she may be so distrained or shall not tender sufficient security for the payment thereof in such manner and form as the said Court or justices shall appoint, then they shall inflict such bodily punishment upon the offender by pillory or whipping as they shall see the cause to deserve. And the intent of this Act is that no person who shall sell or utter any beer or Ale, without lawful license or authority, shall take advantage of his own wrong, but shall be subject to the penalties of this law, if he shall offend against the same."

A reference to the Journals of Parliament, and to the English statutes at large, proves that the subject-matter of these bills underwent much consideration and much legislation in the years 1626 and 1628. The bills, as draughted by Winthrop, however, never became laws ; and the papers in his handwriting are thus proved to be the originals of what was proposed, and not the mere copies of what had been passed. Perhaps they may have been prepared for his intimate friends Sir Nathaniel Barnardiston and Sir William Spring, who were knights for the county of Suffolk in 1628, and whose names are repeatedly found in his correspondence; or perhaps they only indicate that one part of his professional practice was that which is believed to have become of late years the most lucrative occupation of an English lawyer, — the attendance on committees of the House of Commons.

Before leaving the subject of Winthrop's professional practice in England, we may allude to Cotton Mather's story, that he was made a justice of the peace at eighteen years of age. The story does not seem probable; but there is ample evidence that he held the commission for many years before coming to America. He describes himself expressly as a justice, in a paper still extant, as early as 1619. In another paper, written in New England, he alludes to having had " twenty years' experience in the Commission of the Peace; " referring, as it would seem, in round numbers, to his experience in Old England. The religious confessions, too, which have been heretofore given, refer more than once to the exercise of his duties as a magistrate. Meantime, the following letter from his mother to her son-in-law, Emanuel Downing, proves that he did not hold the office continuously, and that " many good men were desirous to have him in againe," when he had withdrawn from the commission for a time. Unfortunately, there is no date to the letter; but it was certainly after 1622. It will have an interest, perhaps, as one of the few remaining letters of Winthrop's mother. At all events, it will serve as a welcome conclusion to this long chapter.

Anne Winthrop to Emanuel Downing.

" To her lovinge Sonne Mr. Emanuell Downing, these.

"Good Sonne,—I am forst now to doe that I have hetherto bin ashamed to doe, that is to trouble you with my dull head and scriblinge hand. The matter is I am suspected & accused to be a means to make you unwilling & to denye your helpe for my Sonns comming into the commission againe ; indeed for his owne part I was very willing to have him out, but hearing the great want that is of him in the country, and so many good men so desirous to have him in againe, I cannot but indevour my self to further ther desires what lies in me ; therefor I pray you, good sonne, that at my request you would doe so much as to speake a good word in the cause. I will not use many words to perswaid you as though I did mistrust your kindness, when as I assure myselfe to have so much interest in your love that you will at my request speake a word, especially when it shall be to the good of many & no hurt to your selfe. Only your word shall satisfie me. I am very glad to hear that you cam well to your iournies end ; your children they are all well. I pray God grant you all still the blessinge of healthe & all other good blessings. Thus with the remembrance of my love to your selfe & your second selfe, I cease to trouble you any further. *Vale in Christo.*

" Your loving mother,   " ANNE WINTHROP."

CHAPTER XII.

WE give up the greater part of this chapter to letters, some of which are of doubtful date, but all of which seem to belong to the period between September, 1626, and June, 1627. The first was addressed by Winthrop to his wife, when she had gone again to visit her old home in Essex County. The others passed between them while he was engaged in professional business in London, or on the circuit, leaving her to take care of the household at Groton Manor. They are all new letters, never before published, and which have probably remained undisturbed in the old family file since the death of their writers. They deal but little with either public or private affairs; but all the more do they illustrate that spirit of Christian love which is so beautiful an element in the characters of them both. The faithful and affectionate Margaret will not often appear to greater advantage than in one or two of these letters. It will be observed that we have interrupted the conjugal correspondence at one point, to introduce two letters written by Forth Winthrop to his father from the University of Cambridge. But we reserve the apology for that interruption until it occurs.

John Winthrop to his Wife.

" To my verye lovinge wife Mrs Winthrop at. Chemsye house in G^t Maplested,

    " MY SWEET WIFE, — The grace & blessing of the Lorde be wth thee ever, & wth us bothe, for the continuance & increase of o^r mutuall love in all truethe & holinesse; whereunto let us strive by prayer & stirringe up each other, that we may have full assurance of o^r beinge in Christ, by o^r livelynesse in Christianitye; that we may live that life of faithe, wch onely affords true peace, comfort, & contentatiō : & if by this meanes the world shall disclaime us as none of hirs, & shall refuse to hould out to us suche full breasts as she dothe to others, this shall not need to trouble us, but rather may give us matter of ioye in that beinge strangers heere, we may looke for o^r inheritance in a better life. I feared thou shouldst take could & therefore I have sent thee another garment. I knowe not certainely when I shall. come for thee, but as soone as conveniently I can : in the meane tyme, be sure, my heart is wth thee, & so I comende thee againe to the protection, blessinge & direction of o^r heavenly father, farewell —   " Thine &c :   " JOHN WINTHROP.

    " from SUDBURYE Sept : 26.

    " Remember my dutye & love to all as thou knowest I owe them."

Margaret Winthrop to her Husband.

    " To my very lovinge Husband John Winthrope Esquire, these &c.

    " MOST DEARE HUSBAND, — I did thinke to have ritten no more to you, hopeinge to see you shortly; and yet I am so much indebtted to you for your· lovinge and longe letters, that I must nedes rite a word or two to show my thankfulnesse and kind exceptance of them, allthoughe I can doe nothinge to equall them or to requit your love; and so I thinke I had better doe a littell then not at all, that I may shew my willingnesse to doe it thoughe I am ashamed I can doe no better. And now I shall longe for that happy hour when I shall see you

and injoy my sweet and deare husband; the Lord send us a
comfortable meetinge. I am sory the wether is so bad. I pray
be as carefull as you·can of takeinge colde. — I send up by John
a pece of plate, and a turkey for my brother Fones. I pray
remember my love to my brothers and sisters and my sonne
John, and thus with my dearest and best affections to my
beloved. husband, desireinge the Lord to send you a safe and
prosperous journey, I commit you to the protection of almyty
God who is onely able to keepe you.

" Your lovinge and obedient wife

"February 13.   " Margaret Winthrope.

" I pray if you doe not think this peece of plate which I have
sent up good enufe, that you would make choyce of a better
your selfe when you come home ; you shall have it with a very
good will."

Margaret Winthrop to her Husband.

" My most deare Husband, — I have no way to manifeast
my love to you but by these my unworthy lines, which I woulde
intreate you to except from hir that loveth you with an unfayned
hart. I shall now know what it is to want a loveing husban
that I may more prise and esteme of him when I have him ;
my mother is cominge to you aboute a weake or fortnight
hence and so I shall be depryved of you booth. I pray God
I may by fayth la holde on Christ Jesus and his benefites, that
he may be instead of husband and mother and all other frends
by the comfort of his holy Spirit. I prayse God we are all
heare in helth. Mr Ley is gone home and returneth no more
till thursday com senight. I pray remember my love to my
brothers and sisters and cosins ; my blessings to my sonne
John and my daughter Mary, thus with my best love to your
selfe, desiringe to be remembred in your prayers, I commit
you to the Lord and rest   Your Obedient Wife

" 10 Apurel.   " M. W.

" My mother remembreth hir love to you all. You shall
receve by the caryer your bedding and a cupple of capons."

John Winthrop to his Wife.

" To my very lovinge Wife M⁻ Winthrop iun. at Groton in Suffolk.

" MOST SWEET WIFE, — Thy kinde Lettre was sent to me this eveninge from London : how welcome it was to me I cannot expresse. I am sorye I am so streightened in tyme as I cañot write to thee as I would : God be blessed for his mercye towards thee & thine & all oʳ famylye, & oʳ selves also in oʳ iorneye & businesse, wᶜʰ hath hitherto had successe beyonde oʳ expectation : We must attende at the Court again to morrow, when I hope we shall knowe how things will goe. The Lo : in mercye be still wᵗʰ thee & all thine & sende us a comfortable meetinge. Remember my duty to my mother, my brother salutes thee etc : farewell mine owne sweet heart.

" Thy faithfull husband   " JOHN WINTHROP.

" From KINGSTON neere HAMPTON COURT this tuesdaye eveninge."

Margaret Winthrop to her Husband.

" MOST DEARE AND LOVINGE HUSBAND, — I receved your most kinde and comforttable letters and the things you sent, for wᶜʰ I hartyly thanke you. I prayse God for the continuanc of yᵒʳ helth and all the rest of our frends. I am glad to heare that my sonne Henrys voyage is like to be for his good. I pray God goe out with him and send him a safe returne that wee may have cause to blesse God for him. My good husban I thanke you for putinge me in minde to be chereful, and to put my trust in my good God who hath never fayled me in time of nede. I beseech him to continue. his mercy stil to me and grant that my sinnes may not provoke his anger against me : for he is a just God and will punnish offenders. The lord give me grace to make my peace with him in Jesus Christ our lord and onely Saviour, who siteth at the right hand of God a mediator for us. I did send Mr. Weny the little boxe uppon Wensday night, but he sayd it came to late ; he should have had it in the morning. I have not yet receved any monye to paye Gage but as soune as I have I will paye him ; Chot was with

me for monye and had a little; I knew not his want and
thought I had better let him have sume then drive him to steal
and offend God. My mother will come up the next weake if
the wether be any thinnge warme (or elce not) and bringe little
Luse and James;[1] she sayth that she shall use y^{or} horses, and
so my brother Jennye[2] can not have any; she sayth that John
shall nede goe no further then Witham, for ther she will meete
Ipswich·Coach. I pray tell my good sonne John that I thanke
him for my Booke and for my boyes tokens, and thus with my
mothers and my owne true love remembred to you all in the
best maner we can expresse, and so intreating you to be mindfull of me and myne in y^{or} prayers I commit you to the lord
our good God and rest

    " Your obedient wife allways   " MARGARET WINTHROPE.
" APURIL 17.

    " Heare was with me Thomas Axden[3] and brought a letter
from Forth wch I send you; he did aske me if you sayd nothinge
to me about his tutors quarterage and I told him I would right
to you about it; he came over to see Thomas Calewe and is
returned back againe. We are all heare in helth I prayse God,
my brother Goslinge and sister remember thear love to you all,
he cometh up with my mother."

Forth Winthrop seems to have written to his father
more particularly, soon afterwards, on the subject mentioned in his mother's postscript. The letter is still
extant, with a date which serves to fix that of his
mother's letter. But it is especially interesting from its
allusion to Hobson, the Cambridge carrier, whom Milton
has immortalized by two epitaphs, and whose name will
live longer in the proverb, " Hobson's choice," than even

---

1 These were undoubtedly the Downing children, who were then residing at Groton.
2 George Jenney of London married Mary Clopton, a sister of Winthrop's second
wife. — *Clopton Pedigree, from the British Museum.*
3 Thomas Archisden, who was Forth's chum at Cambridge.

in Milton's poetry. Hobson was now eighty-three years of age, and was within three years of the time when he sickened and died, because the prevalence of the plague had compelled him to suspend his weekly journeys to London. He had carried letters and parcels for all the wits of the University for more than sixty years; and was evidently a great favorite of Milton, with whom Forth Winthrop was contemporary at Cambridge, though of a different college. A letter which was actually carried up to London by old Hobson is certainly worth preserving and printing, — and here it is; and with it another, from the same pen and place, which shows how much safer it was to send by the good old carrier, of established name and fame, than by the unknown hand, which probably undertook to push him aside as super-annuated:[1] —

Forth Winthrop to his Father.

"MOST LOVINGE FATHER, — I received your letters by Sr Neuton & doe thanke you for yor good counsell & for yor kinde token; I delivered your token to my chamber-fellow,[2] whoe wth thanks retournes his servis: I had sent to you a fortnight agoe, but that my Tutor beinge at London I hoped he had spoken wth you consearninge o^r quarttridge. I spoke wth him about it, who saieth he sent you a bill of both o^r expenses; he tould me y^t we weare behinde wth him 3^{lb} 13^s, & now an other month is come in since, which maketh it up 4^{lb}. If you will send us money for him, you may safely deliver it to Hobson, the Cambridge carrier, by whom I send up now, markinge the letter for a mony letter:

---

[1] Professor Masson gives a most interesting account of Hobson in the fourth chapter of his Life of Milton.

[2] Doubtless the origin of *chum*.

" My tutor remembreth his love to you, whoe said he had thought to have come to Groton this Whitsontide, but his inexpected journey to London staid the other : My mother & grandmother are in helth frō whome I heard lately. Sᷓ Harcoote senior (for the iunior is in the Country) thanketh you for yoᷓ kind remembrance of him, & remembreth his service to you : Thus wᵗʰ my duty remembred to you, & my love to all my friends in generall, allwaies desiringe yoᷓ blessings & praiers for a blessinge on my studies, I humbly leave you & yoᷓ affaires to the blessinge of the Allmighty, & rest

" Yoᷓ Obedient Sonne   " FORTH WINTHROP.

" ffrom CAMBRIDGE·May 1. 1627.

" I would intreate you to send me downe some stuffe by the Carrier for a sute, for I have great neede of one : "

Forth Winthrop to his Father.

" MOST LOVINGE FATHER, — Havinge such an occasion as the cominge downe of Tho : Archisden my chamberfellow & Sᷓ Caly, I thought good, though in some hast, to wright to you by reason of the sooddan iourney of these 2 : I hope you are all in health as I am here (blessed be God Allmighty) whom I humbly beseech to assist me most graciously by his holy spirrit to run the waies of godlyness & to shun the venomous & contagious vices of these outragious times, wherein I once was intangled, but hope by the good spiritt of God to fly them more & more ; although by my selfe I am utterly unable, yet I will not cease to put up my humble petitions & praiers to him yᵗ is the keeper of Israell, & doe likewise desire yoᷓ praiers for the same : My Tutor sent downe a letter to you a while since by one Devurux who received it of Tho : Arkisden, I not knowinge of it ; now since this Devurux sent a note to Tho : Archisden that he had forgot the letter, & his owne letter, for belike he sent one to you : I would desire you to send word whether you have received them or noe : for that Devurux, as I heare say, doeth use to take in hand the cariage of letters & opens them & not delivereth them : I suppose you have heard of the news of o^r colledge businesse about the alteringe of a statute of the library, also y^t the Duke is about to make for the University; if not, these 2 : Sr Caly & Tho : Ark : can certify you of them :

"Thus wth my humble duty remembred to yo^rselfe & my mother, & love to the rest of my friends, allwaies desireing yor praiers & blessings, in haste I rest

"Yo^r dutifull & obedient Sonne   "F. Winthrop.

"I would desire you to send me the shoes for w^ch 'I wrote you : I have need of some clothes, for these are worne out : wherefore I would entreat you, sometime when you shall see fitt, to send me up some stuffe for to make me clothes, or otherwise as you shall see most convenient : "

We proceed now with the remaining letters between Winthrop and his wife belonging to this period.

Margaret Winthrop to her Husband.

"My deare Husband, — I received thy most kinde Letter and thanke thee for it. I wish thy imployments coulde suffer thee to come home, but I must wayt the time till I may enioy thee, though it cannot be without much want of thy beloved presence, which I desyre alwayes to have with me. I see it is the will of God that it shoulde be so, wch makes me beare it the more paciently, and not any want of love in my beloved Husband. And now my deare I have nothinge to right of to thee but my love which is all ready knowne to thee, and it ware needeles for me to make relation of that which thou art so wel assured. I will leave off this discorce for this time. I shalbe glad to heare of my daughter Mary, how hir mach goeth forwarde. Wee are all heare in reasonable good health I prayse God, wch is the best nuse I can right to thee of. I heare that Mr Apulton is dead that lived at S^r R C ; [1] he dyed

---

[1] John Appleton, about 1610, married Francis Crane, of Chilton, and resided at Chilton Hall, the seat of Sir Robert Crane. — *Appleton Memorial*, p. 57.

very suddaynely on Saterday being well over night : and thus with my best love to thyselfe, brother and sister Downinge, my sonne I & daughter M, I desyre the Lord to continue all your healthes and prosper all your affayres and send us a happy metinge. I \being sleppy, as you may see by my righting, bid my good Husban good night and commit him to the safe protection of almyty God and rest

" thy faythfull and obedient wife
" MARGARET WINTHROP.

" I am doutfull whether to send thy horsses this weeke or stay till I here from thee."

John Winthrop to his Wife.

" MY SWEET WIFE, — I hope it will please o^r good God now soone to fullfill o^r desires in comfortinge us in the wished enioyinge of each others presence, wch tyme the neerer it drawes the more it ioyes me to thinke of it : for such is my love to thee (my deare spouse) as were it not that my imployment (whereto Gods providence hath disposed me) did enforce me to it, I could not live comfortably from thee halfe thus longe : & I shall now hasten home so soone as my businesse will give me leave, therfore lett John be heer on Saturdaye, & I hope (God willinge) to be wth thee on teusdaye. I have nothinge to write to thee of, but that wch wilbe the moste wellcome newes to thee, y^t through Gods mercye I am in health, & all o^r friends heer, & I trust to heare of the like blessinge upon thee & all o^r familye. The Lorde make us more truely thankfull : & so wth my love & dutye to my good mother, hearty salutations to all o^r good freinds, Mr Leigh & his wife, brother Gostlin & sister, & all as thou knowest, wth my blessings to o^r children, I comende thee earnestly to the grace & blessinge of o^r heavenly father, so I kisse my sweet wife & rest alwayes

" Thy faithfull husband   " JOHN WINTHROP.

"From my chamber at the TEMPLE GATE, June 12, 1627."

Margaret Winthrop to her Husband.

"To my very lovinge Husband John Winthrope Esquire at Mr Downinge house in fleete strete neere the coundite these del^r.

"MY MOST KINDE & LOVINGE HUSBAND, — I did receve your most sweet Letter by my brother Goslinge, and doe prayse God for the continuance of your health, and the rest of our frends. I thanke the Lorde wee are also in health, and thinke longe for your coming home. My good husband y^or love to me doeth dayly give me cause of comfort, and doeth much increce my love to you, for love liveth by love. I ware worse then a brute beast if I should not love and be faythfull to thee, who hath deserved so well at my hands. I am ashamed and greved with my selfe that I have no thinge within or without worthy of thee, and yet it pleaseth thee to except of both and to rest contented. I had need to amend my life and pray to God for more grace that I may not deceve you of those good hopes which you have of me, — a sinfull woman, full of infirmyties, continually fayleinge of what I desire and what I ought to performe to the Lorde and thy selfe. I hope in God wee shall now shortly meet with comfort, for which I shall pray. — Your horse shal be at London upon Saterday and we shall see you I hope on tuesday. I will send you up by John that you did rite for, and if you thinke good you may change it for a nue one, but doe as you thinke best; if I have any thinge that may plesure you at any time you shall willingly have it, and if the carier doe call heere this weeke I will send my sister Downinge some puddings to make hir some part of amense, because hir share was so small in the last. My mother and my selfe and brother and sister Goslinge remember our love to you and all the rest of our frends; my brother Jenney remembers his love to you and woulde intreate you to deliver this letter heare inclosed; and thus with my love and best affections even with a love incresinge I take my leave and commit you to the Lord, who is alsoficient and able to preserve you from all danger and send you safe home. Your lovinge and obedient wife

"MARGARET WINTHROPE.

"I pray remember my blesinge and love to my sonne John."

John Winthrop to his Wife.

"MY MOST DEARE & SWEET SPOUSE, — I received thy kinde Lettre, the true Image of thy most lovinge heart, breathinge out the faithfull desires of thy sweet sowle, towards him that prizeth thee above all thinges in the world: & blessed be o^r good God & heavenly father, who of his rich mercye is pleased still to afforde us matter of ioy & thankfullnesse in the good newes of each others wellfare, & of those wch are neere & deare unto us: our onely care must be how to be answearable in o^r thankfullnesse & walkinge worthy his great mercies. We continue all in health, I prayse God: I had a Lettre wthin these 2 dayes from my sonne John who hath been out at sea in verye stormy weather, but is returned safe to Portsmouth: Heer is no newes; the Duke is gone to Portsmoth, & 2 or 3 Londoners comitted about the Loane. Thus hoping in God that we shall meet on teusdaye or Wensdaye next, I comende thee & all ours to the grace & blessings of the Lorde, & wth my duty to my good mother, & all o^r lovinge salutations to thy selfe, my blessings to o^r children, & salutations to all o^r friends, I kisse my sweet wife & rest

"Thine as his owne "J : W :

"LONDŌ June 15 1627."

In the last of these letters, it will be observed, Winthrop informs his wife that "his son John had been out at sea in very stormy weather, but had returned safe to Portsmouth;" whither, he adds, "the Duke is gone." We shall find an interesting explanation of this statement in the next chapter.

CHAPTER XIII.

THE YOUNGER JOHN WINTHROP'S NAVAL ADVENTURES. FAMILY
CORRESPONDENCE. — 1627–8.[1]

THE idea of an early marriage having been abandoned,
and the practice of the law not being altogether to his
taste, the younger Winthrop now turns his thoughts to
foreign travels and adventures. His father would seem
to have applied to one of his relatives, the Downings,
for advice and counsel on the subject; and the two
following letters from Joshua Downing (a cousin of
Emanuel), who evidently was much concerned with
either the mercantile or the military marine of England
at that period, furnish ample information as to what was
proposed and what was decided upon: —

Joshua Downing to John Winthrop.

" To my verie Worthie ffreind John Winthrop Esquyer — give theise,
London.

" GOOD S^R, — I received yor kinde & comfortable letters,
ffor wch I render yo^u hartie thanckes ; hoping that the lord will
enable me to a pacient waiting upon his will, & that he will,
in his good tyme, make all thinges to worke for the best for
me, according to his good pleasure. I shalbe right glad to
enioy yor company, wth my Cosins, at yor best leisure.

---

[1] All the letters in this long chapter, except six, are here printed for the first time.

" Concerning M^r. John Wenthrops inclinacion to the Sea, I
will use my best endeavours for hym; but I have no parte in
any shipping that goes ffor Turkie, & the marchants that are
owners, doe 'comonly place their owne servaunts for pursers;
but if he pleaseth to goe alonge in those shipps as a passinger
to see the Contries; the Chardges of his Dyett shall not be
great, & I will comitt hym to the care of them, that wilbe tender over hym, so shall he have more libertie for hymselfe, &
have all occasions to make the best observacions for his owne
good. But what if yo^u send him nowe out in this ffleet wth the
Duke; the lord Harvey is rear admyrall, & I thinck a well
disposed gentleman; The Captain under hym is Captain Best;
in whome I have some interest. If yo^u shall please to thinck
well of it, advize me speedily, & I will deale wth Captain Best
accordingly. Thus wth myne, & my wife's hartie love to yor
selfe, M^{ris} Wenthrop & yor mother, wth Mr. John, & all yo^{rs}, I
desier the benefite of yor prayers to God for us; & so comend
us to his fatherly proteccion, & rest ever

" Yo^r assured loving friend to Comaund,

" JOSUA DOWNYNG.

"CHATHAM DOCK. 24th Aprill, 1627."

Joshua Downing to John Winthrop.

" SIR, — I have not seen Captain Best since I received yor
letters (althoughe I have expected hym heere dayly;) neither
doe I suppose to see hym before his voyage, in regard that I
understand the shipps are to depart speedily into Tilburie hope;
— Therefore I have written a letter to hym, which I send you
unsealed, inclosed in this letter. When y^{ou} have perused it, if
y^{ou} shall please to make use of it, seale it upp, & send it by y^{or}
sonne. Otherwise keepe it at yor pleasure. If (in any thinge)
I can doe yo^u any kindness I will thinck myselfe happy in doinge
it. Thus wth my hartie love to y^{ou} & my Cosen Downyng wth
all yo^{rs}, I rest

" Yo^r assured faithfull frend   " JOSUA DOWNYNG.

"CHATHAM DOCK 4th May, 1627."

In accordance with the suggestion contained in the first of these letters, John Winthrop, jun., entered at once into the naval service of the kingdom, and joined the expedition, under the lead of the Duke of Buckingham, for the relief of the French Protestants at Rochelle. He seems to have acted as the secretary of Capt. Best, of the " Due Repulse," under the command of Rear-Admiral Lord Hervey. Among his papers is found the following original letter from Lord Hervey to his captain: —

Rear Admiral Lord Hervey to Captain Best.

"LONDON. Aprill, 15. 1627.

" CAPTAIN BEST, — this is to advertise you that the Duke hath bin at Chatham to see in what forwardness the ships are wch are to goe this Vyage, & finds that they wilbe all ready to take in ther victuals this weeke cominge, part at Rochester, the rest from London, wch is presently to be sent unto them ; — and our ship I hope wilbe none of the latermost : one thinge I find to be slakly cared for, and that is the Guñer wth his stores, — and it is caused by the change of the Guñer, he that is chosen beinge absent from the ship, thother that belonged to the ship neglectinge his affaires, by reason he is put by for the present. —

" I wish I might speake wth you concerning that matter, that order might be given in dew time — Otherwise our ship wilbe unprovided, when thothers wilbe to sett saile — The Master Cole came to London on Thursday last wth intent to have acquainted you wth all thinges there, but findinge you were out of Towne returned to Rochester again. When I shall speake wth you, I will acquaint you wth the particulars. The Duke makes all the hast that may be. This is all I have for the present, and therefore wth my kindest wishes unto you I leave remayninge

" Your assured Lovinge frend,   " W. HERVEY."

Here, too, are some instructions for the fleet, prepared for Capt. Skipworth, but probably communicated to all the other captains. They are found in the younger Winthrop's handwriting, and show that the "Due Repulse," with which he was associated, was one of the principal vessels of the fleet. They also give an example of discipline and vigilance which might well be followed in some of the expeditions of other lands and later days.

"Instructions for Captaine Skipworth by vertue of order receyved from Sr John Watts who is authorised thereunto from the Right Ho^{ble} the Duke of Buckingham, Lord High Admirall of England.

"1 That you attend his Ma^{ts} Ship the Due Repulse to goe to the Westward & there to spend such tyme as is & shalbe assigned to us by future Comands betweene the Isle of Wight & the Coast of France & at Convenient tymes to put into Stoak bay both to give intelligence of all occurrences & to receive further direction.

"2 And for better performance of o^r Duties I do recomend you these few provisions.

"3 That all the Day you birth yourselves as neere as you may South South east & North North West crosse the Chanell some five or six miles one from the other & so from the Repulse each ship to take his birth as it shall fall out keeping the Distance, And if any man shall discover a saile or sailes presently to give chase first setting once his maine top saile & Shoote of one peece & so the next to ster and then the rest if there shalbe Cause that so all may take knowledge, & in case of diverse Chases at once then each man to aply him selfe for the best as his advantage doth give leave, and upon the end & finishing of the businesse to make p^{r}sent repaire unto the Repulse to give an accompte of all past, That so my Lord Admirall from me may be informed according to my Instructions. And if any man take any ship and have lost the Repulse that then he direct himselfe and prise to Portsmouth or for the Downes to eyther as wind will best permitte, and presently upon his arrivall to eyther to advise my Lord Admirall.

"4 If it shall happen that any man loose Cōmpanie of the Repulse that then upon sight eyther of me or any of oʳ fleet then to hoise and strike twice, and all other ships to her to doe the like.

"5 The nights short and you understanding; small Instructions will suffice. At night to gather your selfes about the Repulse that so you may attend upon the light, and when the Dawning apeares about two of the Clocke to disperse yourselves according to these my Directions.

"And these for this our short imployment I take to be sufficient.

"If it shall happen that in giving of Chase I cast of oʳ long boate or any other of oʳ boats that then if you be neerest to her you take her up & when you may to bring her to us. *Vale.*"

The Duke of Buckingham sailed from Portsmouth on the 27th of June, 1627; probably after as many delays and postponements as proverbially attend great expeditions by sea and land, in all ages and climes. The elder Winthrop dated his parting letter to his son three weeks earlier. It was not of a character to spoil by keeping. It would serve as well for one going to fight the battles of his country to-day, as it did two hundred and thirty-five years ago. Nothing could be nobler in substance, or more exquisite in expression, than the counsel which it conveys.

" Only be careful," says the father, " to seek the Lord in the first place, and with all earnestness, as He who is only able to keep you in all perils, and to give you favor in the sight of those who may be instruments of your welfare; and account it a great point of wisdom to keep diligent watch over yourself, that you may neither be infected by the evil conversation of any that you may be forced to converse with, neither that your own speech or behavior be any just occasion to hurt or insnare you. Be not rash, upon ostentation of valor, to adventure yourself to unnecessary dangers; but, if you be lawfully called, let it appear that you hold your life for Him who gave it you, and will preserve it unto the farthest period of his own holy decree. For·you may be resolved, that, while you keep in your way, all the cannons or enemies in the world shall not be able to shorten your days one minute."

Winthrop could hardly have known much about Shakspeare's "Hamlet," though it was played and published about twenty years before this letter was written; but no one, who is familiar with that great tragedy, can fail to be reminded, by the passage just quoted, of the parting precepts of Polonius to the young Laertes: —

> " Give thy thoughts no tongue,
> Nor any unproportioned thought his act.
> .　.　.　.　.　Beware
> Of entrance to a quarrel; but, being in,
> Bear it that the opposer may beware of thee.
> Give every man thine ear, but few thy voice;
> Take each man's censure, but reserve thy judgment.
> .　.　.　.　.　.　.　.
> This above all, — to thine own self be true;
> And it must follow, as the night the day,
> Thou canst not then be false to any man."

A religious reader might, perhaps, give the preference

to Winthrop's prose over even the matchless blank-verse
of Shakspeare. But we must give the whole letter: —

John Winthrop to his Son.

" To my loving Son, John Winthrop, attending upon Capt. Best, in his
Majesty's Ship the Due Repulse, at Portsmouth.

" MY GOOD SON, — I received your letter from Gravesend,
and do bless God for your safe arrival there; but I heard not
from you since, which I impute to the sudden departure of your
captain out of the Downs upon the duke's coming thither. But
I hope to hear from you soon, for I long to understand how you
fare, and what entertainment you find with your captain, that
accordingly I may be stirred up to prayer for you, and to bless
God for his mercies towards you. I know not what further
advice to give you, than you have already received, and your
own observation, upon occasion, shall direct you. Only be
careful to seek the Lord in the first place, and with all earnestness, as he who is only able to keep you in all perils,
and to give you favor in the sight of those, who may be instruments of your welfare; and account it a great point of wisdom,
to keep diligent watch over yourself, that you may neither be
infected by the evil conversation of any, that you may be forced
to converse with, neither that your own speech or behavior be
any just occasion to hurt or ensnare you. Be not rash, upon
ostentation of valor, to adventure yourself to unnecessary dangers; but, if you be lawfully called, let it appear, that you
hold your life for Him, who gave it you, and will preserve it
unto the farthest period of his own holy decree. For you may
be resolved, that, while you keep in your way, all the cannons
or enemies in the world shall not be able to shorten your days
one minute. For my part, as a father, who desires your welfare as mine own, I cease not daily to commend you to God,
beseeching him to preserve, prosper, and bless you, that I may
receive you again in peace, and have assurance of enjoying you
in a better life, when your course here shall be finished. Your

friends here (I praise God) are all in health, and are daily
mindful of you. Let me hear from you so soon and oft as you
may conveniently. Remember my love and service to your good
captain. The Lord bless you ever. So I rest

      " Your loving father,   " JOHN WINTHROP.
" LONDON, June 6, 1627."

How well the younger Winthrop conformed himself to
the counsel of his father, in this expedition, we have no
means of knowing; but here is a letter of his, from the
very scene of conflict, which gives an interesting account
of what was going on. It has, unhappily, no date; but
another of his papers, of a merely formal character, shows
that he was in the Road of St. Martin's, where the letter
was evidently written, about the end of October, 1627.

     John Winthrop, Jr., to his father.

  " To the worp^ll John Winthrop Esq. at his house in Groton.

  " SIR, — My humble duty remembred to your selfe with my
mother & Grand mother, with the remembrance of my love to
my brothers, & sister, & the rest of my freinds. I wrote unto
you the last opportunity which I found by two severall messen-
gers, whether they came to your hands I know not : but yet I
dought not but you have had so full Intelligence of our proceedings till y^t tyme that it should be needlesse to write any thing
thereof : As touching our affaires now you shall understand
now thereof : Our army lieth still the most part at St. Martins ;
Some few garrisons in other parts of the Iland. The Cittadel is
now Intrenched round. Our trenches come in some places
within a stones quoite of the enemies, the centinels on both sides
continually playing with their small shotte, watching as narrowly as the fouler after a bird how they may come at a shotte,
the great Ordinance on both sides shoote not so often as they
did at first : every day there come some running out of the

Castle who bring divers & uncerteine reports what they thinke
of the tyme it can hold out, but it is thought they had yielded
it up by this tyme had it not beene for 3 or 4 boats which in a
darke & foule night stole over undiscovered of the ships, but tis
thought they could not furnish them with much victuals, & if
that be spent there is such order taken that they shall very
hardly get any more, for besides the ships which lie there close
together, & our boats scouting out all night, they have made
a boome with masts chained together which lieth crosse that
place where they should go in, so that they must needs be foule
eyther of the ships or that. Those boats which gatt over were
garded by two Dutchmen who riding among our ships had taken
notice of the order of our fleet & the likeliest place they might
come by them without discovery; they are now taken and to be
executed. We tooke the other night two boats which were
going to the Castle with victualls, some other there were which
escaped backe againe. We have now arrived 2400 soldiers out
of Irland & doe expect a supplye of ships & men out of England. When they be come I hope we shall not stay here long
after. I thinke soone after Michaelmas we shall be at home.
The King of France hath had an army about Rochell ever since
our coming, they are reported to be 12000 men, but the towne
and they were upon good tearmes till the 30th of August, & then
they began to fall out with some store of great shott on both
sides, but they feare not the kings forces so long as our fleet
keepe the sea open to them. When I had well veiwed the
towne I marveiled not that it holds out so long seige, for I think
it almost Impossible to take it by force if they be not shutt up
at sea as well as by land. It is a very deare place for strangers, & St. Martins is dearer by reason of our army, and that
all we have brought in commeth from Rochell. I am (I thanke
God) hitherto in good helth and our ship hath bene generally
helthfull: thus my duty againe remembered, & desiring your
dayly prayer & blessings I comend you to Gods protection and
rest   "Your obedient sonne

                                              "JOHN WINTHROP.

" I pray remember my love to my uncle Gostlin & aunt with Mr Lee & the rest of our freinds." [1]

An original account of this Expedition by Lord Herbert of Cherbury has recently been published in England, edited by Lord Powis, and dedicated to the Philobiblon Society, in which it is said that the Duke of Buckingham had " a navy of an hundred sayle, whereof tenn were royal, the rest merchants' ships." [2] But we need hardly remind our readers that it proved a disastrous failure, and was completely broken up before the year was at an end.

The elder Winthrop had doubtless gone down to London to attend upon the courts, and pursue his professional practice, in November, 1627, when the two following letters from his wife were written. She had given birth to another son a few months before ; and we find the child alluded to by name in the first of the letters. How prettily and piously she tells her husband, in the second, " I have many reasons to make me love thee, whereof I will name two : First, because thou lovest God ; and, secondly, because that thou lovest me " ! We find no letters from her husband which seem to correspond to this precise date.

---

1 This little certificate, in the hand of John Winthrop, jun., is only important as fixing the date of the foregoing letter : —

" To the Right Wor^ll Sr Sackfeild Crow Treasurer.

"Whereas Robert Atkins was removed out of the Seahorse into his Maj^ie Shippe the Repulse at Portsmouth June 26. 1627 these are therefore to Certify that the s^d Robert Atkins continued in the s^d Shippe of his Ma^ie in the Roade of St Martins till the 26 day of October the yeare aboue written and then falling sicke was discharged.

                                                                         " J. Best.

"The Road of St. Martins Octob: 27. 1627."

2 The Expedition to the Isle of Rhé, by Edward Lord Herbert of Cherbury, K.B. London, Whittingham and Wilkins, 1860.

Margaret Winthrop to her husband.

" MOST DEAR AND LOVING HUSBAND, — I cannot express my love to you, as I desire, in these poor, lifeless lines ; but I do heartily wish you did see my heart, how true and faithful it is to you, and how much I do desire to be always with you, to enjoy the sweet comfort of your presence, and those helps from you in spiritual and temporal duties, which I am so unfit to perform without you. It makes me to see the want of you, and wish myself with you. But I desire we may be guided by God in all our ways, who is able to direct us for the best ; and so I will wait upon him with patience, who is all-sufficient for me. I shall not need to write much to you at this time. My brother Gostling can tell you any thing by word of mouth, I praise God, we are all here in health, as you left us, and are glad to hear the same of you and all the rest of our friends at London. My mother and myself remember our best love to you, and all the rest. Our children remember their duty to you. And thus, desiring to be remembered in your prayers, I bid my good husband good night. Little Samuel [1] thinks it is time for me to go to bed ; and so I beseech the Lord to keep you in safety, and us all here. Farewell, my sweet husband.

" Your obedient wife,   " MARGARET WINTHROP."

Margaret Winthrop to her husband.

" MY MOST SWEET HUSBAND, — How dearly welcome thy kind letter was to me, I am not able to express. The sweetness of it did much refresh me. What can be more pleasing to a wife, than to hear of the welfare of her best beloved, and how he is pleased with her poor endeavors ! I blush to hear myself commended, knowing my own wants. But it is your love that conceives the best, and makes all things seem better than they are. I wish that I may be always pleasing to thee, and that

---

[1] Samuel was baptized Aug. 26, 1627.

those comforts we have in each other may be daily increased, as far as they be pleasing to God. I will use that speech to thee, that Abigail did to David, I will be a servant to wash the feet of my lord. I will do any service wherein I may please my good husband. I confess I cannot do enough for thee ; but thou art pleased to accept the will for the deed, and rest contented.

" I have many reasons to make me love thee, whereof I will name two : First, because thou lovest God ; and, secondly, because that thou lovest me. If these two were wanting, all the rest would be eclipsed. But I must leave this discourse, and go about my household affairs. I am a bad housewife to be so long from them ; but I must needs borrow a little time to talk with thee, my sweet heart. The term is more than half done. I hope thy business draws to an end. It will be but two or three weeks before I see thee, though they be long ones. God will bring us together in his good time ; for which time I shall pray. I thank the Lord, we are all in health. We are very glad to hear so good news of our son Henry.[1] The Lord make us thankful for all his mercies to us and ours. And thus, with my mother's and my own best love to yourself and all the rest, I shall leave scribbling. The weather being cold, makes me make haste. Farewell, my good husband : the Lord keep thee. " Your obedient wife, MARGARET WINTHROP.

" GROTON, November 22.

" I have not yet received the box ; but I will send for it. I send up a turkey and some cheese. I pray send my son Forth such a knife as mine is. Mrs. Hugen would pray you to buy a cake for the boys.

" I did dine at Groton Hall yesterday ; they are in health, and remember their love. We did wish you there, but that would not bring you, and I could not be merry without thee.

---

[1] The first and best news from Henry, who had sailed for the West Indies, came in a letter from him, dated " from the Berbethes in the West Indyes, this 22 of August, 1627."

Mr. Lee and his wife were there; they remember their love. Our neighbor Cole and goodman Newton have been sick, but somewhat amended again. I fear thy cheese will not prove so good as thou didst expect. I have sent it all, for we could not cut it."

The younger Winthrop was again in London not long after his return from the Isle of Rhé; and then we find four more of his father's letters addressed to him. They show, that, at this date, the father was proposing to remove to London, for the more convenient practice of his profession; and one of them contains directions for the commencement of a suit in which he was engaged as counsel. The minute directions contained in the second letter of the series, for procuring a supply of *tobacco*, seem to prove that some of the Puritan families did not wait until they came over to the New World before yielding to the fascinations of the Virginia weed. A decided taste for it must certainly have prevailed at Groton Manor. It will be seen, however (in another chapter), that Winthrop renounced the use of it not long afterwards, at least for a time. The fourth letter indicates that the younger Winthrop was contemplating a voyage with " a religious company," and with some view of settling in a new plantation. This was undoubtedly a voyage to New England; and John Winthrop, jun., was contemplating the idea of embarking with Endicott, who sailed for New England in the " Abigail," on the twentieth day of June, 1628. The elder Winthrop " was loath," it seems, that his son " should think of settling there as yet; " but he suggests that it is best " to be going and coming awhile, and afterward to do as God shall offer occasion." Evidently, the idea that New England was to be the permanent abode of himself and his family had not dawned upon him.

John Winthrop to his Son.

" To my lovinge sonne John Winthrop at the three fawnes in the Olde Baylye, London.

" SONNE JOHN, — I prayse God we came home well on thursdaye at night & this daye I was at the Choyce of o^r knights at Ipswich ; what o^r successe was you may knowe by my lettre to either of yor unckles, as likewise for other affaires. I purpose now to send you up the rest of the writings, wch Mr. ffeatherston may make use of, as he shall think fitt : I would be lothe to come up before the terme except there be necessitye : yet I thincke to be there about a weeke before, because my horse must be at Houndsloe heathe the 23 of Aprill, & likewise to take order about my removall, wch I am now (in a mañer) resolved of, if God shall dispose for us accordingly : for my charge heere grows verye heavye, & I am wearye of these io^rnies to & fro, so as I will either remove or putt off my office. I would have you enquire about for a house at Tower hill or some suche open place, or if I cant be provided so neere, I will make tryall of Thistleworthe : I would be neere churche & some good schoole. If you can finde how to sende to yor brother Hen : let me knowe that I may provide shoes &c : for him, & for other things I will leave them to yor care. We are all in good healthe (I prayse God). Deane hathe had the smale poxe, but laye not by it, & Sam : was verye sick & in great danger, but God hathe delivered him. Yo^r grandmother & mother salute & blesse you : the Lorde blesse, guide, & prosper you in all yor wayes, that you may feare him & cleave to him, & so consecrate yor life & youthe to his service, as yor life may be of use for his glorye & the good of others.   farewell.

" Yo^r lovinge father   " Jo : WINTHROP.

" Remember me verye kindly to Capt. Best & his wife, to Capt. Downinge & the rest of that familye (when you see them.)   Com̄ende me to M^r. ffeatherston & desire him to prepare his assurance by a weeke before the terme, if he thinke good, & if yor host shall require it ; otherwise at the beginninge of the terme.

"Looke out amonge the booksellers in Duck lane, & if you can finde an English bible in 4to for 7 or 8^s : buye it & sende it downe ; & remember the stockfishe.

"FEB : 25. 1627."

John Winthrop to his Son.

"To my loving Son, John Winthrop, at the House of Mr. Downing, near the Conduit, in Fleet Street, London.

"LOVING SON, — I received your letter, and I bless God for your welfare, begging of him daily, that your soul may prosper as your body doth ; and if this care be in your heart, (as I hope it is,) you shall do well, for this rule God hath set us to walk by, — first to seek the kingdom of heaven, then will he see to us for other things. So as I dare avouch it as infallible truth, that he who doth otherwise takes a preposterous course to happiness, and shall not prosper. Should not a man trust his Maker, and rest upon the counsel of his Father, before all other things ? Should not the promise of the holy Lord, the God of truth, be believed above all carnal, false fears and shallow ways of human wisdom ? It is just with God to harden men's hearts in their distrust of his faithfulness, because they dare not rely upon him. But such as will roll their ways upon the Lord, do find him always as good as his word. I bless his name, we all continue in health, and this day I expect your brother from Cambridge. I wish you could meet with some safe means to send to your brother Henry. I have found two sturdy youths, that would go to him. If Capt. Powell return not soon, I shall fear he hath miscarried, and then shall we see God's providence, that your brother returned not with him.

"I cannot come up till the week after Easter ; but you may know Mr. Featherstone's resolution in the mean time. I pray, inquire how things go in the parliament, and write to me of

them ; but things which are doubtful, let pass. If the commission for the navy be dissolved, what employment hath your captain then? for it seems he was lately put into it. When you
see him or her, commend me kindly to them.

" We want a little tobacco. I had very good, for seven shillings a pound, at a grocer's, by Holburn Bridge. There be two
shops together. It was at that which is farthest from the bridge,
towards the Conduit. If you tell him, it is for him that bought
half a pound of Verina and a pound of Virginia of him last
term, he will use you well. Send me half a pound of Virginia. I
would gladly hear of a chamber in the Temple, or in some other
convenient place ; for that I have is much too dear.

" I have many letters to write : therefore I end ; and, with
my love and blessing to you, I commend you to the protection
and good government of the Lord, and rest

" Your loving father,   " Jo. Winthrop.
"March 18, 1627.

" I think to send my brother Downing a greyhound."

John Winthrop to his Son.

" To my very loving Son, John Winthrop, London.

" Son John,—I received your letter and the books you sent,
for which I do thank you. I bless God for the continuance of
your health and welfare, which, through his mercy, we all here
also enjoy ; only myself have a sore hand, which makes me that
I cannot write.[1] For the note, which you mentioned in your
letter, I received it not. I desire to hear from you concerning
Mr. Featherstone's resolution, and whether you have inquired
out a chamber for me, or else to take order, that I may have
that I had before. I pray send me down six of Mr. Egerton's
cattle. For the stuff for the gowns, you may buy it of some
olive color, or such like. Either let there be several colors,
or else the velvet for the capes of several colors. Remember us
all to your uncles and aunts and the rest of our friends. Pray

---

[1] This letter is in the handwriting of Forth Winthrop.

your uncle Downing to send me an answer of my last week's letter, and thank your aunt Downing for her kind letter and oranges, and excuse my not writing to them all, for my hand is so as I am not able. Your grandmother and mother salute and bless you. So, with my love and blessing to you, I commend you to the protection, direction, and good providence of our heavenly Father, and rest

"Your loving father,   " JOHN WINTHROP.

"MARCH 31, 1628."[1]

John Winthrop to his Son.

" To his loving Son, Mr. John Winthrop, at Mr. Fones's House in the Old Bailey, London.

" SON JOHN, — I received your letter, with the things you sent. I do praise God for the continuance of your health and welfare. For myself, my hand is so ill as I know not when I shall be able to travel. It hath pleased God to make it a sharp affliction to me. I hope he will dispose it for my good, and, in his due time, send me deliverance. For your journey intended, seeing you have a resolution to go to sea, I know not where you should go with such religious company, and under such hope of blessing; only I am loath you should think of settling there as yet, but to be going and coming awhile and afterward to do as God shall offer occasion. You may adventure somewhat in the plantation at the present, and hereafter more, as God shall give enlargement. If Mr. Featherstone will not deal, I will look no further; but your uncle Fones shall have it, and the odd £50 may be for your occasions. Commend me heartily to all your uncles and aunts. Desire them to be mindful of me in their prayers. Thank your aunt Downing for her kind letter. Tell her I see she now means to work upon the advantage in setting me upon the score for letters when I want my hand to free myself. Put your uncle

---

[1] It will be remembered, that, according to Old Style, March 31, 1628, would be only thirteen days after March 18, 1627, — the date of the preceding letter.

Downing in mind again of my chamber, and tell him, that this day my brother Gostling and another shall go about the business he did write of. Tell him also, that Peter Alston is dead. Commend me to Edward, and desire him to get me out a privy seal against John Carver, clerk, and Eliza his wife, at the suit of Mr. Attorney, on the behalf of Thomas Foule. In the business concerning your voyage, I pray be advised by your uncle and other your worthy friends, who are experienced in these affairs; but, above all, seek direction and blessing from God. And so, being forced to use another's pen,[1] so as I am not at that freedom to write as I would, I end; and, with your grandmother's and mother's salutation and blessing unto you, I commend you to the gracious providence, direction, and rich blessing of the Almighty. Farewell.

" Your loving father, " JOHN WINTHROP.
"APRIL 7, 1628.

" As soon as I am able to stir about the house, I will look out those geometrical instruments and books,[2] and send them unto you, and any thing else that you will write for."

Winthrop's allusion to Thisleworth, in the first of the four letters just given (dated Feb. 25, 1627), proves that the following letter of his wife, in which she discusses the proposed removal, belongs to the history of that winter. Thistleworth, now well known as Isleworth, is a parish in Middlesex County, on the Thames, nearly opposite to Richmond. Margaret's grave apprehensions, that, if her husband resided there while engaged in professional business in London, the passage down the river might be dangerous and " the waters perilous," are a little

---

1 This letter, also, is in the handwriting of Forth Winthrop.
2 A copy of the Conic Sections of Apollonius Pergæus, the Great Geometer (Venice, 1537), which belonged to John Winthrop, jun., is in my possession, containing his autograph annotations.

amusing in these days. There was cause enough for them, we doubt not, when her letter was written.

Margaret Winthrop to her Husband.

" To my deare and very lovinge Husband John Winthrope Esquire at Mr. Downings house in Fleet Street right over agaynst the Counduit these deliver — London.

" MY BELOVED AND GOOD HUSBAND, — I must craue pardon for my not righting to you the last weeke. Your letter came so late to my hands upon Tuesday that I coulde not right that night, and hearinge of no other mesenger I have bin constrayned to let it alone till this weeke, and so have had the more time to consider of it. I doe ioyne with you in beseechinge the Lorde to direct our wayes and thoughts aright hearein, and that wee may submit unto his holy will in this and all other thinges, to doe that may be for his glory and the comfort of ourselues and others. I doe see yours and the rest of my frends great love and care of me and of all ours, in that you are so mindfull of our good, wch doeth more and more knet my affections to you. I pray God I may walke so as I may be worthy of all your loves. For the matter of which you right about, of takeinge a house at Thiselworth, I like well in some respect, in regard of the good Minister and good people and teachinge for our children. But I must aledge one thinge, that I feare in your cominge to and fro, lest if you should be ventrus upon the water, if your passage be by water wch I know not, it may be dangerous for you in the winter time, the wether beinge colde and the waters perilous. And so I shoulde be in continuall feare of you lest you should take any hurt. I did confir with my mother about it and she thinkes you had better take a house in the City, and so come home to your own table and familye ; and I am of the same minde, but I shall allwayes submit to what you shal thinke fit. Upon the best consideration I can take, I have resolved to stay heare this winter, in regard that my littel one is very yonge and the wayes very bad to remove such things as wee shall stande in nede of, and we shal leave things very unsetled, and to keepe two famylies will be ƚery chargable to us. And so I thinke it will be our best corce to remove in the springe, and in the meane time commend it to God. It is allredy reported about the countrye that we shal remove and so it will be the lesse strange to them, because they loke for it all ready, and you are to be so much from home.

"I have received y^{or} kinde letter by my brother Goslinge for wch I hartily thanke you and for my good sermon wch you sent with it. You doe dayly manyfeast y^{or} love to me and care for my spirituall good, as well as temperall, wch is best of all. I desire of God I may chuse the better part wch cannot be taken from me, wch will stand me in stead when all other things fayle me. For our condishion here wee have yet Mr Leys helpe in our famylye, but he is to remove very spedily, his house beinge all-most finished, and then we shall want helpe for good exercises. The Lord in mercy upholde us and strenkthen us by his holy spirit. I cannot but with greefe beare y^{or} longe abcence, but I hope that this will be the last time we shall be so long asunder, wch doeth sumwhat stay and comfort me. The Lord grant I may find sweetnesse in Christ Jesus my spirituall Husband, who is alwayes with me and never fayleth me in time of neede, nor will fayle me unto the end of my life or the life to come. My good mother commends hir love to you all and thankes you for hir tobacko. She would pray you to be carefull of y^{or} selfe that you take no colde. I desire to have my love very kindely remembred to my brother Downinge and sister, my brother Foones and sister, and all my cosins. I prayse God we continue stil in helth : our children at home remember thear duty to you. I thinke very longe to heare of our sonnes at sea. I pray God send us good nuse of them. And thus with my best affection remembred to my deare Husband I take my leave and commit you to God.

"Your faythfull and obedient wife

"MARGARET WINTHROPE.

"I have sent you a payr of shoes. My mother would know if she should send up a cupple of geese; thay be resonable good ones. I sent the letter to Mr. Weneiye, but he was not at home. There came one for money for Thomas Arkesden. Grandmother and I payed it. I have payed Sug. and Peyer Haksel, my brother Foones tenant, hath payed 25ˢ and woulde know who shoulde apoynt him out his logs to burne this winter, and he sayth that you have a bil of charges that he layed out; he woulde pray you to put my brother in minde of it. My brother Goslinge will send up the money as soone as he doth heare of a safe mesenger."

The elder Winthrop, in his two last given letters, refers to a serious injury which had happened to one of his hands. His devoted son seems to have sought at once for some prescription to relieve him; and the following letter will tell with what success. It seems that "old women's nostrums" were not unknown to London in those days. His father replies by writing a long letter with his *left hand;* and we will do him the justice to say, that it is quite as legible as many of those written with his right. The son rejoins in a letter containing many interesting items of political information; and then we are able to conclude the series with one of Margaret's sweet letters, in which she tells him most tenderly, "I will not looke for any long letters this terme, because I pitty yᵒʳ poore hande: if I had it heere I would make more of it than ever I did, & bynde it up very softly for fear of hurting it." No doubt this would have been the most welcome surgery he could have enjoyed.

John Winthrop, jun., to his Father.

" To the wor" his very loving father John Winthrop Esq. — in Groton.

" SIR, — My duty remembered unto you, I am very sorry to heare that your hand continueth so ill, but I hope, by God's providence, you shall finde helpe by those thinges I have sent you, which I receyved from a woman that is very skilfull, & much sought unto for these thinges.   She is sister to Mr. Waterhouse the linnen draper in Cheape side, by whose meanes, I was brought to her. She told me, if you were at London she made noe doubt but to cure it quicly, but because you cannot come up she therefore gave me these plaisters to send to you, & said that if it were not gangreened she would warrant them by Gods helpe to doe you present good.   The use of them is as followeth : Take the yellow plaister, as much as will cover your sore finger all over to the next joynt below the sore, & on the rest of your finger whereon this plaister doth not lye, lay as much of the blacke plaister as will cover it all over, this must be done twice a day, morning & evening, till it beginneth to grow well, & then once a day.   The other blacke plaister you must lay all over your hand, & that you must shift once in 2 or 3 dayes. You must not wash it, nor lay any other thing to it.   This will draw out the thorne, if any be in, & heale it both.   She will take nothing for it, & therefore I doe the rather credit hir, for she doth it only for freinds, &c.   I pray you therefore use it, & leave of any other course of surgery.   I wish you were here at London where she might dresse it her selfe.   For newes I cannot write so good as the last ; this bearer will fully satisfye you of all proceedings, which every day alter & change, sometime like to be good, by & by crosse againe.

" For my voyage to new England I doe not resolve (especially following my uncle Downings advice) except I misse of the Straights, but I will stay till you have sold the land though I misse of both : thus with my duty remembered againe to your selfe, with my grandmother & mother, & my love to my brothers & sisters & the rest of our freinds, I commend you to Gods protection & rest

   " Your Obedient Son   " JOHN WINTHROP.

" LONDON: April 11 1628.

" My uncle ffones hath paid 10^{lb} to my aunt Branch,[1] he wondered he had no order from you.

" We are all well (God be thanked) they all commend their love to you. You need not send the Instruments."

John Winthrop to his Son.

" MY GOOD SONNE, — As I have alwayes observed your lovinge & dutyfull respects towards me, so must I needs allso now, in that sence which you have of my affliction, & that care & paynes you have taken to procure my ease; wch besides the confirminge of my fatherly affection towards you, wilbe layd by in store wth the righteous Lorde, for length of dayes & blessings upon you in tyme to come. I prayse God my finger is well amended, my Surgeon did his parte well, & stayde the gangreene & tooke out the mortified fleshe, but because your love & peines should not be loste, I have betaken my selfe wholly to your plaister, wch the Surgeon likes well enough of; & I prayse God it goeth well forward. I hope, if God will, to be at London wthin this fortnight. I pray make sure of some Chamber for me, & if you can, gett M^r ffeatherstons resolution, for I will make no new bargaines wth him; if he refuse, speake with your uncle ffones about it, & if he will deale with it, let the writinges be gotten readye ag^t I come up, that you may gett readye for yor voyage, which yet you shall not need to lose for any stay about this. I am verye glad that your Capt. hath recovered his hand, when you see him commend me kindly to him & to Mrs. Best & likewise to Doctor

---

[1] This is one of the payments to which the elder Winthrop referred when he spoke of " 10^{lb} for my A. B.," and which has formed the subject of a footnote on page 213. We know not who this Aunt Branch was.

Burgesse & his sonne. My yellow plaister wilbe spent this week, but of the blacke I have more than I shall use. My naile is almost shotte of, I feare; the short bone under my nayle is putrified, but my finger will not be the shorter for the losse of that bone. We are all in good health I prayse God, your grandmother & mother salute & blesse you. I wish you would finde out Sir Nath: Barnardiston, & remember my service to him, & tell him though I could not write to him, I have sent to know how he doth & his Ladye. Thus beseeching our heavenly Father throughe our Lord Jesus Christ to blesse, guide, & prosper you in all yor wayes, & so to reveale to your soule the glorious riches of Christ & the sweet pleasures of his grace, as being filled & satisfied therewith you may desire no other happinesse, I ende & rest allwayes

" Yo^r lovinge father   " Jo : WINTHROP.
" APRILL 15 1628.

" (This was written with his left hand when his finger of his other hand was sore as mentioned in the letter).[1]

" This trouble of my hand hath so hindered me in the disposinge of my affaires as I must be forced to come downe next vacation, so as it wilbe midsomer ère your mother, etc. can come up."

John Winthrop, jun., to his Father.

" To the wor^{ll} his very loving father John Winthrop Esq. in Groton.

" SIR, — I receyved your letters, my selfe & all our freinds heere much rejoycing to hear from you so good newes of your hand, whereof your former letters put us in noe small feare. I have sent you some more plaisters. I told the gentlewoman of the bone which you feared was putrified; she saith that her plaister will draw it out, if it be, & heale it both without any other thing. I hope you wilbe at London before you shall need any more. The gentleman that my uncle dealt with about the Chamber is not yet come to towne, but I have

---

[1] The passage in parenthesis is in the hand of John Winthrop, jun.

inquired where your former Chamber was; it is already lett out, but you may have a lessei in the same house & cheap. My uncle Downing & aunt commend them to you; he came home late last night from Nelmes, & went this morning to the M^r & therefore desireth to be excused for not wrighting, but sends you this newes — that Mr. Noy hath lately had a triall in the West Countrie at the Assises against the Constables for Cessing of his tenants for the billeting of soldiers, (who for that refused to pay their rents complaining that by reason of those taxes they were not able), & hath recovered against the Constables. My aunt sayth she would write but that she pitieth you that you should write so many letters with your left hand, therefore she will not this weeke provoke you to it by hers. On Munday last the lower house made a speech to the King in the Banquetting house and spake very freely to him about the greivances of the subject. This day & tomorrow are daies of great expectation what conclusion wilbe betweene them, which is hoped to bee well & that there wilbe good agreement, which God in mercy grant. Thus with my duty remembered to your selfe, my mother & grand mother, with my love to my brothers and sister, & the rest of our freinds, I commend you to Gods protection & rest

"Your Obedient Sonne   "JOHN WINTHROP.

"LOND: Aprill 18: 1628.

" My uncle Fones & aunt commend them to you.
" I pray remember my love to my uncle Gostlin & aunt &c.
" The privy seale is in the box &c."

Margaret Winthrop to her Husband.

"LOVINGE AND MOST DEARE HUSBAND, — Now in this solytary and uncomfortable time of your longe absence, I have no other meanes to shew my love but in theese poore fruts of my pen, with wch I am not able to expresse my love as I desire, but I shall endeavor allwaies to make my duty knowne to you in some measure though not answearable to your deserts and

love. Although it pleseth God to part us for a time, I hope he will bringe us together againe and so provide that we may not be often asunder, if it may be for our good and his glory; and now I thinke longe to heare of thee and of your safe cominge to London. I will not looke for any longe letters this terme because I pitty y^{or} poore hande; if I had it heere I would make more of it than ever I did, and bynde it up very softly for fear of hurting it. But I doubt not but you have better helps. I thanke God we are all heare in health, onely little Sam, who hath bin very sick, but I hope he will doe well againne. I am glad I did not weane him for he will now take nothing but the brest. Thus it pleaseth the Lord to exercise us with one affliction after another in love; lest we should forget our selves and love this world too much, and not set our affections on heaven wheare all true happyness is for ever. I thinke to right to thee the latter end of this weeke by Mr Brand, and so I will now rite the lesse. I receved a letter from my sonne John, I pray tel him I thanke him hartyly for it and will take some other time to rite to him though I cannot now. Joseph Cole is come home, & thus with my mothers and my owne best love to you and the rest of our frends, I commit you to the Lord and rest
  " Your Obedient Wife   " MARGARET WINTHROP.
" MAY 1, 1628.

  " I did receave a speach of Sr John Elliott wch I thinke Mr Borros sent you, so I have not sent it up, thinkinge you may meet with the same at London. Forth and Mary and the rest of our children remember theare duty to you, and theare love to theare brother John and all thear cosins."

  This last letter was, of course, addressed to the elder Winthrop, at London; whither he had gone again to attend the Easter Term of Court. The speech of Sir John Eliot, alluded to in the postscript, was undoubtedly one of those fearless utterances against the tyrannical measures of the Crown, on account of which he had already suffered confinement in the Gatehouse, and which not long afterwards cost that noble patriot an imprisonment in the Tower, from which he was released only by death.

An additional illustration of Winthrop's character and habits, at the period included in the chapter which we now close, is furnished by a little autograph volume, found among his papers, in which all the sermons which he heard on Sundays and on prayer-days, during a large part of the years 1627 and 1628, are noted, with the names of the preachers, the texts of their discourses, and the various heads and arguments carefully written out. These notes are often so copious, that it would not be difficult to write out whole sermons, of at least the ordinary length of modern times, from the briefs which this little volume supplies.

CHAPTER XIV.

THE ORIENTAL TOUR OF JOHN WINTHROP, JUN. CORRESPOND-
ENCE BETWEEN HIM AND HIS FATHER, 1628-9.

THE younger Winthrop, having abandoned the idea of
accompanying Endicott to New England, appears to
have departed soon afterwards on an extended European
and Oriental tour. He was absent from England for
more than fourteen months. Three of them he spent
at Constantinople, and at least two at Venice and Padua.
There were but few facilities for land travel in those
days; and his visits seem to have been confined, for the
most part, to places which could be reached by water.
He took passage on board the ship "London," Capt.
Maplesden, which sailed on the 17th or 18th of June,
1628. We hear of him first at Leghorn, in the following letter to his father; to which we append the father's
reply: —

John Winthrop, jun., to his Father.

" To the worp¹¹ John Winthrop Esq. at Groton in Suffolke.

"LIGORNE, July 14: 1628,

" SIR, — I am forced for the more convenient passage of my
letters in a merchants paquet to be more breife then otherwise
I should, but I hope hereby they will come to your hands safe

& with more speed; which, if they were by them selves, would lye long before they could come to you. You shall hereby understand, that we arrived safely (God be thanked for it) at this port the 7 of this month, being but 20 daies since we left sight of the lands end of England and 26 since our departure out of the Downes. We had (I thanke God) both health & faire weather all the way, and are now arrived in a very plesant & temperate Countrie. We spake not with any ships since we lost sight of England save only one English man of Warr upon the coast of Spaine: once we mette 25 saile, but they sprung their luffe & would not speake with us. This place affordeth little newes, at this tyme; from Genoa there is newes that there is free trade granted as is at this towne, & from Marseiles that the Duke de Guise is come to sea with 4 gallioones & 12 sailes of gallies, it is supposed to meete with Sir Chillam Digby,[1] who hath taken 3 or 4 frenchmen, hath beene at Algiers, & redeemed some 20 or 30 Christian slaves, hath man'd his prizes, & is gone againe towards the bottom. The newes of this towne is only of some 200 turkes that the Dukes Gallies have taken and are now heere making ready to set forth againe. Heere is an order from the Duke that no prizes shalbe brought into this port. I find this place very chargeable, & could wish I had brought no English mony with me, for it is foure shillings in the pound losse. Thus with my duty remembred to your selfe, my mother & grandmother, with my love to my brothers & sister, my uncle Gostlin & aunt, & the rest of our freinds, desiring your praiers & blessing, I comend you to Gods protection & rest   "Your obedient Sonne

"JOHN WINTHROP.

"It wilbe yet a month or 5 weeke before we goe from hence; if you write to me after the receipt hereof I pray let it be to

---

[1] Sir Kenelme Digby, with whom the younger Winthrop was afterwards on terms of the most friendly correspondence. — See Letter of Sir K. D., *Hist. Coll.*, vol. x. 3d ser. p. 5.

Constantinople & directed to Captaine Maplesden, or Mr John ffreeman, marchant, or some other way as you thinke it may come safe to my hands as you shall have occasion.

"I pray remember my service to uncle Tindall & aunt when you see them, & to Captaine Best."[1]

John Winthrop to his Son.

"Sonne John,—I received from you 3 : Lettres, one from Plimmouth & 2 from Legorne : the last dated Aug : 11 : by wch I understande of y^{or} wellfare & good successe in y^{or} voyage, for wch my selfe & all yor freinds heere doe muche reioyce & heartyly thanke the Lorde for his mercye towards you : I mervaile you recieved not my lettre wch I wrote to you in June, & lefte it at Mr Soanes to be sent to you. I wrote to Mr. Soane also for a Lettre of Credence for you, & appointed to come to him about it, but before I could goe, he was forthe of towne : Yo^r unckle Downing wrote to you also : I am now at Groton, & therefore am bould wth yor unckle D : to trouble him wth procuringe you Lettres of credence for 20^{lb} that it may be ready for you at yor returne to Legorne. I suppose you have heard before this of the D : of Buck : his deathe,[2] & such other thinges as have fallen out heare : I cannot now write muche to you, but when I come at London, (God willinge) I will write more largely of suche occurrents as are certaine, & fitt to be written. We are all in healthe as you lefte us (God be praysed). Yo^r grandmother & mother salute & blesse you, yor brothers & sister salute you : & yor unckle Gostlin & Aunte : Now the good Lorde who hathe pleased of his great mercye to take care of you from the Cradle hitherto, & hathe, in his most wise & holy providence, disposed of you in this course of life, preserve,

---

1 On the back, the father writes, "This Lettre came to London about the 12 of Aug."

2 The Duke of Buckingham had been assassinated by Felton, Aug. 23, 1628. Felton was a Suffolk man, and had served under the duke as a lieutenant in the same expedition to the Isle of Rhé in which we have seen the younger Winthrop engaged.

blesse, & prosper you therein, so as yor life may be improved to his glorye, the good of the Churche, & yor owne comfort & salvatiō, Amen. Remember my lovinge salut^n to Captaine Maplesden: Have care of yor healthe, especially of yor soule & conscience. ffarewell.   " Yo^r lovinge father

                             " Jo : WINTHROP.

" GROTON. Septemb: 30: 1628. beinge the 2: daye after I received yor last lettre."

We hear of the young traveller next in the following letters from Constantinople, which· tell their own story sufficiently : —

John Winthrop, jun., to his Father.

" To the wor^ll his very loving father John Winthrop Esq. in Groton Suff^k.

                   " CONSTANTINOPLE Octob: 18 1628.

" SIR, — My duty remembered to your selfe, my mother & grandmother, with my love to my brothers & sister, my uncles & aunts & all our good freinds — may it please you to understand that we arrived at Constantinople the 13th day of September all in good health (God be thanked,) hoping the same of yourselfe & all our freinds. When I came to this place I found the gentleman to whome my letter of credit was directed to be absent, beinge gone down to Smyrna, his returne expected now every day, but have been furnished with monyes from his Assignee ; — the bill of exchange I shall not send till his returne. I shalbe forced to take up more then willingly I would, by reason of our going to Venice, where we are likely to stay a good parte of the winter, & our long stay heere, & some places we touch at in the way : What I shall pay a dollar I know not yet, but the dollar goeth very high heere by exchange, being worth 5^s : 4^d : English : By the next vessell I shall God willing write againe, & at Venice shall hope to heare from you. If you write thither, it be best to direct it to Capt : Maplesden.

The newes heere is of the Taking in of Esrom by the Grand
Seignior which was kept by a rebell; the grand Seignior's
forces are now in seige of Bagdat, alias Babilon, which the
Persian holdeth. Heere have been lately many fires in Constantinople. One burnt downe twelve thousand houses. Thus
with my duty againe remembered, desiring your prayers &
blessing, I rest   "Your Obedient son
                                        "JOHN WINTHROP.

"We shall, God willing, depart hence about a fourtnight or
3 weekes hence."

John Winthrop, Jr., to his Father. ·

"To the wor^ll his very loving father John Winthrop Esq. in Groton
                        Suffolk.

·"CONSTANTINOPLE Nov. 15. 1628.

"SIR, — May you please to understand that I wrote to you
dated Octr 18., sent by way of Venice, giving you notice
therein of my safe arrivall at this place, wch was about the 13
of September. My stay at this place wilbe I thinke about a
fortnight longer, & then (God willing) I shall goe for Venice
with the ship in wch I came out, wch hence is thither bound.
Having no acquaintance there, nor letters of credit, I am
forced to take up the 200 dollars for wch I had credit heere,
wch doth amount by Exchange at 5^s 4^d p^r dollar to 53^lb 6^s 8^d.
The bills I have charged home upon my uncle Downing, it
being Mr. Soane his order in his letter to Mr. ffreman : there
be three bills signed to goe by three severall occasions, the first
goeth with these letters. Sir I have not yet heard from you
since my comming out of England, but hope of your welfare,
whereof I desire you to certify me by your letters at my coming
to Venice, as also whether I shall returne by the next occasion
or stay till the London returneth, wch wilbe neere a yeare
hence. So with my duty remembred to yourselfe, my mother
& grandmother, with my love to my brothers & sister, my
uncles & aunts, & all the rest of our good freinds, wch for

brevity I may not particularize, desiring your praiers & blessing, I humbly take my leave & rest

"Your Obedient Son   "JOHN WINTHROP.

"The Embassador from the Emperour was receyved this day into this Citty & cometh to conclude peace.

"I am, God be thanked, in good health."

The younger Winthrop seems to have contemplated a visit to Jerusalem before leaving the East; but, finding no fit companionship or convoy, he leaves Constantinople at the close of December, and sails for Venice. We find among his papers a careful copy, in his own hand, of a " Relation of the practizes of the Jesuites against Cyrillus, Patriarch of Constantinople, & the cause of their banishment, penned by Sir Thomas Rowe, kn^t: English Ambassadour at Constantinople, 1627," with a brief addition of his own, — proving what was the character of his studies. We find, also, the rough draughts of a few letters of his, which show what were his personal associations in Constantinople. We give two of these letters just as they are found.

John Winthrop, Jr., to Sir Peter Wich, Lord Ambassador at Constantinople.[1]

"RIGHT HONORABLE, — After the exhibition of my service to your lordship and my lady, I crave pardon, if these rude lines presume to kiss your honor's hands. My duty and respect to your honor urgeth me to give some testimony thereof; and

---

[1] It has been suggested by Mr. Savage, that the younger Winthrop may have accompanied this very celebrated minister to Constantinople as Secretary of Legation, or Private Secretary. This idea is hardly substantiated by the facts furnished in this chapter; but we shall see reason for thinking, that, on his way back from the East, he was invited to join the party of the ambassador's wife, the Lady Wich, who was returning to England.

your noble favors have obliged me to present this as a small earnest of my thankfulness, and the service which I owe, and desire to perform, whensoever your lordship shall please to command. Here is no news worth your honor's intelligence. We are this day setting sail from the Castles. So, wishing your honor a happy beginning and prosperous continuance of this new year, and many more to succeed, I humbly take my leave, resting, etc.

"CASTLES OF HELLESPONT, December 26, 1628."

John Winthrop, Jr., to Mr. John Freeman at Constantinople.

"NOBLE SIR, — We are now to set saile from the Castles of Sestos & Abidos, & these lines waite for a prosperous gale to clime up the streames of Hellespont, that they may anchor in the desired port of your kind acceptance. I have in them imbarked my love, which at their arrival shall present it selfe to you not in the colored habit of painted words but in the simple vest of true friendship; wch I shall endeavor wth my whole power to mainteine, desiring the continuance of yours, if the unworthiness of the obiect make you not iudge it ill placed. When I come to Venice I shall hope to heare of your welfare, wch shall allwaies be most welcome newes to me. For your many kindnesses I shall remaine alwaies thankfull, & shalbe ever ready to doe you any service wch my best Endeavors can be able to performe. So wishing you a merry Christmas & a happy nue yeare, I commend you to the Divine protection & rest

"Your lovinge freind ready to serve you

"JOHN WINTHROP.

"from aboard the London ridinge neere the Castles of Sestos & Abidos. Decemb: 26."

The reply of his friend Mr. Freeman to the letter last given is not wholly without interest. It was addressed to our young traveller at Venice, where we hear of him next in a letter to his Uncle Downing; and where, it seems, he was detained a whole month in " the purgatory of the Lazaretto." Then follow two other letters to Mr. Freeman, together with a letter from a Mr. Judah Throckmorton, who would seem to be contemplating a voyage to New England. Our traveller is traced next to Amsterdam by a letter written to his father on his arrival there; and, finally, we have evidence that the long tour was successfully completed in the month of August, 1629, by another letter to his father, dated at London, and announcing his safe arrival there on a day of the month which is left blank. The letters are given in their order, both as illustrating the family history and as furnishing an authentic account of the course of travel at that remote period.

John Freeman to John Winthrop, Jr.

" To his approved good frend Mr. Jn° : Winthrope, Gent : In Venice.

"In Constanp^{ll} : 7 : ffebruary 1628.

"Mr. Winthrop, and my approved good frend, — my last letter, bare date ye 12 of Jan^y ; in answere to yo^{rs} frō ye Castles & Gallipoli ; & there inclosed sending yo^u the draught of my Statues at Chius, wishing yo^u to shewe it, upp & downe, in Ittaly as yo^u went, & if any did proffer any mony for the things themselfes, I desired yo^u to advise mee, this was ye effect of my last. Since wch tyme, wee have had no newes of yo^u : neither by letters nor reports, but ou^r hope is yo^u have a good passage, & by this, are att Vennice arrived, frō whence I may shortly, I hope, expect yor letters, then ye wch nothing would be more gratefull to me ; for occurrences, either, private or publique, nothing of note, hath succeeded since yor departure ; if yo^u had remained heere till nowe, yo^u should have had, a comodious passage for Jerusalem, the wch by Mr.

Hamilton, y⁰ Scotch gent: is imbraced, & wᵗʰin this three Dayes, is to Departe : — his passage is on a Gally for Cyprus, under conduct of y⁰ Basa of that place, & frō thence is recōmended unto certayne Greek Caloyeres ¹ (by y⁰ Patriarch) yᵗ goe in his Company ; a better occasione could not have happned in seaven yeares, & then hee's like to thither just at Easter, the tyme of all y⁰ Ceremonies. Thus wishing us a happie meeting agayne, either here or in Engᵈ or in both places, Cōmitt yoᵘ to Gods Divine protection restinge

"Yoʳ true frend & true serᵗ to Cōmand

"JOHN FREMAN.

"I pray p̓rsent my service unto Mʳ Price, Mʳ Throckmʳton, Mr. Mildmay &c."

John Winthrop, Jr., to Emanuel Downing.

" To the Wopˡˡ Emanuell Downing.

"MARTII 9: 1629. DE VENETIA.

"WORTHY Sᴿ, — May you please to understand that I am now arrived in Venice ; the day of oʳ arrivall was the last of Janʸ, having beene from Constantinople about 6 weekes. I should have wrote to you long since, but coming from a place where the plaugue was very great, we could not be admitted to come into this citty, till we had spent all february as prisoners in their Lazaretto (a place a great way distant from the Cytty appointed to such purposes) till it was apparent that we were cleere from all infection : so that not knowing any by whom I might have my letters conveied, I could not write till my cōming into the Citty. My charges there were excessive ; I find them little lesse since my cōming into the Citty, so that I shall have skarce to beare my charges hence, but may have credite heer for more when I want : It may be thought I am a very ill husband, but none can beleeve the charges in these Countries but he that hath expᵈ them. The exchange also maketh them the deeper, paying neere 6 for 4 & would be more if I should take

---

¹ Monks of the Greek Church. — *Worcester's Dictionary.*

up any heere. This maketh me desirous to hasten into England; by sea I find no occasion, by land I might have a good oportunity wth the Lady Wake, wch I heare would be very chargeable. I deffer to resolve till I have receyved letters from Legorne wth I heare are theare for me, wch I gladly expect dayly, hoping to heare from you & my other good freinds of your welfares, wch since my departure from England I have had noe notice of. Heare is little newes of Importance, saving of the French King's coming into Italy, wch is thought heare cannot but bring forth some notable effect; he hath allready made peace between Mantoa & Savoi, & it is thought entendeth to goe ag^{t} Genoa. Thus wth the remembrance of my duty & love to your selfe & my aunt, wth my salutations to my cozens and freinds, I comend you to Gods protection & rest

"Your loving Cosen to command   "JOHN WINTHROP."

John Winthrop, Jr., to John Freeman.

"VENICE, Martii 28 Stilo novo. 1629.

"MR. FREMAN & MY APPROVED GOOD FREIND, — I wrote unto you bearing date the 13 of March, *stil: nov:* being then newly come out of the Lazaretto, where noe man coming at us, nor knowing noe man to send my letters to be conveied, I deferred writing to you till my liberty gave me better occasion. I advised you of o^{r} arrivall heere the 9 of feb: after 6 weeks at sea, having touched at Zante by the way & some other ports. Yesterday I receyved yours of the 7 of feb: then wch nothing could have beene more welcome, being very glad to understand of your welfare. Therein I understand of another from you of the 12 of January, wth the draught of your Statues inclosed, wch never came to my hands, wch had I met w^{th}all I would have used much diligence therein, espetially in Venice, Padoa & those Citties heereabout, where only I have spent my tyme, since I came hither. — Further into Italy I think I shall not goe, nor stay heere long, but thereof I shall not be resolved till the next weeke. The Lady Wake being to depart very shortly for England, & much good Copany going along, I doubt I shalbe drawne that way, but thereof I shall further advise you when I know more certainly. I found Mr. Prise in Padoa to whome I delivered your letter, who was very glad to heare & receive a letter from so good a friend. He spoke to me of the great friendship between yourself & him. Mr. Petty is also at Padoa but I have not seene him; he staieth to passe wth my Lady into England. I hear that there is a booke got out of some of the inscriptions of his antiquities by Mr. Selden in England, wthout his knowledge. The cheife newes heere is of the ffrench king, who since his coming into Italy hath taken the Spanish Generall prisoner, succored the casell a castle neare Mātua beseiged by the Spaniard, made a peace betwixt Savoi & Mantoa, is now in Savoi, & is thought will goe ag^t Genoa : he filleth world wth great expectations of his actions what the event of them may be. He hath had the Cytty of Orange delivered up to him by the treachery of the Governour selling it into his hands for a great summe of money. It is rumored that the Hollanders have againe taken some caracks of Portugal worth over the 6000000 ducats. Of the former I suppose you have heard, being old newes when we came to Zante. So wth my love & service remembred, I commend you to the Divine tuition & rest

              " Your truest friend to serve you

                                      " JOHN WINTHROP.
" I pray present my service &c."

John Winthrop, Jr., to John Freeman.

" GOOD S^R, — I am now arrived in Christendome : the ninth of feb : *stil : nov :* was the day that we came into the Harbour of Malamoco neere Venice, from whence you had heard from me sooner had we not beene deteyned in the Purgatory of the Lazaretto a whole month, (the continuall expectation to be at liberty every day after the first weeke, confidently hoped for, making me defer lettres, knowing no man in Venice by whose meanes I might have them sent on to you,) before I could have liberty to enter the Citty. Mr. Throgmorton & the Dutch

Gentleman being also partakers in the same penalty. To write you of the particulars of o^r Voyage, it would be frivolous, remembring nothing that passed worthy your Intelligence, only in generall you shall understand that from the Castles to Zant we were in 5 daies, where we staied about a weeke; there I delivered your letter to Mr Hobson : we found the Hector there bound for England, in wch Mr. Throgmorton had gone but for feare of long detention &c.

"The second parte of our voiage was very longe & tedious wth continuall tempests & foule weather, being a month in the way betwixt Zant & Venice. I have sent your letters for Legorne. I understand since that Mr. Harvy is gone for England. Mr. Hide at the receipt of your letters hath kindly offered to furnish me wth monies where I shall have occasiō, wch I thankfully acknowledge as a fruite of your love for wch I confesse myself deeply indebted to you, having found such extraordinary kindnesses at your hands whilst I was wth you that to proportion my thanks wth your deserts would be too difficult for my pen to endeavor, only I pray beleeve that I am ever your true friend to doe you any service wch may lye in compasse of my best endeavours."   [JOHN WINTHROP.]

Judah Throckmorton to John Winthrop, Jr.

"To my worthy and very good ffreind Mr. John Winthrope this In Zante.

"NOBLE S^R, — The pardon y^u crave for not takeinge leave belonges to mee; but the occasion wch hindered me from bringeinge y^u aboard, will I hope cause y^u to make a favourable construction of that neglect, wch by no other meanes I should have lett slipp. I sent y^r letter the next day as y^u desired, but heare of noe letters from Leghorne; if any hereafter come to my hands I will keepe them safe for y^u, & should have bine glad to have done y^u some such service in England, if it had pleased y^u to have writte by me; but y^u hope your vioadge wilbe more speedy, wch I allsoe wishe y^u, wth all safety; and all other contentment, w^{ch}, now y^u are ridd of a troublsome companion,

I doubt not but y[u] shall enioy. The bootes y[u] left, if I had bine assured of y[r] touchinge at Zant, I had sent, but havinge some doubt thereof I may happily make bould wth them, & remaine y[r] debtor for another paire till we meete. The stay wee have at ffranckfort (be it more, or lesse) I will imploy to find y[r] booke; Soe wth my love & service to y[r] selfe I take leave and rest

"Your truly loveinge ffreind to command

"JUDAH THROCKMORTON.

"VENICE the 17th: of Aprill, 1629.

"I hope we shall certainely begin our ioyrney the first or second of May; but I feare it twilbe longe and doubt I shall finde it more chargeable then I did expect: but when I shall arrive I will enquier for y[u], to take some better instructions for New England w[ch] must I suppose be my way, or some such course to recover my expences; and to get some settled place."

John Winthrop, Jr., to his Father.

"Worp[ll] his very loving father John Winthrop, In Groton.

"AMSTERDAM, July 28: *Stilo vet:* 1629.

"SIR, — My duty remembered to your selfe, with my mother & grandmother, with my love to my brothers & sister & the rest of our good freinds, may you please to understand that I am yesterday safely arrived in this Citty of Amsterdam. — God be ever praysed for his mercies, that he hath given us a prosperous & safe passage, in this tyme of much danger. I feare you may be doubtfull of my safety, being now foure monthes since my last letters weere written from Venice; having beene so long from thence in the way most at sea, saving that we touched at Zant & staied there a while for the company of 2 other ships. I hoped we should have touched in some place in England, & so have found meanes to come home, but too favorable winds crossed my desires: I am heere without acquaintance & our long passage hath eaten out all the money that I receyved at Venice, whereof by the foresaid letters you have understood, if they came to your hands ; therefore I pray you to send me a letter of credit from some merchant to some man in Flushing, or Middleborough, which because I thinke you may be in the Country, & so cannot so readily doe, I have written to my Uncle Downing to desire him to doe it ; because the longer I stay heere the more I shall runn in debt. Therefore I would, as soone as I can receive answeare from you or my uncle, returne with all speede home. I have not since my departure out of England heard from you neyther by letter nor otherwise, therefore I long much to heare of your welfare, & of the rest of my good freinds. If you write to me, I pray conscribe it to be delivered in Flushing at the house of Mr. Henry Kerker, for I purpose God willing to goe shortly thither, where I shalbe neere to take my passage upon all occasions. For newes I understand little since my coming, the Shertogen-bos [1] that the prince hath beleagered, it is hoped will shortly be taken in, they having noe powder in the Citty : the Enemy is on the other side close by this place, that they feare he hath some designe for some place in Holland : thus with my duty againe remēbered, desiring your praiers & blessinge I comend you to Gods tuition & rest

      " Your Obedient Sonne   " JOHN WINTHROP."

John Winthrop, Jr., to his Father.

" To the worpⁿ his very loving father John Winthrop Esq. In Groton.

" SIR, — My humble duty remembred unto your selfe & my mother : may you please to understand that I am (God be thanked) yesterday safely arrived in London, now first understanding of the death of my grandmother & uncle ffones, to my great & unexpected greife, but we shall one day meet againe with greater joy. They are already in the haven, we saile towards it dayly. I wrote unto you at my coming to Amster-

---

[1] Hertogenbosch, now Bois le Duc. It was yielded to Henry, Prince of Orange, Sept. 4, 1629

dam, then not thinking I should have found so speedy occasions
to come over; but coming to Flissing where I thought I should
have expected answeare of my letters, & finding an English
Ship of good force ready to depart, instigated with a great
desire to understand of your welfare, I presently imbarqued
my selfe, on Munday morninge last; but my trunke I could
not get with me on board, but have left it with a pinke which
will shortly be in London, whose coming I must expect; for I·
must send over by the M^r thereof some mony which I there
owe, being about 12 pounds : I rejoyce much to heare of your
welfare, & shall thinke longe till I may see you & our good
freinds with you : So desiring your praiers & blessinge, I commend you to the Almighties tuition & humbly take my leave
resting   "Your Obedient Sonne   " JOHN WINTHROP.

"LONDON Aug: Friday 1629:

" My brother Henry I heare is in towne, but I have not yet
seene him.   I pray remember my love to my sister his wife,
with all my brothers & sisters & cozens.

" Also to my uncle Gostling & aunt with Mr. Lee & all our
good freinds.

" My Aunt Downing desired to remember her love to you,
having no leysure to write this weeke."

Perhaps there is nothing more striking, in the account
of the tour which is here closed, than the fact, mentioned in the last letter but one, that not a single line
from England had reached the young traveller during
an absence of fourteen or fifteen months.   We know
how prolific a letter-writer his father was; and that it
was not through any default of his, that no tidings from
home, and no words of affectionate interest and advice,
had been received by a son who was so deservedly dear
to him.   But there were no facilities for correspondence
with the absent and the distant in those days; and both

the elder and the younger Winthrop must have written their letters in great uncertainty whether they would ever reach their destination. Hence there was but little inducement to our traveller to make his letters the vehicle of any elaborate account of his observations or experiences. Some fragments are found among his papers, which look as if he had made careful note of what he saw and learned; but there is nothing preserved in a condition for being printed. He returned to find many changes in the family circle, to some of which he touchingly alludes in the letter announcing his arrival. But we shall find a more appropriate place for noticing them in the next chapter.

Meantime, we may conclude the present chapter with the following brief but characteristic entry in the elder Winthrop's autograph "Experiences." It may serve both to give some idea of the amusements of his other children at Groton during their brother's absence, and to illustrate once more the father's unfailing recognition of a Divine Hand in all the events and accidents of life.

"Aug: 1628. It pleased God to preserve my sonne Adam in a very g^t danger, his broth: Step: & Ben: Gostlin beinge neere the danger also: for they standinge togither closse to the stable doore, their broth: fforth shootinge at a marke a g^t waye from them, his arrowe came full amonge the children, so as, to my thinkinge, it must needs strike into Adams side; but it pleased God, it missed him a very little, & struck into the wall by him.

"Soone after, my sonne Deane fell backward from a high stoole & pitched upon his head, so as we feared his necke had been broke; but, through Gods mercye, he had no harme."

CHAPTER XV.

WINTHROP'S SERIOUS ILLNESS. THE DEATH OF HIS MOTHER. THE
LOSS OF HIS OFFICE. CORRESPONDENCE WITH HIS WIFE.

WE have deviated somewhat from the order of dates,
with a view to include in the preceding chapter all that
was connected with the younger Winthrop's Oriental
tour. Many events had occurred in the family circle
during his absence; and to these we must now recur, in
explanation of the correspondence which follows.

About the end of November, 1628, the elder Winthrop
had been taken seriously ill in London, while there in
attendance upon the terms of Court. He seems to
have concealed his condition from his wife and children
at Groton, until he was out of immediate danger; and
then we have the following brief letter: —

John Winthrop to his Wife.

" MY SWEET WIFE, — I can now no longer dissemble wth
thee, & I blesse o^{r} most gratious & heavenly father, in o^{r} most
holy Lo : Jesus Christ, that I may yet rather tell thee how I
have been, than to have feared thee wth the relation of my condition, when it was uncertaine what the issue would be : I have
had an ague these 8 : or 9 : dayes. I cañot saye it is quite
gone, but I prayse God it is so well abated, as I hope to be
abroad againe over a fewe dayes (if God will). I am heere
amonge such lovinge freinds, as will suffer me to want nothinge,
especially the Lord beinge pleased to be wth me allso in the

favo^r & light of his countenance; yet were it not winter, I could want thee; but (my sweet wife) have a little more patience & God will restore me to thee soone: I must persuade, & chardge thee, not to thinke of cominge up, for, if it should befall thee other wise than well, it would be worse to me than all this, & much more. Writing is now wearinesse; I leave thee to supply all duty, love etc. Praye for me; the Lord blesse thee & all o^{rs}. I kisse thee — farewell.

" This THURSDAY EVENINGE.

"If Jack Pease his father & mother will let him goe over to Henryé, let him be sent up by Jarvais next weeke; if they will not let him goe, they shall have him home. If Anth: Deathes boye will goe, let him come up allso."

The true-hearted Margaret was not to be deterred, it seems, by any remonstrances founded only upon considerations of her own convenience or comfort, from going at once to take care of her husband; and she sets off, with no other attendant than her maid-servant (Amye), on a wintry journey to London. She was undoubtedly the bearer of the following little note from Winthrop's mother, written with a trembling hand, and, as it proved, on the very verge of her own grave: —

Anne Winthrop to her Son.

"MY DEARE AND ONELY SONNE, MY MOST LOVING SONNE, — I am very sory for thy sicknes and pray to God night & day for thy good recovery which I desire with the most intire affection of my hart, and wish my selfe present with thee. I have no balme to send thee, but I will offer up to (the) Lord the prayers of a true mornfull mother's hart till (I) se thy face with Comfort, which God in his riche mercie grant me poore soule. I pray, Sonne, remember me to your brother and sister.   "Your mornfull mother,   "A. W."

A few weeks afterwards, Margaret was obliged to return to the care of her children at Groton, leaving her husband happily convalescent; and then we have the two letters which follow, showing that other anxieties awaited her at home.

Margaret Winthrop to her Husband.

" To my very loving Husband John Winthrop Esq. at Mr. Downings.

" MY MOST DEARE AND LOVEINGE HUSBAND, — I doe blesse and prayse God for the continuance of your health, and for the safe delivery of my good sister Downinge ; it was very welcom Nuse to us. I thanke the Lord wee are all heare reasonably well. My pore Stephen is up to day. Amye hath had a very sore ague but is well againe. I hope the Lord will heare our prayers and be pleased to stay his hand in this visitation, wch if he please to doe we shall have great cause of thankfulnesse : but I desire in this and all other things to submit unto his holy will ; it is the Lord, let him doe what semeth good in his owne eyse. He will doe nothinge but that shall be for our good if we had harts to trust in him, & all shall be for the best what so ever it shall please him to exercise us withall. He wounds & he can heale. He hath never fayled to doe us good, & now he will not shake us off, but continue the same God still that he hath bin heare to fore. The Lord sanctify unto us what soever it shall please him to send unto us, that we may be the better for it & furthered in our corce to heaven. I am sorye for the hard condishtion of Rochell : the Lord helpe them & fite for them & then none shall prevayle against them or overcome them. In vaine they fite that fite against the Lorde, who is a myty god & will destroye all his enimyes. And now my deare husband I have nothinge but my dearest affections to send thee — with many thankes for thy kinde letters, prayinge you to except a little for a great deale : my will is good but that I want abilite how to show & expresse it to thee as I desire. I pray remember me to my brothers & sisters, & tel my brother Foones I thanke him for the thinges he sent, & so I bid my good husband farewell & commite him to God.

"Your loveinge & obedient wife,
"MARGARET WINTHROPE.

"I send up a turkeye & 2 capons & a cheese : the carier is payde."

John Winthrop to his Wife.

"MY DEARE WIFE, — I received thy most lovinge & well-come Lettre, & doe heartyly reioyce & blesse o^r heavenly father, acknowledging his most gratious providence, & great love towards us, as in all other thinges, so in this mercy, in bringing thee home in saftye, & preservinge all o^r family in peace to thy cominge : we see how faithfull & true he is in all his promises. O that we could make use of all o^r experience to relye more upon him, & cast o^r owne cares upon him, caringe onely to please & serve him : I am sorrye for Amye her sicknesse, but praysed be God, who hath disposed so well of it, that the trouble is fallen in o^r owne house, for it would have been far more burdensome & inconvenient if it had fallen heer : I doubt not of thy care of her, that she may want neither meanes nor attendance, & I trust the Lord will restore her againe in due tyme. I prayse the Lord, I am now growne indifferent well, & doe gather strength daylye, & doe hope (through his mercy) we shall have a happy meetinge erelonge, for w^{ch}, & for the continuance of all other blessinges (especially those wch con-cerne the good of o^r soules), let us be constant in prayer, & in a carefull endeav^r to walke in all well pleasinge before him. Remember my duty to my good mother, my blessinge to all o^r children, & kinde Salut^s to all o^r freinds particularly at Groton Hall & to Mr Leigh ; thanke him for his kind & Christian Let-tre : O^r freinds heer are all in health & desire to be remembered to you all : for newes I referre you to my neighbo^r Newton : we have received all the thinges you sent, my sister & my selfe thanke thee for them. I will followe thy Counsell, & rest in thy love for as kinde acceptance of these, as thy pretye sweet short Lettre had wth me, so I kisse my sweet wife & comend thee & all o^{rs} to o^r most mercifull Lord & heavenly father in Christ; so I kisse my sweet wife & rest .

      "Thy faithfull husband   "Jo: WINTHROP.

"JAN'Y 22, 1628."

And now we are able to give, in this connection, another brief passage from the little autograph volume; in which Winthrop has made the following record of his experiences during the severe illness from which he had just recovered. His tribute to his "honest and able physician," and his testimony against the immoderate love of tobacco, with his renunciation of the use of it, will not be unobserved.

"Decemb: 1628. At London in the ende of Mich. terme, I fell into a dangerous hote malign^t feaver, wherein the Lord shewed me exceedinge much mercye. ffirst he sanctified it unto me, by discoveringe many corruptions wch had prevayled over me, givinge me Repentance, & pardon for them, thereby subduinge the fleshe & givinge more strengthe to the spirit: It pleased him to reveale his favo^r & goodnesse abundantly towards me, so as I never had more sweet Comunion wth him, then in that afflictiō; & when in my selfe & the judgm^t of others I was under the sentence of deathe, it pleased him to restore me to life, by providinge me fitt meanes, an honest & able phisician, Doctor Wright, (whose care of me, & kindnesse in refusinge any rewarde &c, I may not forgett), & in blessinge the meanes to their desired ende. Among other benefits I reaped by it, this was one: deliverance from the bondage whereinto I was fallen by the immoderate use & love of Tobacco, so as I gave it cleane over. Another was the experience of the love of his people towards me in all places where I was known, testified by their muche inquiringe after me, mourninge for the feare wch was conceived of my deathe, & earnest prayinge for my recoverye : But the greatest of all was, the assurance he gave me of my salvation, & grace over some corruptions wch had gotten masterye of me, wch increased my experience of his trueth & faithfullnesse in disposinge the worst condition of his children to their best good. I did likewise observe the experience of his good providence, that my sicknesse fastned not upon me till I had finished my lawe businesse, & he restored my healthe so as I was able by the beginninge of the next Terme to followe it againe : The Lord give me grace, never to forgett this kindnesse, but to cleave fast unto him, & to holde that resolution of obedience &c, wch he wrought in me. Other favours I founde accompanyinge the former, as preservinge & prosperinge my wife & those who came up & returned wth her, & especially so disposinge as o^r mayd servant, who came up wth her, continued in healthe all the tyme of her staye, but in their returne at Chelmsford fell sicke, & gettinge home was neere unto deathe, but it pleased God to recover hir : His holy name be praysed for ever, for all his mercyes. AMEN."

The next letter, in order of date, is addressed to his son Henry, who had made a voyage to the West Indies in the spring or summer of 1627, and had established himself there, with a company of servánts, as a planter of tobacco. Henry had evidently been rather a wild youth; and his adventurous and speculative turn had occasioned his father much anxiety and expense. The letter contains a good deal of sound advice and serious remonstrance. It contains also some interesting details of local and general history. But Henry had left his plantation for a time, and embarked for home, before it reached its destination.

John Winthrop to his son Henry.

" Son Henry, — It is my daily care to commend you to the Lord, that he would please to put his true fear into your heart, and the faith of the Lord Jesus Christ, that you may be saved, and that your ways may be pleasing in his sight. I wish also your outward prosperity, so far as may be for your good. I have been sick, these seven or eight weeks, near unto death; but the Lord hath had mercy on me to restore me; yet I am not able to go abroad.

" I sent you by Capt. Powell a letter, and in it a note of such things as I likewise sent you by him, in a chest with two locks, whereof the keys were delivered to his brother, who went master of the ship. The things cost me about £35; but, as yet, I have received nothing towards it. I sent divers times to Capt. Powell about your tobacco, but my man could never see it, but had answer, I should have it, or money for it. But there was ten pounds of it, by your appointment, to be delivered to one and the worth of four lb to another, which made me that I knew not what course to take; besides, I found, by the rolls you sent to me and to your uncles, that it was very ill-conditioned, foul, and full of stalks, and evil colored; and your uncle Fones, taking the judgment of divers grocers, none of them would give five shillings a pound for it. I desired Capt. Powell, (coming one day to see me,) that he would help me with money for it, which he promised to do; but, as yet, I hear not from him. I would have sent you some other things by Mr. Randall; but, in truth, I have no money, and I am so far in debt already, to both your uncles, as I am ashamed to borrow any more. I have disbursed a great deal of money for you, more than my estate will bear. I paid for your debts since you went, above £30, besides £4. 10s. to Annett and Dixon, and now £35. Except you send commodity to raise money, I can supply you no further. I have many other children that are unprovided, and I see my life is uncertain. I marvel at your great undertakings, having no means, and knowing how

much I am in debt already.   Solomon saith, He who hasteth
to be rich, shall surely come to poverty.   It had been more
wisdom and better becoming your youth, to have contained
yourself in a moderate course, for your three years ; and by
that time, by your own gettings and my help, you might have
been able to have done somewhat.   But this hath been always
the fruit of your vain, overreaching mind, which will be your
overthrow, if you attain not more discretion and moderation
with your years.   I do wonder upon what ground you should
be led into so gross an error as to think, that I could provide
ten such men as you write for, and disburse a matter of £200,
(when I owe more already than I am able to pay, without sale
of my land,) and to do this at some two or three months' warning.   Well, I will write no more of these things.   I pray
God, make you more wise and sober, and bring you home in
peace in his due time.   If I receive money for your tobacco
before Mr. Randall go, I will send you something else ; otherwise you must be content to stay till I can.   [If you send over
any more tobacco, take order it may be delivered to me, and if
you will have others to have shares out of it, let me have the
disposing of it ; for this last course of yours makes me jealous
of your intent, as I can be no less, when you gave me such
particular directions for the best improvement of it, and yet
underhand appoint another to dispose of a good part of it.
Well, enough of this.[1]]   Your brother (as I wrote to you)
hath been in the Levant above this half year, and I look not
for him before a year more.   Your friends here are all in
health.   Your uncles and aunts commend them to you ; but
they will take none of your tobacco ; only your uncle Tindale
and aunt (whom you write your kinswoman upon the outside
of your tabacco) thank you for theirs.   I sent you, also, two
boys, (for men I could get none,) such as Capt. Powell
carried over ; but I knew not what to do for their binding,

---

1 The passage in brackets was omitted in the letter as contained in the Appendix
to the "History of New England."

being not able then either to walk or write, and they being
but youths. For news, here is little but what, I suppose,
this bearer can tell you. We shall have peace with France.
The Dutch have taken from the Spaniard, in the West Indies, a very great prize of silver, gold, etc., and have brought
it safe home. The king of Bohemia, and his oldest son,
going aboard to see it, in their return were cast away. The
king was saved, but the prince and many others were lost.

"Sir Nathaniel Barnardiston, and Sir William Springe, are
knights of the parliament for Suffolk. All the gentlemen have
been long since set at liberty. Sir Francis Barrington is at
rest in the Lord. Sir Henry Mildmay, of Graces, is sheriff
of Essex, and Mr. Gurdon for Suffolk.

"I have staid sending my letter above a week since I
wrote it, expecting some money from Capt. Powell, according to his promise, that I might have sent you some other
things; but I hear of none. Therefore I will end, and defer
till some other occasion. So, again, I commend you to the
blessing, protection, and direction of the Lord, and rest

    "Your loving father,   "Jo : Winthrop.
"London, this 30 of January, 1628."

We have next a delightful letter of sympathy and
consolation to his sister-in-law, Priscilla Fones, in London, occasioned by the protracted illness and approaching
death of her husband, Thomas Fones. It was written
from Groton, whither Winthrop had returned after his
recovery, and after finishing another term of Court.

John Winthrop to Priscilla Fones.

" To my very loving Sister Mrs. Fones, at her House in the Old Bailey, London.

"My good Sister,—I have been too long silent to you,
considering mine own consciousness of that great debt, which
I owe you for your love and much kindness to me and mine.

But, I assure you, it is not through want of good will to you ; but having many letters to write weekly, I take my ease, to include you in my brother's.

"I partake with you in that affliction, which it pleaseth the Lord still to exercise you and my good brother in. I know God hath so fitted and disposed your mind to bear troubles, as your friends may take the less care for you in them. He shows your more love, in enabling you to bear them comfortably, than you could apprehend in the freedom from them. Go on cheerfully, (my good sister,) let experience add more confidence still to your patience. Peace shall come. There will be a bed to rest in, large and easy enough for you both. It is preparing in the lodging appointed for you in your Father's house. He that vouchsafed to wipe the sweat from his disciples' feet, will not disdain to wipe the tears from those tender, affectionate eyes. Because you have been one of his mourners in the house of tribulation, you shall drink of the cup of joy, and be clothed with the garment of gladness, in the kingdom of his glory. The former things, and evil, will soon be passed ; but the good to come shall neither end nor change. Never man saw heaven, but would have passed through hell to come at it. Let this suffice as a test of my true love to you, and of the account I make of the happiness of your condition. I commend you to his good grace, who is All-sufficient ; and so, with my mother's, my wife's, and mine own salutation to yourself, and my good brother, and all my cousins, I rest

"Your loving brother, 　　"Jo : WINTHROP.

"MARCH 25, 1628.[1]

"I pray remember my love to your brother, Mr. Burgesse.

"I pray tell my brother, that his tenant Gage desires him to forbear him £10 till Whitsuntide."

---

[1] The date should plainly have been 1629, of which year (according to the old style) March 25 was the first day.

And now we have a series of letters, called forth by a strange combination of domestic events. Thomas Fones, a brother-in-law to whom Winthrop appears to have been strongly attached, died in London on the 15th of April, 1629. Winthrop's own mother, who had always lived under the same roof with himself, and for whom he must have had the deepest affection and veneration, died at Groton only four days afterwards. He was doubtless at home to receive her farewell blessing, and to pay his last tribute to her remains. But he must have been obliged to hurry down to London immediately afterwards, to attend the Easter Term of Court; and there, on the 25th of the same month, his son Henry, who had just returned from Barbadoes, was married to his cousin, Elizabeth Fones, with a view of taking her from her now desolate home to his plantation in the West Indies. The letters written by Winthrop to his wife, under these circumstances, are full of the loftiest strain of religious faith and devotional fervor; and it was in no spirit of levity, we may be assured, that Margaret replies to one of them, " Those serious thoughts of thine did make a very good supply instead of a sermon." The first letter was evidently sent by Henry and his bride, on their visit to Groton, immediately after their marriage.

John Winthrop to his Wife.

"My good Wife, — Although I wrote to thee last week by the carrier of Hadleigh, yet, having so fit opportunity, I must needs write to thee again; for I do esteem one little, sweet, short letter of thine (such as the last was) to be well worthy two or three from me. How it is with us, these bearers can inform thee, so as I may write the less. They were married on Saturday last, and intend to stay with thee till towards the end of the term; for it will be yet six weeks before they can take their voyage. Labor to keep my son at home as much as thou canst, especially from Hadleigh. I began this letter to thee yesterday, at two of the clock, thinking to have been large, but was so taken up by company and business, as I could get but hither by this morning. It grieves me that I have not liberty to make better expression of my love to thee, who art more dear to me than all earthly things; but I will endeavor that my prayers may supply the defect of my pen, which will be of best use to us both, inasmuch as the favor and blessing of our God is better than all things besides. My trust is in his mercy, that, upon the faith of his gracious promise, and the experience of his fatherly goodness, he will be our God to the end, to carry us along through this course of our pilgrimage, in the peace of a good conscience, and that, in the end of our race, we shall safely arrive at the haven of eternal happiness. We see how frail and vain all earthly good things are. There is no means to avoid the loss of them in death, nor the bitterness which accompanyeth them in the cares and troubles of this life. Only the fruition of Jesus Christ and the hope of heaven can give us true comfort and rest. The Lord teach us wisdom to prepare for our change, and to lay up our treasure there, where our abiding must be forever. I know thou lookest for troubles here, and, when one affliction is over, to meet with another; but remember what our Saviour tells us : BE OF GOOD COMFORT, I HAVE OVERCOME THE WORLD. See his goodness; He hath conquered our enemies beforehand, and, by faith in him, we shall assuredly prevail over them all. Therefore, (my sweet wife,) raise up thy heart, and be not dismayed at the crosses thou meetest with in family affairs or otherwise; but still fly to him, who will take up thy burden for thee. Go thou on cheerfully, in obedience to his holy will, in the course he hath set thee. Peace shall come. Thou shalt rest as in thy bed; and, in the mean time, he will not fail nor forsake thee. But my time is past; I must leave thee. So I commend thee and all thine to the gracious protection and blessing of the Lord. All our friends here salute thee; salute thou ours from me. Farewell, my good wife. I kiss and love thee with the kindest affection, and rest

"Thy faithful husband, "Jo. WINTHROP.
"APRIL 28, 1629.

"Let John Bluet ¹ be satisfied for his horse."

John Winthrop to his Wife.

"MY GOOD WIFE, — I wrote to thee by my Sonne, & therefore will take lib^{tye} to be briefe now, havinge many other Lettres to write, & verye little leisure. Blessed be the Lorde o^r good God that in this tyme of o^r absence from each other, we may yet heare of one anothers welfare, & have comfort in o^r mutuall love, wch through his grace is so setled, as neither tyme nor absence can alter or deminishe : O^r freinds heere are in reasonable health (I prayse God), & desire to be kindly remembred to thee : my sister Downinge will expect Mary Morten this next weeke ; she may come up by Colchester wagon verye well. I will take a tyme to conferre with my sister Downing about thy clothes ; she weares no mourninge apparrell, but I & my man are in it. I praye thee send to Cambridge so soone as may be. Comende my love & blessinge to my son & daughter : I thanke thee for thy readynesse to entertain them, but I would not have thee to make them over great a charge. Tell him that Mr. Gurdon desires to comende a man to him for his plantatiō, whoom I would have him to entertaine, for it seemes he is honest & trustye, & fitt to doe service, & such he shall have neede of: let him speake with Mr Gurdon about him.

"Let John Samford speake wth Milburne, & tell him that he hath a brother, who should hire a mill of Sr Hen : Mildmay at

---

¹ He was, two years before, steward of the manor of Groton, of which Winthrop was lord.

56^{lb} per añ., who offers Sr Henry, that his brother of o^r towne shall be bounde wth him for his rent; knowe of Milburne if he be willinge to be bound for his brother & lett me knowe his answeare by thy next Lettre, that I may certifye Sr Henry of it.

" There is a boxe to come downe by the carrier wth some thinges for my sonne & daughter.

" Sende these Lettres inclosed, as they are directed, speedy-lye.

" Heere is litle newes; that wch is, my neighbo^r Newton will acquainte you wth. Com̄ende my love to all o^r freinds, Mr Leigh & his wife, brother & sister Gostlinge & all the rest. So wth my heartiest salutations to thy sweet selfe, my love & blessinge to all o^r children, I com̄ende thee & them to the gratious protection & blessinge of o^r heavenly Father, so I kisse thee & wish thee Farewell.

" Thy faithfull husband   " JO : WINTHROP.
" MAY 1 : 1629.

" If Mary come up by the wagon, she may have a porter to carrye her thinges & to direct her to my brother Downinges."

Margaret Winthrop to her Husband.

" For my very loving Husband, John Winthrop, Esq., these deliver.

" MOST LOVING AND GOOD HUSBAND, — I have received your letters. The true tokens of your love and care of my good, now in your absence, as well as when you are present, make me think that saying false, Out of sight out of mind. I am sure my heart and thoughts are always near you, to do you good and not evil all the days of my life.

" I hope, through God's blessing, your pains will not be altogether lost, which you bestow upon me in writing. Those serious thoughts of your own, which you sent me, did make a very good supply instead of a sermon. I shall often read them, and desire to be of God's family, to whom so many blessings belong, and pray that I may not be one separated from God, whose conscience is always accusing them. I shall not need to write to you of any thing this week. My son and brother Gostling can tell you how we are. And I shall think long for your coming home. And thus, with my best love to you, I beseech the Lord to send us a comfortable meeting in his good time. I commit you to the Lord.

"Your loving and obedient wife,

"MARGARET WINTHROP."

John Winthrop to his Wife.

[Fragment.]

"The largeness and truth of my love to thee makes me always mindful of thy welfare, and sets me on work to begin to write before I hear from thee. The very thought of thee affords me many a kind refreshing : What will then the enjoying of thy sweet society, which I prize above all worldly comforts?

"Yet, such is the folly and misery of man, as he is easily brought to contemn the true good he enjoys, and to neglect the best things, which he holds only in hope, and both upon an ungrounded desire of some seeming good, which he promiseth to himself. And if it be thus with us, that are Christians, who have a sure word to direct us, and the holy faith to live by, what is the madness and bondage of those who are out of Christ? Oh! the riches of Christ! Oh! the sweetness of the word of grace! It ravisheth my soul in the thought hereof, so as, when I apprehend but a glimpse of the dignity and felicity of a Christian, I can hardly persuade my heart to hope for so great happiness. Let men talk what they will of riches, honors, pleasures, etc.; let us have Christ crucified, and let them take all besides. For, indeed, he who hath Christ, hath all things with him; for he enjoyeth an all-sufficiency, which makes him abundantly rich in poverty, honorable in the lowest abasements, full of joy and consolation in the sharpest afflictions, living in death, and possessing eternity in this vale of misery. Therefore bless we God for his free and infinite mercy, in bestowing Christ upon us. Let us entertain and love him with our whole hearts; let us trust in him, and cleave to him with denial of ourselves, and all things besides, and account our portion the best in the world; that so, being strengthened and comforted in his love, we may put forth ourselves to improve our life and means to do him service. There are very few hours left of this day of our labor : then comes the night, when we shall take our rest. In the morning we shall awake unto glory and immortality, when we shall have no more work to do ; no more pains or grief to endure ; no more care, fear, want, reproach, or infirmity ; no more sin, corruption, or temptation.

"I am forced to patch up my letters, here a piece and there another. I have now received thine, the kindly fruits of thy most sweet affections. Blessed be the Lord for the welfare of thyself and all our family.

"I received letters from my two sons with thee. Remember my love and blessing to them, and to my daughter Winthrop, for whose safety I give the Lord thanks. I have so many letters to write, as I cannot write to them now. Our friends here are in reasonable health, and desire to be kindly remembered to you all. Commend me to all my good friends, my loving neighbors goodman Cole and his wife, to whom we are always much beholden. I will remember M—— her gown and petticoat, and the children's girdles. So, with my most affectionate desires of thy welfare, and my blessing to all our children, I kiss my sweet wife, and commend thee and all ours to the gracious protection of our heavenly Father, and rest

"Thy faithful husband,
"still present with thee in his most unkind absence,
"Jo. Winthrop.
"May 8, 1629.

"I am sorry for my neighbor Bluet's horse; but he shall lose nothing by him. Tell my son Henry I will pay the money he writes of."

Margaret Winthrop to her Husband.

" To my very loving Husband John Winthrop these deliver.

" MY SWEET HUSBAND, — I rejoice in the expectation of our happy meeting; for thy absence hath been very long in my conceit, and thy presence much desired. Thy welcome is always ready; make haste to entertain it.

" I was yesterday at a meeting at goodman Cole's upon the going of the young folk to Dedham, where many thanks were given to God for the reformation of the young man, and amendment of his life. We had also a part in their prayers. My dear husband, I will now leave writing to thee, hoping to see thee shortly. The good Lord send us a comfortable meeting. And thus, with my due respect to thyself, brother and sister D., sister Fanny,[1] son John, and the rest. My daughter remembers her duty to you all; thinks long for her husband. I received the things you sent, and thank you heartily for them. I will take order with my man to buy some trimming for my gown. And so I bid my good husband farewell, and commit him to the Lord.

" Your loving and obedient wife,

" MARGARET WINTHROP.

" I pray buy a Psalter for Deane. I can get none here."

John Winthrop to his Wife.

" MY GOOD WIFE, — I prayse the Lord for the wished newes of thy welfare & of the rest of our companye, & for the continuance of ours heer : it is a great favour, that we may enjoye so much comfort & peace in these so evill & declining tymes, & when the increasinge of our sinnes gives us so great

---

[1] Mr. Savage suggests that this name may have been inaccurately copied from the original. It was undoubtedly written *Fones.* I have more difficulty about the " son John," as he did not return from his tour in the East until August.

cause to looke for some heavye scourge & Judgment to be
cominge upon us : The Lorde hath admonished, threatened,
corrected, & astonished us, yet we growe worse & worse, so as
his Spirit will not allwayes strive with us, he must needs give
waye to his furye at last : He hath smitten all the other Churches
before our eyes, & hath made them to drinke of the bitter
cuppe of tribulatiō, even unto death.   We sawe this, & humbled not ourselves, to turne from our evill wayes, but have
provoked him more than all the nations rounde about us :
therefore he is turninge the Cuppe towards us also, & because
we are the last, our portion must be, to drinke the verye dreggs
which remaine :   My dear wife, I am veryly persuaded, God
will bringe some heavye Affliction upon this lande, & that
speedylye : but be of good comfort, the hardest that can come
shall be a meanes to mortifie this bodye of corruption, which is
a thousand tymes more dangerous to us then any outward tribulation, & to bring us into nearer comunion with our Lord
Jesus Christ, & more assurance of his kingdome.   If the
Lord seeth it wilbe good for us, he will provide a shelter & a
hidinge place for us & others, as a Zoar for Lott, Sarephtah
for his prophet, &c : if not, yet he will not forsake us : though
he correct us with the roddes of men, yet if he take not his
mercye & lovinge kindnesse from us we shalbe safe.   He onely
is allsufficient ; if we have him, we have all things : if he seeth
it not good to cutt our portion, in these thinges belowe, equall
to the largenesse of our desires, yet if he please to frame
our mindes to the portion he allotts us, it wilbe as well
for us.

"I thanke thee for thy kinde letter.   I am going to Westminster, & must heere breake off.   I would have my sonne
H——— to be heere on teusdaye that I may goe out of towne on
Wensdaye or thursdaye next.   If Marye her gowne be made I
will send it downe by Smith this weeke, or els next, with other
thinges : all our freinds heer are indifferent well, & desire to be
comended to thee, so with my hearty salut⁸ to all our freinds
with thee, my love & blessinge to my sonnes & daughters, in

very much hast, I ende & com̄ende thee & all ours to the gratious protectiō & blessinge of the Lorde — so I kisse my sweet
wife, & thinke longe till I see thee — farewell.

     " Thine   " Jo : WINTHROP.

" I thanke thee for our Turkye.

" MAY 15. 1629."

John Winthrop to his Wife.

" To my verye lovinge wife Mrs. Winthrop at Groton in Suffk.

" Thou mayest mervaile that thou haddest no Letter from
me by my Sonne, but I knowe thou wilt not impute it to any
decaye of love, or neglect of thee ; who art more pretious to
me than any other thinge in this worlde ; but the uncertainty
of his ioᵣnye, & the dislike of his ill course, which made me
estrange my selfe towards him. I prayse God I came safe
hither, & am in good health as all our friends heere are (who
desire to be kindly remembered to thee). I hope my sonne
hath putt awaye his man, for he promised he would, & that he
would amende his life : I beseech the Lorde to give him grace
so to doe ; otherwise he will soone be undone. I am still more
confirmed in that course wᶜʰ I propounded to thee, & so are my
brother & Sister D : the good Lo : direct & blesse us in it.

" I received a lettre from fforthes Tutor, wherein he com-
playnes of his longer absence, wᶜʰ he findes doth him much
hurte both in his learninge & manners, & wisheth me to sende
him speedylie, for he sayth he hath provided him a chamber in
the Colledge. I praye thee speake with him, & doe as may be
fittest, for if he intendes not the ministerye, I have no great
minde to sende him any more ; if he doth, let him goe so soone
as he can. I have now received thy sweet lettre, wᶜʰ I heartyly
thanke thee for, & doe with all thankfullnesse acknowledge the
goodnesse of the Lord towards us in his blessinge upon thee &
all ours, which I shall labour the continuance of to the best of
my power, & so farr as my poore prayers can give furtherance.
I am sorye I cannot write to thee as I desire, but thou wilt

beare with me the rather for that I thinke my Office is gone, so
as I shall not wronge thee so much with my absence as I have
done. I will send thee some pepper in my sonnes boxe, & so
with my blessinge to my sonnes & daughters, salutations to
all our good friendes, & my most intire Affections to thy selfe,
I comend thee to the grace & blessinge of the Lord & rest
                   " Thy faithfull husband   " Jo : Winthrop.

" Thou shalt receive in the boxe a book of the newes this
weeke.

" My sister ffones & her children will be with thee after the
Terme.

" June 5. 1629.

" Sende me no linnen for I have enough heere."

John Winthrop to his Wife.

" My good Wife, — I received thy most kinde Lettre. I
blesse the Lord for the continuance of thy wellfare & of all oᵣ
family. Thou desirest an excuse for thy brevitye; thou shalt
need no other then this, that I am forced to the like : but such
Apologies are needlesse between us, where there is so good
assurance of the trueth of each others love : I blesse God for
thee allwayes, in that sweet comfort & content I have in thee ;
but I must breake off these discourses, though I delight much
in them.

" My sonnes man is come up, but I knowe not upon what
termes, for nobodye writes a word about him. fforth may goe
to Camb : now or at my returne, for all will be one, if he
meanes not to continue there. My Sonne Henry must come
up before the ende of the terme, for he can doe nothinge out of
terme, but his wife needs not come.

" The gent who were in prison, are like to be delivered, &
some of them have libᵗʸᵉ already to goe abroad. Oᵣ freinds
heere are all well, God be thanked, only my sister ffones is
much troubled wᵗʰ the toothach, they all desire to be comended

to thee. So wth my true love to thy sweet selfe, my blessing to all o^r children, & salut^{ns} to all o^r freinds, I comende thee to the Lord & rest in hast   " Thy faithful husband

"Jo : WINTHROP.

" ffor Whales, he hath so often broke promise wth me, as I will trust him no more.

"JUNE 12. 1629."

Margaret Winthrop to her Husband.

" To hir very lovinge Husban John Winthrope Esqr these dd. '

" MY DEARE HUSBAND, — Havinge so fit opertunity I cannot omit it, but rite a word or two to thee that you may understand of our healths. I prayse God we are all well, and I think very longe for y^{or} returne home. I hope to hear this weeke when you will come home. I have received y^{or} sweet letter, and thanke thee for it. My sonne will be at London before the end of the terme : he and his wife purpose to goe to my brothers Tyndall some time this weeke and I thinke he will goe from thence to London. I may chance to goe alonge with them, my daughter beinge a stranger thear : if I go I shall not right ainy more this weeke without I can send from thence. Thou seast how bold I am to take leave to goe abrode in thy abcence, but I presume upon thy love and concent, or elce I wolde not doe it. I hope I shall take order that all thinges shalbe wel looked to for the time I stay. I will not trouble thee with relatinge any thinge to thee, but leave all maters till I see thee. I loth to be thus short in rightinge to thee, but that it is night and I must send awaye my letter, and part with my beloved and good Husban, and have nothinge but my best love and all due respect to send him which my pen can not exprese or my tounge utter, but I will endevor to shew it as well as I can to thee, and to all that love thee. I pray remember my love to brother and sister Downinge, sister Fones. I hope I shall see them all heare this sommer, and thus I must leave thee and bid my sweet Husban good night and commit him to God.

" Your faythful and obedient wife

"MARGARET WINTHROPE.

"Our sonnes and daughters remember thear duty. I will not right any thing·now about my sonnes man, haveinge no tyme. You shall know when you come home. I thinke my son Forth will goe to Cambridge this weeke and talke with his tuter but I thinke he is resoulved to be no longer thear."

John Winthrop to his Wife.

"To his verye lovinge wife Mrs Winthrop at her house in Groton, Suff'k.

"MY GOOD WIFE, — I received thy most kinde Lettre, & doe prayse God for the good newes of thy wellfare & of all our familye : which I beseech him in mercye to continue & blesse unto us. I like well of thy iournye to Maplested, for thou hadst need of some refreshinge among thy many cares & troubles. Our best comfort is, we shall rest in heaven. I cannot write much to thee for I am going to Westminster : neither can tell thee when I shall come home, but my love towards thee will hasten mee. Our friendes heere are in health, yet my sister ffones is not well. They desire to be rememb : to thee. So in much hast with my love & blessing to my children, salut^{ns} to all our good friendes & my best Affections to thy selfe, I comende thee to the blessinge & protection of the Lord & so I kisse my sweet wife & rest

"Thy faithfull husbande,   "Jo : WINTHROP.
"JUNE 17. 1629.

"Let this lettre inclosed be delivered into Mr. Motts owne hands."

John Winthrop to his Wife.

"To his very loving Wife, Mrs. Winthrop, at her House in Groton.

"MY GOOD WIFE, — I wrote to thee this week by Roger Mather, but shall expect no other letter from thee, because of thy journey to Maplested, from whence I hope thou art safely returned. Blessed be the Lord, our good God, who watcheth over us in all our ways to do us good, and to comfort us with his manifold blessings, not taking occasion by our sins to punish us as we deserve. Through his mercy it is, that I continue in health, and that, to my great joy, I hear well of thee and our family. The Lord teach us the right use of all his blessings, and so temper our affections towards the good things of this life, as our greatest joy may be, that our names are in the book of life, that we have the good will of our heavenly Father, that Christ Jesus is ours, and that by him we have right to all things. Then, come what will, we may have joy and confidence.

" My sweet wife, I am sorry that I cannot now appoint the time, that I hope to return, which cannot be the next week; though, it is like, my sister Fones, or some of her company, will come down then; but you shall hear more the beginning of next week.

" For news I have but one to write of, but that will be more welcome to thee than a great deal of other. My office is gone, and my chamber, and I shall be a saver in them both. So, as I hope, we shall now enjoy each other again, as we desire. The Lord teach us to improve our time and society to more use for our mutual comfort, and the good of our family, etc., than before. It is now bed time; but I must lie alone; therefore I make less haste. Yet I must kiss my sweet wife; and so, with my blessing to our children, and salutation to all our friends, I commend thee to the grace and blessing of the Lord, and rest,   " Thy faithful husband,   " Jo. Winthrop.

" My brother D. and sister, and sister F. commend them to thee."

John Winthrop to his Wife.

" My good Wife, — Blessed be the Lord o^r God for his great mercye still continued to us & o^{rs}. O that we could consider aright of his kindnesse, that we might knowe o^r happinesse in being the children of such a father, & so tenderly beloved of the All sufficient, but we must needs complaine. Oh this flesh, this fraile sinfull flesh, that obscures the beauty

& brightnesse of so great glorye & goodnesse! I thanke thee
for thy most kinde & sweet Lettre, the stampe of that amiable
affection of a most lovinge wife : I assure thee, thy labour of
love (tho' it be very great) shall not be lost, so far as the
prayers & endeavours of a faithfull husbande can tende to
requitall.   But I must limitt the length of my desires to the
shortnesse of my leysure, otherwise I should not knowe when
to ende.   I trust, in the Lorde, the tyme of o^r wished meetinge
wilbe shortly, but my occasions are such as thou must have
pacience till the ende of next weeke, thoughe I shall strive to
shorten it, if possible I maye : and after that, I hope, we shall
never parte so longe againe, till we parte for a better meetinge
in heaven.   But where we shall spende the rest of o^r short tyme
I knowe not : the Lorde, I trust, will direct us in mercye ; my
comfort is that thou art willinge to be my companion in what
place or conditiō soevere, in weale or in woe.   Be it what it
may, if God be wth us, we need not feare ; his favour, & the
kingdome of heaven wilbe alike & happinesse enough to us &
o^{rs} in all places.   [*torn*] is in London, but I have seen him but
twice, I knowe not what he doth nor what he intendeth, I
mourne for his sinnes & the miserye that he will soone bringe
upon himselfe & his wife.   Our freinds here are all in health
(God be praysed) & desire to be com͞ended to thee, so wth my
love & blessinge to o^r children, salutatiō to all o^r freinds, my
brother & sister Gostlin &c, I com͞ende thee to the good Lorde
& kisse my sweet wife & rest

    " Thy faithfull husband   " JO : WINTHROP.

" JUNE 22. 1629.

 " Send me no horses except I send for them."

John Winthrop to his Wife.

" To his verye lovinge Wife, Mrs Winthrop the elder at her house in
Groton in Suffolk.

 " MY GOOD WIFE, — I received thy kinde Lettre, & doe
blesse our good God that I heare of thy wellfare & of all o^r

familye; myselfe am likewise in health (I prayse the Lorde) &
hope to be wth thee shortly, with my sister ffones & all her company: We intend (God willinge) to sett forth of London on
Wenesdaye next, & so to be at Groton on thursdaye. The
Lorde directe & prosper all o^r iorneye. I am so streightened in
tyme as I can write no more, but must leave the rest to be supplied when I come; the good Lorde & o^r most mercifull father
blesse & keepe thee & all o^rs. So with the kinde salutations of
all o^r freinds heer to thee, & mine owne to all o^r freinds w^th
thee, I kisse my sweet wife & rest

"Thy faithfull husband   "Jo: WINTHROP.
"JUNE 26. 1629.

"Let this lettre inclosed be delivered into his owne hands."

It will be observed, that, in the letter of June 5, Winthrop says to his wife, "I thinke my Office is gone;"
and that, in a subsequent letter (without date), he tells
her distinctly, "My Office is gone & my chamber both."
We know not the circumstances under which he ceased
to be an Attorney of the Court of Wards. His oppo-
sition to the course of the Government at this period,
and his manifest sympathy with those who were suffering
under its unjust exactions and proscriptions, may have
cost him his place. Or he may have resigned it volun-
tarily, in view of the new plans of life, which more than
one of his letters would seem to indicate that he was contemplating. It is evident that he felt that a crisis was at
hand in the condition of England, and that he was
anticipating a personal share in the sufferings to which
the friends of civil and religious freedom were about to
be subjected. When he says to his wife, in the last
letter but one, "Where we shall spend the rest of our

short time I know not, — my comfort is that thou art willing to be my companion in what place or condition soever," — we seem to find the first foreshadowing of the great decision which will be developed in our next chapter.

The present chapter may be concluded, like the last, with a little scrap from the private " Experiences ;" which corresponds exactly to the period we have reached.

" July 28 : 1629. My Bro : Downing & myselfe ridinge into Lincolnshire by Ely, my horse fell under me in a bogge in the fennes, so as I was allmost to the waiste in water ; but the Lorde preserved me from further danger. Blessed be his name."

New England may well say Amen to this blessing. That ride to Lincolnshire was on an eventful errand. Beyond a question, Winthrop and Downing were on their way to Sempringham to visit Isaac Johnson, and consult with him about the great Massachusetts enterprise. There is a letter from Johnson to Downing, found among Winthrop's papers,[1] dated just twenty days before, inviting them to do so. The Lady Arbella was doubtless at home to administer the hospitalities ; and Winthrop may have promised her, in some playful compliment, that, if she would be of the party, the ship should bear her name. But the interview was almost too serious for compliments of any sort ; and we are anticipating events which belong to a later page.

---

1 Mass. Hist. Coll., 4th series, vol. vi. p. 29.

CHAPTER XVI.

WINTHROP DECIDES FOR NEW ENGLAND. HIS SON'S LETTER APPROV-
ING THE DECISION. THE CONSIDERATIONS AND CONCLUSIONS.

WE have at length reached the period of a decision, which has made the life of John Winthrop a part of the public history of New England and of America. We devoted the last chapter to the changes which had occurred in his domestic circumstances and condition during the absence of his eldest son in the East, and to the correspondence which relates to that period. These changes had undoubtedly co-operated with other and more public considerations in preparing his mind for the great step which he had now resolved upon, and which was announced to the younger Winthrop, by a letter from Groton, immediately on his arrival in London. Unhappily, this letter is missing from the family file, and cannot be recovered. No doubt, it explained the reasons why the father could not hasten in person to London, to welcome his son home again after so long an absence. No doubt, it told him of the momentous meeting which was to take place at Cambridge a few days afterwards, and from which nothing could excuse him for staying away. No doubt, it gave him a summary sketch of the original springs and motives of his determination to quit his native land, and to become the leader of the great emigration to the New World.

Most fortunately, the son's reply has been preserved; and the beauty of its style and thought is only surpassed by the importance of its substance. It is a memorable letter in New-England history. It is certainly a memorable letter in the correspondence of those between whom it passed. Fresh from a protracted pilgrimage in distant lands, the younger Winthrop condenses into a single sentence the whole philosophy of his travels. In another sentence, he expresses his confident belief that the whole disposition of the business in hand is " of the Lord; " and, in a third, he dedicates himself unreservedly to the work, with an earnestness and a solemnity which could only be equalled by the diligence and fidelity with which the pledge was redeemed in his subsequent career.

But the letter will speak sufficiently for itself; and we give it without further comment.

John Winthrop, Jr., to his Father.

" SIR, — My humble duty remembered to you and my mother, may you please to understand, that I received your letters, that by William Ridley on Wednesday, and your other yesterday, rejoicing much to hear of your welfare, with the rest of our good friends, which I desire much with my own eyes to behold. Therefore I purpose, God willing, to make all haste down the next week, hoping to accept of Mr. Gurdon's kind offer, if I can.

" For the business of New England, I can say no other thing, but that I believe confidently, that the whole disposition thereof is of the Lord, who disposeth all alterations, by his blessed will, to his own glory and the good of his; and, therefore, do assure myself, that all things shall work together for

the best therein.   And for myself, I have seen so much of the
vanity of the world, that I esteem no more of the diversities
of countries, than as so many inns, whereof the traveller that
hath lodged in the best, or in the worst, findeth no difference,
when he cometh to his journey's end ; and I shall call that my
country, where I may most glorify God, and enjoy the presence
of my dearest friends.   Therefore herein I submit myself to
God's will and yours, and, with your leave, do dedicate myself
(laying by all desire of other employments whatsoever) to the
service of God and the Company herein, with the whole endeavors, both of body and mind.

"The CONCLUSIONS, which you sent down, I showed my
uncle and aunt, who liked them well.   I think they are unanswerable ; and it cannot but be a prosperous action, which is
so well allowed by the judgments of God's prophets, undertaken by so religious and wise worthies of Israel, and indented
to God's glory in so special a service.

"My aunt Goulding remembereth her love to you.   She
saith, it is not yet discharged, that she knoweth.   Here is certain news, that the Dutch have taken Wesel.   So, desiring
your prayers and blessing, I commend you to the Almighty's
protection, and rest   "Your obedient son,
                                        "JOHN WINTHROP.
"LONDON, August 21, 1629.

"I pray remember my love to my brothers and sisters and
all our friends, whom I hope shortly to see."

It would not be easy, at this late day, to identify the
precise paper which was enclosed in the letter of the elder Winthrop, and to which the son alludes, under the
title of "the Conclusions."   The original may have disappeared, and perhaps may have perished, with the letter
in which it was communicated.   Yet, more probably, it
was returned to the father's hands, after it had been

examined and' considered; and it may be among the
mass of manuscript matter from which this Biography
is compiled. There can be no doubt, certainly, that we
have the substance of it, if not the original or an exact
duplicate, in one or both of the papers which will now
be given.

And, first, we have a paper, a considerable portion of
which has been already published in Hutchinson's "Collection of Original Papers relative to the History of the
Colony of Massachusetts Bay," under the title of "General Considerations for the Plantation of New England,
with an Answer to several Objections." It will be observed, by those who may desire to institute the comparison, that this document, as we now give it from a
careful copy found among Winthrop's papers, differs
essentially, both in its title and in its text, from the version which fell into the hands of Hutchinson. Not only
are the various heads of the argument differently ar-
ranged, but many of them are carried out into much
greater detail. One might doubt whether the differences were the result of an attempt to amplify, or of an
attempt to condense, an original draught; but it is manifest that there was a common original for them both.
As an authentic cotemporary exposition of the views
which brought Winthrop and the whole Massachusetts
Company over to New England, and as unquestionably
prepared by himself, it belongs to his biography in the
amplest form in which it is found among his papers.
We give it accordingly, as follows: —

" Reasons to be considered for iustifieinge the undertakeres of the intended Plantation in New England, & for incouraginge such whose hartes God shall move to ioyne wth them in it.

" 1. It will be a service to the Church of great consequence to carry the Gospell into those parts of the world, to helpe on the comminge of the fullnesse of the Gentiles, & to raise a Bulworke against the kingdome of AnteChrist wch the Jesuites labour to reare up in those parts.

" 2. All other churches of Europe are brought to desolation, & o^r sinnes, for wch the Lord beginnes allreaddy to frowne upon us & to cutte us short, doe threatne evill times to be comminge upon us, & whoe knowes, but that God hath provided this place to be a refuge for many whome he meanes to save out of the generall callamity, & seeinge the Church hath noe .place lefte to flie into but the wildernesse, what better worke can there be, then to goe & provide tabernacles & foode for her against she comes thether :

" 3. This Land growes weary of her Inhabitants, soe as man, whoe is the most pretious of all creatures, is here more vile & base then the earth we treade upon, & of lesse prise among us then an horse or a sheepe : masters are forced by authority to entertaine servants, parents to mainetaine there owne children, all townes complaine of the burthen of theire poore, though we have taken up many unnessisarie' yea unlawfull trades to mainetaine them, & we use the authoritie of the Law to hinder the increase of o^r people, as by urginge the Statute against Cottages, & inmates, & thus it is come to passe, that children, servants & neighboures, especially if they be poore, are compted the greatest burthens, wch if thinges weare right would be the cheifest earthly blessinges.

" 4. The whole earth is the Lords garden & he hath given it to the Sonnes of men wth a gen^l Comission : Gen : 1 : 28 : increace & multiplie, & replenish the earth & subdue it, wch was againe renewed to Noah : the end is double & naturall, that man might enioy the fruits of the earth, & God might have his due glory from the creature : why then should we stand striving here for places of habitation, etc, (many men spending as much labour & coste to recover or keepe sometimes an acre or twoe of Land, as would procure them many & as good or better in another Countrie) & in the meane time suffer a whole Continent as fruitfull & convenient for the use of man to lie waste wthout any improvement?

" 5. We are growne to that height of Intemperance in all excesse of Riott, as noe mans estate allmost will suffice to keepe saile wth his æqualls : & he whoe failes herein, must live in scorne & contempt. Hence it comes that all artes & Trades are carried in that deceiptfull & unrighteous course, as it is allmost impossible for a good & upright man to mainetayne his charge & live comfortablie in any of them.

" 6. The ffountaines of Learning & Religion are soe corrupted as (besides the unsupportable charge of there education) most children (even the best witts & of fairest hopes) are perverted, corrupted, & utterlie overthrowne by the multitude of evill examples & the licentious governm^t of those seminaries, where men straine at knatts & swallowe camells, use all severity for mainetaynance of cappes & other accomplyments, but suffer all ruffianlike fashions & disorder in manners to passe uncontrolled.

" 7. What can be a better worke, & more honorable & worthy a Christian then to helpe raise & supporte a particular Church while it is in the Infancy, & to ioyne his forces wth such a company of faithfull people, as by a timely assistance may growe stronge & prosper, & for wante of it may be put to great hazard, if not wholly ruined :

" 8. If any such as are knowne to be Godly, & live in wealth & prosperity here, shall forsake all this, to ioyne themselves wth this Church & to runne an hazard wth them of an hard & meane condition, it will be an example of great use both for removinge the scandall of worldly & sinister respects wch is cast upon the Adventurers ; to give more life to the faith of Gods people, in their praiers for the Plantation ; & to incorrage others to ioyne the more willingly in it.

" 9. It appeares to be a worke of God for the good of his
Church, in that he hath disposed the hartes of soe many of his
wise & faithfull servants, both ministers & others, not onely to
approve of the enterprise but to interest themselves in it, some
in their persons & estates, other by their serious advise & helpe
otherwise, & all by their praiers for the wealfare of it.   Amos
3 : the Lord revealeth his secreat to his servants the prophetts,
it is likely he hath some great worke in hand wch he hath revealed to his prophetts among us, whom he hath stirred up to
encourage his servants to this Plantation, for he doth not use
to seduce his people by his owne prophetts, but comitte that
office to the ministrie of false prophetts & lieing spiritts.

" *Diverse obiections wch have been made against this Plantation, wth*
their answears & Resolutions:
    " Ob : 1 : We have noe warrant to enter upon that Land
wch hath been soe longe possessed by others :
    " Ans : 1 : That wch lies comon, & hath never beene reple-
nished or subdued, is free to any that possesse & improve it :
ffor God hath given to the sonnes of men a double right to the
earth ; theire is a naturall right, & a civill right.   The first
right was naturall when men held the earth in comon every
man sowing & feeding where he pleased : then as men & theire
Cattell encreased, they appropriated certaine parcells of Grounde
by inclosinge & peculiar manuerance, & this in time gatte them
a civill right : such was the right wch Ephron the Hittite had
in the feild of Mackpelah wherein Abraham could not bury a
dead Corpes wthout leave, though for the out parts of the
Countrie wch lay comon he dwelt upon them, & tooke the fruite
of them at his pleasure : the like did Jacob, who fedde his
Cattell as bouldly in Hamors Land, (for he is said to be Lord
of the Countrie) & in other places where he came, as the native Inhabitants themselves : & that in those times & places
men accompted noething theire owne, but that wch they had
appropriated by theire owne industry, appeares plainely by this,
that Abimileckes Servants in there owne Countrie, when they

ofte contended wth Isaackes servants about welles wch they had digged, yet never strove for the Land wherein they weare : Soe likewise betweene Jacob & Laban, he would not take a kidde of Labans wthout speaciall contracte ; but he makes noe bargaine wth them for the Land where they fedde, & it is very probable that if the Countrie had not beene as free for Jacob as for Laban, that covetous wretch would have made his advantage of it, & have upbraided Jacob wth it as he did wth his Cattell : As for the Natives in New England, they inclose noe Land, neither have any setled habytation, nor any tame Cattle to improve the Land by, & soe have noe other but a Naturall Right to those Countries. Soe as if we leave them sufficient for their use, we may lawfully take the rest, there being more then enough for them & us :

" 2. We shall come in wth the good leave of the natives who finde benifight allreaddy by o^r neighbourhood, & learne from us to improve a parte to more use then before they could doe the whole : & by this meanes we come in by valuable purchase, for they have of us that wch will yeeld them more benefight, then all that Land wch we have from them.

" 3. God hath consumed the Natives wth a great Plauge in those parts, soe as there be few Inhabitants lefte.

" Ob : 2 : It will be a great wrong to o^r Churche & Countrie to take awaye the good people, & we shall lay it the more open to the Judgm^t feared.

" Ans : 1 : The departinge of good people from a Countrie doe not cause a Judgment but forshewth it, wch may occasion such as remaine to turne from there evill waies, that they may prævent it, or to take some other course that they may escape it :

" 2. Such as goe awaye are of noe observation in respect of those whoe remaine, & they are likely to doe more good there then here, & since Christs time the Church is to be considered as universall wthout distinction of Countries, soe as he that doeth good in one place serves the Church in all places in regard of the unity.

" 3. It is the revealed will of God that the Gospell should be preached to all nations, & though we know not whether these Barbarians will receive it at first or noe, yet it is a good worke to serve Gods providence in offering it to them (& this is fittest to be doone by Gods owne servants) for God shall have glory by it though they refuse it, & there is good hope that the Posterity shall by this meanes be gathered into Christs sheepefould.

" Ob : 3. We have feared a Judgment a great while, but yet we are safe, it weare better therefore to stay till it come, & either we may flie then, or if we bee overtaken in it we may well content o^r selves to suffer wth such a Church as ours is :

" Ans : It is likely that this consideration made the Churches beyound the Seas as the Pallatinate, Rochelle, etc, to sitt still at home, & not looke out for the shelter, while they might have founde it ; but the woefull spectacle of theire ruine may teach us more wisdome to avoide the Plauge when it is fore-seene, & not to tarry as they did till it overtake us. If they weare now at their former liberty we may be sure they would take other Courses for theire safty ; & though halfe of them had miscarried in their escape, yet had it not beene soe misera-ble to themselves nor scandalous to Religion as this desperate backsliding & abiureing the trewth, wch many of the ancient Professours among them, & the whole Posteritie wch remaine are now plundged into :

" Ob : 4 : The ill successe of other Plantations may tell us what will become of this :

" Ans : 1 : None of the former sustained any great damage but Virginia, wch happned through there owne slouth & secu-rity.

" 2. The argument is not good, for thus it standes : Some Plantations have miscarried, therefore we should not make any ; it consists of particulars & soe concludes noethinge. We might as well reason thus ; many houses have beene burnt by killes, therefore we should use none : many shippes have beene cast awaye, therefore we should content o^r selves wth o^r home commodities & not adventure mens lives at Sea for those thinges wch we might live w^thout : Some men have beene undoone by being advanced to great places, therefore we should refuse all præferment, etc :

"3. The fruite of any publike designe is not to be discerned by the immediate successe ; it may appeare in time that tlie former Plantations weare all to good use.

"4. There weare great & fundamentall errors in the former wch are like to be avoided in this : ffor : 1 : their mayne end was Carnall & not Religious : 2. They used unfitt instruments, a multitude of rude & misgovernd persons, the very scumme of the Land : 3 : They did not establish a right forme of government.

"Ob : 5. It is attended wth many & great difficulties :

"Ans : Soe is every good action ; the Heathen could say *Ardua virtutis via*, & the way of Gods kingdome, wch is the best waye in the world, is accompanied wth most difficulties, Streight is the gate, & narrow is the waye, that leadeth to life : againe the difficulties are noe other then such as many dayly meete w^th, & such as God hath brought others well through them :

"Ob : 6. It is a worke above the power of the undertakers :

"Ans : 1. The wealfare of any body consists not soe much in quantitie as in a due proportion & disposition of parts, & we see other Plantations have subsisted diverse yeares & prospered from weaker meanes :

"2. It is noe wonder for great thinges to arise from smale & contemptible beginnings ; it hath beene often seene in kingdomes & States, & may as well hould in townes & plantations. The Waldenses weare scattred into the Alpes, & mountaines of Peidmont, by small companies, but they became famous Churches whereof some remaine to this day, & it is certaine that the Turckes, Venetians, & other States weare very weake in their beginninges :

"Ob : 7 : The Countrie affordes not naturall fortifications :

" Ans. Noe more did Holland & many other places wch had greater enimies & neerer at hand, & God doth use to place his people in the middest of perills, that they may trust in him & not in outward meanes of safety ; soe when he would chouse a place to plante his onely beloved people in, he seated them not in an Iland or other place fortified by nature, but in a plaine Countrie, besette wth potent & bitter enimies rounde about, yet soe longe as they served him & trusted in his helpe they were safe ; soe the Apostle S^{nt} Paull saith of himselfe & his fellow labourours, that they weare coumpassed wth dangers on every side & weare dayly under the sentence of death, that they might learne to trust in the livinge God :

" Ob : 8 : The place affordeth not comfortable meanes to the first planters, & o^r breedinge here at home hath made us unfitte for the hardshippe we are like to endure there.

" Ans : 1. Noe place of itself hath afforded sufficient to the first Inhabitants ; such thinges as we stand in neede of are usually supplied by Gods blessing upon the wisdome & industry of man, & whatsoever we stand in neede of is treasured up in the earth by the Creator, & to be feched thense by the sweate of o^r browes :

" 2. We must learne wth Paull to want as well as to abounde ; if we have foode & raym^t (wch are there to be had) we ought to be contented, the difference in the quality may a little displease us but it cannot hurt us.

" 3. It may be God will by this meanes bringe us to repent of o^r former Intemperance, & soe cure us of that desease wch sends many amongst us untimely to o^r graves & others to hell : Soe he carried the Isralites into the wildernesse & made them forgette the fleshpotts of Egipt, wch was some pinch to them at first but he disposed it to their good in the end, Deu. 8 : 3 : 16 :

" Ob : 9. We must looke to be præserved by miracle if we subsiste, & soe we shall tempt God.

" Ans : 1. They who walke under ordinary meanes of safety & supply doe not tempt God, but such will o^r condition be in this Plantation, therefore the proposition cannot be denied ; the assumption we prove thus, that place is as much secured from ordinary dangers as many in the civill parts of the world, & we shall have as much provision beforehand as such townes doe use to provide against a seige or dearth, & sufficient meanes for raising a sufficient store to succeed against that be spent. If it be denied that we shall be as secure as other places, we answeare that many of o^r Sea townes, & such as are upon the confines of enimies countries in the continent, lie more open & neerer to danger then we shall ; and though such townes have sometime beene burnt or spoiled, yet men tempt not God to dwell still in them, & though many houses in the Countrie amongst us lie open to robbers & theeves (as many have found by sad experience) yet noe man will say that those that dwell in such places must be præserved by miracle :

" 2. Though miracles be now ceased, yet men may expecte a more then ordinarie blessing from God upon all lawfull meanes where the worke is the Lords & he is sought in it according to his will, for it is usuall wth him to encrease or weaken the strength of the meanes as he is pleased or displeased wth the Instruments & the action ; else we must conclude that God hath lefte the goverm^t of the world & comitted all power to the Creature, that the successe of all thinges should wholely depend upon second causes.

" 3. We appeale to the iudgm^t of Soldiers if 500 men may not in one mounth raise a fortification wch wth sufficient munition & victuall they may not make good against 3000 for many mounths, & yet w^thout miracle :

" 4. We demand an instaunce of any Prince or State that hath raised 3000 Soldieres, & hath victuald them for vi or viii mounths wth shippinge & munition answerable to invade a place soe far distant as this is from any forraine enimie, & where they must runne on hazard of Repulse, & noe bootie or iust title of soveranitie to allure them :

" Ob : 10. If it succeed ill, it will raise a scandall upon o^r profession :

" Ans : It is noe rule in Philosophie much lesse in divinity to iudge the action by the successe ; the enterprize of the Israelites against Beniamin succeeded ill twice yet the action was good & prospered in the end. The Erle of Beziers in ffrance & Tholosuge miscarried in the defence of a iust cause of Religion & theire hereditarie right against the uniust violence of the Earle Montford & the Popes Legatt : The Duke of Saxony & the Landgrave had ill successe in the defence of the Gospell against Charles the 5ᵗʰ, wherein the Duke & his Children lost their whole Inheritance to this day : The Kinge of Denmarck & other Princes of the union had ill successe in the defence of the Palatinate & the Liberty of Germanie, yet their profession suffered not wᵗʰ their persons, except it weare wᵗʰ the adversaries of Religion, & soe it was noe scandall given."

The paper thus given is in the handwriting of Forth Winthrop, who, as there is abundant evidence, was frequently employed as a copyist for his father. Serious doubts have sometimes been expressed, whether the elder Winthrop was the author of this paper. Hutchinson seems to ascribe its authorship to Francis Higginson.[1] The name of John White has also been given in connection with it. Indeed, a copy of the paper has recently been found among the Colonial Documents of Her Majesty's State-paper Office, in London ; on which is indorsed, " White of Dorchester his instructions for the plantation of New England." But this version is even more abbreviated and condensed than the one given by Hutchinson. Meantime, we find an original draught of the earlier portion of the paper, with marginal alterations and suggestions, in the handwriting of the elder Winthrop,

---

[1] Hutchinson's Collection of Papers, p. 24.

indorsed " For New England, May, 1629 ; " proving that he had it under consideration several months before it was submitted to his son, and that he was probably preparing it about the time when he wrote the letter to his wife, dated May 15, 1629 (given in the last chapter), which has so many sentiments and expressions in common with these Observations. We find, moreover, another portion of the paper in Winthrop's handwriting, distinctly indorsed, " Objections Answered, *the first draught;* " together with still other autograph manuscripts of his, which were evidently preparations for the same composition.

Undoubtedly, the paper was submitted to the consideration of others interested in the enterprise to which it related ; and it may have been altered and amended after a comparison of opinions with the leading friends of the movement. Copies of it were probably made in its original shape, and sent to such men as White and Cradock and Saltonstall and Isaac Johnson and Humphrey and Higginson ; if Higginson, indeed, had not left England before it was the subject of consideration.[1] These may be the copies which found their way into Hutchinson's collection, or were communicated to the British archives from the papers of White. But the testimony now furnished by the family papers of Winthrop would seem to settle the question, in default of any positive evidence to the contrary, that the paper was prepared by him.

In confirmation of the idea that copies of the paper were submitted by Winthrop to the consideration of some

---

[1] Higginson sailed in April, 1629.

of his friends and neighbors, we give, next, an interesting letter, without date, address, or signature, but in the
unmistakable chirography of Robert Ryece, of Preston,
in the county of Suffolk. Robert Ryece, says an old
manuscript in the Herald's College, relating to the antiquities of Suffolk, was " an accomplished gentleman, and
a great preserver of the Antiquities of this County. He
had his education some years in the house of Mr. Theodore Beza, at Geneva. He set up in Preston the Royal
Arms of England, in a fair table, and in glasse the
names of the most ancient Knights and Esquires of
this County, of which the most remain this 25th of March,
1655." [1]

The letter contains a running commentary on the various heads of the paper last given, which had evidently
been submitted to him by Winthrop ; and concludes with
some friendly, though not altogether encouraging, suggestions in regard to the New-England enterprise. But it
contains some other allusions also, which will require
further elucidation at its close.

Robert Ryece to John Winthrop.

"*For the fyrst tracte of the* 7 : *general articles.*

" There is no woorke deemed more lawefull & more requisite,
then y⁰ plātatiō & establishinge of a true church : for y⁰ propa-
gatinge of true Religeō & y⁰ christian faythe; but yett in y⁰
due tyme & place, wᵗʰ a wary regarde of all necessary circū-
stances belonginge to the same, & wᵗʰ a due respecte to all

---

[1] Ryece married Mary, the eldest daughter of Thomas Appleton, Esq., of Little
Waldingfield; and his Will, together with some account of his career, will be found in
the Appleton Memorial, privately printed, Boston, 1850, pp. 71–82.

future contingencies, that insteade of buyldinge thère bee not an overthrowenge.

"This service of reisinge, & setlinge a particular church, is suche a woorthie woorke, & carries suche a bewtifull pretexte, that it doothe anticipate ye awnswere to all obiections, & drawes a concession for sondrye reasons averred. Yett ye furtherance of a particular church is not to be preferred before ye betteringe of some smalle parte of a church allredy setled, that by absence of wonted care & respecte, the same maye suffer a defecte & diminution in recession. ffor, for wante of wonted assistaunce the state of ye church decayeth, wch in progression, by p^{r}sence of all the partes, prospereth.

"It is not denied, but ye newe church once truly settled in ye due tyme & place, maye throughe a sympathie bothe of nature & grace, bee of more use & comforte to hir moother church in future tymes of calamitie, the suche whō shee doothe styll noryshe in hir owne bosome; ffor it is ye conditiō of ye church some tymes to wanze, not allwayes eminently to growe; but sometymes to be ecclipsed in parte, darkened or persecuted; when as it is iuste to seeke refuge for saftye, especially where safest hope may be founde.

"To leave a place of lesse consideration, for a charge of greter consequence, imposed by ye generall callinge of ye better sorte, maye no dowte be allowed, especially as thinges stande heere at this daye, where ye inferiour magistrate, yf he be true & stricte for ye due execution of his place, especially ag^{te} poperye, or ag^{te} the common synnes of the tyme, is alltogeth^r discoraged & discowntenanced.

"And so many instanees may be given, how p^{r}vate persons of this kinde have iustely derelinquished there places, even wth good successe, for ye comon benefyte & better service of God.

"*ffor the second tracte of : 5 : perticuler respectes.*

"If ye State of thinges be so farre gone, y^t wthowte yor p^{r}sence, the cheefe und^{r}takers of this plantation, (men of g^{te} goodness, qualitie & wysdome) wyll no wayes stirre in this buysynes : And yf ye invitation of sondry devynes, m^te deere unto you, Juditious & of g^te understandinge, wth ye calle of supreame auc^te, rectefyenge & awnsweringe all impedim^ts & obiections whatsoev^r, wch was no wayes knowē to yor friendes in these partes, wch wyshed & prayed for yor good, as entyrely and respectyvelye as any others : there is no reason, & lesse conscience, for a particular uncertayntie & an uncomfortable charge heere at home, to omytte & overthrowe a woorke of so eminente consideration & consequence abroade, wherein more service maye be doone to God, ye com̄on benefyte & yor owne particular, wch it were g^te indiscretion to neglecte nowe ye doore is opened, & were a g^te forgettfull unthankfullnes to the lorde, to refuse imploym^ts in so hie an ordināce.

"And therefore yor friends doe now rath^r encorage yo^u to proceede, & do entreate the Allmightye Lorde of Hostes, to goe wth yo^u, to blesse & governe yo^u in all yor wayes.

"Somewhat breefelye for the thyrde tracte.

"It is agayne acknowledged, there can be no woorke or service of great^r consequence, then to plante ye ghospell in ye remote partes of ye woorlde, even for a Rebutter ag^te An̄christe : & ye more for that wee see, y^t m^te parte of ye protestante churches of Europe are destroyed, wherew^th if ye same lotte cometh upon this lande, as longe synce hathe byn feared, how woonderfull is ye lorde in mercye, that hathe reysed this newe plantatiō, for so comfortable a refuge, for all suche whom he hathe exempted oute of that generall divastation, wch o^r Synnes have so muche deserved.

"This contrye riche in ye plenty of a longe peace, & full wth ye surfetts of a contynewall ease, hathe longe synce growē weary of hir Inhītants, especially ye poorer sorte, reputed but as ye burden of ye State. And indeede thinges are growne, to suche a transcendente heighte of excesse in all intemperāce & ryotte, that no mās meanes are enoughe to keep sayle wth his equalls, wherein who so ever can not doe as oth^r men doe, oh wth what scorne & contempte doothe he lyve in? Now from this it befalleth y^t wee see suche fraude & deceipte in all artes & trades, y^t it is deemed allm^{te} impossible for a good & an uprighte mā, to maynetayne his charge, & to lyve comfortably amonge any of them.

"Agayne ye fowntaynes of all learninge Religiō, & ye wonted places for educatiō of youthe, are so corrupted, & so exceedingly chargeable, y^t the fynest wyttes of beste hope, throwghe infynite ill examples of debauched seminaries & governours, are utterly spoyled & overthrowen.

"All this is confessed wth the reste of yor argum^{ts}, wch I forbeare furth^r to wryte, bycawse y^t in suche a flourishinge church & comōon welthe (as the blinde lightes of this lande do p^{r}tende) where every place mourneth for wante of Justice, where ye cryenge synnes goe unponished or unreproved, crueltye and bloode is in o^r streetes, ye land aboundeth wth murthers, slawghters, Incestes, Adulteryes, whoredom, dronkennes, oppression & pride, where well doinge is not mayntayned, or ye godly cherished, but Idollatrye, popery, & what so ever is evyll is countenanced : even the leaste of these is enowghe, & enowghe to make haste owte of Babylon, & to seeke to dye rather in ye wyldernes then styll to dwelle in Sodome, Mesheck, & in the tents of Kedar.

"And now bycawse I see a constante resolutiō for this expeditiō, I praye yo^u yett geve me leave, by waye of cawtiō to enforme yo^u, what I have observed, frō others of g^{te} Judgem^{te}, wysdome, & longe experience in those remote affayres, not in the leaste sorte to contradicte y^r intention, but to make yo^u more warye to provyde for these difficulties.

"No sonner were thes partes discovered, but every one earnestly called for plātatiō, in ye wch ye Margāve had evermore a cheefe hande, stirrīge up auc^{te} & Nobyllytie for ye glory of ye Kingdome, & all godly well disposed persons to contribute, & to collecte, many g^{te} Sumēs, wth these bewtifull pretextes, ye honor of ye Crowne to have newe accesses to ye same, ye enlargem^{te} of Gods church where ye christian faythe was never yett preched, & the g^{te} good of ye lande, to employe so many

ydle heere at home, for trade & traffacke, whereas for there
owne particular benefyte, (wch was ye ende of all these allega-
tions, & wch hathe byn ye sole overthrowe of all these plantations) they never once mētioned. ffor there shall yo^u observe,
yf ye Marchants sawe not p^{r}nte gayne, Supplie promised was
eyth^r totally denyed, or so longe delayed, that they were all
starved & consumed.

"Thay observed lykewise from ye beginninge of this discoverye plantations often attēpted, but never succeeded, unto
wch it wylbe awnswerd, the hystories relate sondry cawses
thereof, of all wch the p^{r}sente generatiō wyll have good cawse
to bewarre. The evill happe of form^r fundamentall errors, may
not hinder ye successe of ye latter. ffor perfection of thinges
is not founded in ye beginnynges, but from ye beginninges men
proceed to those thinges wch are perfectt.

"Thay suppose that untyl there bee, by more lengthe of
tyme, a setled State, wth good hope of certayntye, for a quiett
enioyēge of the same, from so neere & potente an adversary,
who ev^r lysteneth & gapeth for nothinge more thē when those
partes shall once become fytte for his praye, this is no tyme fytt
to adventure there for furth^r plantation.

"But suppose ye lande peopled, ye comowelthe established,
o^r lawes there setled for governm^{te}, as it is heere at home. Hathe
not form^r experience showed, y^t discōtented myndes seinge a
Presidente of weake Judgem^{te} in dangers, & lesse industry in
peace, wth too hie a cariadge in his place, how soone he is dis-
tasted, evē wth ye Cownsell, Soldiers & Mariners, upō ye successe of proceedinges in ye Colonye, how he is cōtemned, his
auc^{te} not regarded, alledgēge he hath no auc^{te} in that place,
beinge no acquired, hereditary or cōquered, setled, or established place, as heere at home, & therefore the great^r number
procede to depose hȳ & to choose a newe Presidēte : ffor inso-
lente cariadges in eminente auc^{te}, ag^t particular persons, may
by longe patience be endured & by strēgthe borne owte : But
whē errors towche the publicke, every member is sensible of
wronge, & putts his hande to his downefall.

"Yea ye Cownsell so often deryded by factions, throughe misgovernm^{te}, whē weake Presidentes appoynte unskyllfull officers in places wch belonge to thē who have spente longest tyme in the service of those partes — whē ye harvest is not duly gathered, the provision in store is moche spoyled or secretly solde to the enemyes, when pryvate Soldiers for victualls do sell there swoordes, there powd^r & shott, to trade wth the Savages, when others of lesse woorthe & regarde then hymselfe, as he deemeth, who never was acquaynted wth those affayres, to be advaunced to the place of gov^rm^{te}, himselfe & his service so longe tyme in those discoveries reiected, he murmureth, mutineth, & secretly conspireth wth p^rvie confederates, for ye primacye.

"Therefore ye beste direction of actions is cownsayle & wysdome to respecte ev^ry one in his place.

"Whē throwghe ye Presidents improvidence, ye Store is not wysely guyded or tymely renewed, from tradinge wth the Savadges, and whē usuall supplie of those partes of all vitualls & necessaryes cometh not soone as was expected, this wyll breede at the leaste suspicion & infinite discōtente, yf not anarchy.[1] ffor thē necessitie is neyth^r ruled by lawe, nor overruled by pow^r, hir force is so g^{te}, not only in ye passive resistance ag^{te} all harde Impressions, but in actyve & vyolente impetuositie, that throwghe all obstacles and dayngers, she wyll fynde a waye, or make it.

"Many in these partes havinge spente there estates, & ashamed heere to stryke sayle, have gone for this plantation, thinkinge there for to lyve at a lower rate, wth some thinge remayninge; but changinge only ye soyle & not ye cowrse of these degenerate tymes, to waste all in drynke & Tobacco, then when ye 2 hands can not feede one mouthe, nor clothe one backe, then they soone starve & pyne awaye. And when the Presidente & Cownsell admitteth ȿuche to lyve there, as can not woorke, but lyve ydlye, nor have any to woorke for them,

---

[1] We have followed the ancient abbreviations in almost every word except this, which in the original is "&^rch"! We claim some credit for the translation; which is obvious enough after it is once suggested, but certainly not before.

nor able there to compasse any meanes, whereupō lyve & setle hymselfe, What shall become on them ! Wysdome is not geven to sytt styll, & to lyve ydlye, but it doothe directe to all vertuous endeavoures. And Slothe & Idleness, wch is the norsery of all evill in a comō wealthe, hasteneth ye ruyne & dissolucion of ye wholl bodye & frame of ye State.

" To proceede furth^r in this sorte were teadious, but to a Judgem^t so quicke & apprehensyve it is in vayne ; only where so many dangers maye appere, to take ye leaste, ever dowbtinge what maye befalle : ffor in pollicie, dowbte is ye mooth^r of good successe, & he y^t feareth the woorste, p^{r}venteth it soonest. Yf you doe well, I shalbe moste gladde. That yo^u maye ever do well, I beseeche ye allmighty. And when you have dooṇe well, I shall infinitely reioyce & prayse the lorde, to whose blessed protection I ever more do leave yo^u in all yor wayes."

Winthrop is entitled to the sympathy of posterity, if all the responses to his communications about New England were in as crabbed characters, and in as lukewarm a strain, as this particular response of the Suffolk Antiquary. But the letter of Ryece is full of interest and value, nevertheless, as furnishing unequivocal evidence in regard to the papers submitted to his consideration. There were evidently three " Tractes " communicated to Ryece ; and they were probably the same in substance with those which were sent to the younger Winthrop. One of them was plainly the paper which has already been given ; to which Ryece refers as " the thyrde tracte," and of which he quotes a part of the precise language. The other two " Tractes" will be no less readily identified as the two brief series of *Conclusions*, which are found in Winthrop's own hand, and which are here printed for the first time, as follows : —

" Some Genl Conclusions shewinge that persons of good use heere (yea in publike service) may be transplanted for the furtherance of this plantation in N : E :

" 1 : It is granted that the worke is lawfull & hopefull of success for the great good of the Churche.

" 2 : It must be advaunced by persons, gifted (in some competent measure) suiteable to the worke.

" 3 : Every one who hathe meet gifts, hath not a will to the worke, & no bonde of Conscience or other compulsarye call can ordinaryely be imposed upon such as have no minde to it.

" 4 : The service of raysinge & upholdinge a particular Churche is to be preferred before the betteringe some parte of a Churche alreadye established.

" 5 : Of workes of the same kinde, that is most to be furthered, which (by common intendment) is of largest extente.

" 6 : The exercise of an Office of lesse consequence, whereinto any is putt by ordinarye callinge, may be lefte, upon the like call to some other imployment of greater consequence : especially where there followeth no violatiō of the rule of Righteousnesse.

" 7 : A future good, if it be greater, may be preferred before a present good that is lesse : & in this respecte, the members of that Churche may be of more use to their mother Churche heere, than manye of those whom she shall still keepe in her owne bosome ; so when the Churche in the Rev : 12 : was presented by the dragon, her sonne was taken from her, not regarding so muche what losse she should have of him for the present, as the future good he should be reserved for.

" 8 : It may be instanced in divers publike persons, & in many others of great use, that have lefte the places where they have been settled, & their changes approved.

" 9 : The takinge off a scandall from a wholl Churche & Religion itselfe is to be preferred before the betteringe of the same Churche : It is a Scandall to our Churche & Religion, that professinge in all o^r Plantations, the Conversion of those

Barbarians, yet we declare to the world, that we intende not that, but o^r owne profitt, in that we imploye not persons meete for suche a worke, but onely such as are a burden to us, or, for the most parte, suche as we can well spare, while the Papists in their like attempts, sticke not to send forthe of their most able & usefull Instruments.

" 10 : Our constant practice in matters of like nature may be a rule in this : for all forraine expeditions, we sticke not to imploye of o^r best Statesmen : & we grutche not to want their service at home (though never so usefull) while they are imployed for the good of other Churches abroad.

" Particular Considerations in the case of J : W :

" 1 : It is come to that issue as (in all probabilitye) the wellfare of the Plantation dependes upon his goeinge, for divers of the Chiefe Undertakers (upon whom the reste depende) will not goe without him.

" 2 : He acknowledges a satisfactorye callinge, outwarde from those of the Plantation, inwardly by the inclination of his own hearte to the worke, & bothe approved by godly & iuditious Devines (whereof some have the first interest in him), & there is in this the like mediate call from the Kinge, which was to his former imployment.

" 3 : Though his means be sufficient for a comfortable subsistence in a private condition heere, yet the one halfe of them being disposed to his 3 : elder sonnes, who are now of age, he cannot live in the same place & callinge with that which remains ; his charge being still as great as before, when his means were double : & so if he should refuse this opportunitye, that talent which God hath bestowed upon him for publike service, were like to be buried.

" 4 : His wife & suche of his children, as are come to years of discreation, are voluntarylye disposed to the same Course.

" 5 : Most of his friends (upon the former considerations) doe consent to his change."

One of these little " Tractes" must have undergone
some modification after it was submitted to Robert Ryece;
as "the 7: general articles" have become 10 in the copy
which has here been given.   But "the Particular Considerations in the case of J: W:" are plainly just what
they were when the Suffolk Antiquary referred to them
as "the second tracte of 5: perticuler respectes."   The
fourth of these considerations could hardly have been set
forth so unqualifiedly until after the younger Winthrop
had given his assent to the plan; but, with this exception, there can be little room for doubt, that the papers
which have been here printed are substantially "the
Conclusions" to which he alludes in the admirable letter
at the beginning of this chapter.   That letter could not
have failed to encourage the heart and confirm the purpose of his father, at the most critical moment of his
deliberations on the subject; and it is hardly too much
to ascribe to its noble spirit a very material influence on
the result which so soon followed.   We shall see, that,
a few days only after it was received, the name of John
Winthrop (the elder) was affixed to the memorable
agreement, entered into at Cambridge, by twelve of the
leading friends of the Massachusetts Plantation, for embarking for New England, — " to inhabit and continue"
there.   Winthrop's name stands ninth on the list of
signers to this agreement; the name of Sir Richard
Saltonstall being at the head.   But the order of names
in the Massachusetts Records, so far as Winthrop is concerned, will soon undergo a very marked alteration.

We must not bring this chapter to a close, long as it
is already, without exhibiting Robert Ryece, the old Suf-

folk antiquary, in a more attractive aspect than that in which he appears in the letter of his which has already been made the subject of so much comment. He seems to have been consulted by Winthrop more than once in regard to his purpose of going over to New England, and to have written at least one other letter of remonstrance. This second letter, however, while it earnestly attempts to dissuade Winthrop from the enterprise, is full of the kindest and most complimentary expressions. Indeed, we should hardly know where to look for a more striking tribute to Winthrop's character and consequence at the period of his leaving Old England, or to the estimation in which he was held by his neighbors of Suffolk County, than is furnished by this letter of Robert Ryece. Such passages as the following are certainly full of significance : " The Church and Commonwealth here at home hath more need of your best ability in these dangerous times than any remote plantation." " All your kinsfolk and most understanding friends will more rejoice at your staying at home, with any condition which God shall send, than to throw yourself upon vain hopes, with many difficulties and uncertainties." " Plantations are for young men, that can endure all pains and hunger." " How hard will it be for one brought up among books and learned men to live in a barbarous place, where is no learning and less civility ! "[1]

---

[1] We have modernized the spelling of these quotations, though we leave the letter itself in its original form.

Robert Ryece to John Winthrop.[1]

"To the Woorshipfull his moche respected good friende Mr. Wynthrop at Bury, geve these.

"SIR, — Were I able to ryde so farre, I woolde wyllingly haue attended you this daye, not for the leaste abyllytie of any service which I can performe, but to shewe the beste of my affection to so deservinge a good friende. ffor the subiecte you wrytte of, breefely & playnelye to shewe you my mynde, what so ever other saye, I pray you geve mee leave in one woorde to shewe you. The Church & Common welthe heere at home, hathe more neede of your beste abyllytie in these dangerous tymes, then any remote plantation, which may be performed by persons of lesser woorthe & apprehension, which I ooolde shewe, yf I had tyme to thinke vpon dyversities of reasons which mighte be produced. Agayne, your owne estate wylbe more secured in the myddest of all accidents heere at home, then in this forreine expedition, which discovereth a 1000 ship-wrackes which may betyde. All your kynsfolkes & moste vnderstandinge friendes wyll more reioyce at your stayenge at home, with any condition which God shall sende, then to throwe your selfe vpon vayne hopes, with many difficulties & vncertayn-ties. Agayne, you shalbe more acceptable in the service of the Hieste, & more vnder His protection whiles you walke charely in your vocation heere at home, then to goe owte of your vocation, comyttinge your selfe to a woorlde of dangers abroade. The pype goeth sweete, tyll the byrde be in the nett; many bewtifull hopes ar sett before your eyes to allewer you to danger. Plantations ar for yonge men, that can enduer all paynes & hunger. Yf in your yewthe you had byn ac-quaynted with navigation, you mighte haue promised your selfe more hope in this longe vyadge, but for one of your yeeres to

---

1 This letter is printed in the sixth volume, Fourth Series, Massachusetts Historical Collections, pp. 392–393, for which it was furnished in advance of the publication of the present volume.

vndertake so large a taske is seldome seene but to miscarry.
To adventure your wholle famylly vpon so many manifeste
vncerteynties standeth not with your wysdome & longe experience.   Lett yonger yeeres take this charge vpon them, with the
advyse of that which elder yeeres shall directe them vnto, the
losse shalbe the lesse yf thay myscarry ; but there honor shalbe
the more if thay prosper.   So longe as you sytt at the helme,
your famylie prospereth, but yf you shoold happen to fayle,
your flocke woolde be at the leaste in hazarde, if not totally to
myscarrye.   Yonge mens directions thowghe sometymes with
some successe, do not all wayes succeede.   These remote partes
will not well agree with your yeeres ; whiles you are heere you
wyll be ever fytter by your vnderstandinge & wysdome to supplye there necessities.   But if it shoolde happen that you
shoolde gett safely thither, you shall soone fynde, how necessitie wyll calle for supplie from these partes.   I pray you
pardon my boldnes, that had rather erre in what I thinke, then
to be sylente in that I shoolde speake.   How harde wyll it bee
for one browghte vp amonge boockes & learned men, to lyve
in a barbarous place, where is no learnynge & lesse cyvillytie.
I beseeche the Lorde to directe you, & to keepe you in all your
wayes.   Thus in haste with the beste remembrance of my true
affection vnto you, I leave you to the protection of the Allmightye and do reste
            " Yours ever in all true affection
                                    " ROBT. RYECE.
" PRESTON, this 12 of Auguste, 1629."

This letter, it will be observed, bears date only a fortnight before the memorable Agreement at Cambridge,
to which we have just referred.   It was undoubtedly
written in reply to an invitation to attend a previous
meeting at Bury St. Edmond's for consultation upon the
same subject.   Certainly, if John Winthrop made any
mistake in coming over to New England, the old Suffolk

antiquary stands fully acquitted of not having given him seasonable and abundant warning of the error he was about to commit. Nor can we altogether wonder at the counsel which he gave, or at the opinions which he expressed. A grave and prudent person, as Robert Ryece seems to have been, would hardly have taken the responsibility of advising a man of Winthrop's age and standing to pluck up his stakes so summarily in his own land, with a view of planting them again in a remote and desolate wilderness. And even we, at this day, might regard it as having been a step of more than doubtful wisdom, did we not keep always in view the motives by which it was induced, and the results by which it was followed.

CHAPTER XVII.

DOMESTIC CORRESPONDENCE. WINTHROP CHOSEN GOVERNOR OF
THE MASSACHUSETTS COMPANY. THE CIRCUMSTANCES AND
CHARACTER OF THAT ELECTION.

THE earnestness and zeal with which the elder Winthrop
devoted himself to the New-England enterprise, after he
had once embarked in it, are abundantly manifested by
his letters at this period, and by those of his wife and
children. He was in London during a large part of the
month of October, 1629, busily occupied in the service
of the Massachusetts Company; and he had little leisure
for writing to any one. But his brevity is full of significance ; and whatever he enlarges upon has a special
interest and importance.

We give eight letters in the present chapter, six of
them new, as introductory to a consideration of Winthrop's peculiar relations to the great cause to which his
life and fortunes were now so solemnly consecrated. One
of the letters is from his son John, and another from his
wife. The others are his own ; and the last but one of
them contains a modest and parenthetical allusion to an
important event, which had occurred on the very day on
which the letter was written. No letter in our collection
— none, certainly, among those which have recently come
to light — would have been less willingly spared from the
personal memoirs or the public history of its writer.

John Winthrop to his Wife.

"MY DEAR WIFE, — I praise the Lord that I hear of thy welfare, and of the rest of our family. I thank thee for thy most kind letter, and especially that sweet affection, from whence it flows. I am sorry I cannot come down to thee, as I hoped; but there is no remedy. The Lord so disposeth as I must stay yet (I doubt) a fortnight, but, assure thyself, not one day more than I must needs.

"I pray thee have patience. God, in his due time, will bring us together in peace. We are now agreed with the merchants, and stay only to settle our affairs. I have not one quarter of an hour's time to write to thee. Therefore thou must bear with me, and supply all defects of remembrances. The Lord bless thee, my sweet wife, and all ours. Farewell.

"Thy faithful husband,

"Jo. WINTHROP.

"Send not up my horses till I send for them.

"OCTOBER."

John Winthrop, Jr., to his Father.

"SIR, — My humble duty remembred, hoping that you are in health, as God be thanked wee are all heere at this present. I thought I should have come to you to London on Saturday next, but because you wrote at the end of your letter to my mother that I should not need come till tuesday, I purpose to stay till then; but we did not well understand whether my brother Forth should need come up wth us to come downe wth my aunt Fones, wch you may please to certify my mother of wth your next letters. I understand that my brother [Henry] doth meane to returne from the Barbathoes wth the first occation, & then to goe wth his wife into New England. If he returne so soone, his voyage will but gaine him expenses & bee to noe purpose when he hath done for: except hee will continue there,[1] (wch I thinke would be the ruine of his soule to live among such company), he must be forced to trust some frend at his returne, wch he may doe as well now, & may make his estate as sure as any other merchants that are forced to commit all to others trust. Besides he may this winter sell his land & make provitions to goe wth you in the Spring, or at least to sende some stocke over, if my sister should not be ready to goe so soone. Therefore I pray S^r, if you see it fitting, counsell him to stay, or if my counsell hath prevailed wth him, be pleased to approve thereof. So desiring your praiers & blessing I humbly take my leave & rest

> "Your obedient sonne
>
> "JOHN WINTHROP.

"GROTON. Oct: 5: 1629.

"I pray remember my duty & love to my uncles & aunts, wth my love to my cozens. My sister Winthrop[2] & my brothers & sister remember their duty to you.

"I suppose if you please he may keepe it private."

John Winthrop to his Son.

"[To] his loving Son, John Winthrop, at Groton, Suffolk.

"SON, — I received your letter, and do heartily bless the Lord for the continuance of your welfare, beseeching him to sanctify you more and more, for his glory and your own salvation.

"For the business you write of concerning your brother, I have conferred with him, and shall be as glad as any of his stay here, if he can take any good order for his estate there. What he will do, I know not yet; but I think he will be with you soon. I would gladly have you here betimes next week; but, being it will be Monday sennight before we shall get forth of

---

1 At "the Barbathoes."
2 This was the wife of Henry, to whom the suggestions in the letter had reference.

town, it will be chargeable to keep all the horses here so long. Therefore, if you can find any company to come up with, you may be here on Tuesday or Wednesday; otherwise, you may stay a day or two the longer, and let John come with you; for I would not have you ride alone. I have sent down all the late news from New England. I would have some of you read it to your mother, and let Forth copy out the observations and all that follows from the ☞, and the letter in the end, and show it to Mr. Mott and others, that intend this voyage.[1] Your uncle and aunts are all in health, and salute you and the rest of ours, etc. Commend me to your uncle G. and A : and all the rest of our loving friends, that ask of me. So, with my love and blessing to yourself, your brothers and sister, salutations to our young company, I end, and rest

     "Your loving father,   "Jo. WINTHROP.
"OCTOBER 9, 1629."

John Winthrop to his Wife.

                    "OCTOB. 9 : 1629.

"My SWEET WIFE, — We heare yet of no lettres from Groton, wch makes us to mervaile, & we shall longe to heare how you all doe. I prayse God we are all heere in health, but we are not like to gett out of towne before mundaye señight : I wish my sonne John were heere before but that it wilbe verye chargeable to keepe horses so longe in towne; but if he can light upon any good company, he maye come on mundaye or teusday next, & John may bringe up the other horses on Saterdaye.

     "I sende thee herew^{th} some papers concerninge N : E : when thou lookest upon them, thou wilt beare wth the brevitye of my lettres : I would have Forth reade the booke to thee : for the loose papers let him write them out better, & then reade them.

---

[1] Mr. Savage, in the Appendix to Winthrop's History of New England, from which the letter is taken, says that this probably refers to the letters received a few days before from Higginson. — See Young's Chron. of Mass., 235, *et seq.*

I would have him copye out so much of that in the booke, as is from the hande in the [blank] leafe to the ende, & shewe it to Mr. Mott, my neighbo^r Childe & others that have a minde to N : E : especially that gratious lettre in the ende : wch I wish thee & the rest to reade seariously over.[1]

"This morninge I received thy sweet lettre ; I heartyly blesse o^r good God for the wellfare of thy selfe & all o^r familye, & doe much reioyce in thy love : I shalbe as loth to leave my kinde wife behinde me, as she wilbe to staye ; but we must leave all to the Lords good providence. I send downe by Jervais two peeces of Lokerum, 26 : elles of one peece, & 18 : of the other, cloth for a sute & Cloake for Forth : & for a night gowne for thy selfe, wth bookes for the children. Lett me knowe what triminge I shall sende for thy gowne.

"My sonne Hen : wilbe at Groton soone ; he is like to putt of his business in Barbethe^s & staye to goe to N : E : the occa- siō comes from my sonne John, as by this lettre I send you may appeare. The good Lo : dispose all for the best in his rich mercye. The Lord blesse thee (my sweet wife) & all o^r chil- dren & familye. My brother & sister salute thee, & all thy Companye. Farewell my good wife,

"Thy faithfull husband   "J : W :"

Margaret Winthrop to her Husband.

"MY DEARE HUSBAND, — I received thy sweet and most welcome letter very late this munday night, and doe blesse God for thy helth and welfayre. I have hearde reade the Nuse from

---

[1] This letter to his wife, it will be observed, bears the same date with the letter to his son which precedes it; and they allude to the same "news from New England," and to the same "papers concerning N : E : " In the footnote to the former letter, we have referred to the opinions of Mr. Savage and Dr. Young, as to what these papers were. We were at first not entirely without misgivings, that the "Observations" to be copied by Forth were those which were given in full in our last chapter: yet the rough draught of a large part of that paper, in the Governor's own hand, indorsed " May, 1629," would seem inconsistent with such an idea; and we only allude to it to prove that it has not been dismissed without consideration.

N : E : and much reioyce in it, the good Lord still continue his mercy to that plantation, and blesse us in our intended purpose that way. We see how the Lord giveth us his warent and daly incoragement that way ; wee may I hope trust him for a blessinge upon us and ours : For my sonne H. his stay from Barbatus, if his pretence be good, it had bin pittye he should have gon to have indangered the good of his soule, by beinge partaker of the sines of the rest of that wicked Company : the Lord I hope hath rowght some good worke in him, which I be-seech him to confirme in his due tyme ; I have read my daughters good letter to him, and shall love hir the better whilst I live. It is now late and bed time and I must bid thee good night before I am wilinge, for I could finde in my hart to sit and talke with thee all night. Though I am a bad wacher, I could wel spare a nights sleepe to doe any thinge for thee. I wish my sister F. ware at home, for Mary is sick and I feare it will prove the smale poxe or mesels or such like ; if she should doe otherwise then well in hir mothers abcence, it would be a great grefe to me, but I leave to yᵒʳ decrecion whether you will tell hir of it or no, and so I bid thee farewell : the Lord keepe thee

" thy unworthy wife   " M. W.

" I have not yet received the things you sent, when I see the cloth I will send word what triminge will serve. I hope you shall not nede to tell my sister Fones of M. sicknesse, it will prove but the meseles at the most."

John Winthrop to his Wife.

" To his verye lovinge Wife Mrs. Winthrop, the elder at Groton, Suff.

" MY DEARE WIFE, — I received thy sweet lettres wᶜʰ were most welcome to me, & I doe heartyly blesse the Lorde for thy wellfare. I am so exceedingly streightened in tyme, as I cañot write to thee wᵗʰ any content ; I have been all this daye till 8 : of the clocke this eveninge abroad about businesse, & yet have dispatched but little : [1] therefore let not John come up wth the horses till Saterday next, for it wilbe mundaye senight before I can come out of towne, or my sister Fones : she is well wth the rest of o^r freinds & company heere, who all desire to be remembered to thee & the rest of o^r companye. The good Lorde blesse thee & keepe thee & all o^{rs} : so wth my best affections to my most sweet wife, my love to my daughter, my blessinge to all o^r children & salut^s to the rest & to all o^r freinds, I comende thee to the Lorde & rest ·

" thy faithfull husband   " Jo : Winthrop.

" Octo : 15. 1629.

" We received the Boxe &c, for wch we thanke thee."

John Winthrop to his Wife.

" To my verye lovinge Wife, Mrs Winthrop the elder at Groton, Suff'k

" My deare Wife, — I am verye sorye that I am forced to feed thee wth lettres, when my presence is thy due, & so much desired : but my trust is, that he who hath so disposed of it, will supply thee wth patience, & better comforte in the want of him whom thou so much desirest : The Lord is able to doe this, & thou mayst expect it, for he hath promised it. Seeinge he calls me into his worke, he will have care of thee & all o^{rs} & o^r affaires in my absence : therefore I must sende thee to him, for all thou lackest : goe boldly (sweet wife) to the throne of Grace ; if anythinge trouble thee, acquainte the Lord wth it ; tell him, he hath taken thy husband from thee, pray him to be a husband to thee, a father to thy children, a master to thy householde, thou shall finde him faithfull : thou art not guilty of my departure, thou hast not driven me awaye by any unkindnesse, or want of dutye, therefore thou mayst challenge protection & blessinge of him.

---

[1] The Records of the Massachusetts Company show that there was a General Court held this day, at which Winthrop was present.

"I prayse the Lorde I am in health & cheerfull in my course, wherein I find God gratiously present, so as we expect, he wilbe pleased to direct & prosper us. We have great advantage because we have many prayers.

"Bee not discouraged (deare heart) though I sett thee no tyme of my returne; I hope it shall not be longe, & I will make no more staye then I needs must.

"So it is that it hath pleased the Lorde to call me to a further trust in this businesse of the Plantation, then either I expected or finde myselfe fitt for, (beinge chosen by the Company to be their Governor). The onely thinge that I have comforte of in it is, that heerby I have assurance that my charge is of the Lorde & that he hath called me to this worke: O that he would give me an heart now to answeare his goodnesse to me, & the expectation of his people! I never had more need of prayers, helpe me (deare wife) & lett us sett o^r hearts to seeke the Lorde, & cleave to him sincearly.

"My brother & sisters salute you all: my sonne remembers his dutye to thee, & salutations to all the rest. Comende me kindly to all o^r freinds at Groton hall, & to Mr Leigh & his wife, my neighbo^r Cole & his wife, o^r freinds at Castleins & all that love us. So the Lorde blesse thee & all o^r children & companye. So I kisse my sweet wife & rest

"thy faithfull husband   "JO: WINTHROP.

"OCTOB: 20 1629.

"I would faine knowe if thou shalt be like to goe wth me, for thou shalt never have so good opportunity. Let John enq^r out 2: or 3: Carpenters: & knowe how many of o^r neighbo^{rs} will goe, that we may provide shipps for them."

John Winthrop to his Wife.

"To his verye lovinge wife Mrs Winthrop the elder at her house in Groton, Suff.

"MY DEARE WIFE, — I received thy most kinde letter, & doe blesse our good God for his gratious protection over thee

& all our Familye, beinge much incouraged by the daylye experience of his goodnesse & providence, that he will continue to be our God to the ende, & will carrye us safe through all the difficultyes & dangers we may meet with in this enterprise. I blesse his holy name, I was never in better health then at this tyme, & my minde now well setled; I wante only a thankfull heart for so great favour. All in this familye are in health also, & desire to be kindly remembered, viz: my brother & sisters, to thy selfe & all with thee : my sonne John remembers his love & dutye etc : Let John be heer with the horses on thursdaye, that my sister Fones & I may be at home on Saterday through Gods assistance. My sister would have her cloke & faurgard sent up. I have no leysure to looke after newes : neither can I doe any thinge for Crabbe, my sonne beinge gone home : So hoping to see thee shortly, to be refreshed with the sweet comfort of thy wished presence, I commend thee & all our children & family to the blessinge & protection of the Lord & rest "Thy faithfull husbande

"Jo: Winthrop.

"Octob: 22. 1629.

"Commend me to all our freindes etc."

And now, while Winthrop is once more at Groton, seeking rest and refreshment from the cares and labors which the business of New England has brought upon him; and while he is taking sweet counsel, not unmingled with sadness, with the faithful Margaret, as to the hopes and fears of their future pilgrimage, — we may find an opportunity to consider the circumstances and character of the office to which he has just been elected. " So it is," says he in his letter of Oct. 20, " that it hath pleased the Lord to call me to a further trust in this business of the Plantation, than either I expected or find myself fit for, — being chosen by the Company to be their Governor." It will be interesting to examine briefly into the nature of this public capacity, in which Winthrop was about to embark for America.

At " a General Court, holden for the Company of the Mattachusetts Bay in New England at Mr. Deputy's house,[1] on Tuesday, the 28th of July, 1629," after other business had been disposed of, Matthew Cradock, the Governor of the Company, " read certain propositions conceived by himself; viz., that for the advancement of the plantation, the inducing and encouraging persons of worth and quality to transplant themselves and families thither, and for other weighty reasons therein contained, to transfer the government of the plantation to those that shall inhabit there, and not to continue the same in subordination to the Company here, as it now is."

In this not altogether grammatical, but entirely intelligible paragraph, from the original Records of the Governor and Company of the Massachusetts Bay, is found the first authentic suggestion of the memorable movement, at the head of which John Winthrop came over to America.

The language of the paragraph sets forth, clearly and exactly, the existing condition of things in the Plantation, and the radical and almost revolutionary change which was contemplated. The Government then existing in New England is styled a Government " in subordination to the Company here ; " namely, in London. It is pro-

---

[1] The Deputy was Thomas Goffe.

posed, that this Government shall no longer be " continued " " as it now is," but that it shall be " transferred to those that shall inhabit there."

The proposition of Gov. Cradock was altogether too important to be acted upon immediately. " It occasioned," as the Records inform us, " some debate ; but, by reason of the many great and considerable consequences thereupon depending, it was not now resolved upon." The members of the Company who were present at the meeting were desired to consider of it " privately and seriously," " and to set down their particular reasons in writing, *pro et contra ;* and to produce the same at the next General Court ; where, they being reduced to heads and maturely considered of, the Company may then proceed to a final resolution thereon : and, in the mean time, they are desired to carry this business *secretly*, that the same be not divulged." This suggestion of private and serious consideration ; this demand for particular reasons on both sides, set down in writing ; this solemn injunction of secrecy, — all indicate sufficiently that the Company were not ignorant how important and how bold a step their Governor had submitted to them. It was no mere measure of emigration or colonization. It was a measure of government, of self-government, of virtual independence ; and its adoption clearly foreshadowed that spirit of impatience under foreign control, which, at a later day, was to pervade not only the Colony of Massachusetts Bay, but the whole American continent.

The General Court of the Company now adjourned, as usual, for a month. They met again to consider this momentous proposition, on the 28th day of August, 1629 ;

but the interval had not been unimproved by those who desired to have it wisely and rightly decided. It had cost them, we may well believe, many an anxious hour of deliberation and consultation; and, two days only before the meeting of the Court, an agreement had been finally drawn up and subscribed, which undoubtedly settled the whole question.

This agreement (to which we have more than once referred already) was entered into and executed at Cambridge, beneath the shadows, and perhaps within the very walls, of that venerable University, to which New England was destined to owe so many of her brightest luminaries and noblest benefactors. It bore date Aug. 26, 1629; and was in the following words: —

The Agreement at Cambridge.

"Upon due consideration of the state of the Plantation now in hand for New England, wherein we, whose names are hereunto subscribed, have engaged ourselves, and having weighed the greatness of the work in regard of the consequence, God's glory and the Church's good; as also in regard of the difficulties and discouragements which in all probabilities must be forecast upon the prosecution of this business; considering withal that this whole adventure grows upon the joint confidence we have in each other's fidelity and resolution herein, so as no man of us would have adventured it without assurance of the rest; now, for the better encouragement of ourselves and others that shall join with us in this action, and to the end that every man may without scruple dispose of his estate and affairs as may best fit his preparation for this voyage; it is fully and faithfully AGREED amongst us, and every one of us doth hereby freely and sincerely promise and bind himself, in the word of a Christian, and in the presence of God, who is the searcher of all hearts, that we will so really endeavour the prosecution of this work, as by God's assistance, we will be ready in our persons, and with such of our several families as are to go with us, and such provision as we are able conveniently to furnish ourselves withal, to embark for the said Plantation by the first of March next, at such port or ports of this land as shall be agreed upon by the Company, to the end to pass the Seas, (under God's protection,) to inhabit and continue in New-England : Provided always, that before the last of September next, the whole Government, together with the patent for the said Plantation, be first, by an order of Court, legally transferred and established to remain with us and others which shall inhabit upon the said Plantation ; and provided, also, that if any shall be hindered by such just and inevitable let or other cause, to be allowed by three parts of four of these whose names are hereunto subscribed, then such persons, for such times and during such lets, to be discharged of this bond. And we do further promise, every one for himself, that shall fail to be ready through his own default by the day appointed, to pay for every day's default the sum of £3, to the use of the rest of the company who shall be ready by the same day and time.

" (Signed)	RICHARD SALTONSTALL,	THOMAS SHARPE,
	THOMAS DUDLEY,	INCREASE NOWELL,
	WILLIAM VASSALL,	JOHN WINTHROP,
	NICHOLAS WEST,	WILLIAM PINCHON,
	ISAAC JOHNSON,	KELLAM BROWNE,
	JOHN HUMFREY,	WILLIAM COLBRON."

The leading *proviso* of this memorable agreement must not fail to be noted : —

" Provided always, that before the last of September next, *the whole Government*, together with the patent for the said Plantation, be first, by an order of Court, legally transferred and established to remain with us and others which shall inhabit upon the said Plantation."

This was the great condition upon which Saltonstall
and Dudley and Johnson and Winthrop and the rest
agreed " to pass the Seas (under God's protection), to
inhabit and continue in New England."

They were not proposing to go to New England as
adventurers or traffickers ; not for the profits of a voyage,
or the pleasure of a visit; but " to inhabit and continue "
there.   And they were unwilling to do this while any
merely subordinate jurisdiction was to be exercised there,
and while they would be obliged to look to a Governor and
Company in London for supreme authority.   They were
resolved to carry " the whole Government" with them.

Accordingly, at the meeting of the General Court on
the 28th of August (two days after this agreement was
executed), Mr. Deputy, in the Governor's absence,
acquainted the Court " that the especial cause of their
meeting was to give answer to divers gentlemen, intend-
ing to go into New England, whether or no *the chief
government* of the Plantation, together with the patent,
should be settled in New England, or here."   Two Committees were thereupon appointed to prepare arguments,
the one "*for*" and the other " *against*" " the settling
of the chief government in New England," with instructions to meet together the next morning, at seven of the
clock, to confer and weigh each other's arguments, and
afterwards to make report to the whole Company.   On
the next morning, at the early hour which had been
appointed, the committees met together, and debated
their arguments and reasons on both sides ; and, after a
long discussion in presence of the Company, Mr. Deputy
put it to the question as followeth : —

"As many of you as desire to have the patent and the government of the Plantation to be transferred to New England, so as it may be done legally, hold up your hands ; so many as will not, hold up your hands."

And thereupon the decision of the question is thus entered upon the Records : —

"Where, by erection of hands, it appeared, by the general consent of the Company, that the government and patent should be settled in New England, and accordingly an order to be drawn up."

At the next meeting of the General Court after that at which this momentous resolution had been adopted, held on the 19th day of September, 1629, the name of " John Wynthropp " appears for the first time on the Records of the Governor and Company of the Massachusetts Bay in New England. It appears not, indeed, as the name of one of those who were present at the meeting, but as one of a committee, chosen by the Company, to consider of certain differences which had fallen out, in the Plantation at Salem, between its worthy local Governor, John Endicott, and two of his councillors, John and Samuel Browne, and which were brought before the chief government in London for adjustment.*

The first meeting of the General Court at which Winthrop is recorded as having been personally present took place on the 15th of October, 1629 ; when he was appointed one of a committee to arrange articles of agreement between the adventurers in the joint stock in England and those who intended to go over in person to

---

* Records of Massachusetts, vol. 1, p. 51.

the Plantation.   On the 16th, 19th, and 20th of the same
month, his presence is also noted on the Records of the
Assistants or of the Company.

On the last of these days (namely, the 20th of October, 1629), the Governor (Mr. Cradock) "acquainted
those present that the especial occasion of summoning
this Court was for the election of a new Governor,
Deputy, and Assistants; the government being to be
transferred into New England, according to the former
order and resolution of the Company;" and soon afterwards, some other business having been previously
transacted, the Records proceed as follows:—

"And now the Court, proceeding to the election of a new
Governor, Deputy, and Assistants, — which, upon serious
deliberation, hath been and is conceived to be for the especial
good and advancement of their affairs; and having received
extraordinary great commendations of Mr. JOHN WYNTHROP,[1]
both for his integrity and sufficiency, as being one every (way)
well fitted and accomplished for the place of Governor, — did
put in nomination for that place the said Mr. John Winthrop,
Sir R. Saltonstall, Mr. Is. Johnson, and Mr. John Humfry:
and the said Mr. Winthrop was, with a general vote, and full
consent of this Court, by erection of hands, chosen to be Governor for the ensuing year, to begin on this present day; who
was pleased to accept thereof, and thereupon took the oath to
that place appertaining."

Mr. John Humfrey was then, in like manner, chosen
Deputy-Governor; and Sir Richard Saltonstall, Mr. Isaac
Johnson, Mr. Thomas Dudley, Mr. John Endicott, and
fourteen others, were chosen to be Assistants.

---

[1] The name of Winthrop is spelt three or four different ways in these Records.
This very paragraph uses *y* in one line, and *i* in others. And so it is with other names.

Nothing could be more significant of the estimation in which Winthrop was held by the Massachusetts colonists, and of the importance which was attached to his embarking with them as their leader, than the circumstances of this election. He was a comparatively new comer into their enterprise. His name was not with those of Saltonstall and Humfrey and Endicott and Cradock and Johnson, in the original charter of Massachusetts, signed by Charles I. on the 4th of March, 1628–9. Nor is there any evidence that he had been associated with them as an adventurer in the joint stock of the Company: while, as to any purpose of crossing the ocean as a planter, we have seen him, only two years before, expressly advising his son against such a course; and it is hardly possible that he could have contemplated it for himself. Yet now, when a great responsibility has been assumed by the Company, and when a great step is about to be taken in transferring the patent and the whole government to New England, Winthrop would seem to have been summoned in at once to their councils, and, at the earliest practicable moment, to have been invested with their chief-magistracy.

He said of himself, on the most solemn occasion,[1] a few years after his arrival in New England, " I was first chosen to be Governour without my seeking or expectation, there being then divers other gentlemen, who, for their abilities everyway, were far more fit." This was said, too, by him, in the very face of those who had been

---

[1] Letter of Winthrop to the General Court of Massachusetts, in vindication of his Accounts, Sept. 4, 1634. — See Savage's Appendix (B) to Winthrop's Hist. of N. E. vol. i. p. 474.

acquainted with all the circumstances of his election, and some of whom, perhaps, would have been not unwilling to convict him of having been ambitious of office and power. He had used the same language, it seems, in a letter to his wife, on the very day of his election.

It would be difficult, we think, for any one to review the facts which have thus been given, without coming to the conclusion, that there was something in the character and capacity of John Winthrop which had inspired peculiar confidence in the minds of those who 'were engaged in promoting the settlement of New England, and which led them to seek him out as the leader of their enterprise. How far this confidence was justified, we shall be able to judge as we proceed with his career. Meantime, it is certain that his connection with the Massachusetts Company in their great emigration seems to have been noted and remarked upon, in Old England and in New England alike, as an event of more than common importance and interest. Thus Sir Simonds D'Ewes, in his Autobiography,[1] under date of 1634, in describing the New-England Colonies, after a word or two about previous emigrations, speaks thus: —

"Yet these chiefly then aimed at trade and gain, till about the year 1630, in the spring, when John Winthrop, Esq., a Suffolk man, and many other godly and well-disposed Christians, with the main of their estates, and many of them with their entire families, to avoid the burthens and snares which were here laid upon their consciences, departed thither; where they, having in the first place taken care for the honor and service of God, and next for their own safety and subsistence, have, be-

---

[1] Vol. ii. chap. v. p. 116.

yond the hopes of their friends, and to the astonishment of their enemies, raised such forts, built so many towns, brought into culture so much ground, and so dispersed and enriched themselves, as all men may see, whom malice blindeth not nor impiety transverseth, that the very finger of God hath hitherto gone with them and guided them."

And the following passage of the letter of Deputy-Governor Dudley to the Countess of Lincoln, dated Boston, March 12, 1630-1, bears a still more striking testimony to the importance attached at the time, and by those best capable of judging, to the fact that Winthrop had become associated with the Massachusetts Company: —

" And the same year, (1628,) we sent Mr. John Endecott, and some with him, to begin a Plantation, and to strengthen such as he should find there, which we sent thither from Dorchester, and some places adjoining. From whom the same year receiving hopeful news, the next year, 1629, we sent divers ships over, with about three hundred people, and some cows, goats and horses, many of which arrived safely.

" These, by their too large commendations of the country and the commodities thereof, invited us so strongly to go on, that Mr. Winthrop, of Suffolk, (who was well known in his own country, and well approved here for his piety, liberality, wisdom, and gravity,) coming in to us, we came to such resolution, that in April, 1630, we set sail from Old England with four good ships. And in May following eight more followed ; " &c., &c.

Thomas Dudley, who, as we may find hereafter, was not always disposed to regard Winthrop too favorably, would thus seem to imply that his " coming in " on this occasion was the very hinge of the great Massachusetts movement.

We may add here, in the same connection, the notice which was taken of the arrival of Governor Winthrop and his Company by Nathaniel Morton, in his " New England's Memorial," first published in 1669.

"1630. This year it pleased God, of his rich grace, to transport over into the bay of the Massachusetts, divers honorable personages, and many worthy Christians, whereby the Lord began in a manifest manner and way to make known the great thoughts which he had of planting the gospel in this remote and barborous wilderness, and honouring his own way of instituted worship, causing such and so many to adhere thereunto, and fall upon the practice thereof; — among the rest, a chief one amongst them was that famous pattern of piety and justice, Mr. John Winthrop, the first Governor of the jurisdiction, accompanied with divers other precious sons of Sion, which might be compared to the most fine gold." [1]

In view of the various but concurrent testimony which has thus been furnished, Winthrop may be exonerated, we think, from any imputation of vanity, when he says of himself, in his statement of the particular considerations which induced him to join the Massachusetts Company, " It is come to that issue, as (in all probability) the welfare of the Plantation depends upon his going; for divers of the chief undertakers (upon whom the rest depend) will not go without him." [2]

---

[1] Morton's Memorial, pp. 157-8. The title of "first Governor of the jurisdiction," given to Governor Winthrop by Nathaniel Morton, in a work published as early as 1669, will not fail to be noted. Morton was at Plymouth, and eighteen years old, when Winthrop arrived; and he continued in New England till his death. No better authority could be adduced as to the contemporaneous opinion on a recently vexed question. We may perhaps find occasion to refer to this subject again.

[2] In Winthrop's rough draught of this paper, the same idea is stated as follows: " It is come to that issue, as, in all probabilitye, the wellfare of the plantation depends upon my assistance: for the maine pillars of it, beinge gentlemen of high qualitye & eminent parts, bothe for wisdom & Godlinesse, are determined to sitt still if I deserte them."

CHAPTER XVIII.

PREPARATIONS FOR NEW ENGLAND CONTINUED. LETTERS TO IN-
VITE CO-OPERATION, &c. DOMESTIC CORRESPONDENCE.

WINTHROP allowed himself but a short time for his first
visit to Groton, after his election as Governor ; and his
mind must have been much occupied, even while there,
with his new obligations and responsibilities.   Immediately after his return to London, we find him preparing
a circular letter to some of the Puritan ministers of England, to invite their co-operation in the enterprise to
which he was now pledged.   There is, also, among his
papers, a rough draught of a note to his neighbor, Mr.
Gager of Little Waldingfield, inviting him to join the
Company as a sort of family physician.[1]   We give these
letters just as we find them, — both of them without signature, and the first without address, but both throwing
light on the measures which were adopted by the Governor and his Assistants to provide for the spiritual and
temporal necessities of the Company over which they
had been called to preside.[2]

---

[1] William Gager accepted the invitation, came over with Winthrop, and became a
deacon of the First Church at Charlestown, but died on the 20th September, 1630. He
was called by Gov. Dudley "a right godly man, a skilful chyrurgeon." Winthrop's
Hist. of N. E., vol. 1, p. 34, and Savage's note.

[2] Of the twenty-two letters in this chapter, seventeen are here printed for the first
time.

John Winthrop and others to ——

" Sir, — We conceit you may have heard of the resolution
of divers of us to engage our persons & estates in the planting
a Colony in New England, for divers ends concerning the glory
of God & the service of his Church : Unto the furthering of
this worke we finde the Lorde strongely overwaying & enclining
the spirits of many of his servants to offer themselves willingly
unto him for this service ; only we want hitherto able & sufficient Ministers to joyne with us in the worke : the reasons whereof we finde to be the Conscience of the Obligation by which
they stand bound unto this Church for the service in which most
of them are imployed att present, & want of a sufficient calling
unto the employment for which we desire them. Wherefore
that we may in all things submitt ourselves to be guided by the
will of God in a worke of soe great importance, we resolve not
to leave to our owne Wisdome the choyce of the men whom we
desire for this worke, & for y^t cause earnestly request the assistance of divers godly Ministers to judge of the persons & corses
of such of their brethren of the Ministry whom we shall desire
to single out for this employ^t. We doe therefore earnestly
desire, & in the name of God as you tender the furtherance of
soe great a service, require, your assistance for Counsell &
direction in this weighty Cause : and entreate you for y^t purpose to afford us your presence in this Citty the ninthe day of
November, to joyne with such other of your brethren as we
shall likewise request to be present heere att the same time for
ye same busines. We assure ourselves of your readines to
answer our desire herein, & therefore expecting your presence
heere att that time, in the meane & for ever we commend you
to the grace of God resting

" Your very loving freinds

" London. Octob : 27 1629."

John Winthrop and others to William Gager.

" To our loving friend Mr. Gager at little Waldingfield in Suffolk.

" Sir, — Beinge informed of your good inclination to the furtherance of this work which (through the Lords good providence) we are in hand with for the establishing of a Churche in N : E : & having sufficient assurance of your godlinesse & abilityes, in the arte of chirurgerye, to be of much use to us in this worke ; being informed also, that the place where you live dothe not afforde you such sufficiente & comfortable imployment as your giftes doe require, we have thought good to offer you a call to joyne with us, & become a member of our familye : your entertainement shalbe to your good contente ; if you like to accepte this motion, we desire you would prepare to goe with us this springe. If you come up to London we shal be readye to treat further with you, & so with our hearty salutations we commit you to the Lord & rest

" Your loving friends "

We give next, in the order of date, two of the Governor's letters to his wife, and two of her replies, which will tell their own story, without preamble or explanation.

John Winthrop to his Wife.

" To his very loving Wife, Mrs. Winthrop the elder, at Groton, Suffolk.

" My dear Wife, — I must needs write to thee by this bearer, though I can write little in regard of my much business. I praise God, I came safe hither, where I found all in health, and so (through his mercy) we continue. I have sent down my horses, because I am like to stay somewhat longer than I made account of ; but I shall make what haste I can back. Here is much news : Divers great personages questioned and committed; but the cause yet uncertain. St. Christopher's is taken by the Spaniard, and the English there honestly sent home. The same is reported of the Barbethes, but not so certain; but, if it be, the people are all safe. Some would discourage us with this news; but there is no cause, for neither are we in the like danger: and, besides, God is with us, and will surely keep us. I shall take time to write to thee again in the end of the week. So, for this time, with all our hearty salutations to thyself, my good sister Fones, and the rest of our friends, with my love and blessing to all our children, I commend thee to the Lord. So I kiss my sweet wife, and rest

"Thy faithful husband,   "Jo. WINTHROP.

"NOVEMBER 11, 1629.

"My son remembers his duty to thee and his aunt, and love to all, etc."

Margaret Winthrop to her Husband.

"My DEARE HUSBAND, — I knowe not how to expresse my love to thee or my desyres of thy wished welfayre, but my hart is well knowne to thee, which will make relation of my affections though they be smalle in apperance: my thoughts are nowe on our great change and alteration of our corce heare, which I beseech the Lord to blesse us in, & my good Husband cheare up thy hart in the expectacion of Gods goodnesse to us, & let nothinge dismay or discorage thee; if the Lord be with us who can be against us: my grefe is the feare of stayinge behinde thee, but I must leave all to the good providence of God. I thank the Lord wee are all heare in reasonable good health, I receved a letter since you went from my sonne John, wᶜʰ brout good Nuse from Nue E: I pray thanke him for it, I wil rite to him if I have time, & thus with my best respect to thy selfe, brother & sister D: I commit you to God and rest

"Your faythfull wife   "MARGARET WINTHROPE.

"Your servante remembers hir service to you, our sonnes & daughters remember there duty. You shall receive by Smith the caryer a rundelet of syder, the carage is payed, if you like it send for more."

John Winthrop to his Wife.

· "MY SWEET WIFE, — I received thy most kinde Lettre, & blessed be o^r good God that giveth us still cause of reioycinge in the newes of each others wellfare, & of those wch are deare to us : & blessed be God, who hath given me a wife, who is such a helpe & incouragem^t to me in this great worke, wherein so many wives are so great an hinderance to theirs : I doubt not but the Lorde will recompence abundantly the faithfullnesse of thy love & obedience, & for my selfe, I shall ever be mindfull of thee, & carefull to requite thee.

"Our businesse comes so fast upon us heer, as I cañot yet appointe when I shall returne, but I will make what hast I maye.

"I would have my daughter M : come up in the ende of next weeke, I hope to come downe the weeke followinge : I thinke it would be good for my sonne H : to come up wth her, that he may looke after his men & provisions wch were to goe to the Barbethes. Let John speake wth Cole the constable of Boxford & tell him, that I have gotten a place for his kinsman wth Sir Richard Saltonstall, who will entertaine him presently if he will come up. Let John or my sonne Hen : speake to Holder to lett alone the timber till I come home.

"Our freinds heer salute thee & all wth thee. Comende my love to my good servant, & tell her, I think I must be forced to write to her this weeke ; if Mr Payinter come downe, he is a reverend man & a good preacher, let him be kindly entertained, he will preach wth you if he come. The good Lord be wth thee (my deare wife) & blesse thee & all o^{rs}, so wth wonted salutations I rest

"thy faithfull husband   "Jo : WINTHROP.

"Nov: 12 1∧∧∧,"

Margaret Winthrop to her Husband.

"MY DEARE HUSBAND, — I reioyce in thy welfayre, & in the expectacion of thy presence wch I hope shortly to enioy. I send up my daughter M. somewhat the soner by reson of Mr. P. cominge up, and would pray thee to send word this weeke when I shall send up thy horsses. I pray make what hast you can for the hart of your good servant is fallen so loe, that she say^th if you doe not com home presently you will never lift it up agayne. But I think hir desyre is that she may confir with you about Mr. P. whome I thinke she will scarce have power to deny. He preached with us the last Lords day and did very well. He seemeth to be a very godly wise man, but I am sure my sister will not make any promise till she hath confired with thy selfe and the rest of hir frends. Coles kinsman shal come up next weeke. Kingesbery will goe for N: E: his wife and two children. You must pardon me that I am so short in righting to you, for my affections are longe enough if I had time to expresse them. But I must leaue thee for this time, beinge in hast. Desyringe the good Lord to prosper all thy businesse and affayres and send us a comfortable meetinge, I commend my best love to thee and commit you to the Lord and rest

     "Your faythfull and obedient wife
         "MARGARET WINTHROPE."

The allusion to Mr. Painter, in the two last of these letters, furnishes a fit occasion for introducing two letters which Winthrop received about this time from his sister-in-law, Priscilla Fones. The second of them has particular reference to Mr. Painter, whom, notwithstanding the reluctance which she expresses to change her condition, she soon afterwards married. There is something peculiarly quaint and pretty in the coyness, not to call it

coquetry, of the second letter; and we shall catch still
another glimpse of it, before she finally yields to the
importunity of her worthy and reverend suitor.[1] Her
first letter has no date, but must have been written a
month or two before the second.

Priscilla Fones to John Winthrop.

"To the right Wor[ll] her verie lovinge brother John Winthrop Esq.
these be dd at his house in Groton.

"MY GOOD BROTHER, — I was kindly salluted with a letter
from you which cam to my hands that day senet I cam to Sutton, & was not a littel wellcom to me. I would gladly have
returned you thankes for it before this time, but that I could
not hear of any messenger to send by all the while I was at
Sutton, which bred me much grife & troubel of mind in the
midst of all my comforts, & more would have done had I not
bin well perswaed[d] that your love would judge the best of me.
My absence from you hath bin now much longer then I intended, my father being so loth to part with me ; & truly it was
no easie thing for me to part with such a father, having not bin
with him in ten yeres before ; but now throughe Gods goodnes
I cam safly to London on Saterday last, whear I thankfuly
recaived your loving letter, which did much refrech me after my
weary jurny. I had a purpose then to have sene you this
weke & did much reioyce in the hope I had of inioying your &
my good sisters compeny, with my pore children whom I much
long after ; but before I could take my fill of these thoughts, that
heavi nuse of your going for new England cam to me. How
much grife it hath cost me I spare to relate at this time, but I
see the Lord is about to take away my props that I may wholy
rely upon himself. These nuse hath made me now to looke out
for a house which I intended not before, & so my coming is

---

[1] Rev. Henry Painter, of Exeter, was one of the Assembly of Westminster Di-
vines, 1644-5.

defered till the next weke : in the meane time I earnestly crave
your prayers, & so with the remembrance of my best love and
affections to your selfe, my good sister, all yours and mine, I
take my leave of you for this time & rest

           " Your very loving sister   " Pris. Fones.

"I would faine have written to my daughters, but time is
very precious with me in London. I pray remember me to
them both and to my maid whose care of my pore Mat I shall
not forgit."

Priscilla Fones to John Winthrop.

"To the right Worshipfull my very loving brother John Winthrope
esquire London.

"My dere brother, — Such is my love to you & my
respect of you as I cannot but take kindly from you this motion
of which I was desierous never to have heard more of. And
as well as I could indure to spake of such a busnes, I intrated
your help to that end when I parted with you ; but see my
answear toke not that efect which I ded desier, which hath bred
me much grife & troubel of mind, my selfe being very fearfull
to chang my condition. All my friends perswade me it will be
best for me to chang, but myselfe hath no hart to it. In the
man I see that which I chefly ame at in a husban, which is
grace & godlynes with gifts sutabel to his calling ; though in
outward estate he coms short of any that hath bin yet moved
to me. These things, with his importunity & paines in coming
so fare, hath bred such destraction in my mind as truly I know
not what to doe, but mine eis are towards the Lord for derec-
tion in this waity busnes. Good brother help with your prayers
& best advise, for I have now cast myselfe uppon you & my
father & Mr White, to whom I pray make knowen this busnes
& crave his councel in it. I have only given him this answer,
that I will doe nothing without the advise of my freinds. Good
brother I know your love to be such towards me as I shall not
nede to intreat your care in this, but now my request to you is

that you would make all the hast home you can, for we all long for you. Myselfe which could not so prise the benefit of your good company as I ought, have now larned to prise it by the want of it. The Lord give me grace to make beter use of it when he shall be plased to restore it to me againe — and thus with remembrance of my best love and servis to yourselfe, my good brother and sister, and the rest of my frinds, I comit you and all your affares to the Lord & so I rest

       " Your ever loveing sister and faithful servant

                         " PRIS. FONES.

" NOVEMBER 17."

It is not a little odd, that, on the very same day on which Priscilla was thus writing so interesting a letter to our Governor in regard to a proposed matrimonial arrangement of her own, his son Forth should also have been engaged in addressing him a similar epistle in regard to his affection for his cousin Ursula, Priscilla's daughter.[1] The Governor must have had his hands full, when these two appeals for advice and counsel, on the tenderest domestic topics, reached him at the same moment, and in the midst of all the occupations and consultations in which the business of New England had involved him. But Forth's letter is too good and too characteristic to be lost. It is at least worth preserving as an illustration of the deference which the young men of that day paid to the opinions and wishes of their parents. Forth, be it remembered, had now finished his

---

[1] Ursula Sherman has sometimes been supposed to have been a daughter of Rev. Henry Painter by his first wife; but Forth speaks of her as his cousin, and as his Aunt Fones's daughter, before the marriage, or even the engagement, of Priscilla Fones to Painter. She must have been a daughter of Priscilla by a husband, before Fones, whose name was Sherman.

collegiate course, and was nearly twenty-one years of age. We shall see but too soon what was the end of all his plans of domestic happiness.

Forth Winthrop to his Father.

"MOST LOVINGE FATHER, — The consideration of that saying *literæ non erubescunt*, hath moved me to cause you to understand that by letters, wch bashfullnesse would not suffer me to utter, but sealed up my mouth in silence. The heathen could say *Tu nihil invitâ dices, faciesve Mynervâ*. I would be loath soe far to violate the lawes of nature or infringe the præcepts of nurture & education, as to undertake any enterprize of moment w^thout yor leave, knowledg, consent, & license. That therefore I may have yor councell & direction I desire that from me you may understand, that I doe beare affection in such sort as God may approve, & wth yor agreem^t may in time blesse wth his holy ordinance of Mariage, to my cosen Ursula, my aunt ffones her daughter, yet have I made noe mention of any such thing, nor till I shall knowe yor will, pleasure & advice heerin, will I. To yor wisdome therefore doe I most humblye submitte myselfe, & earnestly desiring yor prayers, that God may direct me for the best, I shall awaite the expectation of yor councell, instruction, & direction, what best you in yor wisdome shall see most fittinge for me to be done or lefte undone ; & soe committinge this to you & you to the protection of the allmighty, wth my most humble duty remembred to yo^rselfe, my Uncle & Aunt Downing, wth my love to my cosens, I rest & remaine

"Yo^r Obedient Sonne
"FORTH WINTHROP.

"ffrom GROTON Novemb: 17, 1629."

We come next to another letter which is without address, and some portions of which are supplied with difficulty, but which again exhibits the zeal of the Governor in urging the cause of New England upon all who were within the sphere of his influence. It would seem to have been written to some humble dependant or tenant of his, whom he designed to enlist in the great emigration which he was preparing to conduct. It will be followed, without further explanation, by two more letters to his wife, which tell their own story sufficiently. The allusion to his friend " Mr. Cotton, of Boston," in the postscript to the second of them, will not escape observation.

John Winthrop to —— ——.

" I expected to have seene you at London and imparted that to you by conference wch cannot be done by Lettres, but better thus then not at all. I suppose you have heard howe it hathe pleased the Lord to dispose of me, for my transplanting into New England & making me to longe to sett down there. If I could meet wth you, I doubt not I could give you good satisfaction, & perchance I would convince or would perswade you to goe wth us, if you would yield yo^{r}selfe to be informed of the cause of the work, & then let God dispose yor minde as he please. If you come up to London, when I am not there, I wish you would repaire to one Mr. Nowell a merchant in Philpott lane at the house where Sr Tho : Smithe sometymes dwelt, & let him knowe that you come from me, & he will acquaint you fullye wth all thinges : I heare you are removinge from Stewards ; [1] I would desire you therefore, that such hangings as I lefte there, wch are worthe the removinge, you would

---

[1] The manor of *Stewards*, in Romford Town Ward, Essex, about twelve miles from London, was the birthplace of the celebrated Francis Quarles, author of the Emblems, in 1592; and is believed to have continued in his family at least until his death, in 1644. — *Excursions through Essex*, vol. i. p. 168. It would seem, from this letter, as if Winthrop had once occupied apartments at this place, or some other bearing the same name, perhaps in order to be nearer London for the practice of his profession and the discharge of his official duties. — See his letter of Feb. 25, 1627; *ante*, p. 152.

sende them up to me, if you have no use of them, & for the other householde I lefte, give me for them what you please. I am heare full of businesse, & cañot write as I desire, onelye knowe, that I doe earnestly desire (if it may be the Lords good pleasure) to have yor company into N : E : & o^r good Dames (who may be of great use there), & so wth my hearty salutations to you both, I comēde you to the Lorde, & desiringe yor prayers I rest

" Yo^r assured friend   " Jo : WINTHROP.

"LONDON. Nov. 20: 1629."

John Winthrop to his Wife.

" MY DEARE WIFE, — I blesse o^r good God for the continuance of thy wellfare & the rest of o^r familye, & for his good providence & mercye towards us in all o^r affairs : I thanke thy sweet heart for thy kinde lovinge Lettre, & doe longe as much to be wth thee, as thou dost to enioye me, the Lorde in his good tyme will bring us togither wth comfort, as he hath done ofte heretofore : Let my horses be sent up on Saterdaye or mundaye come señight, except I write to the contrarye in the meane tyme, for I will make what hast I can.

" Comēde me to my brother Jennye, etc, & excuse my not answearinge his kind lettre for wante of leysure, & and so for my neighbo^r Child, if he come to you.

" My businesse dothe so take up both my tyme & thoughts as I cañot expresse myself to thee as I desire, but I knowe thou wilt beare wth me, — so wth all lovinge salutat^s to thy selfe, to all o^r good freinds wth thee, & my blessinge to all o^r children, thankinge the Lord for the recoverye of o^r Saml, I comēde thee & all o^{rs}, & all o^r Affaires to his grace & good providence. So I kisse my sweet wife & rest,

" thy faithfull husband   " Jo : WINTHROP.

"LONDON Nov^r: 20. 1629."

John Winthrop to his Wife.

" MY DEARE WIFE, — Blessed be the Lord o^r good God, that I still heare of the health of thee & o^r familye, & that he is pleased to continue health & peace to us heer. I have nothinge to write to thee of, but havinge so fitt opportunitye, I could not let it passe wthout a lettre to my best beloved : I know thou wilt consider how it is now wth me in regard of businesse, wch so takes up my tyme & thoughts, as I can no more but let thee know that I have a desire still to be writinge to thee; though I cañot expresse my love so largly to thee as I was wonte to doe : I hope (if God will) to be wth thee the beginninge of next weeke ; therefore let John be heer wth my horses on Saterdaye. All o^r freinds heer salute thee : Comende me kindly to my good servant, & all o^r freinds : The Lorde blesse thee & all o^r children & companye : So I kisse my sweet wife & rest

" thy faithfull husband, " Jo : WINTHROP.

" It may be Mr Cotton of Boston will come see thee on thursdaye or fridaye. Gett him to staye a night if thou canst.

" LONDON Novemb: 24. 1629."

Winthrop presided at the General Court of the Massachusetts Company in London on the 30th of November ; and was doubtless at home a few days afterwards, agreeably to the promise in the letter just given. As the records of the Company show that he was absent from the meeting held on the 15th of December, he probably spent his last Old-England Christmas holidays with his wife and children at Groton Manor. At any rate, we hear nothing more of him until the middle of January ; when the following letter to his wife, evidently from

London, implies that he had been there for some time, and that he was proposing to return home again the next week : —

John Winthrop to his Wife.

" MY DEAR WIFE, — I have many things to thank thee for this week, — thy most kind letter, fowls, puddings, etc. ; but I must first thank our heavenly Father, that I hear of thy health and the welfare of all our family ; for I was in fear, because I left thee not well. But thus is the Lord pleased still to declare his goodness and mercy to his unworthy servants. Oh that we could learn to trust in him, and to love him as we ought !

" For my care of thee and thine, I will say nothing. The Lord knows my heart, that it was one great motive to draw me into this course. The Lord prosper me in it, as I desire the prosperity of thee and thine. For this end, I purpose to leave £1500 with thy friends, if I can sell my lands, which I am now about, but as yet have done nothing. I purpose (if God will) to be at home the next week. I am forced to keep John here for my business, which now comes so heavy upon me, as I can spare no time for aught else. The Lord in mercy bring us well through all our troubles, as I trust he will. Thou must bear with my brevity. The Lord bless and keep thee, and all our children, and company. So I kiss my sweet wife, and rest
" Thy faithful husband,
" Jo. WINTHROP.

" My brother and sister salute you all. Let the cow be killed against I come home ; and let my son Henry provide such peas as will porridge well, or else none.
" JANUARY 15, 1629."

And now we have a letter of a widely different character from all which have preceded it. It is from John Winthrop, jun., to his father, giving an account of some labors and experiments of his own in the service of the

Massachusetts Company. It begins with an allusion to his having been engaged in taking the dimensions of a fort near Colchester, and of his having made a perfect plot of it.[1] The letter then proceeds with an elaborate account of a windmill, which the younger Winthrop had invented for the benefit of New England. We dare not pronounce on the scientific merits or the practical value of the invention; nor do we know whether such a windmill was ever set up by its inventor, either in Massachusetts or Connecticut. We certainly doubt whether this letter would have established the claim of its writer to be enrolled (as he was about forty years afterwards) among the founders of the Royal Society; but it affords a pleasant illustration of the earnestness with which he exerted whatever ingenuity or skill he possessed, for the one great end to which he had so recently and so solemnly devoted himself.

John Winthrop Jr. to his Father.

" To the Wor[ll] his very loving father John Winthrop Esq. at Mr. Downings house in Peterborough Court over ag[t]: the Conduit in fleet Street, London.

" S[R], — My humble duty remembred, I receyved your letters, reioycing much to understand of the continuance of your welfare. Wee are heere (God be praised) all in good health. I am glad you have made an end wth my brothers businesse upon so good termes; he & she are both very glad of it: it would have bred much trouble if it could not now have bene put of,

---

[1] The importance attached to this work may be inferred from the postscript of a letter of Isaac Johnson to Gov. Winthrop, written a few weeks earlier, and printed in the Mass. Hist. Coll., vol. vi., 1st series, p. 32.

besides what hinderance it would have bene to themselves. I was last weeke at Colchester wth Mr. Heath the Kinges Workman, who made the fort at Langer point. I have now a perfect plot thereof, wth the dementions of the whole & parts, I will have it ready ag^t you come downe.

"I have now made a rude modell (as only to shew that it is feasable) of that wind motion, wch I tould you of, then only imagining it speculatively, but now have seene the experience of it, and doe affirme that an Instrument may be made to move wth the wind horizontally to equall if not to exceed the ordinary verticall motion of the windmill sailes, both in swiftnesse & force : for the wings of it (wch may be eyther 4 : 6, or 8, or as many as the workman will) in the one semicircle shalbe allwaies wth their broad superficies oposite to the wind, the other semicircle (allowing only such bredth as for strength the timbers of the wings shall require) shall be in respect only liniarily oposite to the same, & where there is any broad superficies pressed upon by the violence of winds we may conceive the force it carrieth by the great weight that it moveth, as ships, &c : & where it is placed upon a center, & farr distant from the same, we may iudge wth what violence it would whirle round, by the effect it worketh upon ships sailing close by a wind (wch tendeth towards a round motion save that it continually as it declineth changeth his center, & falleth on a new one) that sometyme through the force of it, it oversetteth them though poised wth reasonable weight. Swiftnesse must needs proceed proportionably from force. I conceive it may be aplied to many laborious uses as any kind of mills, Corne mills, saw mills &c., & I thinke a cornemill of this to performe wth the ordinary verticall mills may be made for little more cost then a good horse mill, & so may hold proportionably in the other sorts, as saw mills, oyle mills, &c, wch are not made eyther for wind or water wthout great cost ; ·for this may be made as low as the workman will, whereas the verticall mills must be made very highe, wch maketh them so chargeable : And one spetiall property wilbe in them that they allwaies stand right for the wind wheresoever it

bloweth: If there may be made any use of it, I desire New
England should reape the benefit for whose sake it was invented.
Et soli Deo gloria.

"Heere was to day a youth from Polsted to be enterteyned
for New England, but knowing you were full I bid him not
loose his labour to come any more to speake wth you, etc. I
pray remember my duty & love to my Uncle & Aunt Downing,
wth my love to my Cosens & freinds. Thus desiring your blessing & praiers I comend you to Gods protection & rest

			"Your obedient sonne			"JOHN WINTHROP.

"GROT. Jan: 18: 1629."

We may bring this somewhat miscellaneous chapter to
a close with a series of seven more letters, which passed
between the elder Winthrop and his wife, after he had
paid her another brief visit at Groton, and had returned
to London again to pursue his preparations. They are
full of significance as to the work in which he was
engaged. There is a hurried brevity in some of them,
and a touching pathos in others, which betoken at once
the pressure of business on his time, and the heavier
pressure of care and sorrow, at the prospect of "the
long parting," upon his heart. Both his wife and his
eldest son, with others of the family, were to remain
behind for the present; and he had thus to make preparations, at the same time, for their comfortable continuance in England, and for the outfit and voyage of the
Company and of himself. The perils of the ocean were
to be encountered, and the privations of a wilderness to
be endured. No wonder that he "could write little, in
regard of his much business." No wonder that what he
did write bore so strong an impress of mingled anxiety

and affection. No wonder that his " head was dissolved into tears," as he read one of his wife's little replies, alluding to the " solemn leave " which they were so soon to take of each other. The dates of the two first letters prove, that, by some magnetic sympathy, they were writing to each other on the same day.

We reluctantly break the series at one point, for the admission, in its chronological order, of a letter from Forth ; which indicates that the custom-officers of Old England were already taking cognizance of the Governor's movements.

John Winthrop to his Wife.

" My dear Wife, — I praise God, we came safe to London, and continue in health, and found all well here. Thus it pleaseth the Lord to follow us with his blessings, that we might love him again. I find here so much to do, as I doubt I shall not come down these three weeks ; but, thou mayest be sure, I will stay no longer than my occasions shall enforce me.

" I must now begin to prepare thee for our long parting, which grows very near. I know not how to deal with thee by arguments ; for if thou wert as wise and patient as ever woman was, yet it must needs be a great trial to thee, and the greater, because I am so dear to thee. That which I must chiefly look at in thee, for a ground of contentment, is thy godliness. If now the Lord be thy God, thou must show it by trusting in him, and resigning thyself quietly to his good pleasure. If now Christ be thy Husband, thou must show what sure and sweet intercourse is between him and thy soul, when it shall be no hard thing for thee to part with an earthly, mortal, infirm husband for his sake. The enlargement of thy comfort in the communion of the love and sweet familiarity of thy most holy, heavenly, and undefiled Lord and Husband, will abundantly recompense whatsoever want or inconvenience may come by the

absence of the other. The best course is to turn all our reasons and discourse into prayers; for he only can help, who
is Lord of sea and land, and hath sole power of life and
death.

" It is now near eleven of the clock, and I shall write again
ere long (if God will). The good Lord bless thee and all thy
company. My broth. and sister salute you all. Commend my
hearty love to my good sister F. and all the rest. Tell her
I wrote to Mr. Dummer so soon as I came to town; and, if I
can, I will speak with him, before John go down. So I kiss
my sweet wife, and rest

            " Thy frail, yet faithful husband,

                         ." JO. WINTHROP.

" JANUARY 31, 1629."

Margaret Winthrop to her Husband.

" MY MOST DEAR HUSBAND, — I should not now omit any
opportunity of writing to thee, considering I shall not long have
thee to write unto. But, by reason of my unfitness at this
time, I must entreat thee to accept of a few lines from me, and
not to impute it to any want of love, or neglect of my duty to
thee, to whom I owe more than I shall ever be able to express.
My request now shall be to the Lord to prosper thee in thy
voyage, and enable thee and fit thee for it, and give all graces
and gifts for such employments as he shall call thee to. I trust
God will once more bring us together before you go, that we
may see each other with gladness, and take solemn leave, till
we, through the goodness of our God, shall meet in New England, which will be a joyful day to us. I send thee here enclosed letters from Mr. P. My good sister F. remembers her
love to you, and, it seemeth, hath written so earnestly to Mr.
P. not to come, that he doth forbear to come till he hear more.
I think she would have you send him word to come as soon as
he can, being desirous to speak with him before you go; but it
must not come from herself, for she will write to him to stay

still.[1]   She saith, that he shall not need to provide any thing but a house, for she will furnish it herself.   And thus, with my best wishes to God for thy health and welfare, I take my leave, and rest

" Thy faithful, and obedient wife,

" MARGARET WINTHROP.

" JANUARY the last."

Forth Winthrop to his Father.

" MOST LOVING FATHER, — S^r, my uncle Gostling received a letter from Colechester to my brother John, & thinkinge it had concerned some businesse about the carriage of yor goods thither, brake it open, wherein perceiving that there was declared the Scearchers demande custome, & my Lord Chamberline his warrant, or else to search the goods, (as you shall see expressed in that letter, wch I have sent you enclosed in this,) my uncle Gostlinge desired me to write to you, to entreate you to send downe directions to us what you would have done in this businesse ; & if you have my Lord Chamberline his warrant (if you shall see soe fitting) to send it downe, y^t the Scearchers may see it for there satisfaction :   Thus hopinge of yor wealfare, desiringe yor prayers & blessinge, & beseeching Allmighty God to blesse & prosper you in these yor waighty affaires, entreatinge you if you can conveniently to send me downe an hatte of wch I stand in need, & to remember my service to my uncle & Aunt Downing & my love to my brothers wth you.   Wth my most humble duty to yor selfe remembred I rest & remayne

" Yo^r obedient Sonne   " FORTH WINTHROP.

" ffrom GROTON ffeb : 2. 1629 :

" My Aunt Fones desires to be remembred to you, & my cosen Ursula wth her duty remembred beseecheth yor praiers & blessinge."

---

[1] The letter of Priscilla Fones, which has already been given in this chapter, will sufficiently show that all this diplomacy had reference to her approaching engagement to Mr. Painter.

John Winthrop to his Wife.

" To my very lovinge Wife Mrs Winthrop the elder at Groton, in Suffk.

" MY SWEET WIFE, — Thy love is such to me, & so great is the bonde betweene us, that I should neglect all others to hold correspondencye of lettres wth thee : but I knowe thou art willinge to dispense wth somewhat of thine owne right, to give me lib^{ty} to satisfie my other occasions for the present, wch call me to much writinge this eveninge.   Otherwise I would have returned a larger answeare to thy sweet lettre.   I prayse God we are all in health, & we goe on cheerfully in o^r businesse : I purpose (if God will) to be with thee upon Thursdaye come senight, & then I must take my Farewell of thee, for a Sumers daye & a winters daye.   The Lorde o^r good God will (I hope) sende us a happye meetinge againe in his good tyme : Amen.   Comende me kindly to my good sister ff : I would have written to her, but I canot, havinge 6 : Lettres to write.   I wrote to Mr P. Tell my sister that her mother is brought in bedd & the child dead, & she in great danger.   Among other thinges let the brassen quart in the Larder howse be putt up ; & my gray cloake & the coate wch was my brother ffones : & let this warrant inclosed be sent to Colchester to Mr Sam^{ll} Borrowes by the next tyme the carte goes.   The Lord blesse thee my sweet wife wth all o^r children : my brother & sister salute you all : my sonnes remember their love & dutye : comend my love to all, farewell.

" Thy faithfull husband,   " Jo : WINTHROP.

" Lett Mr Dudleys thinges be sent up next week.

": FEB : 5. 1629.

" Remember to putt me up some Cardons & Card^{ns} seed.[1]
" Beinge now ready to send away my Lettres, I received thine ; the readinge of it *has dissolved* my head into tears.   I

---

[1] *Cardoon*, a plant used for soups and salads. — *Worcester.*

can write no more.   If I live I *will see thee* ere I goe.[1]   I shall parte from thee with sorrowe enough ; be comfortable my most sweet wife, oᵣ God wilbe wᵗʰ thee.   Farewell."

John *Winthrop to his Wife.*

"To my verye lovinge Wife Mʳˢ Winthrop the elder at Groton in Suffk.

"MY SWEET WIFE, — I must now answeare 2 : Lettres of thine, wᵗʰ one shorte one : Let this make some supplye, that (if God will) I wilbe wᵗʰ thee on thursdaye next, therefore let John come up wᵗʰ my horses on Mundaye.   Blessed be the Lorde oᵣ heavenly father, for all his mercye & goodnésse towards us ; that we may yet heare thus comfortably each from other, & hope of a meetinge soone in peace, to be an embleme to us of oᵣ sweet & 'happy meetinge in N : E : by the same power & mercye of oᵣ heavenly Father : but I must ende : oᵣ freinds heer salute thee & all the rest.   Com̄ende my love & blessinge to oᵣ children & to all oᵣ freinds.   The Lorde be wᵗʰ thee my sweet wife : farewell.

"Thy faithfull husband   "JO : WINTHROP.
"FEB : 11. 1629."

Margaret Winthrop to her Husband.

"MY DEARÉ HUSBAND, — I received thy sweet letter, and doe blesse God for all his mercyes to us, in the continuance of thy health and welfayre, and the rest of us heare.   I am glad to heere you wil come home this weike, for I desire to enioy thy sweete presence as ofte as I can, before that longe partinge come wᶜʰ I desyre the Lord to fit us for, and give me fayth and pacience to submite unto his will in all thinges wᶜʰ he requires at my hands.   I trust he wil sanctify it to me and give me a right use of it, that I may theareby learn the more to depend

---

[1] The words in italics are almost illegible; the paper having evidently been wet, — it may be, with the very tears of which he writes.

upon him; when other comforters fayle me, I hope, he will supply by the comfort of his holy spirit in the assurance of his love in Jesus Christ our Lord and Savior. I see thy love to me and mine, my good Husband, is more then I can deserve, and thou art more willing to grant then I forward to desyre: the good Lord requit thee all thy kindnesse to me, but I will say no more of this till you come home. I beseech the Lord to send us a comforttable meetinge, and thus with my best love to thy selfe, my brother and sister Downinge, & all the rest of our frends, I desyre the Lord to send thee a good end of al thy troubles and inable thee to goe through them cherefully, as I trust he will not fayle thee, into whose hands I commit thee and rest "thy faithful and obedyent wife
"MARGARET WINTHROPE.

"My sister Fones, my sonnes and daughters, remember thear love and duty to you and brother and sister D."

John Winthrop to his Wife.

"MY SWEET WIFE, — I wrote to thee yesterdaye: & this day o^r Company hath spent in prayer & fastinge, & the Lorde hath been pleased to assist us gratiously; blessed be his name: I doubt not but thou & all o^r familye shall have parte in the answeare of o^r prayers. This eveninge about 10: of the clocke Mr Painter came to me: he intendes to be at Groton on teusdaye next. I expect my horses on teusdaye night, & so (if God will) I purpose to be at Groton on thursdaye night, or els at Mr. Gurdons on fryday at noone. Nowe the good Lord blesse & keepe thee & all thine. So wth all o^r salut^s to you all in hast I ende & rest
"Thy faithfull husband: "JO: WINTHROP.

"I sent downe by Jervais some rice, & 2: couple of o^r N: Engl^d fish.

"Let Brease, Mr Huggins sonne in Lawe, have notice to send up his tooles this weeke.

"FEB: 12. 1629."

John Winthrop to his Wife.

"MY SWEET WIFE, — The opportunity of so fit a messenger, and my deep engagement of affection to thee, makes me write at this time, though I hope to follow soon after. The Lord our God hath oft brought us together with comfort, when we have been long absent; and, if it be good for us, he will do so still. When I was in Ireland, he brought us together again. When I was sick here at London, he restored us together again. How many dangers, near death, hast thou been in thyself! and yet the Lord hath granted me to enjoy thee still. If he did not watch over us, we need not go over sea to seek death or misery: we should meet it at every step, in every journey. And is not he a God abroad as well as at home? Is not his power and providence the same in New England that it hath been in Old England? If our ways please him, he can command deliverance and safety in all places, and can make the stones of the field and the beasts, yea, the raging seas, and our very enemies, to be in league with us. But, if we sin against him, he can raise up evil against us out of our own bowels, houses, estates, etc. My good wife, trust in the Lord, whom thou hast found faithful. He will be better to thee than any husband, and will restore thee thy husband with advantage. But I must end, with all our salutations, with which I have laden this bearer, that he may be the more kindly welcome. So I kiss my sweet wife, and bless thee and all ours, and rest

"Thine ever,   "JO. WINTHROP.

"FEBRUARY 14, 1629.

"Thou must be my valentine, for none hath challenged me."

CHAPTER XIX.

WINTHROP'S LAST VISIT TO GROTON. HIS RETURN TO LONDON, ON HIS WAY TO SOUTHAMPTON TO EMBARK FOR NEW ENGLAND. FAREWELL LETTERS TO HIS WIFE, AND OTHER CORRESPONDENTS.

WINTHROP returned to Groton for the last time soon after the date of the letter which closes our last chapter. The time for " the long parting " had at length arrived. His final departure from the old homestead, which had been the scene of his earlier as well as of his maturer years, and where were the graves not only of his father and mother, but of others who had been nearer and dearer to him still, took place during the last week of February, 1630. He went down to London by the way of Maplested, the seat of his wife's family; and soon after proceeded to Southampton, where he awaited the arrival of the ships which were to bear the Massachusetts Company to New England. He embarked at length on the 22d of March; but the ships were detained by bad winds at Cowes, and again at Yarmouth, in the Isle of Wight. His letters from all these places to his wife and others are full of interest, not merely as showing the tenderness of his affections and his unfailing trust in God, but as containing many incidents connected with the outset of this memorable embarkation. There is something of poetical beauty, as well as of pious sentiment, in the agreement, which is more than once referred to as having been made between his wife and himself, that they would remember each other every Monday and Friday evening, between the hours of five and six, and " meet in spirit before the Lord." Shakspeare, not long before, had put the same thought into the mouth of Imogen, when, on having parted with Posthumus, she complains that her father's angry entrance had interrupted her —

> " Ere I could tell him,
> How would I think on him, at certain hours,
> Such thoughts, and such; . . .
> . . . or have charged him,
> At the sixth hour of morn, at noon, at midnight,
> To encounter me with orisons; for then
> I am in heaven for him."

But Posthumus was not in his forty-third year, as Winthrop was; nor Imogen in her thirty-ninth. And certainly we doubt whether the language of real affection on a real occasion was ever more ardently and exquisitely expressed than in the following passage of John Winthrop's letter to his wife, " from aboard the Arbella, riding at the Cowes, March 28, 1630:" —

" And now, my sweet soul, I must once again take my last farewell of thee in Old England. It goeth very near to my heart to leave thee; but I know to whom I have committed thee, even to Him, who loves thee much better than any husband can; who hath taken account of the hairs of thy head, and puts all thy tears in his bottle; who can, and (if it be for his glory)·will, bring us together again with peace and comfort.. Oh, how it refresheth my heart to think, that I shall yet again see thy sweet face in the land of the living! — that lovely countenance that I have so much delighted in, and beheld with so great content! I have hitherto been so taken up with business, as I could seldom look back to my former happiness; but now when I shall be at some leisure, I shall not avoid the remembrance of thee, nor the grief for thy absence. Thou hast thy share with me, but I hope the course we have agreed upon will be some ease to us both. Mondays and Fridays, at five of the clock at night, we shall meet in spirit till we meet in person. Yet if all these hopes should fail, blessed be our God, that we are assured we shall meet one day, if not as husband and wife, yet in a better condition. Let that stay and comfort thine heart. Neither can the sea drown thy husband, nor enemies destroy, nor any adversity deprive thee of thy husband or children. Therefore I will only take thee now and my sweet children in mine arms, and kiss and embrace you all, and so leave you with God. Farewell, farewell. I bless you all in the name of the Lord Jesus."

There are other passages in these letters, of almost equal pathos and beauty; but no reader will fail to discover them for himself.

Among the letters never before printed, that of March 10, from London, is of peculiar interest; recounting, as it does, the parting kindnesses which had been shown him, not only by the Lady Mildmay and the Downings, and others of his friends and neighbors, but by some who had been "meer strangers" to him; and showing how " the eyes and hearts of all good people " were upon him and the Company, " breathing many sweet prayers and blessings after them."

In neither of the letters from Southampton is there any allusion to the presence of John Cotton, or to the sermon which he is said to have preached there; but such an omission is by no means conclusive evidence that Winthrop was not among the edified listeners to that memorable discourse. His letters from there are very brief; and he says, as an excuse for not writing more fully, " Here I meet with so much company and business, as I am forced to borrow of my sleep for this." And so we will still trust that his heart was encouraged by hearing the faithful minister of Old Boston, who was so soon to become his companion and pastor in New Boston, deliver " God's Promise to his Plantation," [1] and follow it with his prayers and benedictions.

John Winthrop to his Wife.

" To my very loving Wife, Mrs. Winthrop, at Groton.

" MINE OWN SWEET SELF, — I bless God, our heavenly Father, we are all come safe to Maplested, where we find all in health. I have nothing to write to thee, but an expression of my dearest and most faithful affection to thee, and my dear children and friends with thee. Be comfortable and courageous, my sweet wife. Fear nothing. I am assured the Lord is with us, and will be with thee. Thou shalt find it in the needful time. Cleave to thy faithful Lord and Husband, Christ Jesus, into whose blessed arms I have put thee, to whose care I have and do commend thee and all thine. Once again I kiss

---

[1] This discourse was printed at London in 1630, with a preface signed "J. H.;" undoubtedly written by John Humphrey. The principal authority for the statement that it was delivered before the Massachusetts Company at Southampton is Joshua Scottowe, in his Narrative of the Planting of the Massachusetts Colony, first published in 1694, and reprinted in Mass. Hist. Soc. Coll., vol. iv., fourth series, pp. 279, 290–5. Contemporaneous testimony is found in the following passage from the "Diary of John Rous," a Suffolk man, under date of 1630: "Some little while since, the Company went to New England under Mr. Wintrop. Mr. Cotton, of Boston in Lincolnshire, went to theire departure about Gravesend, & preached to them, as we heare, out of 2 Samuel, vii. 10. It is said that he is prohibited for preaching any more in England then untill June 24 next now comming." — "Diary of John Rous," Camden Society's Publications, No. 66, pp. 53, 54.

and embrace my sweet wife. Farewell; the Lord bless thee and all thy company. Commend me to all, and to all our good friends and neighbors, and remember Monday and Friday between five and six.

"Thy faithful husband,   "Jo. WINTHROP.

"My son Henry must come by Maplested to seal a writing, which I left there."

John Winthrop to his Wife.

"To Mrs. Marg. Winthrop at Groton with haste.

"MINE OWN DEAR HEART, — I praise God, we are all in health at Chelmsford this morning. My son F. came to us last night about ten of the clock. Our two boys are lusty travellers, and God's providence hath fitted them with so good means for their carriage, as we could not desire better. I thank thee for thy kind tokens. I have nothing to return thee but love and prayers for thee and thine. The blessing of the Lord be upon thee and them. My son Hen. must go by Maplested. Pray him to call to my brother Tindale for £100, and bring it with him. It is in gold. Send John Hardinge when thou wilt. Commend us to all our friends, broth. G. and sister, Mr. Leigh, goodwife Cole, all at Castleins, and all that love us. We all here salute you all. You must divide it at leisure, with my love and blessing to all our children and the rest in our family. Farewell, my sweet wife, and be of good comfort. The Lord is with us. He hath sent his servants to bless us, & we shall be blessed. Kiss me, my sweet wife. Farewell.

"Thy faithful husband,   "Jo : WINTHROP.

"This SATURDAY MORNING."[1]

---

[1] The date of 27th November, 1627, is affixed to this letter in the Appendix to Winthrop's History of New England; but we were convinced that some mistake must have occurred in regard to it. The letter bears internal evidence of belonging here. Chelmsford was his next stage to Maplested, in this last journey from Groton to London. While this chapter is going through the press, the original letter has come to light, and our conjecture is sufficiently verified. The Governor himself has given no date to the letter; and the date of November, 1627, is indorsed by a very modern hand.

John Winthrop to his Wife.

" MY DEARE WIFE, — I prayse God we came all safe to
London & continue in health : I thinke we shall not goe from
London till the ende of this weeke or the beginninge of the
next : & therefore I hope to write to thee againe from hence.
I am full of businesse & cañot write as I desire : I knowe thy
love will accept of any thinge. The Lorde in mercye blesse &
keepe thee & all thine. Comende my love to all, farewell my
deare Wife & be of good comfort in the Lorde.

    " Thy faithfull husband   " Jo : WINTHROP.
" MARCH 1: 1629.

" The monye thou hast it were not amisse if thou didest sende
the most of it & of thy plate to my brother Gostlings in some
stronge chest."

John Winthrop to his Wife.

           " LONDON, March 2, 1629.

" MINE OWN DEAR HEART, — I must confess, thou hast
overcome me with thy exceeding great love, and those abundant expressions of it in thy sweet letters, which savour of more
than an ordinary spirit of love and piety. Blessed be the Lord
our God, that gives strength and comfort to thee to undergo
this great trial, which, I must confess, would be too heavy for
thee, if the Lord did not put under his hand in so gracious a
measure. Let this experience of his faithfulness to thee in this
first trial, be a ground to establish thy heart to believe and
expect his help in all that may follow. It grieveth me much,
that I want time and freedom of mind to discourse with thee
(my faithful yokefellow) in those things, which thy sweet letters
offer me so plentiful occasion for. I beseech the Lord, I may
have liberty to supply it, ere I depart ; for I cannot thus leave
thee. Our two boys and James Downing, John Samford and
Mary M. and most of my servants, are gone this day towards
South Hampton. The good Lord be with them and us all.

Goodman Hawes was with me, and very kindly offers to bring his wife to Groton about the beginning of April, and so stay till thyself and my daughter [1] be in bed; so as thou shalt not need take care for a midwife. Ah, my most kind and dear wife, how sweet is thy love to me! The Lord bless thee and thine with the blessings from above and from beneath, of the right hand and the left, with plenty of favor and peace here, and eternal glory hereafter. All here are in health, (I praise God,) and salute thee. Remember my love and blessing to our children, and my salutations to all as thou knowest. So I kiss and embrace thee, and rest

"Thine ever,   "Jo. Winthrop."

John Winthrop to his Wife.

"To my verye loving Wife Mrs. Winthrop the elder at Groton, Suffolk.

"London March 10: 1629.

"Mine owne, mine onely, my best beloved, — Methinkes it is verye longe since I sawe or heard from my beloved, & I misse allreadye the sweet comfort of thy most desired presence : but the rich mercye & goodnesse of my God makes supplye of all wants : Blessed be his great & holy name. Ah my good wife, we now finde what blessinge is stored up in the favour of the Lorde; he only sweetens all conditions to us, he takes our cares & feares from us, he supports us in our dangers, he disposeth all our affaires for us, he will guide us by his counsell in our pilgrimage, & after will bringe us to glorye.

"John is returned from S: Hampton, where he lefte our boyes well & merrye : & this morninge we are ridinge thither, & from thence I shall take my last farewell of thee till we meet in new E : or till midsomer that it please God our shipps returne. My deare wife be of good courage, it shall goe well

---

1 Doubtless this was Henry's wife. Her daughter Martha was baptized at Groton, May 9 following.

with thee & us, the hairs of thy head are numbred, he who gave his onely beloved to dye for thee, will give his Angells charge over thee : therefore rayse up thy thoughts, & be merrye in the Lorde, labour to live by thy Faith ; if thou meet with troubles or difficultyes, be not dismayed ; God doth use to bringe his children into the streights of the redd sea &c, that he may shew his power & mercye in makinge a waye for them : All his courses towards us, are but to make us knowe him & love him ; the more thy heart drawes towards him in this, the freer shall thy condition be from the evill of Affliction.

"Our friends heer are all in health (blessed be God) & desire to be heartyly comended to thee. I am exceedingly beholdinge to my good brother & sister D, I can fasten no recompence upon them for all the chardge my selfe & my company have putt them to. I have received much kindnesse also from my Lady Mildmay & from others, whereof some have been meer strangers to me, the Lord reward them : It doth much incourage us to see, how the eyes & hearts of all good people are upon us, breathinge many sweet prayers & blessings after us. Comende my hearty love to all our friends, I cannot now name them, but thou knowest whom I meane. Nowe I beseech the Lord & father of mercye to blesse thee & all thy companye, my daughter W : Ma : Mat : Sam : Deane, & the little one unknowne, Tho : Am :[1] & the rest : Tell Am : I am very much beholdinge to her brother, desire her to give him thanks for me : tell my n : Culproke I am beholdinge to his sonne in lawe for oysters he sent me, but could not see him to give him thankes. My deare wife farewell, once againe let us kisse & imbrace, so in teares of great Affection I rest

　　　　"Thine ever　　　　　　　　"Jo : WINTHROP."

---

[1] The persons indicated by *Tho:* and *Am:* were undoubtedly his servants Thomas and Amy. The others, previously alluded to, were Henry's wife, his own daughter Mary, Martha Fones (afterwards the wife of his son John), and his sons Samuel and Deane.

John Winthrop to his Wife.

" MINE ONLY BEST-BELOVED, — I now salute thee from South Hampton, where, by the Lord's mercy, we are all safe ; but the winds have been such as our ships are not yet come. We wait upon God, hoping that he will dispose all for the best unto us. I supposed I should have found leisure to have written more fully to thee by this bearer ; but here I meet with so much company and business, as I am forced to borrow of my sleep for this. I purpose to redeem this loss before I go hence, and to write to divers of my friends. I must entreat thee to supply this defect by remembering me in the kindest manner to them all. And now (my dear wife) what shall I say to thee? I am full of matter and affection toward thee, but want time to express it. I beseech the good Lord to take care of thee and thine ; to seal up his loving kindness to thy soul ; to fill thee with the sweet comfort of his presence, that may uphold thee in this time of trial ; and grant us this mercy, that we may see the faces of each other again in the time expected. So, loving thee truly, and tender of thy welfare, studying to bestow thee safe, where I may have thee again, I leave thee in the arms of the Lord Jesus, our sweet Saviour, and, with many kisses and embracings, I rest

" Thine only, and ever thine,

" Jo. WINTHROP.

" SOUTH HAMPTON, March 14, 1629.

" The good Lord bless our children and all thy company.

" Do thou bless these here, and pray, pray for us.

" Give Mrs. Leigh many thanks for her horse, and remember to requite it."

John Winthrop to his Son.

" To my verye lovinge sonne Mr John Winthrop at Mr Downing's house
in fleetstreet neere the Conduitt, London.

" MY GOOD SONNE, — The Lord blesse thee ever.

" It hathe pleased him of his riche mercye to bringe us all
hither in safetye, blessed be his name.   Our shippes are not yet
come about ; so as we knowe not when we shall departe, but o^r
eyes are towards o^r God, who hath putt us into his service, &
wilbe wth us to the ende : I have not yet any leysure, & therefore cañt write to suche of my good freinds as I desire, but I
hope to gett tyme before we goe : make what convenient hast
you can to y^r mother, & that love & dutye you owe to me,
exercise it towards her & y^r brothers & sisters, (I have no
cause to doubt of it, neither doe I), the Lord will reward all y^r
goodnesse this waye.   Mr Dudlye was gone to the Wight before we came, & Sr Rich^d [1] is not yet come to us.   The Lord
poure downe his blessings upon you, bothe the blessings of the
right hand & the lefte, & let the blessings of yor father be increased above the blessings of o^r ancestors, upon the head &
heart of my deare sonne, so I rest

" Yo^r lovinge father   " Jo : WINTHROP.

" S : HAMPTON March 14. 1629.

" If you spare any money lease it wth your unckle, for I
feare I shall want some."

John Winthrop to his Son.

" To my very loving Son, Mr. John Winthrop, at Groton, Suffolk.

" MY GOOD SON, — We are now going to the ship, under the
comfort of the Lord's gracious protection and good providence.
I pray have care so to walk with God in faith and sincerity, as,
by his blessing, we may meet with joy.   There is newly come

---

[1] Sir Richard Saltonstall.

into our company, and sworn an assistant, one Sir Brian Janson of London, a man of good estate, and so affected with our society, as he hath given £50 to our common stock, and £50 to the joint stock. He desires to be acquainted with you.

"I pray pay Bulbrooke of Wenham such money as his provisions cost him, about 30 or 40s. and receive £12 of goodman Pond for the rest of his son's two cows, (I had £10 before,) and ask him for their passage £10. You shall receive £5 for Edward Palsford, which John S. hath order for. I pray pay Mr. Goffe such money as you shall receive direction for from your uncle Downing.

"We are now come safe (I praise God) to the Cowes. The wind is now very fair, (God be praised,) and we are preparing to set sail this night. The Lord in mercy send us a prosperous voyage. Farewell, my dear son. The Lord bless you and all my children and friends. Commend me to them all, as if I named them; for I am in great straits of leisure. So I rest

"Your loving father, "Jo. Winthrop.

"March 22, 1629."

John Winthrop to his Wife.

"My dear Wife, — I wrote to thee, when I went from South Hampton, and now I must salute thee and take leave together from the ship. God be blessed, the wind is come very fair, and we are all in health. Our children [1] remember their duties and desire thy blessing. Commend me to all our good friends, as I wrote in my former letter, and be comfortable, and trust in the Lord, my dear wife, pray, pray. He is our God and Father; we are in covenant with him, and he will not cast us off. So, this once more, I kiss and embrace thee and all my children, etc., etc.

"Thy faithful husband, "Jo. Winthrop.

"From aboard the Arbella, riding at the Cowes, March 22, 1629."

---

[1] Henry, Stephen, and Adam.

John Winthrop to his Wife.

" To Mrs. Marg. Winthrop, the elder, at Groton.

"MY FAITHFUL AND DEAR WIFE, — It pleaseth God, that thou shouldst once again hear from me before our departure, and I hope this shall come safe to thy hands. I know it will be a great refreshing to thee. And blessed be his mercy, that I can write thee so good news, that we are all in very good health, and, having tried our ship's entertainment now more than a week, we find it agree very well with us. Our boys are well and cheerful, and have no mind of home. They lie both with me, and sleep as soundly in a rug (for we use no sheets here) as ever they did at Groton ; and so I do myself, (I praise God). The wind hath been against us this week and more ; but this day it is come fair to the north, so as we are preparing (by God's assistance) to set sail in the morning. We have only four ships ready, and some two or three Hollanders go along with us. The rest of our fleet (being seven ships) will not be ready this sennight. We have spent now two Sabbaths on shipboard very comfortably, (God be praised,) and are daily more and more encouraged to look for the Lord's presence to go along with us. Henry Kingsbury hath a child or two in the Talbot sick of the measles, but like to do well. One of my men had them at Hampton, but he was soon well again. We are, in all our eleven ships, about seven hundred persons, passengers, and two hundred and forty cows, and about sixty horses. The ship, which went from Plimouth, carried about one hundred and forty persons, and the ship, which goes from Bristowe, carrieth about eighty persons.[1] And now (my sweet soul) I must once again take my last farewell of thee in Old England. It goeth very near to my heart to leave thee ; but I know to whom I have committed thee, even to him who loves

---

[1] The ship from Plymouth was the "Mary and John," which carried Maverick, Warham, and Roger Clap. From Bristol came the "Lion;" William Pierce, master.

thee much better than any husband can, who hath taken account of the hairs of thy head, and puts all thy tears in his bottle, who can, and (if it be for his glory) will bring us together again with peace and comfort. Oh, how it refresheth my heart, to think, that I shall yet again see thy sweet face in the land of the living! — that lovely countenance, that I have so much delighted in, and beheld with so great content! I have hitherto been so taken up with business, as I could seldom look back to my former happiness; but now, when I shall be at some leisure, I shall not avoid the remembrance of thee, nor the grief for thy absence. Thou hast thy share with me, but I hope the course we have agreed upon will be some ease to us both. Mondays and Fridays, at five of the clock at night, we shall meet in spirit till we meet in person. Yet, if all these hopes should fail, blessed be our God, that we are assured we shall meet one day, if not as husband and wife, yet in a better condition. Let that stay and comfort thy heart. Neither can the sea drown thy husband, nor enemies destroy, nor any adversity deprive thee of thy husband or children. Therefore I will only take thee now and my sweet children in mine arms, and kiss and embrace you all, and so leave you with my God. Farewell, farewell. I bless you all in the name of the Lord Jesus. I salute my daughter Winth. Matt. Nan. and the rest, and all my good neighbors and friends. Pray all for us. Farewell. Commend my blessing to my son John. I cannot now write to him; but tell him I have committed thee and thine to him. Labor to draw him yet nearer to God, and he will be the surer staff of comfort to thee. I cannot name the rest of my good friends, but thou canst supply it. I wrote, a week since, to thee and Mr. Leigh, and divers others.

      "Thine wheresoever,   "Jo. WINTHROP.

"From aboard the ARBELLA, riding at the COWES, March 28, 1630.

"I would have written to my brother and sister Gostling, but it is near midnight. Let this excuse; and commend my love to them and all theirs."

John Winthrop to his Wife.

" To my very loving Wife, Mrs. Winthrop, the elder, at Groton, in
Suffolk.

" MY LOVE, MY JOY, MY FAITHFUL ONE, — I suppose thou
didst not expect to have any more letters from me till the return
of our ships ; but so is the good pleasure of God, that the
winds should not serve yet to carry us hence.   He will do all
things in his own time, and that shall be for the best in the end.
We acknowledge it a great mercy to us, that we went not out
to sea on Monday, when the wind was fair for one day ; for we
had been exposed, ever since, to sore tempests and contrary
winds.   I praise God, we are all in good health, and want
nothing.   For myself, I was never at more liberty of body and
mind these many years.   The Lord make me thankful and wise
to improve his blessings for the furtherance of his own work.
I desire to resign myself wholly to his gracious disposing.   Oh
that I had an heart so to do, and to trust perfectly in him for
his assistance in all our ways.   We find him still going along
with us.   He hath brought in the heart of the master of our
ship to afford us all good respect, and to join with us in every
good action.   Yesterday he caused his seamen to keep a fast
with us, wherein the Lord assisted us and our minister very
comfortably ; and when five of the clock came, I had respite to
remember thee, (it being Friday,) and to parley with thee, and
to meet thee in spirit before the Lord.   After supper, we discovered some notorious lewd persons of our own company,
who, in time of our fast, had committed theft, and done other
villanies, for which we have caused them to be severely pun-
ished.

" I am uncertain whether I shall have opportunity to send
these to thee ; for, if the wind turn, we shall soon be gone.
Therefore I will not write much.   I know it will be sufficient
for thy present comfort, to hear of our welfare ; and this is the
third letter I have written to thee, since I came to Hampton, in

requital of those two I received from thee, which I do often
read with much delight, apprehending so much love and sweet
affection in them, as I am never satisfied with reading, nor can
read them without tears; but whether they proceed from joy,
sorrow, or desire, or from that consent of affection, which I
always hold with thee, I cannot conceive. Ah, my dear heart,
I ever held thee in high esteem, as thy love and goodness hath
well deserved; but (if it be possible) I shall yet prize thy virtue at a greater rate, and long more to enjoy thy sweet society
than ever before. I am sure thou art not short of me in this
desire. Let us pray hard, and pray in faith, and our God, in
his good time, will accomplish our desire. Oh, how loath am I
to bid thee farewell! but, since it must be, farewell, my sweet
love, farewell. Farewell, my dear children and family. The
Lord bless you all, and grant me to see your faces once again.
Come, (my dear,) take him and let him rest in thine arms, who
will ever remain,

" Thy faithful husband,   " Jo. Winthrop.

" Commend my love to all our friends at Castleins,[1] Mr.
Leigh and his wife, my neighbor Cole and his wife, and all the
rest of our good friends and neighbors, and our good friends at
Maplested, when you see them, and those our worthy and kind
friends at Assington,[2] etc. My brother Arthur[3] hath carried
himself very soberly since he came on shipboard, and so hath
Mr. Brand's son,[4] and my cousin Ro. Sampson.[5] I hope their
friends shall hear well of them.

" From aboard the ARBELLA, riding before YARMOUTH,
     in the Isle of Wight, April 3, 1630."

---

[1] This was a manor-house in Groton, the seat of the Cloptons.

[2] Assington was the residence of the Gurdons.

[3] He was a son of Sir John Tindall, father of the writer's wife.

[4] The Brands were of Polstead Hall, in Polstead or Edwardston, — parishes close to Groton.

[5] Robert was the son of John Sampson, who married Bridget Clopton, sister of Winthrop's second wife. The Sampsons were an ancient knightly family of Sampson's
Hall in Kersey, near Groton.

John Winthrop to his Son.

"To [my very loving Son,] Mr. [John Winthrop,] Groton, in Suffolk.

"My good Son, — I received two letters from you since I came to Hampton, and this is the second I have written back to you. I do much rejoice and bless God for that goodness I find in you towards me and mine. I do pray, and assuredly expect, that the Lord will reward it plentifully in your bosom; for it is his promise to prolong their days, (which includes all outward prosperity,) who give due honor to their parents. Trust him, son, for he is faithful. Labor to grow into nearer communion and acquaintance with him, and you shall find him a good God, and a master worth the serving. Ask of any who have tried him, and they will justify him in his kindness and bounty to his servants. Yet we must not look that he should always give us what we think might be good for us; but wait, and let him take his own way, and the end will satisfy our expectation.

"Our ship and the Talbot are now at Yarmouth; but the Jewell and Ambrose are put back unto the Cowes. We have had very tempestuous weather, with the wind at S.W., so as some ships, which went out at the Needles before us, are driven back again; and we intend not to stir till we see the wind settled. I would wish women and children not to go to sea till April, and then to take shipping at London. If we had done so, it had eased us of much trouble and charge. There lie now at Cowes two ships of Holland, bound one to the Streights and the other to the East Indies, of one hundred tons a piece, which, putting to sea in February, spent their masts, and, with much difficulty, and loss of near a hundred men, are come in hither. There came in lately by us a ship from Virginia, laden with tobacco. The master came aboard us, and told us, that they want corn there. She was fourteen weeks outward, and yet lost but one man. I pray certify me, by the next occasion, what the wine cost for the common use, and if you have laid out any more in that kind, that I may perfect my account.

"I pray prepare money so soon as you can, that I may be clear with Mr. Goffe and others, and that my part in the joint stock may be made up.

"Sir Nath. Barnardiston desired to put in money into our joint stock. Remember my love and respect to him, and if he will put in £50, take it as part of the £200 which I have put in already, except you have money enough to supply more.

"Yesterday we kept a fast aboard our ship and in the Talbot. Mr. Phillips exercised with us the whole day, and gave very good content to all the company, as he doth in all his exercises, so as we have much cause to bless God for him.

"In the Talbot a woman was lately delivered of a son, and both like to do well.

"For other things, which concern my affairs at home, I refer them to your care and the good providence of the Almighty.

"Commend my love to all our good friends, as you have occasion, — to my daughter Winthrop, your sister and cousin, and to Mr. Leigh, Mr. Nutt,[1] and that family, and to all at Castleins, and the rest, whom I can't now name; and the Lord bless, direct, and prosper you in all your ways. So farewell, my good son.

"Your loving father,   " Jo. Winthrop.

" From aboard the Arbella, riding before Yarmouth, April 5, 1630.

"Our long stay here hath occasioned the expense of much more money than I expected, so as I am run much in Mr. Goffe's debt. I pray get up some money so soon as you can, and pay him £150, or so much as you can get."

We must not omit, before closing this chapter, to give another of Winthrop's parting letters; of which the original draught, or it may be a rough copy, in his own

---

[1] Undoubtedly Mr. Newton and his family.

handwriting, has survived the ravages of time. It is a letter to his friend Sir William Spring, then serving in Parliament with Sir Nathaniel Barnardiston, as Knight for the County of Suffolk. It contains many striking passages, altogether characteristic of the writer; and certainly indicates a depth of feeling and a warmth of sympathy such as *men* rarely express, even if they ever feel, towards each other in these latter days. It seems to have been written in answer to a request from Sir William for a farewell word of consolation and counsel.

John Winthrop to Sir William Springe.

"WORTHY SIR, and to me a most sweet friend, — I know not how to frame my affections to write to you. I received your letter, nay, *merum mel non epistolam a te accepi.* I am in suspense, whether I should submit my thoughts in the sweetness of your love, or sit down sorrowful in the consciousness of mine own infirmity, as having nothing precious in me, or any way worthy such love or esteem; — But that which I have found from yourself and some others, whose constance and good trust hath made me some time proud of their respects, gives me occasion to look up to a higher Cause, and to acknowledge the free favor and goodness of my God, who is pleased to put this honor upon me (a poor worm and raised but yesterday out of the dust) to be desired of his choicest servants : I see his delight is to show the greatest bounty where he finds the least desert, therefore he justifies the ungodly, and spreads the skirt of his love upon us, when he finds us in our blood unswathed, unwashed, unseasoned — that he might shew forth the glory of his mercy, and that we might know how he can love a creature.

"Sweet Sir, You seek fruit from a barren tree, you would gather knowledge where it never grew : If to satisfy your desire, I should bundle up all that reading and observation hath

put into me, they will afford but these few considerations — 1.
Joshua his best piece of 'policy was, that he chose to serve the
ablest master; Mary's, that she would make sure of the best
part; and Solomon's, that he would have wisdom, rather than
riches or life: 2. The clear and veriest desire of these, was
never severed from the fruition of them: the reason is clear,
the Lord holds us always in his lap, as the loving mother doth
her froward child, watching when it will open the mouth, and
presently she thrusts in the teat or the spoon: Open thy
mouth wide (saith the Lord) and I will fill thee. O! that
Israel would have hearkened to me, I would have filled them
&c. O! that there were in this people an heart &c. O! Jerusalem, Jerusalem, how often would I have gathered thee &c.
He filleth the hungry soul with good things. 3. Even our
Grace hath its perfection begun in this life: All true colours
are good, yet the colour in grain is in best esteem, and of most
worth: meekness of wisdom, poverty of spirit, pure love, sim-
plicity in Christ &c., are Grace in Grain: 4. For all outward
good things, they are to a Christian as the bird to the fowler,
— if he goes directly upon her, he is sure to miss her: riches
takes her to her wings (saith Solomon) when a man pursues
her: he that will speed of this game, must seek them *quasi
aliud agens*, or (more freely) *aliud cogitans*. I have known
when three or four have beat the bushes a whole day, with as
many dogs waiting on them, and have come home weary, empty
and discontented, when one poor man going to market, hath in
an hour or two dispatched his business, and returned home
merry, with a hare at his back. Of all outward things life hath
no peer, yet the way to save this is, to lose it; for he that will
save his life shall lose it. Where is now the glory and greatness of the times past? even of yesterday? Queen Elizabeth,
King James, &c. — in their time, who but they? Happy he
who could get their favour! Now they are in the dust, and
none desire their company, neither have themselves one mite
of all they possessed — only the good which that Queen did for
the Church hath stamped an eternal sun-lustre upon her name,

so as the Londoners do still erect triumphant monuments of her in their churches. — If we look at persons of inferior quality, how many have there been, who have adventured (if not sold) their souls, to raise those houses, which are now possessed by strangers? If it be enough for ourselves, that we have food and raiment, why should we covet more for our posterity? It is with us as with one in a fever, the more nourishment we give him, the longer and sharper are his fits : So the more we cloy our posterity with riches (above competency) the more matter will there be for affliction to work upon : It were happy for many if their parents had left them only such a legacy as our modern spirit of poetry makes his motto, *Ut nec habeant, nec careant, nec curent.*[1]

"I am so straightened in time, and my thoughts so taken up with business, as indeed I am unfit to write of these things. It is your exceeding love hath drawn these from me, and that love must cover all infirmities. I loved you truly before I could think that you took any notice of me ; but now I embrace you and rest in your love, and delight to solace my first thoughts in these sweet affections of so dear a friend. The apprehension of your love and worth together hath overcome my heart, and removed the veil of modesty, that I must needs tell you, my soul is knit to you, as the soul of Jonathan to David : Were I now with you, I should bedew that sweet bosom with the tears of affection. O ! what a pinch will it be to me, to part with such a friend ! If any Emblem may express our condition in heaven, it is this Communion in love. I could, (nay, I shall), envy the happiness of your dear brother B.[2] that he shall enjoy what I desire — nay (I will even let love drive me into extacy) I must repine at the felicity of that good Lady (to

---

[1] I was curious to know whom Winthrop called "our modern spirit of poetry;" but the motto eluded my search, until I found, in the recent Life of Milton by Prof. Masson, that it belonged to *George Wither*, whose "Hymns and Songs of the Church" were among the best religious verses in that day, and have been republished in our own. — *Masson's Life of Milton*, Am. edition, vol. i. pp. 364–7.

[2] Evidently Sir N. Barnardiston, then the colleague of Spring, in Parliament, as Knight of the County of Suffolk.

whom in all love and due respect I desire to be remembered) as one that should have more part than myself in that honest heart of my dear friend. But I must leave you all : our farewells usually are pleasant passages, mine must be sorrowful ; this addition of, forever, is a sad close ; yet there is some comfort in it — bitter pills help to procure sound health : God will have it thus, and blessed be his holy name — let him be pleased to light up the light of his countenance upon us, and we have enough. We shall meet in heaven, and while we live, our prayers and affections shall hold an intercourse of friendship and represent us often, with the idea of each other's countenance. Your earnest desire to see me, makes me long as much to meet you : If my leisure would have permitted me, I would have prevented your travel ; but I must now (against mine own disposition) only tell you where you may find me upon Thursday, &c. It is time to conclude, but I know not how to leave you, yet since I must, I will put my beloved into His arms, who loves him best, and is a faithful keeper of all that is committed to him. Now Thou the hope of Israel, and the sure help of all that come to thee, knit the hearts of thy servants to thyself, in faith and purity. Draw us with the sweetness of thine odours, that we may run after thee — Allure us, and speak kindly to thy servants, that thou mayest possess us as thine own, in the kindness of youth, and the love of marriage — Seal us up, by that holy Spirit of promise, that we may not fear to trust in thee — Carry us into thy garden, that we may eat and be filled with those pleasures, which the world knows not — Let us hear that sweet voice of thine, my love, my dove, my undefiled [1] — Spread thy skirt over us, and cover our deformity — Make us sick with thy love — Let us sleep in thine arms, and awake in thy kingdom — The souls of thy servants, thus united to thee, make as one in the bonds of brotherly affection — Let not distance weaken it, nor time waste it, nor

---

[1] Winthrop's familiarity with the Song of Solomon is abundantly evident in this and other passages of the prayer with which he concludes the letter.

changes dissolve it, nor self-love eat it out ; but when all means
of other communion shall fail, let us delight to pray for each
other :   And so let thy unworthy servant prosper in the love
of his friends, as he truly loves thy good servants S. and B.[1]
and wishes true happiness to them and to all theirs — Amen.

" J. W.

"LONDON, Feb. 8, 1629."

Nor were the leave-takings altogether confined to letters.   " That honourable and worthy gentleman, Mr.
John Winthrop, the Governour of the Company " (says
Hubbard), " at a solemn feast amongst many friends,
a little before their last farewell, finding his bowels yearn
within him, instead of drinking to them, by breaking into
a flood of tears himself, set them all a weeping, with
Paul's friends, while they thought of seeing the faces of
each other no more in the land of the living." [2]   Well
did he say, " This addition of *forever* is a sad close to
our farewells."

And thus ends the life of John Winthrop in Old England.   We have traced it, or rather have allowed it to
trace itself, for a period of a little more than forty-two
years.   His ancestry and parentage, his education, his
professional career, his repeated personal trials and afflictions, his religious experiences, all have been exhibited
in succession.   As the mere story of a life two centuries
and a half ago, it could not have been wholly without
interest.   Had that life terminated here ; had the " Arbella " foundered on her weary and perilous passage, and

---

[1] Spring and Barnardiston.   [2] Hubbard's N.E., ch. xxiii.

Winthrop never again been heard of; or had he only landed on the shores of New England, like his excellent friend and associate, Isaac Johnson, to look around for a few months on the wilderness-work which he had undertaken, and then to sicken and die,—we still cannot doubt that there would have been many minds and many hearts to whom his career, as thus far developed, would have been both instructive and attractive. No one could have been willing that these ancient letters and papers, unveiling so much of the domestic life of a period so remote, and which have so mysteriously survived the accidents of time, should have been suffered to perish at last without seeing the light. No true antiquarian, certainly, would have forgiven the suppression even of a. single letter of so distant a date; while any attempt to abridge or condense such materials could only have resulted in depriving them of that quaintness and raciness which constitute so much of the charm of the epistolary style of the olden time.

And now, in his mature manhood, Winthrop is leaving home and friends and kindred and native country, to traverse a vast ocean, and to enter on a most laborious and responsible public service in a remote and unsettled corner of the earth. Had he remained in England, it is easy to imagine that he might have played no undecided or undistinguished part in the great events which were soon to shake that kingdom to its centre. Civil and religious persecutions, alike, were rapidly assuming a shape and an intensity which could not fail to rouse the nation to resistance. The days of ship-money were close at hand, and Laud was soon about to ascend his archiepiscopal throne. In the stern struggles of Puritanism against arbitrary power, whether in Church or in State, Winthrop could not have remained neutral or inactive. All his associations and all his principles would have ranged him on the side of toleration and freedom; and, though his marked moderation of character might have held him back from the extreme measures of Rump Parliaments and Regicides, no one can doubt that he would have gone along with such men as Hampden and Eliot to the battle-field, to the Tower, or even to the block, rather than submit to the tyrannical exactions and oppressions which Crown and Mitre were so soon to vie with each other in dealing out over the land.

But his fortunes are henceforth indissolubly linked with the colonization and civilization of the New World, where he is destined to exercise an influence, second, certainly, to that of no other man of his day, upon the rise and progress of American institutions. Nineteen years are still to elapse between his embarkation on the 22d of March, 1629–30, and his death on the 26th of March, 1649; and the account of his career during that period will furnish ample materials for another volume of this Biography. That career, however, belongs to history, and has been already illustrated by more than one of the historians of the United States and of New England.[1] We can hardly hope to add much to the account of

---

[1] Mr. Bancroft has given a brilliant sketch of Winthrop's life and character in his History of the United States, vol. i. (18th edition) ch. ix.; and nothing could be more admirable, or, as we think, more generally just, than Dr. Palfrey's treatment of Winthrop's career, in his recent History of New England.

this latter part of his life, although we are not without some new original letters and papers pertaining to it. Meantime, the present volume contains all the facts, in regard to his earlier condition and fortunes, which have been brought to light in the recently discovered family papers, and exhibits the whole preparation and discipline through which he passed before entering upon his memorable New-England enterprise. It displays, in greater detail, perhaps, than can be found anywhere else, not merely the outward life, but the inmost thoughts and motives and principles, of one of our most distinguished American Puritans, and unfolds all the circumstances which could have given an impulse and a direction to the course which he ultimately adopted and pursued. It portrays, as he was up to the very moment when he entered upon the solemn trust, the chosen Leader of the fathers and founders of Massachusetts in the transfer of their government from England to America; and shows us precisely of what stuff he was made, and under what stars he was moulded.

In this regard, the present volume is complete in itself, and may not unfitly be given to the public as an independent work. Here, then, we close it; leaving all question as to the earlier or later appearance of another volume to be decided hereafter.

APPENDIX.

APPENDIX.

I.

MEMORANDA FROM THE DIARY OF ADAM WINTHROP,

(Father of Governor Winthrop.)

1595–1610.

Special matters & observations noted in the yere of our Lorde God 1595: by me A. W.

This yere Corne was very scarce vntil haruest, notwthstanding y^t there 1595. was muche wheate & rye brought into Inglande from by yonde the Seas, whereby the price of corne was abated.

Also al other kinde of vitaile was in the begynnynge of this yere sould at great prices.

On Whitsonday I had a great swarme of bees, and on Munday in Witsonweeke ther did come a swarme of· bees flyeng ouer Castleynes heathe into Carters grounde.[1]

The same day & tyme Mr. Gatcheroode, Mr. Walton, Mr. Th. Waldgraue, Mr. Clopton & my selfe were ther present about the bounding of the heathe.

On Thursday the 3. of July, Mr. Brampton Gurdon had a soonne borne to him: who was baptized on Sunday the 13 of July and named John. Sr Wm Waldegraue and old Mr. John Gurdon were godfathers: and the Lady Moore & olde Mris. Gurdon were godmoothers.

This yeare at ye Sommer assises, viz: 22 Julij 1595, diuers Justices of the Peace were put out of ye Comission by the Q. comandement, viz. Mr. Tilney, Mr. W. Foorth, Mr. Doile, Mr. Warren, Mr. Drury.

---

[1] There were many superstitions about bees in Suffolk County; and, among others, that bad luck was portended by a stray swarm of bees settling on one's premises, unclaimed by their owner. — "*The Book of Days*," p. 752.

1595.   This yere the viiith Day of July my brother Roger Alibaster, & my
37 El. sister his wife wth their iij soñes, George, John & Thomas, & Sara their
daughter, tooke their iourny from Hadleigh to goe into Irelande.

The same day it Thundred, hailed & Rayned very sore.

Willm Alibaster their eldest soonne departed from my house towards
Cambrige the ixth of July, malcontent.[1]

This yere harvest begañ not wth vs vn till the xijth of August & con-
tynued vntill the [*blank*] of September.

The 27 of August Mr. Hanam fell sicke & recoüerd the iiijth of
Sept. The same day my brother killed a brocke[2] wth his hounds.

The xxx of August I received a lr̄e from my brother Cotty of
Couentry.

The vth day of Sept. my cosen Marian Rolfe cam̄e to my house.

The xth of Sept. my cosen Hawkyns cam̄e to me.

The xxijth of Sept. my brother Mildmay cam̄e to my house.

The 3, 4 & 5 daies of October Sr Wm Waldegraue mustred all his
souldio^{rs} viz. 400, vppon a hill nere Sudbury.

The 8 day of october my wyfe rydde to her father at Pritlewell in
Essex & returned the xxth.[3]

The xth day of October Adam Seely retourned home, & the same
day I Rec^d a lr̄e from my L. of Bathe.[4]

In the moneth of Octobre, Año 1595, Sr Thomas Heneage died,
Vir bonus & pius, & on the same day & monethe Philip, late Erle of
Arundell died in the Tower of London.

The xxxth day of Octobre Richard Bronde of Boxford sherman,[5]
Departed out of this life, año etatis 59.

The 7 of November the Erle of Hertford was com̄itted to the
Tower.

The xiiijth of Decembre I receyved a lr̄e from my brother Alibaster
written from Tenby in Wales concernynge his ill successe in his Irisshe
iourny.

---

1 For some account of William Alabaster, see p. 16, note 1.

2 A badger.

3 Adam's wife was the daughter of Henry Browne, who is sometimes styled of
Edwardston, and sometimes of Prittlewell. See pp. 47–8.

4 By "my Lord of Bathe" is meant Dr. John Still, Bishop of Bath and Wells,
whose sister was Adam's first wife.

5 "The Cloth-workers were originally incorporated by Edward IV. in 1482 as
shermen (shearers)."—*Timbs's Curiosities of London.*

A festo natiuitatis Domini Anno 1595.

The [*blank*] Day of January the butcher of Netherden woodde was 1595. cruelly murdered viz. his hed was cutt of & his body devided into iiij qr^trs & wrapt in a sheet & layd vpon his owne horse, as he came from Bury markett; & so brought home to his wyfe, who vppō the sight therof pntly died.[1]

The ix^th of January Mr. Sandes was taken sicke *grauiter*.

The xx^th of January my brother Mildmay did sett vppon a Comission at the Whight Lion in Boxford street w^thin Groton.

The third day of ffeb. Carue Mildmay was borne.

The vth of ffeb mother Baker died.[2]

The vij^th of ffeb. I Rec^d a lre from my L. of Bathe.

The xth of ffeb. I was at my ffathers, & the xv^th at my brother Mildmayes.

The xvi. of ffeb. Sara Winthrop was maried to John Froste.

The xix^th of ffeb Robert Brand the phisitōn died, etats 61.

The seconde of Marche Sr Wm Waldegrave kept a Court at Edwardeston.

The xth day of March John Clarke the warde setter died beinge of th' age of lxxvj yeres.

The xvij^th day of Marche Mr. Nicholson was robbed.

The xix^th day Mr. Knewstub preached at Boxforde.

The [*blank*] of Marche Sr Robert Winckfild the ancientest knight in Suff. died & Sr Francis Hynde of Cambridgeshire died the 21 of the same moneth.

The xth of Aprill John Wade died & was buried at Pritlewell.   1596.

The xj of Aprill, being Ester day, the Bell did Ringe at Groton for Mr. Clopton, Año 1596, but he recouered.

The xv^th of Aprill Rich. Spenser asked Mr. Gurdon forgivenesse for Slandringe of him.

The xxiij^th of Aprill E. Aulston was maried to Susan B.

The last of Aprill Sr J. Puckringe, L. keper of the great seale died of the deadde palsey.

The xth of May [*blank*] Grymolde of Nedginge did hange himselfe in his Barne.

---

1 This paragraph has lines drawn over it by a later hand, perhaps to throw doubt or denial on the story.

2 The terms " father " and " mother " will be frequently found in this Diary, applied evidently to aged persons who were probably so called in the neighborhood, but having no reference to any parental connection.

1596.   The xvij^th of May Adam Seely went privilie from my house & caried awaye xv^s wch he did steale from Richard Edwardes, *pro quo facto dignus est capistro.*

The xviij^th of May John Spencer the eld^r died.

The xxviij^th of May Mr. Pie of Colchester died suddenly.

The xj^th of June Sr Wm Waldegraue trayned his whole band of footemen & horsemen on Babar heathe.

The 16 of June my brother Winthrop departed from my house towards Ireland, & my brother Alibaster went wth him.

The xv^th day of June Dr Fletcher B. of London died.

The xxiiij^th of June my ffather Browne came to my house.

The vj^th of July th assises were holden at Bury.

The same day was the Comencement at Cambrige, & Mr. Overall was made D^r of Divinitie.

The 26 day of July my brother Mildmay came to Edwardeston to my house.[1]

The 2^d of August George Alibast^r died, A° 1596.

The ix^th of August my b. Weston p^rched at Boxford *sup.* 13 *Marcū versu vltimo, pie & eloquenter.*[2]

The xx^th of Aug. fell a great Rayne wch made a floud at Boxford.

The xxiij^th of August I dragde my great ponde & tooke out xxxv greate Carpes.

The xix^th of August Tilleson did sett vp the house in the W. Reignolds yarde.

The last of August my wife ridde to Ipsw^ch for phisick & on the same day Clover died.

The xiij^th of Sept. Judithe Pond was dd° of her first soonne being munday, & he was named W^m.

The same day my Cosen Tho: Mildmay retorned, & Ed. Aulson was maryed the xxj^th & my wife rydd to Bury.

The xxvij^th of Sept. my Cozen Alib. came to my house.

The xviij^th daye, being S. Luks day John Hawes rent Mary Pierces peticote & did beate her sister Katherine wth a crabtree staffe.

On Tuesday the ix^th of Novembre Richard Edwards my servant died.

On thursday the xj of Novembre Anna Snellinge was maried to John Duke.

---

[1] Some account of the relations between Adam Winthrop and the Mildmays will be found on pp. 27–8.

[2] See note on p. 34.

On tuesday in the mornynge being the last of November the 1596. wydowe Francs died, & the same Day the goodwyfe Lewes Kyrby was dd of ij childrē.

The vth day of December Susan Bronde the wyfe of Edward Aulston died of childbed.

The [blank] day of December old Simon Laughlinge died.

The [blank] day Anne Nutter the daughter of Willm̄ Nutter died, of the age of xx yeres.

A Register of the Deathes of my frends, & of other things wch haue happened since the feast of the Nativitie, Año 1596.

The iiijth Day of January Mr. Steven Piend died.

The viijth day of January being Saterday, my ffather Henry Browne died, of the age of 76 yeres, & was buryed in Prittle^{wel} Church in Essex.

The seconde of Marche John Hamonde died.

The vijth of Marche I was robbed by false kks, & iij dayes before Mr. Sands was robbed.

The xxixth of Marche Año 1597 John Crab was married to Kathe- 1597. rine Ker my s^rvant who was sicke the same day.

The xvjth day of Aprill Mr. Gawen Harvey the yongest soonne of Mr. George Harvey highe shreve of Essex came to my house & the xixth day he & my nephewe Henry Mildmay depted toward Springfild in Essex.[1]   *

The 22 day of Aprill Grymble my great mastiffe was hanged, a gentle dog in the howse but eyes oft blind.

The xxiijth day of Aprill I sowed Wranglande wth berry barley.

The iij^d of May Mr Robt. Hanhams wife Receyved xx^{li} of the gift of Mr. Hanham his vnckle.

The xth of May I did ryde to my b. Mildmayes & retorned the xvjth of the same & Charles cam̄e to dwell wth me.

The xviijth day of May my Cosen Alib. cam̄e to my howse.

The same day I bought Kembolds grey horse for iij^{li} vj^s viij^d.

The xxth day of May in the mornynge Anne Kembold was deliuered of a girle, & Mr Briggs died at Brettenham.

The xxixth day of May my cosen Bulwer came to my house.

The seconde day of June I was at my Cosen Muskett.

The vth day Charles had his livery cote.

---

[1] See note 1 on p. 38.

A festo Sci Johīs Baptiste Anno 1597.

1597. The last day of June goodman Gosslinge had xx laborers to make the Causey in Claypit-fields, wch was aft^rwards stoned and gravailed.

The vj^{th} of July I received a privie seale to lend the Q. matie xx^{li} for a yere.

The same day Edward Aulston his wife was dd of hir first soonne.

The viijth day of July olde Cant died.

The ix^{th} day I rec^d a l^re from my brother out of Ireland sans date. Mrs Pyne was dd.

The xth of July Tillesons wife Died.

The xj^{th} my cosen Alibast^r came to my house.

The same day Sr John Peyton & Sr Henry North wth their Ladyes came to Boxforde.

The xiij^{th} day my cosen Alib. *fatebatur se esse papistam.* The xiiij^{th} we did ride together to London, & I retourned home the xxijth.

The same day my Daughter Anna came home from my brother Mildmayes.

The xxj^{th} Day of July my cosen Johane Muskett died *Año etatis sue* 59.

The first of August my cosen Alib: depted to Cambridg from my house, & the thirde Day aft^r Priscilla his sister cam to me.

The iiij^{th} of August my brother in lawe Willia^m Hilles Died.

The xxij^{th} of August I did wright vnto my brother in Ireland by George Mawle.

The last of August my Cosen Alib: depted to Camb.

The viij^{th} Day of September Mr. John Payne of Stoke died of the age of xx iiij & iiij yeres.[1]

The viij^{th} day of September Johane Hilles my wiues naturall sister died, & made me her executo^r.

. The xxj^{th} of Sept. being St Mathews Day Thomas Osborne was murdered by John Hawes in the waye betwene Branthm & Thetford, for^r the wch J. H. was hanged at Bury.

The xxvj^{th} day of Sept. Jasp. Laughlings wife died of the bloudy fflux.

The first Day of Octobre I lett my howse at Edwardeston to Wm Brande & the same day John Sure my L. of Bathes stuarde came to me.

---

[1] Probably intended to designate fourscore and four years.

The vth Day of December Willm Brond died.   1597
The vijth day ffather Pierce died.

A note of the books wch I haue lent.

The pambulation of Kent to Mr. Nicholson.[1]
The Termes of the lawe to Mr. J. Grymwade.
Dr. Bright *De Sanitate tuenda* in Latine.
Petrarcha his woorkes Mr. J. G. tooke awaye.
To Mr. Ellyson the Remes Testament.
The Defence of the Apologie to my sister Mildmay.
Eusebius & Socrates in Englishe to my cosen Munnyng.
Item, lent him iij volumes of Lyra, & Googes husbandry.

A feste Circumsitionis Dñi nri Jesu Chri Anno 1600, *et Eliz. R^{na}*
                    xliij^{tio}   1600.

Imprimis the iiijth of January Mr. Powle was arrested at my
brothers suite.

The next day in the mornynge Mres. Samsone was deliuered of her
first sonne John.

The ixth Day my wife was Deliuered of her fowrth daught^r, Lucilla,[2]
& my brother sickened.

The xvth Willm Hilles was maried to Elizabeth Gibson.

The xxth my daught^r was Christened.

The 24th Gardin^r the geld^r died.

The 25 of ffeb. the Erle of Essex was behedded wthin the Tower.

The viij day of Marche my Cosyn Dr Duke & his wife Dyned wth
me.

The xixth Day of Marche my Nephewe Josua Winth. came to Groton & departed the next daye.

The 23 of Marche my Nephew Wa. Mildmay came to me.

The xxth [April] I began to sowe Magotts crofte wth barley, & the 1601.
thirde of August I reaped it.

The last of Aprill beinge thursday, my cosen Adam Winthrops wife April.
was deliuered of her first sonne Adam, to whom I was godfather.

The xviijth of May Thomas Mildmay my cosen Wm Mildmays eldest
sonne came to Groton.

---

1 See pp. 41–2.
2 The same daughter elsewhere called Lucy, and afterwards the wife of Emanuel
Downing, Esq.

1601.   The xx[th] he went to the free schole at Boxford.

The last of May beinge Whitsonday, Richarde Bronde the eldest sonne of John Bronde of Boxforde, clothier, died. *De merore animi ob patris sui iram.*

The vth of June Mr. Powle did shewe me an Infamous libel written in Ryming verses, made as I suppose of P. E.

The xij[th] of July I went to Holton. The same day I dyned at Mr. Manocks, of Gyffords hall.

The 14 of July my cosyn Alibast[r] was removed out of the Tower into Framingham Castle.

The xxvij[th] of July Augustine Podde beinge about $\frac{xx}{iiij}$ & vj yeres[1] olde Died 10 daies after he came out of Bury Gaile, & the first day of Sept next his wife died.

The xxvij[th] of July there was made a Rate by me & Diūs of the townemen of Groton, for the Repaccons of the church, & we viewed the Decay of the leades.

The first of August my cosen Adam Winthrop & my cosen Sara Frost his sister came from London to Groton.

The 3 of Aug. my cosen Adam W. & I did ride to Holton, & viewed the pewter w[ch] was given to his wife & her sister. The same day my brother did ryde towards London.

The v. I sent my Auditt Accoumpt to Ipswich to Tho. Laster to be ingrossed by him in pchem[t].[2]

The vj[th] Day of Aug. Rob[t] Surrey did marry M : P.

The viij day my ij neeces being sisters the daught[rs] of my brother W[m] Winthrop did ride from Groton towards London. The one had not seene the other xxj yeres before.

The 17 day of August Anne Page, that was my se[r]vant iij yeres, died at her mothers in Groton.

The xxj[th] day Sara Cely was maried to Robte Humfrey at Highm̄ Churche w[th]out a license *pr hōiem ignotū.*

The 14 day [Sept.] I was at Hockley at a Court for Will[m] Coe & lay the same night at Mris Bronds.

The 17 day I was at Lanham, before the Escheto[r] for my brother.

The xxv[th] day of Sept. Mr. Clopton kept a Court at Castleyns hall & I was of the *hom* [?].

The iij^{de} of Octobre my brother kept a Court at Groton Hall, where 1601. we had pike to dynn^r that was iij qrt^{rs} of a yarde longe, *vt puto.*

The iiijth day of Oct. Willm Gardin^r did his penance in Groton Churche *sine lodice & valde impenitentem.*

The 23 of Octobre I took vplande for the poore, at Mr. Sampson's Court.

The 24 my brother had a verditt against Powle in the guilde hall in London, & Recoūed C^{li} damages.

The 12 [Nov.] the Erle of Desmond dyed at London.

The 30 being St Andrews Day I was witnesse to Andrew Mr. Dreslyes soonne.

The vth of Decemb. I ridde to Cambridge & beganne the Auditt the 7th beinge Monday.

The xiiijth of Decembre I retourned from the Auditt & did see the sonne in the Eclips, about 12 of the Clocke at noone.

The xxjth being St. Thoms day Robte Humfry & Sara his wife came to my howse in Groton.

The 18 of Decembre my Cosyn Munnyng came to Groton.

The 23 of Decembre I felt an Erthquake.

A° 1601 et
Reginæ
Eliz:
44to.

A festo Nativitatis Dñi ñri Jesu Chrī.

The 2 of Jan. Mr. Mannocke sent me iij yardes of satten for a token January. of this nue yere.

The 22. John Frenche died. The same day I did ryde to Spring-fielde & from thence to London.

The iiijth day of ffeb. Nicholas Strut the Riche Clothier of Hadleighe died beinge not l yeres olde.

The 27 of ffeb. I was at my cosen Muñynges, & fownde him sicke & weake.

The same day Mres Bonde died & made me her executo^r. The 2 of Marche she was buryed.

The xiijth of Marche Mr. Philip Tilney Esqr Died.

The vijth of Aprill I was appointed by Sr Wm Waldegraue & iij other Justices to be one of the oūseers of the poore & one of the Serch- [1602.] ers of Clothe wthin Grotⁿ. *Juratus & obligatus.*

The xijth of Aprill Hen. Hartw. was maryed to E. Rawlyn *in alienis vestibus.*

The 20 of Aprill Martyn Piend died.

The 29 of Aprill Mr. Frith pson of Harwell was here.

1602. The xth of May my daught^r Anne had a nue gowne brought from London, & the next day my wife did ryde early in the morning to Harwell.

The 25 of Maye Diuers houses in Melford were burned.

The 28 day Peter Parson died suddenly.

The last Day I was at the Hundred Court of Baber, where I lent a Rentall of the C. to the Bayliffe.

The [*blank*] of June John Barkers eldest soonne was Drowned in the River behinde the mill of Boxforde.

The last day of June (?) it thundred & lightned a great part of the night, & sett a tree on fyre in Stoke parke, wch burned iiij dayes.

On Saturday the vijth of August my sister Mildmay, my Cosen Thomas her soonne, my Cosen Browne & his wife cāme to my house & Departed the xiijth.

The ixth day my sister Alib^r, [and] my sister Veysye came to my house, where fyve of vs that are brethren & systers mett & made merry, wch we had not doonne in xvj yeres before.

The 26th day of Aug. John Goslings wyfe was buryed.

The tenth day [Sept.] I was at Smalbridge & dined wth olde Sr Wm Waldegrave & had his hand & seale to a Certificate.

The xvth day Sarah Alibast^r died at Colchest^r.

The 16 day the Arbitrat^{rs} betwene my Brother & Powle did meete at the Whighte Lion in Groton, & ther was Powle, Payne & Spenser witnesses for h^m.

The xxth of Sept. Stephen Piend the yongest soonne of mris Piend died of the Pockes.

The xxijth Tho: Piend her [*blank*] soonne died of the same disease.

The xxiijth I sent Tho. Mildmay to Springfilde.

The xxixth Day of Sept. my brother Veysye Departed out of Holton Hall.

This moneth many died of the poxe in Groton, & many were sicke of that disease.

A festo S͂cⁱ Mich͞is Arch^t Aō R͞ne Eliz. xliiij^{to}, et Aō D͂ni 1602.

The last day of Sept. Will͞m Hills entered Holton Hall, & began to dwell there.

The xxjth my sister Weston cāme to my house, & she & my wife parted the lynnen wch my sister Hilles did give to her ij Daught^{rs}.

The 27th day in the mornyng the Bell did goe for mother Tiffeyn, but she recouered.

The firste day of Decembre my cosen Tho. Mildmay died at Spring- 1602.
fild.

The 2ᵈ of December I rode to Cambridge.

The viijth day John my soonne was admitted into Trinitie College.

The xxjth day my brother Alibast^r came to my house & toulde me
y^t he made ctayne inglishe verses in his sleepe, wch he recited vnto me,
& I lent him —— xl^s.

A festo nativitat^s Dñi, A° 1602.

The iiijth of Januarry I rode to Springfild & the vjth I Dyned at
Danbury wth Mr. Humfrey Mildemay, & I retourned home the
vijth

The xth I dined wth Mr. Dr. Johanes at my brother Snellings.

The xvijth day I ridde to the Sessions at Bury to give evidence
against ctein clothiers for strayning.

The xviijth daye Wiltm Gale did give ouer his office of High
Constableshippe, & John Gale of Hadleigh was sworne in his
place.

The ixth of ffeb. I received a lre from my brother, out of Ireland, by
James his man.

The xxjth the Assises were holden at Bury, where Cricke was indited, accused for whitchcrafte.

At the same assises Mr. Rolfe, Mr. [*blank*] & other of the Justices of
the peace were not named in the Comission.

The 23th of ffeb. my cosen Walter Mildmay came to bourde wth me,
& depted the xxxth of m.

The first of March Josephe Brond was maried to Anne Strutte.

The 2 of Marche my soonne went to Cambrige, the same day James   Mr. Aple-
Departed from Groton.   ton died at
                                                               London.

On Wedensdaye the xxiijth of Marche Quē Elizabeth died,[1] & James   „   „   „
the vj^t Kinge of Scotland was pclaymed the next day at London, & on
Saturday the xxvjth at Colchest^r and Sudbury, wth great reioicinge of
all men.

The iiijth of Aprill Mr. Brampton Gurdons wife died in Childbed, of
the xth Childe.

---

1 The date of Queen Elizabeth's death was the 24th, and is given correctly a few
paragraphs after this.

1603.   The vijth of Aprill Robt Surrey wife lay speechelesse, & the bell went for her, but she died the xiijth.

The xjth of Aprill I & my Wyfe Did ride to Bockinge, to the Christening of my Cosin Firmins Childe, who was named Josephe.

The xvijth Day of Aprill I received a lre from my brother, dated from Asmore the 23 of ffeb. 1602, & also another from James Elwell written from London the xiiijth of Aprill. ·

The same day Mr John Coe of Tomblyns came to Groton Churche to mornyng prayer.

Ab anno primo Regni Rs Jacobi primi.

On thursday the 24th of Marche Queene Elizabeth died at Riche-monde of the age of lxvi yeres vj monethes & [*blank*] dayes.

The same daye was James the vjth Kinge of Scotts proclaymed at London, kinge of England, France & Irelande.

The iiijth of Aprill Dr. Nevill M^r of Trinitie College in Cambrige & Deane of Cánterbury went towarde Scotlande to the Kinge, as sent by the Archb. of Cant^rbury, in the name of the Clergie.

The xvjth of Aprill being Saturday the Kinges Mat^y came to the Citty of Yorke.

The xviij of Aprill Mr. Clopton toulde me that the Kinge had sworne the Erles of Northumbland & Cumbland of his privy Counsell, & also the L. Tho. Howard & the L. Mountague, & that the lord Howarde should be L. Chamblayne.

The xth of Aprill the Erle of Southamton & Sr Henry Nevill were deliuered out of the Tower by a lre or warrant sent from the Kinge out of Scotlande, Dated 5° Aprilis.

The [*blank*] of Aprill Sr Robt Cecill & Diūs others went to meete the Kinge at Yorke.

The 21 the Kinge did come to Shrewsbery, the 22 to Nuewarcke, the 23 to Bever Castle.

The xxiijth of Aprill the Justices of the peace were sworne to the Kinge, & appointed Justices by force of a nue Comission.

The 28th day was the funeralles kept at Westm for o^r late Queene Elizabethe.

The [*blank*] day the Kinges ma^{ty} was at Cambrige.

The third of May the K. came to Teboldes to Sr Robert Cicilles howse.

The first daye of May being Sondaye there were iiij howses burned 1603. at Leigham.

The xth Day of Maye Nicholas Coky the yonger was maried to Elizabeth Cooke.

M^d that the K. ma^{tie} sett forthe a proclamation giuen at Theobaldes the vijth of May against licenses granted by the late Q. to private psons of all monopolies, & against prophaning of the Saboth by int'ludes, Bulbaytings & all other games.

The xi of May I sent to Harwell & writt lres to my L. Bisshop of Bathe.

On Munday the seconde of Maye, one Keitley a blackesmythe dwellinge in Lynton in Cambridgeshire had a poore man to his ffather whom he kepte. A gentleman of the same Towne sent a horse to shoe, the father helde vp the horses legge whilest his soonne did shoe him. The horse struggled & stroke the father on the belly wth his foote & ou'threwe him. The soonne laughed therat & woulde not helpe his father vppe, for the wch some that were their put reproved him greatlye. The soonne went forwarde in shoinge of the horse, & when he had donne he went vppon his backe, mynding to goe home wth him. The horse putly did throughe him of his backe against a poste & clave his hed in sonder. M^{ris} Mannocke did knowe the man, for his mother was her nurse. *Graue judiciu Dei in irrisorem patris sui.*

The same daye of May the Bishop of Norw^{ch} came ryding throughe Boxforde towards Norw^{ch}.

The 28 day of May Nicholas Reeve was lett downe into a well of goodman Coles at Holton by a ladd^r, & the ladd^r being pulled vp did fall downe into the well, & bruised him sore on his backe, he being benethe in the well.

The vijth Day of June olde Doare of the age of lxv yeres maried Margarett Coe the pedlers daught^r. The xjth her sister died, & the same day I sawe a grey conye in my woode yarde.

The 14 my cosen Bulwers wife came to my house & toulde me that my cosen T. M. childe was borne at Wetherden, & named Honor.

The 17 of June I rid wth Mr. Powle to Colchest^r to sit vppon a Comission wth Sr Wm Aylofe to inquire of the Wardshippe of Willm Ayletts daughters, but the Jury founde no tenure in Capite for the Kinge. Mr. Powle was in danger to haue bin killed by Gilbt Vintener his wifes brother.

1603. The last of June Mr Alyston vicar of Acton borrowed of me the Remes Testament in Englishe.

The xvijth Day of July Alcocks beastes were in my barley. The same day my wife lent Mres Sands xx^s. vppon a siluer & gilt salt seller, & I lent l^s to Willm Coe the day before.

The 23th daye of July my brother Mildmay was made knight at Whight-hall; my soonne came from Cambrige.

The 25 daye the kinges ma^{tie} was crowned at Westm^r.

The same daie Robt Surrey was maried to John Dogetts maide, Thomasin Hubbard.

The 26 Daye Mr. Bronde kept his Court at Edwardston, & Wm Daye & his wyfe made a S^rrend^r to me, &c.

The vj of Aug. my Cosen Math. Still ridde to Cambrige.

The vth day was celebrated for the kings Deliuerance in Scotland the same Day of the moneth A° [*blank*] from being murdered by the Erle of Gowry. Mr Birde preached at Boxforde vppon the 124 psalme, *pie & docte.*

The vth of August William Wymerkes only soonne was killed at Cambridge wth a peece of a gunne wch brake & killed iij more. he was scholler of Trinitie College: & about xiiij yeres olde.

The xvjth Day M^{res} Waldgrave died.

The xxixth of August Bridgett the wife of G. Fitche, & before of John French & John Gosse, died of a consumption.

The xvijth daye the geñall fast was kept at Boxford, & the xxiiijth at Groton, by the Kinges comandement.

The first of August I beganne to cast the great ponde in the Barne close, & tooke out of it 7 great carpes.

ffrom the 25 of August vntill the first of Sept. there died of the plauge in London & wthout in the Subvrbes m^cm^cm^c xxxv psons.[1]

The iiijth of Sept. my cosen Munnyng came to Groton, & I gaue him iv books of Lewes Granatensis.

The vjth of Sept the fast was kept the 2 tyme at Groton, & Mr. Newton preached his first S^rmon vppon the 4 of Amos, 12.

The xxjth my cosen Alibast^r came to my howse & shewed me his pdon Dated the xth of Septembre.

---

1 Was this intended for 3335 persons?

A festo S^{ct} Mich^{is} Arch^{i} A^o 1603.

The viijth of October my cosen Henry Mildmay came to my howse. 1603.

The [*blank*] day of Octobre Sara my cosen Frosts wife died.

The xxxth of Octobre I was witnesse to Wm Hilles soonne at Holton, named Peter, who was borne the xviijth day of this moneth.

The last day I was at Ipsw^{ch} & acknowleged a Recognisc^e of xx^{li} to Novemb. the kinges ma^{tie} to give evidence against Zachary Vintener at the next Cessions ther holden.

The seconde of Decembre I did ride to Cambridge & retourned home the xiiijth.

The same day one of my Lord Wyndsors men, his fauconer, having byn at the alehouse, as he went home through Stow churchyarde, fell into a deepe drye well wth ij hawkes on his fist, & was fownd dedde the next day, & one of the hawks aliue, but the other was dedde. *Graue judiciū.*

The xijth of January Mr Newton Departed to Cambrige wth his pupilles from my house.

The xvjth of January I was at the Sessions at Bury, where Zach. Vintener was bayled by his father & Mr. Powle.

The viijth of ffebruary my cosen Wa: Mildmaye was at Groton after he was maryed.

The ixth John Grymwade did lye at my house.

The xth my sonne went to Cambrige, & the night before Mr. Cakes wife was safely dd of a Daught^r wch was hir first childe, named Eliz.

The xjth day of ffeb. goodman Plampin of Newton died, & the [*blank*] Lancelott Baker of Stoke died.

The xiiijth of ffeb. Eliz. Bond was maried to W. Swets^r.

The xxjth of ffeb. Sarah Bronde was Baptized. The same day one Sewell was so bruysd through a fall wch he had in Camping, that he died therof.

The xxiiijth H. Cookes wife died of a consumption, and the first of July 1610, he died of a plurisye.

The xxvijth of ffeb. Sr John Higham & Sr Robert Drury of Hawsted, knightes, were chosen knights of the Shire of Suff. for the Parleament wch began the xixth of Marche next followinge, *Anō primo Regni Jacobi Regis.*

The first of Marche Zachary Vintener was arraigned & condemned at the Assises holden at Bury, for burglary comitted in Groton the xxiijth of October last past.

1603.   The same daye & tyme was Bridgett Horneby condemned for kyllinge of her infant nuely borne x^{mo} *Octobris.*

On Tuesday the xxviij of ffeb. D^r. Whitgifte Archb. of Cant. Died at Lambethe.

The xijth of Marche John Speede came to Groton & toulde me y^t he shoulde marry his m^{res}, & I pd him x^{li} of his grandfathers legacie.

The xvjth of Marche Johnson Ryd to Camb. to my soonne.

1604.   The xijth of Aprill Mr. Clopton & Mr. Dogett made an awarde betweene me & Adam Wynthrop my nephew.

The same day Dr. Jones & Mr. Parson dyned at my howse. ·

The xxiiijth of Aprill my sonne retourned from Cambridge. 1604.

The vjth of May my sister Veysye was at Groton.

The xxvjth of May my soonne & my daughter did ride to Springe-field to Sr Thomas Mildmayes.

The same day I Rd a lře from my brother, dated at Corke in Ireland the first of May, by James his man.

The xxixth my cosen Munnyng was at Groton, & shewed me a nue booke in Latine *De Vnione Britaniæ.*

The last of May Dr. Duke & his wife dyned wth me.

The xxiiijth of June John my soonne was witnesse to Robte Surreys first soonne John, & Jane Kedby was godmother.

The [*blank*] of June my Cosen Wm Alibaster was comitted againe to prison for popery.

The third of July Thoms Alston the yonger died.   He lefte vj children borne, & his wife great wth the vij^{the}. The Inventory of his goodes came to — 304-4-8.

The xjth of July th'assises were holden at Nuemarket.

The xvjth I received a lře from my lord B. of Bathe.

The xxvijth my sonne did ride to Cambridge.

The ixth of Aug. my brother & sister Veysey came to Groton, & the xth I began to shere my wheate.

The same day was a Court Baron holden at Groton hall for James Dixey.

The xiiijth of August Sr Isaac Appulton came to speake wth me, & the same day M^r. Coe of Tomblyns gave me warnynge of the first of September to be at Sudbury &c.

The xxth of Aug. M^r. Willm Manocke dyned wth me.

The xxjth my Cosen Muñynge came to Groton.

The xxixth of Aug. Mr. Clopton & I examined the buttalls of Stone medowe by o^r Court Rules.

The same day the Bailiffe of Rayleighe warned me to the Court.   1604.

The xxxth of August Johane Betts my maide did wounde John Wailleys my man in the hed wth her patten, for the wch she was very sory.

The first of Sept. I was before Sr Wm Waldegrave, Sr Tho. Eden & Mr. Gurdon to answere to Coes complaint made against me for occupienge of Stone medowe.

The seconde of Sept. my daught^r Anne was at Ipswche at the mariage of my Cosen Sparrowes maide.

The iiijth of Sept. Henry Cooke th'eld^r did mary Johane Betts my maide, he beinge lx yeres oulde & she xxxv, & his father then livinge of thage of xc yeres.

The vth I was at Bures & dined wth Mr Thoms Waldegrave.

The vijth of Sept. I rec^d a pryvye seale of x^{ll}. The same Day Tho: Kedby was arrested.

The xijth daye of Sept. I first heard of the Death of my sister Cottye, who died the ixth Day of August last beinge of the age of 51 yeres 9 monethes & [*blank*] dayes.

The viijth of Sept. Thomas Coe the eldest sonne of Thom^s Coe of Boxforde, gent. my god sonne died of the age of xix yeres & x monethes.

The ixth of Sept. Mr. Dudley Foscue did hange him selfe at Mres Trimm^{rs} his wiues mothers house nere Cambridgshire, vizt. at Blunts hall in Little Wrattinge.

The xxijth I lent the kings ma^{tie} x^{ll} vppon a privie seale.

The xvjth I was at Hadley & Holton, & dyned at Mr. Wm Manocks in Stoke.

The xxth of Octobre John Speede came to me for the residue of his granfathers legacye.

The 24 I rode towards London & retorned the xxxth of the same moneth.

The same day it was pclaymed that England & Scotland shoulde be   24 Oct. called Great Brittaine.

The vth of Novembre my soonne did ryde into Essex wth Willm Forth to Great Stambridge.

The last of Novemb. I rode to Cambridge to keepe the Audit at Trinitie Colledge, & I ret. the xvth of December.

The xxvjth of Decembre Mr. Tasker died.

The xiiijth of Jan. my Cosen Nath. Still came to G.

The xvth day Josephe Cole & Marye Gale were maried betymes in the mornynge.

1604.   The xv of ffeb. my Cosen Wm Mildmayes late wife Died in the Tower of London.

The xxiij^th T. F. came to Groton, & was maried to my daught^r Anne the xxv^th & they departed toward London, the xxvij^th day of ffeb., 1604.[1]

The vth of March the Wyndmille in Boxforde was blowen downe, & Willm Jarrold & ij others were sore hurt therby, whereof he died the vij of Marche.

The xij of Marche I soulde Mr. Mannocke xxj^ty sheepe for ix^li xij^s.

The xiij^th of Marche the Assises were at Bury.

" The same day Mr. Powles onlie soonne died of th'age of vij yeres, & his wife died the xx^th of Marche.

The xiiij^th I & my soonne viewed ou Mr. John Foorthes land at Carsey & Hadley.

The xxj^th of Marche Mris Powle was buried.

The xv^th of Marche Mres Browne was condemned of petit Treason for pcuringe one Peter Gouldinge to murder her husband, Mr. Browne, for the wch facte the said Peter was hanged & she burned quicke at Pury the xix^th of Marche.

The same daye I received a lre from my brother out of Ireland, dated 2 Martij 1604.

The xxvj^th of Marche I & my soonne did ride to Mr. John Foorthes of Greate Stambridge in Ess^x.

The xxviij^th day my soonne was sollemly contracted to Mary Foorth by Mr. Culverwell minister of Greate Stambridge in Essex. *Cu consensu parentu.*

1605.   *A festo Annc bte Marie Virginis Occurrentia.*

The xxx^th of Marche my brother Wynthrop came to Chelmisford.

The vth my brother came to Groton, after his Retorne out of Ireland, & departed the ix^th of June.

The ix^th my sonne did ryde into Essex.

The xvj^th of Aprill he was married at Great Stambridge, by Mr. Culverwell, *A° etatis sue 17° 3 mensibus & 4 diebus completis.*

---

[1] Thomas Fones was the husband of Adam's daughter Anne. See page 50, and note 1.

The 25 Day of Aprill M^{ris} Anne Clopton was marryed to John 1605.
Mayston of Boxsted gent.

The 27 John Johnson the Taylo^r died.

The viijth of May my soonne & his wife came to Groton from Lon-
don & the ixth I made a mariage feaste, when Sr Tho^{ms} Mildmay & his
lady my sister were pn̄t.

The same day my sister Veysye came to me, & departed on fryday
the 24 of Maye.

My dauter Fones came the viijth of May, & depted home the xxiijth
of Maye.

On Munday the third day of June, John Gosling of Groton & John
Massey of Edwardston died.

The vjth of June Mr. Willm Manocke dined at my house in Groton.

The viijth my Cosen Duke was dd of hir first sonne before her
tyme.

The ixth I did ride wth my brother Wynthrop into Ess. & retorned
the xvijth.

The xxth my brother departed from London towards Irland.

The same day I cutt my bearde. *Male.*

The 26 it thundred & lightened wond^rfullye.

The first of July my Cosen Wa. Mildmay & his wyfe came.

The 3 of July I did ride to Bury to th assises, & the xvth to th
assises at Chelmisford.

The xviijth day of July Mr. Welshe the pcher of Little W. died,
& was buried in the said Churche the xxth of July.   Mr. Knewstub
pched the funerall se^rmon, & he wth other preachers caried his coffin on
ther shoulders.

The xxiiijth of July I & my wife, wth my soonne & his wife did
ride to the Baptising of John Hilles the sonne of Wm Hilles of
Holton.

The next day my soonne & his wife did ride to her fathers in
Essex.

The 29 of July the Sessions were kept at Groton by Sr Wm Waldegraue, Sr Tho: Eden, Mr. Gurdon, Mr. Clopton, Sr G. Waldegraue,
Mr. Cratchreede, Mr. Walton.

The xxxth of July Mr. Clopton kept a Court at Castleines
Hall.

The first of August my soonne Fones came to Groton from London.
The same daye H. M. pched at Boxford a very godly & learned s^rmon
vppon the v chap. of Gen. v. 1. 2. 3.

*my cosyn
Munnings.*

1605.   The iiijth of Aug. Johane Cooke was dd of a girle, an Hermophro-
Abigail dite.
John
        The viijth of August Edward Alstons eldest soñe was borne in Box-
forde & M^{res} Wheeler died.

Jam. 4.   The xxixth Mr. Rogers preached at Boxford. The same day my sonne
1, 2, 3, 4. did ride to Stambridge.

        The third of Sept. Mr. Manock & his eldest sonne dyned at my
house.

        The vth I was sworne at Stowe before Sr Wm Waldegrave & other
Comission^rs for to inquire of Recusants landes & goodes.

A festo scī Michīs Anō RR. Jacobi &c. Tercio.

        The viijth [Oct.] the goodwyfe Lappage was buried.

        The xxixth of Oct. Justine Nicholson was maryed to Josua Stocker
at Edwardston.

iiij^u p An.   The iij^d of Decemb^r I did ryde to the Auditt at Trinity Coll. &
retourned the xvijth.

        The xth of Decemb. Eliz. Piene was maried.

        The iiijth of Jan: Mr. Tomkes a fellowe of Trinitie College was at
my house.

        The xviijth of January my Cosen Wa: Mildmay & iiij oth^r gents
made a great sturre at Bury.

        The xxx & xxxj of Jan. viij traito^{rs} were hanged & Q^rtered, wherof
Ambrose Rookewood of Coldhm hall in Suff. was one.

        On Wedensday in the morning the 12 of ffeb. my soonnes first
soonne was borne in Groton.

        The 23 of ffeb. beinge Sunday my soonnes first soonne was baptized
& named John.[1]

        The seconde of March being Sunday, about vij of the Clocke in the
even7nge the goodwyfe Dogett died.

        The vjth of Marche being Thursday Henry Vinteñ thelder died of
thage of lxx yeres.

        The xvth day of March ther were great stormes of wynde, wch did
muche hurt to howses.

        The same daye Thom^s Humfreys howse was burnt downe at Mel-
fourde.

---

[1] A rich christening robe of embroidered satin, which is said to have been
worn by the future Governor of Connecticut on this occasion, has long been in
possession of the Hon. David Sears, one of his lineal descendants.

The xvth day of Aprill I kept a Court for my brother Snelling at 1606.
Shimplinge.

The xixth of Aprill my sister Snellinge sent me xxiiij^{tie} younge   "
pigeons to store my dove house.

The xxiijth of Aprill Mr^{is} Clopton sent me [blank] pigeons & Steven
Plomb a payre of tame pigeons.

The xxvijjth I kept a Court at Groton Hall.

The iij^d of Maye I putt xlv younge pigeons into my nue Dovehouse.

The vjth of Maye I was at a Court in Hadleighe, & did fealty for a
Tenem̅^t & c̃taine landes.

The viijth of Maye Willm̅ Gale of Hadley died.

The 26 my soonne & his wife wth their soonne did ride to Hadley.

The 27 Mr^{is} Alston & her sister Mary dined wth me.

The 29 Nath. & Phebe were maryed & kept ther dinn̅^r at Deathes
on Horners greene in Groton.

The xth of June John Dixon theld^r died in Groton.

A festo nativitat^s s^{ci} Johis Baptiste.   24 Junij.

On Sunday the [blank] of June the Q. was dd of a Daughter.

The 29 I kept a Court at Shimplinge.

The viijth of July Mr. Brampton Gurdon was maried to his seconde
wife.

The 28 of August Mr. Arminger had a fall of his horse & brake his
legge.

The first of Sept. I did give an estate to my soonne in the house &
lande called Wrights in the ffenne.

The thirde of Sept. we did ride wth Mr. Sands to Stambrige, & the
vjth my sonne tooke an estate.

The ixth of Sept. my Cosen Laysters wife cam̅e to my house, &
the xth goodwife Ponde was dd of hir third soonne.

The same day the great Appletree next the kille house was fyred
for to distroy a hornetts nest.

The xiiijth of Sept. Mr. Sands p^rched at Groton, & dyned wth me.
ye same day Bonde atturned to my sonne.

The xviijth Mr^{is} Alston & her sister dined wth me.

The xixth day John Still cam̅e to my house.

The thirtieth of Sept. Beniamin Bronde was maryed at Ipswich to
[blank] Cutler. The same day I dyned at Mr. Sands.

1606.   The vijth of September the nue howse at Castleynes hethe was sett
vp by Surrey.

A festo sci Michaelis Arch^e A° sup^r Dicto.

October.   The 2 day I kept a Court for Mr. Manocke at Toppesfilde.

The xiiijth Mr. D^r. Goade preched at Boxford.

The xxjth I kept a Court & leete at Shimplinge.

The xxiiijth the Bell went at Groton for fathe^r Cooke & at Boxford
for Zachary Bonde.

The same day I rec^d a lr̄e from my Lady Mildmay & writt her an
answere p̄ntly.

The xxvth day John Cooke of th'age of c yeres died.

The 30 my soonne did ride to London by Stambridge.

November.   The seconde ther fell muche Snowe & Rayne.

The vjth Zachary Bond died.

The ixth Jane Kedby was maryed to Thomas Driffild a citizin &
Grocer of London.

The xiiijth M^{ris} Goodday & M^{ris} Pointell were wth me.

The xvijth of December Stephen Plombe was maried att London.
The [*blank*] daye Tho. Fitch was slayne.

The first of Jan : Mr. Armiger & his wife & her sister Alston dyned
at my howse, with diu^{rs} others.

The viijth of Jan : father Smyth of Toppesfild cam̄e to me, &
brought me a fatt Capon, & James Botts a bottle of secke.   Also M^{ris}
Alston sent me a fatt goose & a bottle of muskadine, on nue yeres daye.

The xj of Jan. Simon Blumfild sent me ij Capons.

The xvth I satt vppon a Com̄ission wth Mr Clopton at Lanhm̄.

The xxth of Jan. was very tempestuous & wyndye, wch did muche
harme to howses & trees.

The 21 of Jan : I & my soonne did give warnynge to Ponde to leaue
the copy landes.

The 16 Mr Nicholas Hubbarde died.

The xviijth I did keepe a Court at Toppesfild.

The xxth the Assises were holden at Bury.

The 26 John Wynthrop was weaned,   The same Day I went to Bret-
tenhm̄ & brought my cosens wyfe to my house.

1607.   The first of Aprill John Bogas th' eld^r died.

The vijth I was at Hadleigh at the mariage of S^r. Wm Waldegraves
man, whereat was a greate offeringe.

The viijth of Aprill Thomas Polley was maryed to Anne Speed, toe 1607. whom I p^d xxv^{ll}.

The xiijth of Aprill my Cosen Nath Still came to my house & brought me a lre from his father.

The xiiijth day I was at Hadley to S^rvey Robert Veysyes howse & lande for my L. BB. of Bathe.

The xxjth of Aprill my sonne & his wyfe did ride into Essex, to hir fathers.

The 26 of Aprill, Richd. Cooke sen. died & was buryed.

The [blank] of June John Robtson died.

The 3 of July Justine Nicholson the wife of John Stocker was dd of her first soonne.

The same day Jo. Nutton did give my soonne a fawne.

The 22 of July I was sworne one of the grande Jury at thassises then holden at Bury, before my L. Coke. Mr. Ryce was the foreman.

The 23 Miles the Inform^r stoode on the pillory, & the next daye Bowman, a promoter. Also Wyles a merch^t of Ipsw.^{ch} was arrayned & condemnd for poysonynge one Aldriche, his wives first husband, who denied the fact at the time of his deathe, 27 Julij, 1607.

The third of Aug. Anne Gosling & Fra. Kedby were maryed.

The 14 of Aug. the bridge in Howfild was made.

The xvth of Sept. my ten^t John Ravens died.

The xvjth Mr. Tho. Waldgraue & M^r. Wm Clopton made an awarde betweene me & Mr. Powle.

The 22th of September I p^d Mr. Powle x^{ll} in full satisfaction of all matt^{rs} in question, & he sealed me a genall releas, Dated the same daye, & I sealed to him a Releas of all acčions psonaly, dated the twentythe of September, in the presence of Mr. Clopton, & my soonne, & James Dixon.

M^d that the 29 of September being Michillmas day, olde Surreys wyfe did fall into the water at Horners brooke, in Groton, & was in danger of drownyng if Podds wyfe had not stept into the water & holden vp her hed vntill more helpe came to pull her out.

A festo Sci Micaelis Archi, año supradicto.

The vjth of October I kept a leete & Court Baron for Mr. Edward Newport at Bromley hall in Essex.

1607.   The 26 of Octobre John Spenser the soonne & heire of Richard
Spenser of Groton, wounded John Peny of Hadley in his hed wth his
dagger, wherof he died the 30th.

The 28 being Weddensday, Elizabeth the wife of Thoms Walton
Esqr died at Hadley.

On fryday the 30th of Octobre my sister Mildemaye had a fall
in her chambre wherof she died the viijth of November followinge.

The 2 of November I did ryde to Springfild, & retourned the 7th &
the 11 I did ryde thether againe to hir Buriall, the wch was on the xvth
of November.

A festo nativitatis Dñi nri Jesu Chri, 1607.

On St Stevens day the first sonne of Mr. Driffild and Jane his wife
was baptized & named Thomas.

The last of Decembr̃ Mr Willm̄ Amyes preached at Boxford vppon
the 80 psalme & first verse. pie & docte.

On fryday the 8 of January Mr. Wm Clopton kept a Court for his
father at Samford in Great Waldingfild, & did give the Charge very
oratorylike.   The same day Manfield caryed an Ashe of the heathe,
&c.

The xiijth of Jan. I did ryde to Stambrige & reto^{r}ned the xixth.

The xxth of Jan. my soonnes second soone Henry was Christened
at Groton, Mr. Sands & my b. Snelling were his godfathers.

The 2. Mr. Tho. Newton p̃ched at Boxford, Jud. v. 5.

The viijth of ffeb. beinge Shrovetuesday, the L. Cokes seconde
soonne maryed the daughter & heire of Sr George Waldegraue at
Hicham.

The xvijth of ffeb. Jane Dryfild & hir childe departed from hir
mothers in Groton, to goe to London.   The night before she was in
danger to haue bin burned in hir bedde, & as she rode throughe Boxford hir childe fell into the water at Boxford bridge. Hæc sunt maloru̅
omina.

The xviijth of ffebruary Amy Veysye was maried.

The last of ffebruary on Munday about ix of the clocke in the forenoone Mr. Lawrence Hargrave, an Attorny of the Comon Place,
Departed this life in the 62 yere of his age, at his howse in Groton.

The xvjth of Marche I did ride to Stambridge, & retorned the xxiijth
followinge. ffather Michelefild died.

The iiijth of Aprill Anne Goslin the wyfe of Nath Warn̄ died of a   1608. Consumption, after she had bin maryed viij monethes.

The ixth of Aprill Josephe Bronde the soonne of Rich John Bronde of Boxford was fownde dead in his Chamber, being wounded wth a paire of shires sticking in his bellye. *Graue judiciū.*

The xth of Aprill my soonne did ride towards Stambridge.

The xjth of Aprill Ezechiel Bonde was putt to schoole to Mr. Barfoote of Edwardston.

The same day ther happened a fire in Bury wch consumed aboue cc howses.

The xiijth my wyfe & my soonne did ryde to London.

The vth of Maye the Erle of Sarisbury was sworne L. Treasorer at Westm̄.

The 17 day of June Willm̄ Sweetman was maried to Eve Cooke, wid̄, by Mr. Deersley in Groton churche.

A festo nativitatis Scī Johīs Baptiste.   24 Junij. ⎫
                                                       1608. ⎭

The xxiiijth daye of June my soonne Fones & his wife cam̄e from London to Groton.

The last of June I made Robt. Waspes will.

The iiijth of July old Mris Gurdon died suddenly.

The vth Mr. Willm̄ Clopton the yonger com̄ensed M^r of Arte at Cambridge.

The same day the Assises began at Bury, & the next day Rich. Spenser of Groton was Indited for beatinge of Sharman the Constable, & fined to pay x^{li} to the Kinge.

On Thursday the vijth of July Mres Gurdon was buryed in Assington Churche, & Mr. Knewstub preached.

The xijth of July I was at Hadley & heard Dr Jones preache at the buriall of the wydowe Gale. Act. 9, v. 36.

The xvijth of July Jane Nicholson my goddaughter was Baptized, *et illa confessus est & non negavit palam,* &c.

The 28 Tho. Turno^r & Abigail Beamond were maryed.

The xxvth of July my lorde Coke chiefe Justice of the com̄on plaeis came to Hichm̄ to Sr G. Waldegraues, *cū magno comitatu amicorū & famulorū stipatus.*   August.

The 2 I was at Melford before the Com̄ission^{rs}.

The xxvth day [of] August Thomas Paine of Charsfield was maried to Elizabeth Alston of Groton, wydowe.

1608.   The xiiijth of Sept. Sr Isaac Appulton, knight, died at little Walding-field.

The 28th the Court was kept at Groton hall by John Potter, the same day my sister Winthrop came to my house, & Eliz. Hilles had a sutor.

A festo sci̅ Michi̅s Archi Año sup^r dicto.

The iijth of Octobre my cosen Nathanaell Still & his brother John were at Groton.

The iiijth Sr Robert Crane sent his Coche for me, my wyfe & my Daught^r Winthrop, to dine wth him at Chilton.

The vjth Mr. Ben: Brond kept Court & leet at Edwardston.

The xth of Octobre my soonne & his wyfe departed from Groton to dwell at Stambridge in Essex.

The xjth day Robert Waspe died & was buryed.

The xxjth my daught^r Jane & Eliz. Hilles went to Chilton hall.

The xxijth my soonne Fones came to Groton. And the xxiiijth in the morninge my daughter his wife was dd̅ of hir first childe, a daughter.

The same day I kept a Court at Bromeley hall.

The xxvjth Sr Robert Crane came to my howse.

The 2 of November my daught^r Fones daught^r was Christened. Sr Rob̃t Crane & his Lady were pn̄t, & she was witnesse wth Mres. Samson & M^{res} Bronde & my selfe. She named the Childe Dorothey.

The xvjth day Mr. Clopton, Mr. B. Gurdon & D^r. Duke were com̃itted to the ffleete by my L. Chancello^r.

The 24 Mr Parson of muche Bentley preached at Boxford.

The seconde day of December I did ryde to Cambridge.

The same day my brother Weston, the Vicar of Wormingforde in Essex died.

The iiijth of December Barnabe Warde, my tenant, died.

The xijth of December I retorned home from the Auditt.

The xixth of Dece̅. my soone Fones & his wyfe wth their little Daught^r Depted towards London. 24° *filia sua in lecto mortua est inventa.*

A festo sci̅ Nativitatis Dn̄i Nri Jesu Chri.

The xijth of January Mr. Sands preached at Boxford.

The xixth Mr Carewe preached at B: & I dyned wth him at Mr. Brondes, & muche snowe fell.

The 26 Mr. Chaplayne did preach at Boxford.   1608.

The 4 of ffeb. I went to Hadley to see my sister Alib. The same
daye John Wynthrop hurt his forhed wth a fall.

The vj^{th} of ffeb. Dr. Some M^{r} of Peter house died, & Dr. Playfere
died the [blank] of January.

The 21 of ffeb. Harry Pease brought me a lre from my soonne.

The last of ffeb. John Rawlinson graffed xx heds for me in my
nue orcharde. The wynde blue very colde & Rough out of the west, &
rigebant oës.

The 2 of Marche Mr. Sands pched at Boxford, after his retourne
from London.

The xj^{th} Sr Henry Mildmay my nephew came to G. & the next day,
being Sonday, he ryd to Bury.

The xiij^{th} th assises were holden at Bury.

The xviij^{th} Sr Willm Waldegrave tooke a geñal view of Diu^{r}s townes
at Assington for the pviding of Armo^{r}.

The last of Marche the Comissioñs did sett at Bury, for the levienge   1609.
of Aide to make the prince knight.

The 3 of Aprill my sister Winthrop came to Groton, wth her Cosen
Thomas Springe.

The vj^{th} goodwife Potter the midwife died.

The xiiij^{th} day my soonne John W. & his wife came to my house
from Stambridge in Essex.

The first of May my wyfe did ryde wth my soonne & his wyfe into
Essex to Stambridge. The same day Mr. Nicholsons soonne was to be
arrayned at the gr^{te} Sessions in Bury. &c.

The xj^{th} of May Mr. Cartar pched at Boxford. Rom. 6. 12.

The first of June my nephew Sr Henry Mildmay was maried to S^{r}
Willm Harris his Daught^{r} of Crickesey.

The 27 thassises were holden at Bury.

The xj^{th} of August my soonne was taken wth a fierce ague, & the
xviij^{th} I rodde to Stambridge to see him, & retorned the xxij^{th}.

The seconde of Sept. Mr. Knewstub preached at Boxf.

The vth of September Thomas Walton, Esqr Died at Hadley of the
age of lx yeres.

The xiij^{th} day I kept a Court at Toppeffilde.   October.

The xviij^{th} day Willm Gale had a house burnt.

The xxv^{th} my soonne kept his first Court at Groton hall, where a
Recouery was sued against Ed. Robtson.

1609.   The first day of Novembre John Rawlinge kept a feast at his nue house, where Mr. Thom̄s Tilney, Mr. Dogett, & diuᵃ others dined.

The viijᵗʰ I did ryde towards London & retourned the xiiijᵗʰ.

The xijᵗʰ I did heare Dʳ Kinge preache a Sermon at Sᵗ Andrewes in Holbrone, vppon the 14. Joh. v. 1. *pie & erudite.*

The xxiijᵗʰ of Novembʳ I went to Lanham to my sister Winthrop.

The xixᵗʰ of December my soonne John Winthrop & my nephewe Abraham Veysie cam̄e to Groton.

The xxxᵗʰ Day of Decembr̄ my sonnes third sonne was borne at Stambridge in Essex.

January.   The 22 & 23 Mr. Dr. Meriton came to speake wᵗʰ me about the resigninge of my office in Trinity College to Mr. Brookes.

The xiiijᵗʰ of Marche I Dyned at Dʳ Meritons in Hadley, & Received of him a xxˡˡ for my Auditoʳshippe.

One Sundaie the 21ᵗʰ of January my daughter Fones was dd̄ of her seconde Daughter.

One thursday the 25ᵗʰ Mr. Dr. Jones preached at Boxf. on the 3 Chap. of Ecclesiastes v. 1, 2, 3, 4, 5, 6, 7, 8.

The 26. Ruthe Sindʳlande was drowned & I inquired vppon hir Death as Coroner.

The 27 I surrendered my Auditorship in Trinitye College to the Mʳ, fellowes & schollers before a pub. notary.

The xiijᵗʰ of ffeb. I was godfather to Jasp Riddlesdals Daughter.

On Wednesday the thirde of Marche Sʳ John Spenser of London Died suddenly, as he was pullinge on his nether-stocks in the mornynge, & was buryed the [*blank*] of Marche.

The xjᵗʰ of Marche Mr. Knewstub preached at Boxford.

The xiiijᵗʰ thassises were holden at Chelmesforde by Baron Althm̄ only, & Sʳ Tho: Mildmay of Barnes in Springfild was highe shrive.

1610.   On Munday the xvjᵗʰ of Aprill Mʳ Rich. Brooke the nue Auditoʳ of Trinity College was at my house in Groton, to whom I dd̄ diuᵃ pap books & Roles towchinge his office.

On ffryday the xviij of May my wife did ride to London wᵗʰ Mres Pyne. Mr. Bronde died suddenly.

On Munday in the morninge Richarde Plum Died, of thage of ₓₓ̄ᵢᵢᵢⱼ vj yeres.

The same daie Thomas Page his wife was dd of ij Children.

On fryday the viijᵗʰ of June Mr. Lovell the preacher died. *Vir bonus ac pius, nulli pietate secundus. Ætatis* 64.

The xiij[th] of June, my Cosen Munnynge & Mr. Marcellyne were at my house, at wch tyme I did give my cosen a Scotch dagger & Mr. Marcellyne a nue knyfe.

The xiiij[th] of June Mr. Rogers preached at Boxford.

The first of July, Henry Cooke my Tenant died of a Pluresye.

The same day my soonne John Winthrop came to Groton.

II.

MEMORANDA FROM THE ALMANACS OF ADAM WINTHROP.[1]

From a copy of Ponde's Almanac for 1603.

1603. March 15. Kinge James, Q. Anne, & Henry ye prince of Wales rode through ye Cytty of London from y[e] Tower to Whighthall.

19. The Parleament began at Westminster, where the K. made an Eloquent Oration to y[e] Lordes & Comons.

March 24. Q. Eliz. died at Richmonde, and K. James was proclaymed, año 1602. The same day S[r] Rob. Cary tooke his journey in post towardes Scotland; and w[th]in three daies he came to Edenburrough, and certified the Kinge thereof, being welneere 300 myles.

26. The K. was proclaymed in Berwicke.

27. The Towne was surrendered to the Kinge's use.

April 6. K. James did enter Berwicke, and tooke possession therof.

April 8. His Ma[ty] did depart from Berwicke, and entered the realme of Englande.

April 10. His Ma[ty] came to Nuecastel, before whom the Bishop of Durham preached.

April 13. He came to Durham: and was entertayned by the Byshop.

April 16. His Ma[ty] came to the Cyttye of Yorke.

April 17. He went on foote from his lodging to the Minster to heare a Sermon w[ch] the Byshop of Lymrick preached.

---

1 It will be perceived that while many of these memoranda relate to incidents which occurred at the moment when the record was made, many others of them give the dates of events long past, and were probably transcribed from a previous diary.

April 25. As he rode backe from Burleigh to Sir I. Harring.[1] His Ma^{tyes} horse fel wth him, and very dangerously bruysed his arme.

April 27. His Ma^{ty} dyned at Sr Anth. Mildemayes.

May 3. Being Tuesday his Ma^{ty} came to Theobaldes, Sr Rob. Cicills house, wher met him the L. Keeper, ye L. Treasorer, ye L. Admyral and most of ye Nobility.

May 7. Being Satterday his Ma^{ty} removed from Theobalds towardes London.

May 11. Being Wednesday his Ma^{ty} went from the Charter house to the Tower of London.

May 13. Being Fryday he created wthin ye Tower Sr Robert Cicil, Sr Rob. Sydney, Sr Wm Knowles, & Sr John Wootten, Barons. The 14 nue Serjantes tooke their othe at Westminster this terme: and kept ye feast in the nue Hal of ye middle Temple.

August 8. Sr George Harvy Lieuten^t of ye Tower died, 1605, æt. 72.

Sept. 4. Robert Dudley, Erle of Leicester, died 1588, at Cornbury in Oxfordshire, Eliz 30.

Sept. 10. Ostende was delivered by Composition unto ye Duke of Burgoigne. 1604.

The 3 of Octobre 1605. Sr Edwarde Lewkenor of Denham in Suff. Knight, died of the smalpocks. *Vir bonus et doctus fuit et patriæ amans.* The lady his wife died two dayes before him.

Oct. 17. Sr Philip Sydney died, 1586.

Oct. 31. George Erle of Cumberlande died, 1605.

Dec. 1. My nephew Th. Mildmay died, 1602.

Dec. 4. Dr. Whytaker died at Cambridge, 1595.

Dec. 12. John Hanham died, 1599.

From a copy of Hopton's Almanac for 1614.[2]

On Nue yeares day the Lady Elizabeth, the County Palatines wyfe, was safely delivered of a Soonne, at Heydelberg in Germany.

Jan. 12. This day my sonne John was b. 1587. 26 yeres since.

Feb. 6. Wm Mildemay my nephew died.

---

[1] Sir John Harrington, soon after created Baron of Exton.

[2] Adam states, on the titlepage of this almanac, that it was the last prepared by "Arthur Hopton, Gent.," and that he died the same year; adding these lines:—

"Hope not to have Hopton againe to write;
For deathe hathe fett away his learned sprite."

Feb. 24. Tho. Lappage died of th' age of 82 y.

Feb. 27. Wm Alibaster my nephew was borne 1567. 46 y. since.

Dum fuerit Romæ, romanam colluit papam:
Sed patriæ rediens, renuit ille papam.

Aprill 6. A general erthquake. 1580. 34 y. since.

April 19, 1614. Sr Robt Jermyn died — *vir pius, et veræ religionis*
amans.

April 26. Dr Perne died suddenly, 1589, 23 y. since.

Qui Christum duro tempore liquit amens.

May 31. Sir Wa: Mildmay died. 1589. 25 y. since.

Vir bonus et prudens, nulli pietate secundus.

June 9. Dr Goldingham died. 1589. 25 y. since.

Qui mihi dum vixit charus amicus erat.

June the 16th day the Erle of Northampton died.

Tempora dura Deus, tempora læta dedit.

July 29. Francys Mildmay my neece was borne. 1591. 23. y. since.

June. 30. Sr Tho: Eden the elder died.

Aug 10. *Ego* A. W. *natus fui* 1548. 63 y. since. *Anno 2 R. Edw.*
VI. Mors mihi grata foret, jamq: satis vixi.

Aug. 26. Sr Wm Waldegrave, th' elder died. 1613.

Vir patriæ charus, sed pietatis inops.

Sept. 4. The Erle of Leicester died. 1588. 27 yeres since.

Mors inopina venit, clausit avaro sinu.

Sept. 9. Mr. St. Pine died.

Sept. 16. Mr. Knewstub & Mr. Egerton did lye at Groton.

Sept. 21. Mr. Jo. Marceline died.

Oct. 15. Nath. Stil was borne. 1579. 35 y. since.

Ad sacrŭ fontem sponsor & testis eram.

Oct. 29. The Lady Mountague died.

Vulnere quam subito mors inopina tulit.

This Lady was borne at little Waldingfielde in Suff. and first maried
to Sr Leonarde Holyday, Knight, who had bin L. Maior of London, and
after his death to Sr Henry Mountague the Kings Maties Serjant at the
Lawe.

Nov. 22. Thomas Garrarde died at Cambr.

Nov. 25. Sr Wm Waldegrave ye yonger died.

Nov. 27. Sr Tho. Gresham died suddenly, 1579. 35 y. since.

Dives in hoc mundo, qui deo pauper erat.

Dec. 12. Tho: Sutton the founder of the Hospital died 1611. 9
Jac. R.

Fœnore, pergrandes accumulavit opes.
Dec. 30.   Forthe Winthrop was borne 1609.

From a copy of Bretnor's Almanac for 1617.

1616 Jan. 12.   This day J. W. the elder is 29 yeares olde.
Feb. 20.   My son's first fit of his ague.
April 13.   John Cooke died.
1617. April 22.   Tho: Doget was maried to Mar. Clopton, Mr. B^d
p^rched.
May 5.   James Death died.
May 9.   Sr Fra: Bacon L. Keeper, came to Westminster-Hall with
a great Company of noble men & others, to take his place in the
Chancery.
May 14.   Sergant Hutton was sworne one of ye Justices of the
Comon Plees.
June 4.   A Court was kept at Groton Hall in the afternoone.
June 7.   Sente ye wid^o Canon 5^s.
June 10.   Mr. Sands was maried at Brettenham.   Mr. Munnynge
preached.
June 18.   John Jannynge died.
August 9.   Mr. W. Clopton died 1616.
August 12.   M^{ris} Bronde th' elder died, 64 y.
Septr 1.   John Plombe beinge sicke, made his testament.
Septr 9.   Th. Gostlin maried the wid: Blomfielde.
Septr 11.   Mr. Egerton & Mr. Knewstub *pernoctabant nobiscum.*
Septr 17.   My son first rid to Maplested.
Octr 4.   Hall the phisition died.
Octr 18.   Judith Spenser died at Colchester 22 y. olde.
Octr 27.   My son rode to London.
Octr 29.   My Cosin Muñinges eldest daughter was maried to
George Salter.
Novr 18.   Sr Hen. Mild: & his lady came to Groton.
Novr 25.   My son returned from London.
Decr 12.   Mr. Rich. Bromel died.
Decr 13.   M^{ris} Judith Gurdon died at Sr Henry Mildmay's in
Essex.
Memorandum, to wright to Sr Henry Mildemay by the goodman
Warde that my Cosen Hamonde who maried the widowe Bronde
came to Groton to talke wth me about her buysines 6 Apr. 1618.

On Fryday the 24th of Aprill 1618. [My] sonnes [third] wife came first to Groton. She was maried to him the [*torn*] day of the same moneth at Greate [Map]lested in Essex. Año 1618.

From a copy of Allestree's Almanacke for 1620.[1]

1619. Jan. 6. My Cosin Henry Mildmay was baptised being 12 daies olde. The same day Mr. Chaplin preached at Boxforde.

Jan. 22. Thomas Alston of Giddy Hall died.

1620. Jan. 23. Sr John Crooke died.

Jan. 24. Mr. Tindal & his wife came to Groton.

Feb. 2. Jo. Potter the Attorney died in London.

March 8. The Assises at Bury, Mr. Muñinge preached before the Juges.

March 15. S^r Jo. Deane & my lady dined wth us.

March 25. The year 1620 beginneth.

Aprill 17. Mr. Rogers of Dedham preached at Carsey.

May 9. Mr. Birde preached at B. & M^{ris} Bacon came to Groton.

June 18. Mr. Smyth of ye K. Colledge preached in Groton. My Cosen Jeremy Raven preached at Boxforde on Sonday in the afternoone. 18 Junij 1620. Psal. 136. v. 15.

August 20. Mr. Daniel Rogers preached at Groton, & my cosen Jer. Raven in ye afternoone.

26. Sr Tho Savage sent halfe a bucke.

Sept. 10. Goodman Bemont died.

Sept. 12. Mr Chamber preached at his burial.

Sept. 16. My cosen Tho: Alibaster died in Assington.

Oct 28. Mr. Sands began to pr. upon Jonah.

Nov. 10. Smith sent a hare, & Hare brought fowre pikerels.

Dec. 9. This daye Mr. Grice preched at Boxforde *ex imp^oviso.*

Dec. 11. Sr Rob: Crane & Mr. Churche were chosen Knights for the Shire.

Dec. 24. Mr. Wm Gurdon died at Cambridge.

---

1 This almanac, which was prepared for Adam's grandson, as described on p. 40 of this volume, is mainly taken up with a statement of the successive preachers at Groton, Edwardston, and Boxford, during the year 1620. Of these preachers, no less than thirty-three names are given; viz., Chaplin, Sherman, Quirles, Butler, Nicholson, Birde, Hankin, Gartwright, Bromel, Layfield, Munning, Vertue, Pilgrime, Webster, Wilmot, Harrison, Carter, Rogers, Watts, Raven, Hawes, Dove, Parson, Sands, Tayler, Smyth, Salter, Chamber, Sterne, Stansby, Paine, Grice, and Wythriel. A goodly variety, certainly, for a single year!

From a copy of Allestree's Almanac for 1621.[1]

Jany 4.   The Thursday sermon ceased at Boxf.

12.   Mr.   Gurdon fel out of his coache in Boxforde Street.

Feb. 10.   G. Winterfloud sen^r died.

Feb. 11.   John Baker of Edw. died.

Feb. 17.   John Wallis died.

Feb 19.   2 Sunnes seene betweene 3 & 4 in the afternoone.

March 1.   We dined at Goodman Coles.

March 5.   M^{ris} Clopton & Eliz. her daugh : dined wth us.

March 15. The assises at Burye, where Porter a minister was condemned for Sodomie.

The Kings Ma^{ty} wrote a most gracious letter to ye Justice of this assise in the behalfe of Mr. Faweather for the punishinge of his false accusers.

April 11.   S^r. Ro : Crane came to Groton.

April 16.   The Q^{ter} sessions at Bury.   J. W. *abijt.*

April 25.   The Widow Carter died.

April 28.   Mr. Brag of Stratf. dined wth us.

May 4.   My son rode to London.   *barbam scidi.*

May 24.   Sr Hen : Mildemay & his Lady dined here.

June 6.   My son & his wife rode to Shrublande hall.

June 11.   Mr. Bachelour the preacher dined with us.

June 21.   My son & his wife went to Stambrige in Essex.

July 18.   The assises at Burye.   J. W. *redijt.*

July 31.   Sir John Deane sent us venison.

August 16.   They of Castleins dined here.

August 21.   Jo : Miller & Susan Rawlin were mar.

August 22.   Mr. Tindal sent a hanche of venison.

August 28.   My son Fones was married at London.

Sept. 2.   There was seene in ye skie a fearful sight.

---

[1] At the foot of the titlepage of this Almanac, Adam pays a tribute to the author in the following verses : —

" Astrologos inter si quis jam laude meretur,
  Allestre est certe, vel puto nullus erat."

The author himself concludes his "Rules concerning Physicall Elections," at the close of his prognostications, with the following prescription in Latin (with an English translation), which may have been supposed to be of more recent origin : —

" Si tibi deficiunt medici, medici tibi fiant,
  Hæc tria, mens læta, requies, moderata dieta :

  Use three Physicians' skill: first, Doctor Quiet;
  Next, Doctor Meriman, and Doctor Diet."

Sept. 18. My nevieu Carew Mildmay was heer.

Sept. 30. M^r. Dan: Rogers preached at y^e. communion.

Oct. 6. Thomas Gale died of ye smale pockes.

Oct. 30. Wm Ponde was married to the widow Havens.

Nov. 12. My sonnes nurse, being 76 yeres olde, came to Groton unto him.

Nov. 15. Brampton Gurdon the third soonne of Mr. Br. Gurdon died at London.

Nov. 18. Benjamin Bronde the brother of Sr John Bronde died of ye smale pockes.

Nov. 26. Rafe Aggar the creple died.

Nov. 29. John Bluet & Joane Kinge were married.

Dec. 5. I dreamed y^t Carew Mildmay was dead.

Dec. 13. Mr. Powle charged a chimney sweeper wth stealing of a silver cup.

Dec. 21. Catharine ye first daughter of Mr. Wm Clopton was borne in Linsey.

Many more Memoranda might have been gleaned both from the Diary and from the Almanacs of Adam Winthrop. Those have been selected which seemed most characteristic of the writer and his times, or which appeared to have any thing of local, personal, or historical interest. We could hardly have hoped to satisfy the genuine antiquary without giving the whole; but this would have occupied too much of our volume. For the general reader, we have more fear of having given too many than too few.

adā woynthorp ꝑ [1]

I am, I assure you

(Gentle Mrs Margaret)

your assured frende Adam Winithrop [2]

this Last of Marche 1618

your louing mother

Anne winthrop [3]

[1] Autograph of Adam Winthrop, the grandfather of Governor Winthrop of Massachusetts, Master of the Clothworkers' Company in 1551; kindly furnished me from the Records of the Company for the year 1546, by Mr. John Calver, late of Clothworkers' Hall.

[2] Autograph of the Governor's father.

[3] Autograph of the Governor's mother.

Thy husband by promise
John Winthrop

Aprill 4. 1618.

Jo: winthrop

Jo: winthrop gou

Your faythfull and obedient wife
Margaret Winthrope

---

[1] Autograph of Gov. Winthrop of Massachusetts at thirty years of age, — the earliest signature found among his papers, — with his seal, bearing the family arms.

[2] Autograph of the Governor at forty-one years of age, with the seal bearing the Dove of promise, which he seems to have used habitually after he had resolved to embark for New England.

[3] From an official signature of Governor Winthrop in New England, in 1639.

[4] Autograph of Margaret (Tyndal) Winthrop, the Governor's third wife, with her seal, showing the *garb* or wheat-sheaf of the Tyndal arms.

¹ The signature of John Winthrop, jun., afterwards Governor of Connecticut, — the eldest son of the Governor of Massachusetts, — with his seal, bearing the arms of Winthrop quartered with Forth.

² The autograph of Forth Winthrop, third son of the Governor of Massachusetts, while a student at Cambridge University, with the seal used by him there.

INDEX.

INDEX.

A.

Admission of John Winthrop, jun., to the Inner Temple, 203.
Alabaster, Dr. William, 16.
Alabaster, Roger, 16, 47.
Alabaster, Thomas, 47.
Allen, Major John, 15.
Allibone: his Dictionary of Authors, 61.
Almack, Richard, F.S.A., 5, 208.
Alston, Peter, death of, 253.
Altham, Edward, Sheriff of London, 14.
Altham, Sir James, Baron of the Exchequer, 14.
Altham, Richard, son of Sir James Altham, 14.
Ames, William, author of Medulla Theologica, 34.
Anecdote respecting the negotiation of John Winthrop, jun., for the Charter of Connecticut, 27.
Appleton, John, 232, 319.
Appleton, Mary, wife of Robert Ryece, 319.
Archisden, or Arkesden, Thomas, 229, 231, 256.
Assassination of Sir John Tyndal by Bertram, 123, 124.
Assington, village of, 1. Parish of, 152. Residence of the Gurdons, 391.
Atkins, Robert, 245.
Autograph manuscript of John Winthrop, 63–122, 145–149, 278, 283, 304.

B.

Babergh, Old Hundred of, 1.
Bacon, Sir Francis, 123, 124.
Bagdat, siege of, 267.
Bancroft, George, sketch of life and character of John Winthrop by, 400.
Bandon, family of, descended from William Winthrop, 16.
Barefoote, Walter, Deputy-Governor of New York, 194.
Barfoote, Dr. John, 194.
Barnardiston, Thomas, 50.
Barnardiston, Sir Nathaniel, 223, 259, 287, 393, 396.
Barrington, Sir Francis, imprisoned for resisting the forced loan, 211, 287.

Belknap's American Biography, 6.
Bertram, assassination of Sir John Tyndal by, 123, 124.
Best, Capt., 237, 249, 258. Letter to, from Lord Hervey, 238.
Beza, Theodore, 319.
Blackheathfield, battle of, 13.
Blomfield, Bishop of London, 170.
Bluet, John, steward of Groton Manor, 291.
Bohemia, King of, 287.
Bowditch, Nathaniel I., suggestion of, relative to the signification of "Winthrop," 11.
Bowen, John, letter from, to John Winthrop, 215.
Boxford, village of, 1, 148.
Boxsted, parish of, 102.
Bradstreet, Governor Simon, 50
Bramston, Sir John, 29.
Branch, Aunt, 213, 258.
Branch, Elizabeth, 213.
Branch, Reynold, 213.
Brent, John, petition in case of, 219.
Browne, Agnes, wife of Henry Browne, 48.
Browne, Anne, daughter of Henry Browne, 47.
Browne, Henry, 4, 26, 47, 48.
Browne, John, 347.
Browne, Samuel, 347.
Buckingham, Duke of, 184, 235, 238, 240, 265.
Burd, Richard, 20.
Burgis, Priscilla, second wife of Thomas Fones, 165.
Burgis, Rev. John, D.D., 165.
Burnel, Lord, 14.
Burton, Joane (or Jane), wife of Adam Winthrop, 14.
Butler, James, 2.

C.

Camden, Britannia of, 2.
Campbell, Lord, Life of Sir Edward Coke by, 54.
Canterbury, Prerogative Court of, 20.
Carver, Eliza, 253.
Carver, John, 253.
Castleins, seat of the Cloptons, 391.
Caulkins, Miss, the historian, 27.